John Muehleisen Arnold

The Koran and the Bible

or, Islam and Christianity

John Muehleisen Arnold

The Koran and the Bible
or, Islam and Christianity

ISBN/EAN: 9783743315549

Manufactured in Europe, USA, Canada, Australia, Japa

Cover: Foto ©Lupo / pixelio.de

Manufactured and distributed by brebook publishing software (www.brebook.com)

John Muehleisen Arnold

The Koran and the Bible

THE

KORAN AND THE BIBLE;

OR,

ISLAM AND CHRISTIANITY,

BY

JOHN MUEHLEISEN-ARNOLD, B.D.,

CONSULAR CHAPLAIN AT BATAVIA,
LATE HON. SEC. OF THE MOSLEM MISSION SOCIETY.

SECOND EDITION.

LONDON:
LONGMANS, GREEN, READER, AND DYER.
1866.

PREFACE TO THE FIRST EDITION.

RECENT events in the East must have convinced us that we have not discharged our whole duty towards the Mohammedan world, by praying once a year that God may have "mercy upon all .... Turks, ... and take from them all ignorance, hardness of heart, and contempt of His word." Nor can it any longer suffice to multiply learned treatises on Islam, without laying before the Church some really feasible proposition, how to reach the 200 millions of Moslems, so large a proportion of whom are under British rule, and who to this day constitute fully one-third of the entire Mission field of the world.

This book avows a purely practical purpose. The foot-notes are intended for the few who might feel disposed to question certain statements, or to pursue the subject still further. The *text* is entirely independent of the notes; and those who wish to ignore them will not, it is hoped, object to being furnished with the authority for every important statement, and the original of every important quotation.

It is not only since the Mahommedans have come so prominently before Europe, but many years ago, that the author first commenced gathering information upon the subject of this volume,—and that, during a sojourn in Egypt, Arabia, Palestine, East Africa, Abyssinia, and more especially in India.

The work is now published with a view to cherish, if possible, the missionary spirit which has been called forth by recent events; and to place some of the leading truths of Christianity antithetically to the falsities and perversions of the Koran, so as to render the comparison available for actual missionary operations.

May God, in His infinite mercy, "stir up," by this, or any other means, "the spirit of the remnant of His people," that they may no longer neglect to do this "work in the house of the Lord of Hosts."

Zell, February 10th, 1859.

PREFACE TO THE SECOND EDITION.

This book first appeared in 1859, under the title of "Ishmael: or, a Natural History of Islamism, and its Relation to Christianity," since which time 800 copies have been circulated. It is now issued with some corrections and alterations, in a cheaper form, and under a less ambiguous title.

The entire proceeds of the volume were devoted, as intimated on the original title-page, towards founding a special Society for Evangelising the Mohammedans. It is now purposed to give all further profits to the *Moslem Mission Society*, which has since come into operation.

The main body of the Work was left intact, excepting only the correction of a few mistakes. The last Chapter of the book, in its original state, chiefly advocated the need of a special Society; the corresponding Chapter now limits itself to a general review of the present condition of the Mohammedan world, and a brief notice of Christian Missions to Moslems, in ancient and modern days.

East Ham, E., Aug. 6th, 1865.

CONTENTS.

PART I.
MOHAMMED AND HIS CREED.

i. THE FORERUNNERS OF MOHAMMED, p. 5—16.

Islam the type of faith adapted to the Arab mind. The mystery of the Incarnation. General denial of the Divine Sonship of Christ in the Apostolic age. Cerinthus and his heresy. The heresy of the Ebionites. Who where the Antichrists in the days of St. John. The Samosatenians. The Arian heresy. Islam absorbed and supplanted all the Christian heresies which previously denied the Godhead of the Redeemer.

ii. THE LAND OF ITS BIRTH, p. 16—45.

Name and character of the land of its birth. The inhabitants of Arabia. Ishmaelite descent of the Arabs. The character of the Arabs predicted. The wild ass or the Dsigetai. Ishmaelites and Israelites: the only two nationalities surviving of ancient days. The Patriarchal faith in Arabia. Admixture of idolatry. The Kaaba at Mecca, the ancient Pagan sanctuary. Composite nature of Islam.

iii. THE AGE, AND CHARACTER OF MOHAMMED, p. 54—99.

Political aspect of the age in which Mohammed was born. His age in a religious point of view. State of Judaism in Arabia. Deplorable state of Christianity in Arabia: deification of the Virgin Mary. Arabia at that time a reputed place of refuge for persecuted heresies. Distraction of the Arabs amidst Christian heresy, Christian orthodoxy, Judaism and idolatry. Honest minds groaning for light. The tribe of Mohammed. His family. His fits in childhood. His private life. Career as a prophet. Struggles and battles. The poisoned lamb of the Jewess. Mohammed's last moments. His appearance and habits. His character. Commenced his career in honest sincerity. Degenerates.

iv. HISTORY AND DOGMAS OF THE KORAN, p. 99—142.

Name of El Koran. Versions of the Koran. Revoked passages. Original collection. Prevailing confusion. Real order of the Suras.

CONTENTS.

The alleged divine character of the Koran. The Unity of the Godhead. Attributes of holiness; omnipotence; mercy; righteousness, Anthropology of the Koran; creation of man; immortality of the soul; fall of man. Doctrine of Angels. Concerning the devil and genii. Resurrection and judgment. Ceremonial injunctions: prayer and fasting. Alms and pilgrimage. Sacrifices and circumcision.

v. WHAT MOHAMMED BORROWED FROM JUDAISM, p. 142—179.

More acquainted with the Jewish traditions than with the Old Testament. Mohammed's interest to borrow. Plagiarism from Judaism. Hebrew names and terms. Hebrew ideas borrowed from the Talmud. Doctrines borrowed. Talmudic demonology. Moral precepts. Historical incidents: patriarchs before the flood and Rabbinical fables. Noah; Hud or Eber; Abraham; Isaac; Ishmael; Jacob; Joseph. Moses a leading figure. Fables. The golden calf lowing or roaring. Korah's riches. Aaron. David and Solomon. Queen of Sheba and Talmudic legends. Elijah; "Jonah the man of the fish." Job and Ezra.

vi. WHAT HE BORROWED FROM CHRISTIANITY, p. 179—218.

More at home in the apocryphal traditions than in canonical Scriptures. The childhood of Jesus. Apocryphal Gospels. Parents of the Virgin Mary. Joseph never named. The birth of Christ. His childhood. The Arabic Gospel of the Infancy. Miracles of Christ. The Ministry of Christ. Denial of the crucifixion. Titianus. Christ's Ascension. Supposed Tritheism of the Christians. The Virgin Mary said to be no goddess. Divinity of Christ denied. Titles given to Jesus in the Koran. The Gospel allowed to come from God. The Gospel of St. Barnabas alleged to have prophesied of Mohammed. Double opinion of Christianity set forth in the Koran: one assuming a perfectly peaceful, the other a hostile relation to Christianity. Importance of disabusing the mind of Moslems.

vii. SPREAD AND SUCCESS OF ISLAM, p. 218—253.

Spread over the whole of Arabia in twelve years. Syria and Palestine. Jerusalem capitulates to Omar. Egypt and North Africa: Alexandria; embassy from Cyrenaica. Irak subdued. Persia. The Omayades. Islam introduced into Syria. The entrance of Tarik into Spain. Reverses in Gaul by Charles Martel. Spread in China and India. Mongols and Tartars found the Ottoman empire. Bajesid: project to feed his horses at the high altar of St. Peter's at Rome.

CONTENTS.

Peaceful spread of Islam by Missionary efforts in the interior of Africa. Causes of success and permanence enumerated.

viii. CHARACTER AND INFLUENCE OF ISLAM, p. 253—315.

Flaws in the legislature of Islam. Oaths wantonly made and broken. Vain oaths and perjury. Injurious effects of the Sonna. Warlike and cruel fanaticism. Lust of persecution. Social and domestic sores. Polygamy, its prejudicial effects. Facility of Divorce. Slavery and Dulocracy. A hint to the Statesmen of the present day. Form of Government. Compulsion and bloodshed. Islam Predestination, its effects. Sects and heresies of Islam briefly reviewed. Mystical Sufiism in Persia. Effects of Moslem sectarianism. Effects upon literature, commerce, arts and sciences. Decay, depopulation, devastation and demoralisation.

PART II.

CHRISTIANITY AND ISLAM CONTRASTED.

INTRODUCTION, p. 316—321.

i. INTEGRITY OF THE OLD TESTAMENT, p. 321—355.

Names, division and number of the books of the Old Testament. Collection of the books. Preservation by the Christians. Christian catalogues. Origin of various Readings. No wilful corruption on record. Wilful corruption impossible. Internal evidence. Historical evidence. Versions: Chaldee, Septuagint, Peshito, Hexapla, Itala, Vulgata. Mysterious absence of Arabic versions. Early Arabic versions destroyed. Their early existence proved.

ii. THE INTEGRITY OF THE NEW TESTAMENT, p. 355—397.

The New Testament Scriptures known to the Apostolic Fathers. Known to the Early Fathers of the Church. Quoted by enemies and heretics. Catalogues of canonical books. Origin of various readings. Collection and preservation. Instance of wilful corruption and how dealt with by the Church. Proved by ancient Manuscripts. Ancient versions. The Peshito; two other Syrian versions; Armenian and Egyptian translations. Latin versions. British versions in the days of Bede. Corruptions morally impossible. Admitted by Moslems.

CONTENTS.

iii. THE BIBLE AND THE KORAN, p. 397—435.

Symptoms of imposture in the one case. Historical feature of the Old Testament shown in detail. Admissions of the Koran. Hint from the Hebrew Scriptures being read from right to left. Organic connection of the Bible acknowledged in the Koran. The Bible a standing miracle of God's power and wisdom. Is the Koran the so-called miracle it is pretended to be? Internal connection of the New Testament Scriptures, and the contradictory character of the contents of the Koran. Absolute mistakes of the Koran which admit of no explanation.

iv. TRINITY AND UNITY, p. 436—447.

Symbolical anthropomorphisms. The moral attributes of God. His metaphysical attributes. Distortion of the character of God in the Koran. Allah a metaphysical deity. The belief in the Holy Trinity. Caution to Christian Missionaries. The dogma of the Holy Trinity above reason. The creeds of the Church do not express the mystery, but seek to protect it against Unitarianism and Tritheism. Matter of fact evidence that neither the Incarnation nor the Trinity are irrational. Metaphysical Monotheism satisfies neither faith nor reason.

v. CHRIST AND MOHAMMED, p. 447—470.

The Divine Sonship of Christ proved from the Koran. The miracles which Mohammed is said by tradition to have performed. If performed he is a lying prophet, since in the Koran he repeatedly denies that he wrought any miracles. Are miracles in themselves a true evidence? The miracles of our Lord. Misapplication of single prophecies in the case of Mohammed. A full system of prophecies fulfilled in Jesus Christ. Why the crucifixion and the atonement are denied.

vi. CHRISTIAN MISSIONS TO THE MOSLEMS, p. 471.

What was done by our ancestors. Raymund Lully, the Martyr of Moslem Missions, and the founder of the Arabic Professorships at Salamanca, Bologna, Paris and Oxford. Other efforts of the Church of Rome. Henry Martyn the modern Apostle to the Moslems. The two Church Mission Societies. The Moslem Mission Society. Syud Ahmed Khan the reformer of Islam and author of a Moslem Commentary on the Holy Bible. Hopes and fears of the Church. Hopeful signs and circumstances. Presentiments and prophesies. Christ first appearing to Hagar. Special promises.

PART I.

MOHAMMED AND HIS CREED.

CHAPTER I.

THE FORERUNNERS OF MOHAMMED.

"Who is a liar but he that denieth that Jesus is Christ? He is Antichrist that denieth the Father and the Son. Whosoever denieth the Son, the same hath not the Father."
1 John II. 22. 23.

1. Islam is the type of faith which of all others was most adapted to the Arabian mind. The Arabs, remained equally unimpressible to the poetry of the Greeks, the Philosophy of Plato, and the teachings of Christianity, but in perfect accordance with the national predominance of the cold intellectual faculties, they threw themselves with enthusiasm into the subtilties of Aristotle. Just so much was adopted of Judaism and Christianity as commended itself to the intellect only, without any regard to the deeper yearnings of the heart.

Hence the unconditional rejection of the doctrine of the Holy Trinity, and of all the leading features of Christianity. The Arab could speak with contempt of the subtle controversies which Nestorius, Entyches and the Monophysites had fomented in the Eastern Church. Islam had no cause to dread similar troubles and comparisons; for it was a creed without miracles, and a faith without mystery.

One of the earliest doctrines of Mohammed was the Unity of Allah; and the assertion that God had no son and no partner was enough to cause the rejection of the whole basis of Christianity. Mohammed, to originate his composite system of belief, purged from the existing creeds all that seemed mysterious and supernatural.

It must not however be supposed that in thus rejecting the *fundamentum fundamenti* of the Christian faith, Mohammed planted an absolutely new heresy. A cursory view of the early heresies of the Church will convince us that Islam gathered the already existing elements of apostacy and reproduced them under a new type and in a new form of misbelief.

2. The mystery of the Incarnation was purposely hidden from the world for a time. If we seek for the popular opinion of our Lord's person and character during His lifetime, we find that Jesus, up to His thirtieth year, was *supposed* to be the son of Joseph. After his baptism Christ was spoken of by Philip "as Jesus of Nazareth, the son of Joseph." When He commenced His public

ministry, the people ask astonished: "Is not this Joseph's son?" At a later period they exclaim: "Is not this the carpenter's son? Is not His mother called Mary?" Only one year before His passion the Jews ask: "Is not this Jesus the son of Joseph, whose father and mother we know?" The same opinions prevailed among the unbelieving masses long after the Ascension of the Redeemer; and even in the days of the Apostles, heresies sprang up within the Church, adopting the views then current, viz., that He was no more than "Jesus of Nazareth, the son of Joseph."

Amongst the heretical teachers who in the apostolic age paved the way for Mohammed, Irenaeus mentions *Cerinthus*, a Jewish convert, who subsequently relapsed and was the first who dared to question the Divinity of Christ, asserting that his entrance into the world was according the ordinary laws of nature:[1] Epiphanius also writes that Christ was considered an ordinary man by the Cerinthian heresy, adding that it admitted His Cross and Passion, but distinctly denied His Resurrection;[2] and this is confirmed by St. Augustine.[3]

---

[1] "Cerinthus quidam in Asia docuit, Jesum non ex virgine natum fuisse, autem cum Joseph et Mariae filium similiter, ut reliqui omnes homines, et plus potuisse justitia et sapientia prae omnibus." Iren. lib. I. cap. 25.
[2] Epiphan. lib. I. tom. II. pag. 53.
[3] Vide August. tom. VI. haeres. That Cerinthus propagated his heresy in the days of the Apostles will appear from the well known incident, which Polycarp is said to have recorded viz., that St. John immediately left the bath at Ephesus on seeing that Cerinthus, "the enemy of the truth," had entered the building. Iren. lib. III. contra haeres. cap. 3.

Another heresy of the same age and tendency as the preceding, was that of the *Ebionites*,[4] who, like the Cerinthians, adopted the popular notion concerning Christ, which was current during His lifetime.[5] There has been much uncertainty as to the minor, and for our purpose less important items of this ancient heresy, but however indefinite and multiform[6] their system of error may have been, one thing was clear and decided, that they denied the Godhead of Christ and lowered him to the level of mortal man. It is but due to Mohammed to add, that he abstained from going to the full length of these early heretics, when he admitted the miraculous entrance of Christ into the world, which was by them denied.[7]

These are the two chief heresies, which gained ground in the days of the Apostles, to refute which, was one of the objects which St. John had in view in writing his Gospel and Epistles. The Evangelist indeed himself assigns a cause for writing as he does, in these words: "These are written that ye might believe, that *Jesus is the Christ, the Son of God,* and that believing, ye might have life through His name."

Irenæus writes: "John the disciple of the Lord,

[4] Ebion is probably the name of the founder of this heresy; some however receive it as a cognomen, from the Hebrew Ebion, pauper.

[5] "Ebionaei ex Joseph Christum generatum esse dicunt." Iren. lib. III. Cap. 24. See also: lib. I. cap. 26. and 59.

[6] Epiphan. lib. I. contra haeres. tom. II. pag. 59.

This was expressly done by Ebion. Epiph. tom. II. pag. 60.

wishing by the preaching of the Gospel to refute the error, which had been spread by Cerinthus and still earlier by those who were called Nicolaitanes, commenced his Gospel with a view to confound and persuade them, that there is one God, who made all things by His Word, and to establish a rule of truth in the Church." [8] St. Jerome says : " Even when John was still in Asia, the seeds of the heretics, Cerinthus, Ebion and others, who deny that Christ came into the flesh, had already sprung up—whom in his Epistle he calls " Antichrists," whom Paul also frequently attacks—and he was compelled by almost all the Bishops then in Asia, and by legates from many Churches to write more deeply concerning the Divinity of Christ." [9]

Hence, what significance passages like these acquire : " Who is a liar, but he that denieth that Jesus is the Christ. He is Antichrist, that denieth the Father and the Son. Whosoever denieth the Son, the same hath not the Father." Again : " Beloved believe not every spirit, but try the spirits, whether they are of God, because many false prophets are gone out into the world." In the second Epistle, he complains of " many deceivers, who confess not, that Jesus came into the flesh. This is the deceiver and the Antichrist. Look to yourselves,

[8] Iren. lib. III. cap. XI pag. 184.
[9] Vide Hieronymus in proxim. Comment. in Matt. In his "Catalog. Script. ecclesiast." Cap. IX. the same Father adds : that St. John wrote the last Gospel "at the request of the Bishops of Asia, against Cerinthus and other heretics, chiefly the Ebionites, who maintained that Christ did not exist prior to Mary."

that we lose not those things, which we have wrought, but that we receive a full reward. Whosoever transgresseth and abideth not in the doctrine of Christ, hath not God; he that abideth in the doctrine of Christ, he hath both the Father and the Son. If there come any among you and bring not this doctrine, [10] receive him not into your house, neither bid him God speed, for he that biddeth him God speed, is partaker of his evil deeds."

3. In the beginning of the second century we have a revival of the above heresies under Carpocrates, Theodotus, and Artemonius. The first was a philosopher of Alexandria, and though his teaching is not clear on all points as far as ecclesiastical writers notice him, yet his disciple Theodotus A.D. 146, a leather-merchant by trade, broadly affirmed the doctrines of the Cerinthians and Ebionites.[11] Artemonious followed in the same track of heretical teaching;[12] whilst Paulus Samosatenus, Bishop of Antioch A.D. 270 admitted that the Word and the Spirit have always existed in God, but denied their personality and self-existence.[13] Had we no other testimony concerning this heresy we should have considered it purely a revival of the Sabellian error; this

[10] Which teaches, that Jesus is Christ the Son of God, 2 John 9. 10. and which the heresies in question rejected.

[11] Eiphan. haeres. 54. pag. 462. Theodoretus lib. II. haeretic. fabul. cap. 5. pag. 220.

[12] Eusebius lib. V. hist. Eccles. cap. 28. It has been suspected that he expunged the passage 1 John V. 7. from some of the ancient Manuscripts. Theodotus and Artemonius were both cut off from the Church, the former A. D. 146., the latter A. D. 191.

[13] Epiphan. lib. II. tom. II. haer. 65.

error would of itself imply a denial of the personal Divinity of Christ: there is however additional evidence that the Samosatenians dated the beginning of Christ from His birth of Mary, esteeming Him a mere man.[14] We must therefore take it for granted that the Word as conceived by Samosatenus, was something altogether different from Jesus Christ, or that his followers carried the denial of Christ's Divinity to a still greater extent, and thus, as is usually the case, out-stripped their leader. The Bishop was deprived of his office and his doctrine branded as heresy, but far from being eradicated, it was only cut down for a time to sprout up again with fresh vigour at a future season.

4. Exactly fifty years afterwards, the Arian heresy arose, as another precursor of Islam; it admitted our Lord to be a personal and self-existing being, but denied that He was "God of the substance of the Father, not made, nor created, but. begotten."[15] Christ according to Arian teaching was a mere creature, but one endowed with gifts and virtues of a superior character; Jesus was the Son of God not by nature, but by adoption, and on account of His excellencies deserved to be called the Son of God in Holy Scriptures: our Lord was therefore considered

[14] "Paulini a Paulo Samosateno Christum non semper fuisse dicunt, sed ejus initium, ex quo de Maria natus est, asseverant, nec cum aliquid amplius, quam hominem putant. Ista haeresis aliquando cujusdam Artimonii fuit, sed cum defecisset, instaurata est a Paulo, et postea sic a Photino confirmata, ut Photiani quam Pauliani celebrius nuncupentur." August, de haeres.

[15] Arius a presbyter of the Alexandrian Church A.D. 320.

not consubstantial with the Father, but of a diverse nature and essence, neither co-eternal, there being a time, when he did not exist. It assumes also that the power He possesses was received from God;[17] that the Son knows the Father or His secrets only so far as was revealed to Him; that He is not to be worshipped in the flesh; that He was inclined to good and evil,[18] and that His kingdom will perish at the end of the world.

This pernicious heresy was condemned at the Council of Nice A.D. 325 where 318 Bishops assembled to establish the faith in "one Lord Jesus Christ, the only begotten Son of God, begotten of His Father before all worlds, God of God, Light of Light, very God of very God, begotten not made, being of one substance with the Father, by whom all things were made."[19] Neither the sudden death however of its founder, nor the condemnation of the heresy could extinguish the flame which had been kindled; under the Emperor Valens it spread over Greece, part of Asia, over Italy as far as Milan, and among the newly converted Goths."[20]

Beryllus, Bishop of Bostra in Arabia, had already prepared the way for Arianism in the Peninsula, denying, as he did, the pre-existence of Christ and with it the Godhead of the Redeemer;[21] hence it was

[17] Athanas. Orat. contra Arianos. [18] Theodoretus lib. I. cap. 9.
[19] Theodoret I. 11. Nicaenum fidei symbolum.
[20] So mightily grew the evil: "ut totus ingemisceret orbis, seque tam cito factum esse Arianum miraretur." Hieronym. adversus Lucifer tom. I. fol. 65.
[21] Euseb. VI. 33. cfr. Orig. comm. ad Titum: hominem dicunt

comparatively easy for Constantius to propagate the Arian creed among the Arabs. He sent Theophilus to the King of the Himyarites with considerable presents to ask permission to build churches; one was accordingly built in his capital, Tapharon, a second at Adena, the now British Aden in South Arabia, and a third in the Persian Gulf.[22]

5. It is the object of these introductory remarks to show that not only in truth, but also in error, remarkable epochs are gradually introduced and systematically fore-stalled. Mohammed's new creed, as far as we may designate it new, did not appear, until the world was in a measure prepared for it by heresies of a cognate and analogous character, such as those we are reviewing. We now arrive at a period extending from the Nicene Council to the rise of Islam. Soon after its condemnation the Arian heresy split up into two distinct sections, which nevertheless agreed in denying the divine character of our blessed Redeemer.

The first section was that of the strict Arians,[23]

Dominum Jesum praecognitum et praedestinatum, qui ante adventum carnalem substantialiter et proprie non exstiterit, sed homo natus patris solam in se habuerit deitatem." Ullmann de Beryllo Hamb. 1835.

[22] This happened 350. Theophilus was a native of India from the Island Divus (Diu) who had been sent as a hostage to Constantine the Great. He became an Arian Monk, and Eusebius of Nicomedia ordained him a deacon. Philostorgius Hist. Eccles. epit. lib. II. 6. lib. III. 4.

[23] The chief leaders were *Aetius*, a deacon of Alexandria; *Eunomius*, described by Ruffinus as a man "corpore et animo leprosus," and *Acacius*. August. tom. VI. haeres. 54.

who not only denied the Son of God to be of the same substance with the Father, but declared Him to be altogether unlike the Father:[24] the Semi-Arians, whilst rejecting the orthodox dogma, that Christ is the substance of the Father, held that He was of a similar nature. It was this latter section which was by far the most powerful and numerous of the two; sufficiently so, to continue to distract the Church in the following ages, till Islam had grown potent enough, to arrest and supplant the heresy altogether.

6. That the creed of Mohammed absorbed the various heresies which denied the Divinity of Christ is evident, from the fact that they vanish from the Church on the rise of Islam; and it is not less remarkable, that they remained dormant till the 13th century, when Islam sustained a fatal blow by the dissolution of the Kaliphate in the year A.D. 1258.[25]

After the days of St. John many Antichrists went

[24] Epiphan. tom. I. lib. III. pag. 388. Photinus, the Bishop of Sirmium being deposed A. D. 351, is said by some to have followed Samosatenus; but according to Augustine, he heartily joined the strict Arians.

[25] Abbot Joachim was the first after Mohammed who denied the Divinity of Christ; his heresy was condemned by the Lataran Council A. D. 1215. Joachim was succeeded by his countrymen Laelius and Faustus Socinus A. D. 1546, from whom sprang the Socinian and Unitarian heresy. The following may serve as a correct estimate of their character: "Ab Ebione enim initium, ab Ario incrementum, a Photino caput erroris hauserunt. Ariani recte dicuntur, quia conveniunt in summo controversiae puncto, quod est, divinitas Christi negatio." Quenstedt Theol. did.-pol. Pars I. cap. IX, pag. 367.

out into the world, who for the space of seven centuries denied that Jesus Christ was the Son of God. As they served merely as forerunners to a still more fatal error, they naturally retired when Mohammed and his successors arose, and presided over that system of error, which destroys the very foundation of our holy faith and brands the confession of Christ being the Son of God as idolatry and blasphemy.

The Moslem admits the law and the Gospel to be of divine origin; he knows however nothing of either, except through the distorted medium of the Koran; and it is just because Islam acknowledges so many truths and borrows so many weapons from the Christian armory that it becomes so dangerous an adversary. We have to do, not with a heresy within the Church, which might be condemned at a general Council, but with a conspiracy against the existence of the Church itself.

The Christian dispensation is declared to have been superseded and abrogated, as if decayed and waxen old; the very identity of the facts and truths recorded in the Koran is destroyed by its misrepresentations, and in asserting that the Bible has been corrupted, Mohammed takes from us the most effectual means of proving his imposture.

In order to give, as far as lies in our power, a correct view of the creed, thus introduced to the reader, we shall next inquire for the land of its birth, and the people among whom it first made its appearance.

CHAPTER II.

THE LAND OF ITS BIRTH.

"For there shall arise false Christs and false prophets; wherefore if they shall say unto you, Behold he is in the *desert*, go not forth,"
Matt. XXIV., 24, 26.

1. A close affinity may be recognised between the religions of the Pagan world and the respective countries, in which they obtain. Whilst true Religion is of a purely spiritual character and admits none of the natural and accidental elements of the country in which it was revealed, or in which it is planted, false creeds ever yield to the physical influences to which they are exposed. We could not conceive for instance that the Hindoo Mythology in all its exuberance could have sprung up in a poverty-stricken country like Arabia.

There are several names descriptive of the position and character of the land in which Islam was reared. In the East it is called Bar-el-Yemen, or the "land to the right," in contradistinction to Bar-esh-Sham, the "land to the left," by which Syria is known. In Chaldea it was called the "land of the evening," and in Europe and Africa it was universally known as the "land of the East."

CHAP. II.] NAME AND CHARACTER OF THE COUNTRY. 17

In the Bible, where it occurs four times it is invariably called Arabia,[54] and the signification which it could alone have to the Hebrew in Palestine, is that of *desert* or *wilderness* and this is by far the most appropriate appellation, the characteristic feature of Arabia being that of an interminable desert.[55]. If there be a fountain, a rivulet, a green spot, a pleasant garden or a fruitful vale here and there, it only the more painfully convinces the traveller, who sets his foot on its sandy wastes, that Arabia is indeed "a desert land", and that no other name could express its physical aspect more correctly. As the country, so the religion; for although Mohammedanism embodies some elements of a spiritual character yet beyond what it borrows from Judaism and Christianity, it only faithfully reflects the nature of the country, in which it originated, being poor, barren, and highly expressive of the rigid severity of the land of its birth.

We have only to travel through the length and breadth of Arabia, and peruse the Koran on our journey, to be convinced of this remarkable analogy between the physical aspect of the country, and the book in question.[56] In the Koran we travel from

---

[54] 1 Kings X. 15. 2 Chron. IX. 14. Isa. XXI 13. Jer. XXV. 4. in the last passage we read of מַלְכֵי עֲרָב, Kings of Arabia; and the Arab is called עֲרָבִי.

[55] עֲרָבָה = desert: the Arabs themselves speak of their native land as Bar el Arab, the land of the Arabs; the same term is used by their neighbours.

[56] A learned Prelate once observed in a letter to the author: "I often felt during my studies of the Koran, as one, who has to

B

Sura to Sura, and all appears like a dreadful and howling desert, with sandy steppes and dark rocky hills without a single vestige of vegetation; we find indeed a few sparks of heavenly truth on its dismal pages, which have been borrowed from the Bible, and which are fairly represented by the solitary fountain, the occasional oasis, and the few green valleys, in which the weary and way-worn reader may repose for a moment.

2. The next point to be considered regards the *inhabitants* of Arabia, who were the first to embrace Islamism. They are either pure Arabs, said to have descended from Joktan [57] the great grandson of Arphaxad, the son of Shem; or Ishmaelite Arabs who were grafted upon the primitive stock. Otherwise they are classified into *Hadesi*, or Arabs who live in fixed habitations; and *Beduins*,[58] who now, as in olden times, are roving about with their flocks and tents in the vast desert between the Euphrates and Egypt. The Hadesi who settled chiefly in Yemen, claimed their origin from Noah through Joktan. It is amongst them we find the ancient kingdom of the Sabians;[59] and according to the Koran the Queen

wade through the endless sands of the desert, and frequently I turned aside to refresh myself at the fountain of Israel."

[57] Respecting these genuine Arabs or aborigines, العرب العاربة the Arabs of the Arabs, compare Joktan יָקְטָן; amongst his sons we find שְׁבָא so well known in Arabia. Gen. X. 26. 27.

[58] Beduin, بداوي from Badia, desert, which they inhabit. In Syriac: *Ber Broie*; hence *Berber*, Barbary.

[59] In the days of Lokman "the kingdom shone like a diamond on the forehead of the universe." The prophecy then: מַלְכִּי שְׁבָא

of Sheba came from thence to hear the wisdom of Solomon. The time however arrived when the kings of Yemen were alternately dependent on Ethiopian and Persian monarchs; and many of the tribes emigrated and spread over the Peninsula. Amongst them there was one family, that of Rebia, which pushed towards the north and conquered Mecca, the sanctuary of the Pagan Arabs; but owing to their corrupting influence it became the seat of a still grosser idolatry. In the year A. D. 464 they were expelled by the Koreishites, who took possession of the old heathen temple at Mecca.

When Nauwash a Jew, the last king of Yemen persecuted the Christians in the sixth century, Nagush came from Abyssinia to espouse their cause. The Abyssinian host obtained a glorious victory and Nauwash threw himself into the sea in despair. Encouraged by their success the victorious army besieged Mecca with a large force including thirteen Elephants; but Abd el Motalleb, a Koreishite hero, saved the town and the sanctuary A. D. 570. The Arabs subsequently counted their time from this "year of the Elephants", as it was called, till it was superseded by a new era in the days of Mohammed.[60] Strange to say it was his grandfather, who saved Mecca from the Abyssinians.

מַלְכֵי שְׁבָא אֶשְׁכָּר יַקְרִיבוּ "the kings of Sheba and Seba shall offer gifts acquires force. Psalm LXXII. 10.

[60] عالم الفيل, era of the elephants. The legend of the battle and its marvels: Wahl pag. 716. note to Sur. CV. which is called "the Elephant".

3. We have above mentioned that the Joktan Arabs were chiefly to be looked for in Yemen, whilst the Ishmaelite Arabs or the Beduins occupied "Arabia deserta" in contradistinction to "Arabia felix" or Yemen. Upon what authority however, may we ask, do we believe that the Arabs in question descended from Ishmael? Josephus in speaking of circumcision as being administered among his own nation, on the eighth day, thus continues: "But the Arabians administer circumcision after the thirteenth year, for Ishmael the founder of their nation, the son of Abraham by his concubine was circumcised at that time of life."[61] According to Origen, "the Ishmaelites, who inhabit Arabia, practise circumcision in the thirteenth year; for this history tells us concerning them."[62] Still more ancient, and more important testimony is found in the Old Testament; there we have the names of the 12 sons of Ishmael,[63] and their dwelling-place in after ages; namely, "from Havilah unto Shur, that is before Egypt as thou goest toward Assyria." This is confirmed by subsequent sacred writers. The Prophet Isaiah mentions Nebaioth and Kedar[64] in connection with Sheba. Again Duma and Tema are

[61] Ἀραβὲς δὲ μετὰ ἔτος τρὶς καὶ δέκατον. Ἰσμαῆλος γὰρ ὁ κτίστης αὐτῶν τοῦ ἔθνους, Ἀβραάμῳ γενόμενος ἐκ τῆς παλλακῆς ἐν τούτῳ περιτέμνεται τῷ χρόνῳ. Flav. Joseph. Antiqu. Jud. lib. I, cap. X. pag. 26.

[62] τοῦτο γὰρ ἱστορεῖται περὶ αὐτῶν. Origen tom. II. pag. 16. Edit. Bened.

[63] Nebaioth; Kedar; Adbeel; Mibsam; Mishma; Duma; Massa; Hadar; Tema; Jetur; Naphish; and Kedemah. Gen. XXV. 13—15.

[64] Isa. LX. 6. 7. "They from Sheba"; "flocks of Kedar"; "rams of Nebaioth".

mentioned in connection with Kedar, and this in a prophecy, conveying the burden upon Arabia.[65] Jetur and Naphish were overcome by the Reubenites in the days of Saul; and their abode was the desert towards the East of Gilead.[66]

Ishmael's posterity on multiplying, soon became mixed with other nations; the six sons of Abraham by Keturah,[67] who had been sent "eastward unto the east country", had in the days of the Judges, so far blended with the Ishmaelites, as to render the terms Ishmaelite and Midianite interchangeable.[68] That the Edomites or Idumaeans mingled at an early period with the Ishmaelites is proved by Strabo, when he says that the Nabataeans or the descendants of Nebaioth were one and the same people.[69]

Thus we see that the promise was speedily fulfilled: "I will make him a great nation"; "behold I have blessed him"; "I will multiply thy seed exceedingly, that it shall not be numbered for multitude".[70] In answer to the prayer of Abraham God promised that Ishmael should become the father of twelve princes analogous to the twelve Patriarchs that sprung from Isaac. A celebrated geographer whose judgment cannot be suspected of partiality, describes Arabia as "a living fountain of men, the stream of which had poured out far and wide to the East and

---

[65] Isa. XXI. 11—27.   [66] 1 Chron. V. 10. 19—21.
[67] Gen. XXV. 6.   [68] Judges VIII. 1. 24.
[69] Ναβαταῖοι δ' εἰσὶν οἱ Ἰδουμαῖοι. Strabo lib. XVI. pag. 10
[70] Gen. XXI. 18. XVII. 20. and XVI. 10. The last words were spoken to Hagar.

to the West for thousands of years. Before Mohammed's time, the Arab tribes had spread throughout Asia Minor. In the middle ages they are found in India. In the whole of North Africa as far as Morrocco spread their wandering hordes; and their ships went through the Indian ocean as far as China; on the Molucca islands and on the coast of Mosambique they had their settlements. In Europe they populated the south of Spain, where they ruled for seven hundred years, and remaining unsubdued themselves, the Arabs ascended more than one hundred thrones beyond their native soil."[71] We have seen that the descendants of Joktan and the posterity of the six sons of Abraham blended with the Ishmaelites, and that all these elements united in the population of Arabia, yet it is beyond doubt that the Ishmaelites gained the ascendency and impressed their character upon the rest. The above testimony may therefore be legitimately adduced to prove that God made good his words to Hagar: "I will multiply thy seed exceedingly, that it shall not be numbered for multitude."

Again the *character* of Ishmael and his Arab-

---

[71] „Arabien ist eine lebendige Menschenquelle, deren Strom seit Jahrtausenden sich weit und breit in's Morgen- und Abendland ergossen hat. Vor Muhammed befanden seine Stämme sich schon in ganz Vorderasien, in Ostindien schon im Mittelalter, im ganzen nördlichen Afrika bis Marokko ist es die Wiege aller Wanderhorden. Durch den ganzen indischen Ocean bis zu den Molucken hin hatten sie schon im Mittelalter Ansiedelungen; ebenso an der Küste Mosambik, wie ihre Schifffahrt über Hinterindien bis China gieng: in Europa bevölkerten sie Südspanien und beherrschten es 700 Jahre lang; und während sie selbst unbezwungen blieben, haben Araber außerhalb ihres Stammlandes mehr als 100 Throne bestiegen." Ritter.

posterity was defined with wonderful precision by the Spirit of Prophecy: "He will be a wild man or a wild ass of a man,[72] his hand will be against every man, and every man's hand against him; and he shall dwell in the presence of his brethren." The "wild ass", to whom Ishmael is here compared is described in the book of Job[73] as a wild, independent and haughty animal, living in the wilderness. He is known in natural history as the Dsigetai;[74] a fine, strong and noble creature; of the size and bearing of a lightly-built horse, light-footed and slender, with a neck resembling that of a stag, which he always carries upright; the forehead is high, the ears long and erect. His colour is cherry brown, cream or grey, with a dark woolly mane, and a coffee brown bushy stripe of hair down the back; his limbs are nimble and his motions swift; he runs like lightning snuffing up the air,[75] and thus easily escapes the hunter. His wild and proud appearance indicates unsubdued power and perfect independence; and indeed no one has hitherto succeeded in taming him. Even when caught young they prefer to die in their fetters, than to submit to the will of man. "For vain man would

[72] וְהוּא יִהְיֶה פֶּרֶא אָדָם and he will be a wild ass-man. Gen. XVI. 12.

[73] "Who has sent out the wild ass free? Or who has loosed the bands of the wild ass? Whose house I have made in the wilderness, and the barren land his dwellings. He scorneth the multitude of the city, neither regardeth he the crying of the driver." Job XXXIX. 5—8.

[74] Vide Naturgeschichte von H. Rebau pag. 320.

[75] "A wild ass used to the wilderness, that snuffeth up the wind at her pleasure." Jer. 11. 24.

be wise, though man he born like a wild ass's colt."[76] Another very remarkable feature in the Dsigetai species is this, that they only exist in treeless and interminable deserts, especially in Central Asia, where they live sociably together in herds from 15 to 100 in number. The strongest and most courageous of the males acts as guide and watchman, who in time of danger gives the signal for flight, running three times round in a circle. If the leader is killed the flock is instantly dispersed and falls a prey to the pursuers.

The Arab bears precisely the stamp of the wild ass, here described. He lives in herds and tribes and is as untamed and untameable. He feels as free as the air, whilst roving through boundless deserts; and delights to wander in wild and unfettered freedom through the wastes of his inheritance. Like the wild ass he "scorneth the multitude of the city;" despising a civilised life with its comforts, and as little as the Dsigetai could he be subdued.[77] Only single portions of the Peninsula have been subjugated for short periods, although every man's hand has been against its wild inhabitants. The Abyssinians,

---

[76] The only parallel passage to the פֶּרֶא אָדָם in Gen. XVI. 12. is in this place of Job XI. 12. :וְאִישׁ נָבוּב יִלָּבֵב וְעַיִר פֶּרֶא אָדָם יִוָּלֵד: and a vain man would be wise although he were born the colt of a wild-ass-man.

[77] "Saraceni nec amici nobis unquam, nec hostes optandi, ultro citroque discursantes, quidquid inveniri poterat momento temporis parvi vastabant Omnes pari sorte sunt bellatores, per diversa reptantes in tranquillis vel turbidis rebus; nec quidem aliquando, sed errant semper per spatia longe lateque distenta, sine lare sine sedibus fixis aut legibus." Ammian. Marcellin. I. XIV. cap. 4.

Babylonians, Jews, Persians, Romans and other nations have made war against them, but by no nation, however powerful, could they at any period be permanently subdued. To rob whomsoever they can, is no crime, for they allege that Ishmael was turned out of his father's house and received the wilderness for his inheritance with permission to take what he could. Like the Dsigetai, each tribe chooses a leader, a Sheich, from among its own people, under whose direction they fight, rob, and rove about from place to place. However united they may appear as a nation they nevertheless present the scene of a "house divided against itself," the respective tribes maintaining the most inveterate and interminable feuds with one another. It is a proverbial saying among them: "in the desert every one is the enemy of the other." That these animosities commenced in the days of Ishmael, we may conclude from the wild and misanthropic disposition, which was first of all exemplified in his own person; and the marginal reading of the account of his death would lead us to infer, that he "*fell*" in the act of fighting.[78] "He grew, we read,

---

[78] "And they, viz. the twelve princes, dwelt from Havilah unto Shur that is before Egypt, as thou goest toward Assyria; *and he fell in the presence of all his brethren.*" עַל־פְּנֵי כָל־אֶחָיו נָפָל Gen. XXV. 18. Having examined all the passages where the verb נָפַל occurs, we find that with, or without qualification, it invariably means, *falling by violent means*. Where this is not the case, it is always specified; and we have no reason to depart from this ordinary sense. Vide Gen. XIV. 10. Exod. XXII. 28. Josh. VIII. 25. Judg. IV. 16. V. 27. VIII. 10. XII. 6. XX. 44. 1 Sam. IV. 10. XIV. 13. The usual term for dying is: וַיִּגְוַע he gave up the ghost; or וַיָּמָת and he died. Then the preposition עַל before פְּנֵי implies opposition; *over, against* the face of all his brethren. See the meaning of עַל

and dwelt in the wilderness and became an *archer*." That there was many a "*cunning hunter*" amongst his brethren, whose hand was against him, we have reason to judge from several incidents, which are recorded of those early days; and it is most natural that the fore-father of the Arabs should have perished or fallen in one of those conflicts, of which he was the author. The meaning of the expression; "He shall dwell in the presence of all his brethren," is determined by the context; it implies not only that Ishmael and his posterity should have a fixed boundary within which they should "*dwell*", but also that they would assume a posture of hostility towards their brethren. There is however another reason for assuming that the dwelling together could not be of so peaceable a nature, as we might suppose from the English version. The words "He shall dwell in the presence of all his brethren", would be more correctly rendered as in most translations; thus, "He shall dwell *against* all his brethren;" signifying, that not only would Ishmael's hand be against every man in general, but even in dwelling with his brethren, he would maintain his characteristic hostility. Not without peculiar significance was it predicted that Ishmael should "dwell opposing all his brethren"; and that his death should be recorded in these words: "He fell whilst opposing all his brethren".⁹⁷ What a

2 Kings XIX. 22. He fell then in the act of opposing his brethren; in resisting them *to the face*.

⁷⁹ The angel saith before Ishmael's birth: עַל־פְּנֵי כֹל־אֶחָיו יִשְׁכֹּן after his death we read: עַל־פְּנֵי כָל־אֶחָיו נָפָל In both cases not: לִפְנֵי as in 1 Sam. XIV. 13. but: עַל־פְּנֵי

marvellous book that of the Bible, to sketch a people's character, to pourtray a nation's destiny so many thousand years in advance with such accurate precision, and in so few, simple, yet graphic words!

5. The word of Jehovah thus set forth the future character of the wild man Ishmael, in it most distinctly fore-shadowing that of His posterity. The fact however which stands out most prominently in the history of the world is this, that out of all the nations of antiquity, only those descended from the two sons of Abraham have preserved their nationality. Phenicians, Egyptians, Assyrians, Babylonians, and Persians have either altogether disappeared, or they exist only in degenerated remnants. The Chinese and Hindoos remain only in two great masses, inert and torpid, their ancient vigour of life having utterly decayed.[60] The Greeks and Romans of the present day are essentially different from the Greeks and Romans of classic times: but the sons of Israel and the sons of Ishmael to this day stand in the world as two separate and distinct nations, unchanged from what they were in the pristine ages of their existence, retaining their ancient manners and customs to a considerable extent, and what is still more remarkable, their distinctive peculiarities of character. That the Ishmaelites should have preserved their independence and nationality in their desert wilds, is indeed less surprising than that the Hebrews should have con-

---

[60] They have moreover mixed with other nations, who have successively conquered them. Each wave of foreign conquest left its deposit upon the native soil.

tinued a separate people after having been dispersed and persecuted from eighteen to twenty four centuries among all nations.

The peculiarity of the Jewish type in matters of religion is a blind adhesion to the vain traditions of their ancestors, as well as to the dead letter of the Old Testament, which has virtually become a sealed book to them.[84] The Ishmaelites with their egotism, their indomitable love of freedom and their ruling principle of embracing everything with the understanding, proved the very soil for the growth of Islamism; and in a religious point of view we may take the Mohammedan as a true type of the Ishmaelite. Of all people therefore, the *Jews* and the *Mohammedans* are the most determined opponents to Christianity; Judaism being the embodiment of a dead orthodoxy and Islamism the personification of a cold religion of the understanding, such opposition is easily accounted for. It is a principle with the Mohammedans to believe only what is intellectually tangible; or to use their own expressive words, they receive nothing with their hearts, "which does not fall into their heads." They are acquainted with some of the leading facts of Divine Revelation, but after having corrupted what they have borrowed, like Ishmael,

---

[84] "They are drunken, but not with wine; they stagger, but not with strong drink; for the Lord hath poured out upon you the spirit of *deep sleep;* and hath closed your eyes. The prophets and your rulers, the seers, hath he covered. And the vision of all is become unto you as the words of a book that is sealed: בְּדִבְרֵי הַסֵּפֶר הֶחָתוּם which men deliver to one that is learned saying: Read, I pray thee and he saith: I cannot for it is sealed." Isa. XXIX. 9--11.

they "*mock*" at the truth. Being inflated with gross superstition, wild fanaticism, inconceivable pride and a special animosity against the Christian, the Mohammedan is far more difficult to convert than even the Jew.

Having noticed the position which these two nations assume with regard to the Church of Christ, we now refer to their distinctive features of nationality. The Ishmaelites cling to the hostile and nomadic habits of their patriarch Ishmael, and up to this day follow exactly the same rude and natural mode of life which existed among them 3500 years ago. They prefer a wild and independent life in the desert to the comforts and conveniences of a civilised state, and no foreign power has ever been able to impose new manners and customs upon them; a fact without parallel in the annals of nations. In the Jews we perceive a finer and more delicate shade of nationality; they are more flexible and of a less untractable spirit than the Ishmaelite. They accommodate themselves more easily to the strangers amongst whom they dwell, without however endangering their national character. With nothing to call forth the higher and more spiritual aspirations of the immortal soul they throw themselves with double zeal and energy upon the material world. The Jews and Ishmaelite Arabs reciprocally indulged in an international hatred, the hand of the latter being especially directed against the posterity of Isaac, whom they supposed to have acquired the blessing, which legitimately belonged to Ishmael, as the first-born of Abraham.

6. After considering the land in which Islamism

was first planted, and the people who first received it, we now revert to the *religion* of the ancient Arabs. If we discover fragments of truth in Mythologies, more remote from the fountain of primitive revelation,"[2] why may we not in Arabia, where there existed proximity of locality, analogy of language, unity of ancient tradition and consanguinity of descent? In the Pagan creed of the ancient Arabs we find a disfigured Patriarchal faith. The celebrated symbol of the Mohammedan creed, "there is no God but one" was known to the Arabs before Islamism existed."[3] In times of peace and security they resorted to idols, their apology, as preserved in the Koran, being, "we worship them only, that they may bring us nearer to God;" but they instinctively fled to the *Most High God* in time of peril and danger. Nor is it difficult to account for their knowledge, superficial as it was, of the true God. We have direct evidence, that the ancient Arabs were brought into contact with revealed Religion, since it is generally admitted, that the book of Job was written in Arabia;[84] if this be the

---

[82] "When we compare the Pagan systems of belief with the most ancient records of the Bible, we discover that the history of the primitive days of the human race and the primary elements of sacred tradition constitute the foundation of every ancient system of Pagan Mythology." Arnold's True and false Religion. Vol. II. pag. 211.

[83] The following was a form of prayer usual amongst them: "I dedicate myself to thy service; O God! Thou hast no companion, except thy companion, of whom thou art absolute Master, and of whatever is his." Abulfarag pag. 160.

[84] Uz the chief part of Idumaea. Lam. IV. 21. Job is not without cause considered the same as king Jobab, the king of Edom. Gen. XXXVI. 31. 32. That Job was a king, a prince, see

case, it doubtless embodies views and ideas, which were current in that land. Again, we can scarcely conceive that Moses could have lived, forty years in Arabia, and leave no good seed behind him. Nor could the host of Israel sojourn forty years amidst the ancient Arabs, who must have heard of the miracles which God had wrought on their behalf, without reviving ancient traditions and exercising a directly beneficial influence upon the inhabitants of that country. Indeed the Rechabites, one of the tribes of Arabia with their zeal for the true God might serve as a testimony, that there was a remnant of God-fearing people among them; the character of Jethro, the father-in-law of Moses, who was a pure Arab, and a Priest of Midian, might also be mentioned. The queen of Sheba's coming from the south of Arabia, where it was customary for women to inherit sovereign power, also confirms the idea, that some light of truth had found its way into the deserts of that great Peninsula. As the wise men are also supposed to have come from Arabia to see "one

Job 1, 2. chap. XXIX. XXXI. 37. His friends are called kings, in the book of Tobit II. 14. and are also found in Idumaea as likewise belonging to the family of Esau. See Gen. XXXVI. Isa. XXXIV. 6. LXIII. 1. Aristeas, a heathen writer, is reported to have said in his "Historia Judaica" that "Jobum ex Esavi liberis in Idumaea atque Arabiae finibus habitasse et cum justitia tum opibus precipuum fuisse." Eusebius lib. IX. praepar. Evang. fol. 251. St. Chrysostomus speaks of Arabia as "terram illam, quae Jobi victoris certamina et crucem omni auro preciosiorem suscepisset." Chryso. homil. V. At the end of Job the LXX interpreters have these words: οὗτος ἑρμηνεύεται ἐκ τῆς Συριακῆς βίβλου, ἐν μὲν γῇ κατοικῶν τῇ Αὐσίτιδι, ἐπὶ τοῖς ὁρίοις τῆς Ἰδουμαίας καὶ Ἀραβίας, προϋπῆρχε δὲ αὐτῷ ὄνομα Ἰώβαβ. λαβὼν δὲ γυναῖκα Ἀράβισσαν, γεννᾷ υἱόν, ᾧ ὄνομα Ἐννών.

greater than Solomon," they doubtless were in possession of the remarkable prophecy of Baalam, which was delivered in Arabia, by an Arab prophet, in the hearing of an Arab king. This is not the place to enter upon the history and character of Balaam; all we wish to maintain is this, that there was in those days still a priest, or a prophet of the true God among the Arabs, who uttered remarkable prophecies in His name. Nor did God disdain to administer counsel to Moses through Jethro his father-in-law. What this priest of Midian taught his Arab countrymen, we may gather from his confession of faith: "Now I know that the Lord is greater than all Gods." [85]

To refer only to one more point. When Ishmael was sent away into the desert with his mother, he doubtless took with him something more than "bread and a bottle of water;" nor can it be supposed that Abraham in sending his six sons [86] by Keturah into Arabia failed to add to the "gifts" which he is said to have bestowed upon them, the parting injunction that they should keep the way of the Lord, which they had learned from their father: "*For I know him, that he will command his children and his household after him, and they shall keep the way of the Lord, to do justice and judgment.*" [87]

---

[85] What makes this the more important was his acknowledgement of the covenant name, *Jehovah;* he said: Exodus XVIII. 11. עַתָּה יָדַעְתִּי כִּי־גָדוֹל יְהוָֹה מִכָּל־הָאֱלֹהִים

[86] Zimran, Jokschan, Medan, Midian, Ishbak, Shuah. Gen. XXV. 2. 6.

[87] Gen. XVIII. 19.

7. Together with the many noble truths, preserved among the first settlers in Arabia, which were subsequently revived by the sons of Abraham, and still later by the sojourn of Moses and the Israelites, an admixture of superstition and idolatry existed. In tracing out these Pagan elements we meet with no small difficulties. The native writers are strangely silent on the subject, and that because they were taught by the Koran[88] to consider themselves superior to any other nation, even in "the time of ignorance," as they call the days prior to Mohammed. It was natural, they should dwell as little as possible on a point, which humbled their national pride. In the Koran however eight idols are mentioned; and as the destruction of these external marks of idolatry formed an essential part in the spread of Islamism, we become incidentally acquainted with several particulars relating to it.

The chief feature seems here, as indeed in all ancient Mythologies, to be a worship of the heavenly bodies; perhaps the noblest effort of man without revelation to represent "the Father of lights," and the least degrading species of idolatry.[89] It was the

---

[88] "Ye are the best nation, that hath been raised up unto mankind." Sura III. 106.

[89] "Lest thou lift up thine eyes unto heaven, and when thou seest the sun and the moon, and the stars, even all the host of heaven, shouldest be driven to worship them and to serve them, which the Lord thy God hath imparted (*meted or measured out* אֲשֶׁר חָלַק), unto all nations under the whole heaven. Deut. IV. 19. This "*meting out*" may be taken in the same sense as the words: ὃς ἐν ταῖς παρῳχημέναις γενεαῖς εἴασε πάντα τὰ ἔθνη πορεύεσθαι ταῖς ὁδοῖς αὐτῶν. Act. XIV. 16.

first step in the downward course of superstition, when Babylon, that "mother of harlots" considered the heavenly bodies as the representatives of the invisible Majesty of the Lord of Hosts. Bel or Belus for instance, throughout appears as the solar deity, whose temple still stood in the days of Herodotus. Another not less celebrated temple of the moon stood at Haran; the well-known sojourn of Abraham. Terah had already taken Abram and Lot from Ur of the Chasdim or Chaldees; and if Chasdim or Chaldees signifies "worshippers of idols" as has been thought by an eminent scholar, we can easily account for the exodus of Terah's family from Ur. When Haran however proved no better shelter from idolatry, as we infer from the early existence of the lunar temple there, Abraham was altogether removed from his native country.[90]

That the Arabs fell into the snare of worshipping the heavenly bodies at an early period, may be gathered from various authorities. Job, himself an inhabitant of Arabia, bears witness to the fact of the existence of this idolatry amongst the Arabs of his day.[91] An Arab author of the eighth century, writes: "The Arabs also held the religion of the Sabians:"[92]

---

[90] Gen. XI. 31. and XII. 1.

[91] "If I beheld the sun when it shined, or the moon walking in brightness, and my heart hath been secretly enticed, or my mouth hath kissed my hand; (an idolatrous practice still in vogue, and witnessed by the author) this also were an iniquity — *for I should have denied the God, that is above.*" Job. XXXI. 26—28. Compare also Ezek. VIII. 16.

[92] وممّن كان بدين الصابية العرب Samsaddin ad-Dimaski in his Kosmography. Zeitschr. der Morg. Gesellschaft Vol. V. 392.

which explains the following admonition: "worship not the sun neither the moon, but worship God, who hath created them; if ye serve Him."[93] Twice occurs the name of "servant of the Sun" in the list of the Himyaretic Kings; for as in the Bible we find the names of God associated with "nomina propria" so the ancient Arabs called themselves the servants, slaves, and property of their idols;[94] according to the Musnad-inscription, Samir Jaras reared a temple to "the Lord, the Sun."[95] In a Sabian Almanac, under the month Subat or February it is stated: "They fast in it seven days, commencing on the ninth day of the month, and this fast is held in honour of the great Lord, the Sun, the Lord of all Good."

According to Strabo, the descendants of Nebaioth offered up sacrifices to the sun on the roofs of their houses. Nor was this luminary alone worshipped by the Arabs; for there existed among them seven temples in honour of the presiding deities of the days of the week, consisting of sun and moon and five planets.[96] Like other nations, the Arabs had proceeded from a more or less pure Monotheism to consider the

---

[93] Sur. XLI. 37.

[94] e. g. יִרְיְתָן from יְהִיָה and נְתָן, given of Jehovah; שְׁמוּאֵל from שָׁמוּעַ (not שָׁאַל as might appear) and אֵל God: "God hath heard." In the same way we have "the servant of the sun" and "the prince of Manat," among the Arabs.

[95] The parallel to this בֵּיתחֲמָשׁי Jer. XLIII. 13.

[96] Sun and moon; Aldabaran, Jupiter, Canopus, Sirius, and Mercury. Abulfarag histor. dyn. pag. 160. See Studien über die vorislamitische Religion der Araber von Dr. E. Osiander; Zeitschrift der deutsch. Morgenländ. Gesell. Band VII. 1853. pag. 463.

heavenly bodies as symbols of the Divine Majesty; the next step was to worship them as self-existing deities; this being done, the third step to actual *idolatry* was rendered comparatively easy. Nor was this new element an entirely distinct form of error. It will be necessary, distasteful as it may be, to glance at the more corrupt form of superstition, which in a measure co-existed with Sabeism and a partial retention of the patriarchal faith. Beginning in the South of Arabia, we meet with a mountain of witchcraft near Hadramaut, in one of the caves of which, resided the master of sorcery, who exercised considerable influence upon the benighted Arabs around him. In Hadramaut itself we find the two idols *Galsad* and *Marhal*. The capital of the Himyaretic Kings contained the colossal and gorgeously ornamented temple of *Gumdan*.[97] The god *Riam* was also worshipped in Sana,[98] to whom sacrifices were offered, and at whose temple oracular information was sought. It is not improbable that we have a parallel of this oracular deity in Baal, of whom king Ahaziah in his sickness inquired.[99] The temple

---

[97] Sahrastani adds these words: على اسم الزهرة, it was dedicated to Venus. Her worship being established in Sana, it is not only probable, but almost certain, that the name Athatar: عَثْتَر so frequent in the Himyaretic inscriptions might be the same as the Phenician idol: עַשְׁתָּרוֹת Judges 2, 14. X. 6. 1 Kings XI. 33.

[98] Riam, the exalted one; in Ethiopic, heaven. It is perhaps not too much to think, that this deity was the same as בַּעַל, if the goddess was עַשְׁתָּרוֹת. They are always put together in Scripture.

[99] 2 King. I. 16.

of Riam was first destroyed on the establishment of the Jewish kingdom among the Himyarites, and a second time, when Islamism was introduced.

Another idol in the Himyar country was *Nasar*;[1] he was worshipped, as his name implies, under the form of an eagle. Two days journey from Sana towards the north, we meet with *Yauk*, another deity mentioned in the Koran;[2] which like Nasar, Waad, Sowa, and Yagut is said by the Koran, to have been worshipped before the days of Noah. He was adored under the image of a horse.[3] *Yagut* had his temple at Djoras or Goras not far from the road leading from Mecca to Sana; and was the deity of the tribe of Madhig, but that his name was revered among other tribes is proved by the fact of its appearing among them as a component part of their surnames. This deity was worshipped under the figure of a lion, and in the choice of this image there may be an allusion to the corresponding sign of the zodiac, as that also was an object of divine worship among the ancient Arabs.[4]

Different from Naser, Yauk and Yagut, who were worshipped under animal forms, are the two

---

[1] نسر; compare with it the Assyrian נִסְרךְ: Isa. XXX. 38. The eagle entered largely into all the systems of ancient Mythology. Nasar is mentioned Sur. LXX. 23.

[2] يعوق, Yauk, the refrainer; deus averruncus.

[3] Horses dedicated to the sun at Jerusalem. Were destroyed 2 King. XXIII. 11.

[4] Ideler Untersuchung über die Stern. pag. 161. The lion is a celebrated religious symbol, and has frequently become an object of religious worship.

other deities, *Sowa* and *Waad*, who are named with the former in the above-mentioned passage of the Koran.[5] Sowa was adored under the image of a woman, Waad under the figure of a man. All five are said to have been antediluvian idols,[6] which being discovered after the flood came to be worshipped by the Arabs. Sowa was worshipped at Ruhat north of Mecca, and Waad on the north east of Arabia among the tribe Kalb, but we notice them in this place, because they were associated in the Koran with the idols, to which we have just alluded. Resuming our northerly route, we proceed from Goras the seat of Yagut, to Talabah, a town four days journey south of Mecca; in this place we meet with the goddess Chalasah,[7] whose temple was of such reputation, as to be considered a rival of the sanctuary of Mecca, and called "the Kaaba of Yemen."

We now enter the province of Hedgas, and in Taif, about sixty geographical miles south of Mecca, a place otherwise important in the history of the Arabs, we find the great goddess of the Takif tribe, Allat,[8] who was represented under a white square

---

[5] Sur. LXX. 23.

[6] They are always mentioned with the addition: صنم لقوم نوح

[7] The temple of Chalasah seems to have been in Yemen what that of Gumdan was in Sana; namely a temple to Venus. The intimation of Fasi that Chalasah was introduced from Syria, is therefore worthy of notice. Sprenger's Life of Muhammed, pag. 7. not. 1.

[8] The name of Allat: اَللَّت was derived by the ill-disposed Meccans from اَللّٰه Allah. Herodotus calls her Ἀλιλατ or Ἀλιττα.

stone, upon which a temple was built. This idol was carried with that of Uzza before the army in battle;[9] and was one of the goddesses, whose names are recorded in the Koran: — "What think ye of Allat, alUzza and Manah that other third goddess." From the fact that Mohammed frequently protested against the goddess Allat, and from other more direct evidence, the importance of her rites and the extent of her worship is sufficiently established. There can be no doubt that this square-shaped idol, called by the Arabs "the Goddess,"[10] represented an astronomical deity; and from reasons, unneccessary here to specify, it could only have been the moon. That this luminary was worshipped among the Takif and the adjoining tribes Beder and Hilal we know from other sources.[11]

In the valley Nahlah[12] we find Uzza, the second great goddess of the Arabs, mentioned in the Koran; she was worshipped under the form of the tree, Samurah.[13] This is not the only instance in which trees were adored by the Arabs. The Koreishites worshipped a palm-tree, offering up sacrifices, and

[9] Caussin de Perceval III. p. 9. Sur. LIII. 6.
[10] Al-Lat, unlike other deities, always has the article. We never hear of a goddess "Lat".
[11] بَدْر name of a tribe means "full moon"; هِلال, Hilal — another tribe, signifies "newmoon".
[12] Valley of dates.
[13] The سَمُرَة — Samurat, species of Acacia, called "spina Aegyptiaca". The sanctuary was called Boss. Uzza is thought to be the lunar deity like Allat.

hanging their arms upon it. At Nagran they celebrated an annual festival in honour of a sacred palm-tree, on which occasion they adorned it with the garments and ornaments of women. The traveller in Arabia may at this day see Acacia trees, hung all over with rags of divers colours.[14] Over the "vegetable" idol of Uzza a temple was built, and when Boss, the name of this sanctuary, was destroyed by Chalid, one of Mohammed's generals, after murdering the priestess, who had rushed forth with her hair dishevelled, and her hands on her head as a suppliant, he uttered these words: "O Uzza, I deny thee, I praise thee not: I have seen how Allah has humbled thee!"[15] When Mohammed heard of the success of the expedition he exclaimed: "This is Uzza, never again shall she be served."

Mecca became the centre of the Ante-Mohammedan religion of the Arabs, about the beginning of the first century B. C. Arab historians have very little to say as to how matters stood during the time of the Gurhamites;[16] except that they took away the golden gazelles, and the weapons which were hung up in the Kaaba, when they were driven away from Mecca.[17] They left however some traces of their idolatry behind, which it is needless for us to examine.

[14] A fine specimen of these rag-clad Acacia trees could be seen some time ago in the desert between Cairo and Suez.

[15] العزى or عزى Uzza, the most mighty and powerful.

[16] Ley, de templi Meccani origine, Berlin 1851.

[17] Remarkable is it that among its ancient kings, we find one with the Christian name, Abd al-Maseeh, "*servant of Christ*".

The Kaaba itself, which was the sanctuary of the *Pagan* Arabs, and remained such after they had embraced Islamism, is a building about thirty four feet high and about twenty seven broad, so called from being almost a perfect square, as the name implies.[18] In this building we find no less than 360 idols, the chief of them, Hubal,[19] was at once the presiding god in the temple, and the principal deity of the Koreishites, who were its guardians. The pre-eminence of this idol was evinced by the fact, that before it, the casting of lots with arrows took place. Prior however to its obtaining this honour, it passed through a term of probation, for we learn upon good authority, that for a considerable period it stood outside the walls of the Kaaba, patiently waiting for its admission.[20] It was probably introduced when the sanctuary of the Koreish tribe was converted into the Pantheon of the whole of Arabia. The name of Hubal remains a mystery.[21] The opinion that it is synonymous with the Babylonian and Syrian Baal or Bel is supported by the testimony of Arab authorities, according

[18] الكعبة, the square or the Kaaba.

[19] Hubal was اعظم اصنامهم the most excellent of the idols; and was said to have been brought from Mesopotamia, by Amru ben Luhai.

[20] The man to whom it was indebted for its promotion was Amru ben Luhai. He according to Sharastani introduced it على ظهر الكعبة

[21] Pocock, who is still the great authority, since his "Specimen historiae Arabum" has not yet been surpassed, derives Hubal from הָבֵל or הַבַּעַל, הָבָל; nor is this derivation to be censured. Vide pag. 97. 98.

to whom Hubal was originally imported from Syria; these do not indeed maintain that Hubal was Baal, but they admit him to be an astronomical deity; there is therefore nothing which militates against the idols being identical.

Again when it is stated by Abulfeda that the image of Abraham occupied the chief place in the Kaaba, and that he was represented by Hubal, we may take it for granted that Hubal had a double character, like Baal, who was both the founder of the Babylonian empire and the solar deity. Nor is the popular notion of the Arabs, which considers Ishmael to be the original founder of the Kaaba, to be entirely rejected. The well-known adherence of that extraordinary people to their ancient customs seems to warrant the high antiquity of that sanctuary. That patriarchal associations were connected with the Kaaba will appear from a practice which is censured in the Koran. The Pagan Arabs used to compass the sanctuary naked, *because* they considered garments to be signs of disobedience to God. Then the celebrated black stone, fixed outside the Kaaba, towards one of the corners, indicates an acquaintance with a Patriarchal custom.[22] The Arabs attribute its introduction to Ishmael himself, and their superstitious regard for it, is just what might

---

[22] Weil gives the following from the Manuscripts Insan and Chamis: Der schwarze Stein war ursprünglich ein Engel, der Adam im Paradiese bewachen sollte, und von Gott nach Adams Sünde in einen Stein verwandelt ward. Er wird aber am Auferstehungstage sich mit Hand, Ohren, Zunge und Augen erheben, und den frommen Pilgern als Zeuge beistehen. Weil pag. 40. Note 45.

be expected from the abuse of the early practice of setting up stones in commemoration of extraordinary mercies, received from God.²³ The black stone is no doubt older than the Kaaba itself.

Not only was Mecca as well as the Kaaba holy ground to the ancient Arabs, but also the adjacent country. The valley of Mina²⁴ was as much the place of religious resort before Mohammed, as it has been since the days of Islamite pilgrimage to the Kaaba. Leaving Mecca and its immediate neighbourhood, we find an idol in Kudaid, a town about seventy three geographical miles north of it, the name of which indicates some connection with the valley of Mina. The goddess Manat²⁵ was worshipped under a large block of stone, over which a sanctuary was constructed. Near Jeddah we find another of these grim-looking monster idols, cut out of a solid rock, which was worshipped in a large sandy plain under the

---

²³ Gen. XXVIII. 18. "Jacob took the stone, that he had put for his pillows and set up for a pillar and poured oil upon the top of it, and he called the name of that place, Bethel." XXXI. 45. And Jacob took a stone and set it up for a pillar. also 52. XXXV. 14. Exod. 24. 4. Josh. IV. 3. 7. 8. הָאֲבָנִים הָאֵלֶּה לְזִכָּרוֹן לִבְנֵי יִשְׂרָאֵל עַד־עוֹלָם: In Josh. XXIV. 26. 27. אֶבֶן גְּדוֹלָה 1 Sam. VII. 12. we have the אֶבֶן הָעֵזֶר of the prophet Samuel. Compare also the Phenician Baclyla or Baelilos; and the traces of holy stones in the West.

²⁴ Mina مِنًى; Amr ben Luhaj raised seven idols in this valley. Reiske, primae lineae p. 124.

²⁵ مَنَاتُ, Manat. As we have no further information touching the character and worship of this goddess, we naturally think of the Chaldean deity מְנִי, Meni; see Margin Isa. LXV. 11. and the lunar goddess M*ηνη*.

name of Saad. Several other Arabian deities were worshipped near Medina,[26] but excepting their names scarcely any thing has been handed down. We have however seen enough to convince us, that the Arabs had widely swerved from their original patriarchal faith. Many of their idols were of a rough and uncouth appearance, square stones, white or black, trees and solid rocks, figures of birds and beasts, images of men and women, all served to represent their imaginary deities. There is however reason to think, that some of the Arab idols were artistically conceived and skilfully shaped. The utter destruction by the Mohammedans of every vestige of Paganism as regards *idolatry*, prevents our forming any accurate opinion upon the subject; but the fact of Arabian poets comparing beautiful women to idols, and the proverb "more beautiful than an idol,"[27] would seem to indicate, that the Arab idols were not all of them without some degree of form and beauty.

In reviewing the religion of the Pagan Arabs we find remnants of the Patriarchal faith, the Sabian worship of the heavenly bodies, and the elements of a more corrupt idolatry, amalgamated together. The custom of visiting the Kaaba; the rite of circumcision; the doctrine of the Resurrection,[28] to be in-

---

[26] We hear of Nuhm, Humam, Halal, Bagir, Ruda, Aud, Awab, Manaf, Gaum, Kais, Durigel, Fuls, Dariban, and others.

[27] احسنُ من الزون and احسن من الدميةِ more beautiful than an idol. Arab. prov. I. pag. 408. prov. 195.

[28] "I know that my Redeemer liveth, and that he shall stand at the latter day upon the earth: and though after my skin worms

ferred from the Heathen custom of tying a camel near the grave of the departed; the belief that demons are transformed into serpents; abstinence from wine; preference for green among the colours; the custom of sacrificing the first-born of the camel; the habit of swearing by religion; the national traditions, especially the stories relating to Abraham, Ishmael, and other early characters of Bible history; these Mohammed already found among his countrymen, and the same motives, which induced him to adopt the ancient sanctuary and the Pagan rites of the Kaaba as the groundwork of the ceremonial part of his religion, would naturally suggest the adoption of Arabian tradition as the basis of his doctrinal precepts in the Koran.

CHAPTER III.

THE AGE, HISTORY AND CHARACTER OF MOHAMMED.

"Who is more wicked than he who forgeth a lie concerning God? or saith, This was revealed unto me, when nothing hath been revealed unto him?" Sur. VI. 93.

1. No ordinary mortal ever exercised such an immeasurable influence upon the human race in a religious, moral and political point of view, and this

destroy this body, yet in my flesh shall I see God. Whom I shall see for myself, and mine eyes shall behold, and not another." Job XIX. 25. 26. 27. This was written in Arabia.

during a period of twelve centuries, as did the man, whose age, history and character we are about to consider. Although not one of these extraordinary individuals, endowed by divine Providence with genius and power to break up long established institutions and to strike out new paths in the history of politics and religion, yet Mohammed, a man of limited powers of mind and apparently too destitute of materials for the formation of a new religion, succeeded in throwing his seemingly indestructable net of doctrine and practice over millions of souls and in impressing a uniform stamp upon the thoughts and actions of the heterogeneous tribes and nations, scattered over Asia and Africa.

The learned Professor Weil, who has done more perhaps towards producing a correct biography of Mohammed than any one else, deems it one of the most mysterious things, that the life of a man who established a religion, which till now flourishes in the most beautiful parts of the old world, should be so little known or studied. Yet such is the case.

It cannot therefore be without interest to trace out some of the details connected with this remarkable character and the age in which he appeared. The period which ushered Islam into the world was marked by great changes and startling convulsions. The Western Empire was already overrun by the Northern Barbarians, whilst the Eastern and Greek portion of it enfeebled by luxury, fell a prey to all its enervating consequences. Persia torn to pieces by intestine divisions both political and religious had now become incapable of any vigorous resistance. Whilst these empires were declining, *Arabia* on the contrary, which had hitherto displayed no conspicuous part in the history of the world, retained the vigour and energy, which characterise nations, untainted by luxurious habits.[31] The attempt of the Pharaohs of Egypt, of the Persians, the Abyssinians, and the Romans to subdue that country was equally unsuccessful.[32] The Arabs continued an independent race, and it was left to God's more special and direct Providence to rouse them, and to accomplish the mysterious purposes of Him, of whom it is written: "The fierceness of man shall turn to thy praise, and the fierceness of them shalt thou refrain."[33]

Islamism being a grand apostacy from the truth it was natural that it should start up, when true and vital religion had reached it lowest ebb. On examining the records of the *Church* at that period, we discover the grossest corruptions in doctrine and practice. The *Western* and *Eastern Churches* being abandoned to the most degrading immorality, became agitated in those days by violent and rancorous controversies, which extinguished all true piety and practical devotion.[34] The earliest simplicity, which flourished

---

[31] The ancient Greeks and Romans, and those very nations which destroyed the Western empire, may serve as examples.

[32] What classic historians record of the successful inroads of Sesostris and Cambyses, Crassus, Aelius, Gallus and Trajan refer only to partial and temporary conquests.

[33] Psalm LXXVI. 10.

[34] We refer to the fierce controversies connected with Arian

among the suppressed and persecuted Christians had passed away. When the Church was no longer exposed to trials, but favoured and honoured by the first Christian Emperors, it began to fade and lose its primitive power; and it was then, to use the words of St. Chrysostom that *the world entered the Church*.[35] Bishops struggled for the highest and most lucrative sees;[36] and as once when the "tree of knowledge" was perferred to "the tree of life" the greatest evil was produced, so now a curious philosophy being substituted for vital godliness, it led to the most lamentable consequences: those who were to feed the Church indulging in fearful controversies, mutual persecutions followed in rapid succession as the contending parties alternately came into power. The interests of Christianity were made the pretext for carrying out ambitious views and vindictive feelings. The worship of Saints and images had reached such a scandalous pitch, that Christian Churches rather resembled Heathen temples, the objects of adoration only, being changed. This humiliating exhibition might well convey the idea that Christianity was

and Semi-Arian heresies, which agitated the Church up to the beginning of the seventh century, when Islamism absorbed them.

[35] "Eratque super his admire facilis, quae donabat, Christianam religionem absolutam et simplicem anili superstitione confundens; in quo scrutanda perplexius, quam componenda gravius excitavit dissidia plurima; quae progressa fusius aluit concertatione verborum, ut catervis antistitum, jumentis publicis ultro citroque discurrentibus per Synodos, quas appellant, dum ritum omnem ad suum trahere connatur arbitrium, rei vehiculariae succideret nervos." Ammianus Marcellinus fine libri XXI. de Constantio.

[36] Ammianus lib. XXVII. records the case of Damasus and Orsicinus.

merely another system of idolatry, a notion still current among Mohammedans, who judge of our faith only by the meaning and vain ceremonial of fallen Churches.[37] When religion was thus turned into faction, and the Church of the East indulged in disputes on mysterious subjects, in deciding abstruse metaphysical questions by seditious councils, in fabricating spurious Gospels, and in anathematizing some of her less corrupt members, God raised up instruments of his displeasure to remove the candlestick from many a place, and to introduce a strong delusion," that she might " believe a lie."[38]

As long as the light of the Holy Scriptures, remained in the Church, the means of ultimate re-

[37] By an oversight the old garbled version of St. Eligius' exposition of the Whole Duty of a Christian in paying tithe and discharge a few ritual observances was formerly here inserted. This was the more blameable as both Dr. Maitland's refutation and Mr. Hallam's retractation were before the public when this work was first published. The truth is that St. Eligius did mention certain formal observances as binding on a good Christian, but that he also at much greater length on those moral and religious duties about which all Christians agree. Mosheim picked up so much as suited his purpose of depreciation, but he had the decency to leave some marks of omission. His English translator left out the marks of omission, and Robertson—who is still read at Oxford—and a host of others copied one from the other, till poor St. Eligius was made to give a description of a perfect Christian altogether unlike what he intended to give.

[38] Thus it happened that some who were most zealous in supporting the interests of their own party, were foremost in abjuring Christianity in toto. Individuals who would not part with an abstruse notion or a favourite term of expression for the peace of the Church, did not hesitate to abandon her community altogether, when it was their worldly interest to do so. Vide Predaux's address to the reader, prefixed to his "Life of Mohammed."

formation was retained, but the "strong delusion" which Islamism introduced destroyed this remedy. The Western Church in preserving the Bible amidst the corruptions to which she fell a prey, preserved the element by which her reformation was alone rendered possible. Both the Eastern and Western Churches however were fallen, and it is not a little remarkable, that judgment began in each at the same period; for Mohammed announced his career as a prophet about the same time, that Pope Boniface V. by virtue a grant from the weak and tyrannical Emperer Phocas assumed the title of Universal Bishop.[39]

Arabia itself presented in the sixth century a most miserable spectacle, being torn by the intestine commotions of civil and religious warfare. Jews and Christians were so numerous and powerful in the country, as to struggle for the government, and each

---

[39] It has been considered by students of prophecy, that these two rival ecclesiastico-political powers were represented by the Eastern and Western horns. Dan. VIII. 5. 9. Be this as it may: the sins of both Churches did find them out, bringing down upon them a corresponding judgment. The *heresy* of the Eastern, and the *superstition* of the Western Church were both visited in one hour; the former received its retribution in the Arch-heresy of Islamism; the latter was chastised by the Spiritual and temporal tyranny of the Pope. As they crynologically coincided as to their rise, so we trace between them points of sympathy and antipathy. What Mohammed was to the East, the Pope became to the West. The "Key of Heaven" to Mohammed was the sword; the Pope held the Keys of St. Peter. Both united in their persons the supreme civil and ecclesiastical power. Both are acting the part of Antichrist by "casting the truth to the ground;" and not without reason is it supposed by many, that as they commenced at the same period, so they will perish together.

party succeeded in raising kings to the throne, who were followers of their respective creeds. We have already adverted to the persecutions of the Christians by the Jewish king of Yemen, in which many who would not embrace Judaism were executed; nor was the Christian prince Abraha, who was placed upon the throne by Nagush, more successful in gaining the esteem and affection of the different sects, extant at that period in Arabia.

Judaism as a religion had greatly degenerated from its original purity. When Mohammed charges the Jews in the Koran with believing Ezra to be the Son of God,[40] we may at least take for granted that they manifested a superstitious reverence for his memory: although they retained the Monotheism of the Old Testament, yet Jehovah, according to their view, was no longer the God of the Universe, but exclusively the God of the Jews. In the Talmud, which was already considered a standard authority in matters of faith, God is represented "as roaring like a lion in each of the three watches of the night, and as shaking his head;"[41] and according to it the "divine Spirit" was heard "moaning like a dove out of grief for Israel" as often as the *Amen* was responded to in the synagogue.[42] Strangers naturally shrank

[40] قالوا لليهود عزير ابن الله "the Jews say: Ezra (Ozeir) was the son of God." Sur. IX. 30.

[41] Talmud I. Sect. 1.

[42] בַּת קוֹל invariably signifies the Divine Spirit in Talmudic Theology.

D*

from the exclusive creed of a hated nation, who had made themselves obnoxious by the spirit of persecuting proselytism,[43] to which we have alluded, and this produced a desire for a religion, whose blessings were not confined to one particular race.

That *Christianity* prevailed in Arabia to a great extent cannot be doubted, when we read of so many Bishoprics having existed in divers parts of the country[44]. When the Jewish Kingdom was destroyed by the Christians about forty years before the birth of Mohammed, a Church was built in Sana eclipsing the temple of Mecca in beauty and magnificence. But how corrupt the doctrines and practices of the Arab Christians were at that period, will appear partly from the Koran[45], and partly from the writings of the Church historian Epiphanius, who speaks of a Christian sect deifying the Virgin Mary, and offering a twisted cake on her altars, from whence their name Collyridians.[46] That Mohammed made use of spu-

[43] Essai sur l'Histoire des Arabes avant l'Islamisme, pendant l'Epoque de Mahomet. Par A. P. Caussin de Perceval tom. 1. p. 128. 129.

[44] "Die Lehre Jesu hatte sehr frühe in Arabien Bekenner gefunden, und es sind daselbst verschiedene Bisthümer und in mehreren Städten Metropolitankirchen errichtet gewesen. Vom dritten Jahrhundert an nahmen auch die in andern Ländern Asiens verfolgten und bedrängten christlichen Parteien ihre Zuflucht und Freistatt in Arabien." Wahl pag. 15.

[45] Jesus is asked whether it was true that he said to men: اتخذونى وامى الهين من دون الله "accipite me et matrem meam in duos Deos praeter Deum." Sur. V. 116. "Again they are certainly infidels who say God is the third of three." Sur. V. 77. to which Jelladin adds: وللاجران عيسى وامه "the others are Jesus and his mother."

[46] Epiphanius speaks of a sect, which he describes as: ἀπὸ

rious Gospels, and that these Pseudo-Gospels countenanced the deification of the Virgin is equally certain.⁴⁷ Amidst the bloody feuds of the Eastern Church, many of its corrupt members fled to the Huns and Vandals in Africa and some into Arabia; in most instances carrying with them nothing but a Christian Paganism; hence their proselytes were but a shade superior to the Pagans. As an additional proof of heretical teaching in those days, may be added, that the mysterious and blessed dogma of the holy Trinity was converted into a positive Tritheism; thus representing, Father, Son and Holy Ghost as three distinct Gods.⁴⁸ From these scanty allusions to the condition of the Eastern Church in general, and to that of Arabia in particular, it will be sufficiently clear, that Christianity in the age in which Mohammed appeared, had been reduced to a mere carcase, and "where the carcase is, there the eagles will be gathered together."⁴⁹

θεοῦ ταυτὴν (i. e. the Virgin Mary) παρεισαγεῖν σπουδάζοντες. Haeres. LXXVIII. 79. And d'Herbelot Orient. Lib. III. 398. observes that the oriental Christians have given to Mary the title: السيدة: *domina*, and that the Greek Father Cyril styled her the supplement of the Trinity. Then the Θεοτόκος which was so stoutly defended, gave cause to corrupt teaching. Vide also the article: "Das Theologumenon vom πνεῦμα ἅγιον als der Mutter Christi." Nitzsch "Theologische Studien". Vol. 1. 1816.

⁴⁷ Origen. in Joan. Vol. IV. pag. 63. ed. de la Rue. Ἐὰν δὲ προσιέταί τις τὸ καθ' Ἑβραίους εὐαγγέλιον, ἔνθα αὐτὸς ὁ σωτήρ φησιν· ἄρτι ἔλαβέ με ἡ μήτηρ μου, τὸ ἅγιον πνεῦμα ἐν μιᾷ τῶν τριχῶν μου καὶ ἀπήνεγκέ με εἰς τὸ μέγα Θάβορ.

⁴⁸ This was done e. g. by the celebrated Joannes Philoponus, who died in 610. the very year of Mohammed's Mission. Leontius de sectis act. V. 6.

⁴⁹ Dr. Grant's Nestorians pag. 267. The Arab independence

Lastly the Arabs themselves at that period were roused and perplexed by the discordant elements of a corrupt Judaism, and a depraved Christian Church, on the one hand, and by native idolatry, blended with noble remnants of a Patriarchal Monotheism on the other. The Jews, they thought, in rejecting their last prophet, had forfeited their ancient dignity; and they considered that the Christians had run into an opposite extreme by ascribing to him a divine character, and surrendering the doctrine of the divine unity. They deemed the time now come for them, to have a prophet of their own, who would restore the religion of Abraham, and put an end to the state of ferment, into which the Peninsula had been thrown by the concussion of Judaism, Christianity, Sabaism, and the idolatry which they inherited from their fore-fathers.

As a proof that such was the state of things we refer to certain signs of dissatisfaction with the state of religion, some years prior to the alleged Mission of Mohammed.[50] On the occasion of a great meeting of the tribe of Koreish four men sat in secret conclave and imparted to each other the following sentiments: "Our fellow-countrymen are in a wrong path, they are far astray from the religion of Abra-

---

of thought displayed itself among the Christians in the acceptance of nearly every kind of heresy. Ebionites, Beryllites, Nazaraeans, Arians, Semi-Arians and Collyridians vied with each other to destroy the Church, which was planted by St. Bartholomew, St. Pantacnus and St. Simon Stylites. Epiph. de Haeres. lib. I, Haer. 40. and Sozom. Hist. Eccles. lib. I, cap. 16. 17. Sale's Prelem. remarks Sect. II. pag. 24. 25.

[50] Lectures on Mahometanism by Cazenove pag. 47.

ham. What is this pretended divinity to which they immolate victims, and around which they make solemn processions? A dumb and senseless block of stone, incapable of good and evil. It is all a mistake: seek we the truth, seek we the pure religion of our father Abraham. To find it, let us quit our country, if need be, and traverse foreign lands."[51] Three of these became acquainted on their travels with the truths of Christianity; but one of them, Zaid, having been kept back by his relatives, who were offended at his evident estrangement from pagan superstition, went day by day to the Kaaba, and prayed the Almighty to enlighten him.[52]

Not knowing the truth, he opposed what he knew to be false, testified against superstition, forbade men to eat the flesh of victims offered to idols, and protested against the practice of destroying their infant daughters. When imprisoned by his uncle he escaped and after wandering from place to place, he heard from a Christian monk, that an Arab prophet was preaching the religion of Abraham at Mecca. Zaid hastened back to hear Mohammed, but was robbed and murdered on the road.[53] Nor were

[51] These four men were Waraca, son of Naufal; Othman, son of Houwayrith; Obaydallah, son of Djahch; and Zaid, son of Amer. The three first became Christians, and thus satisfied their craving after truth.

[52] He might be seen leaning his back against the wall of the temple, repeating the prayer; "Lord if I knew in what way thou didst will to be adored and served, I would obey thy will; but I know it not." Caussin tom. I. p. 321.

[53] This precursor of Mohammed, says M. Caussin de Perceval, has been hitherto almost unnoticed by European Savans.

others wanting during the life-time of Mohammed who sought to control the stream of national feeling, and asserted rival claims. Amongst them we may mention Ommaiah,[54] who died an early death; and Toleicha and Moseilama; the latter was so successful in making disciples; that even to this day an Arab tribe in western Africa trace their religion back to him and his immediate followers.[55]

From this cursory glance at the age which gave birth to Islamism, we can well understand that a creed embodying the elements of all the religious systems extant among the Arabs and yet avoiding their flagrant excesses would be acceptable to the nation: what it desired was, a religion possessing a simple formula of belief, coming apparently from indisputable authority, freely open to all, and affording to believers the enjoyment of a sensual Paradise; and this was most skilfully contrived and adapted by the man, whose personal history we are now to consider.

2. Mohammed[56] was born in the month of April

[54] He was grandfather of Moviah, who usurped the Kaliphate. Dr. Döllinger's Muhammed's Religion" pag. 4.

[55] Relation des voyages de Saunier, à la côte d'Afrique p. 217.

[56] مُكَمَّد or اَحْمَد, from حَمّ, to laud; حَمَدَ laudavit, signifies "laudabilis, multa laude dignus." Compare the Hebrew חָמַד desideravit מַחְמָד and חֶמְדָּה. Gesenius Hebrew Lexicon. Called Muhammed, Mehemet, Mahomet, better Mohammed. This is the pronounciation also of the modern Arabs. The faith which he founded is called by Europeans: Mahommetanism, Mahometism, Mohammedism, or better Mohammedanism; but by himself and his followers exclusively: اِسْلَام, Islam (from سَلِمَ, to spread peace, in the fourth sense: to be saved, to be put in a state of happiness)

A. D. 571 or 286 of the Diocletian era, his biographers however do not agree as to the exact date, being more anxious to chronicle the marvels which are stated to have accompanied his birth, than to ascertain the precise period, when it took place.[57] We are furnished with a genealogical table comprising thirty generations, tracing Mohammeds descent from Ishmael through his second son Kedar. The tribe to which he belonged was that of Koreish, and the family that of Hashem, princes of Mecca and the hereditary guardians of the Kaaba. Hence they were called "Ahal Allah" or "the people of God." Mohammed therefore was "Arab al Araba" or a pure Arab. Yet in spite of his noble descent he inherited only poverty from his ancestors. Abdallah, his father dying two months after Mohammed saw the light of the world, the whole property which remained for the support of his widow, Amena, and her infant son, consisted of a house, five camels, an Abyssinian female slave, a few sheep, and as some say, a slave called Sakran.

Notwithstanding the marvels which are said to have attended the birth of her child, Amena had

which signifies: resignation, submission. The Germans retain the Arabic Islam; the French transform it into Islamisme, and the English generally adhere to Islamism Moslem is the appellation for the believer in the Koran; the plural Moslemin. The transformation into Musselman and Musselmen, is therefore incorrect.

[57] Pagan images fell to the ground, the sacred fires of the Parsees were extinguished, demons were expelled from heaven: the drying up of the lake Sawa, inundation of the desert of Samawa, illumination of the whole earth, white clouds, voices from heaven, and other prodigies are recorded to have solemnised his birth.

difficulty in procuring him a nurse; at last one was found in Halema, a Beduin woman, who failing in her attempt to procure an infant at Mecca, whither according to custom, she had come to seek one to nurse,[58] rather than return without a charge acceptted the orphan prophet; and Amena confided him to her care for the space of two years.[59] On restoring the child to his mother at the end of that time, the nurse for some reason begged, to be permitted to resume her charge for a longer period; in consideration of his health, Amena willingly consented, but to her surprise, within two months the child was returned in consequence of spasmodic fits, which Halema attributed to evil spirits.[60] It is not to be expected, that the biographers of the Pseudo-prophet would allow this period of his infancy to pass over, without ascribing to it events of a marvellous character, and such are gravely recorded upon the authority of his nurse![61]

[58] The Meccan mothers still send their children to the country, to live with the Beduins in tents till they are eight or ten years old.

[59] The time of weaning a child, is after two years. See Lane's modern Egyptians I. 59. Also Sur. II. 234.

[60] The term, which Abulfeda and Sirat Arrasul apply to these attacks, to which we shall have occasion to refer at a future period, signifies to be overcome by misfortune, to be mortally injured, but is specially applied to people, possessed. "*I fear*," said the husband of Halema, "*this child is possessed, take him to his* people before it becomes known." The fable of Mohammed's chest being opened by two angels to remove the tares of lust and to fill it with prophetic light, is assigned to that period. Sur. XCIV. 1. 2.

[61] The mule on which Halema rides home with her charge, tells her that he carries the best of prophets, the Lord of Apostles, and the darling of God and the world. Sheep courtesy to the little

At the age of six, his mother having taken him to Medina to visit his relations, died on her way home. The orphan being now left to the care of the female slave Barakat, was brought by her to his grandfather Abdalmutalib who willingly receives him, and shortly has occasion to take him to a monk near Okaz for the benefit of his eyes, which had been deemed incurable at Mecca.

On losing his grandfather two years later, the young Mohammed was adopted by his uncle Abu Talib, whom he accompanied, in his ninth or twelfth year, on a mercantile journey to Bussora, their caravan was entertained by a Christian monk, called by some Bahira, by other Serdjis, who being so much pleased with the boy predicted his future greatness.⁶²

In his sixteenth year Mohammed accompanies Zubeir, another uncle on a mercantile trip to southern Arabia, and in his twentieth year he is seen on the battlefield with the same relation.⁶³ After this no-

boy, the moon bends down to his cradle; he is endowed with *speech* immediately after his birth, etc. etc. Weil's "Mohammed der Prophet" pag. 26. 27.

⁶² Bahira according to the Sirat al Zuhra quoted in the Chamis of Hussein, Ebn Mohammed was formerly a Jew, and this explains his second name. He was בְּחִיר or בָּחִיר and on his baptism was called Georgius, which name the Arabs changed into سرجِس, Serdjis or Djerdjis. Christian writers mention a Nestorian monk, بَكِيرا, Bahira, who being expelled from his Monastery in Syria, fled to Mecca. After Mohammed had extracted all the information he required, he put him to death to prevent his divulging the secret. Whether these two monks are identical is a disputed point.

⁶³ This war against the Beni Kinanah is called "*vicious*", be-

thing is heard of him till his twenty fifth year, except the facts of his obtaining his livilihood as a shepherd near Mecca,[64] and of his joining the business of a linen-trader named Saib, in whose company he visited the market at Hajasha, six days journey south of Mecca.[65] In the latter place Mohammed makes the acquaintance of Hakim Ebn Chuzeima, who recommended him to his rich widowed aunt Chadija as an honest and trustworthy young man;[66] being compelled by famine, Mohammed offered his services to her as a mercantile agent. Chadija having at that time many goods to send to Syria engaged him in her service and promised him double wages, viz. two female camels.

His success in this transaction was so great, that his mistress made him a present in addition to the promised wages, and as a proof of her confidence subsequently sends him to the south of Arabia upon other business.[67] This occupation of traffic, in af-

cause it commenced in the four holy months, in which wars by ancient custom were interdicted.

[64] Prof. Weil gathered this fact previonsly unknown in Europe from the "Insan Aluyun" by Ali Halebi; M. S. of four folio Volumes, and the „Chamis" by Hossein Ebn Muhammed Ebn Alhasan Addinarbekri in two folio Volumes, M. S.; both being biographies of M. of the sixteenth century, obtained in Gotha. "Mohammed der Prophet" pag. 33.

[65] This also unknown fact is derived from the "Insan Aluyun" and explains how Chadija came to take M. into her service. Ali Halibi has it from the Uyun Alather by Hafiz Abul Fath.

[66] M. had already acquired the cognomen: "Amin", the trustworthy.

[67] Tradition endows the journey to Syria with strange marvels. In Bussora M. meets Nestor, another monk, who recognises a

fording Mohammed an opportunity of acquiring a knowledge of the world became in after life of the greatest service to him.[68] Mohammed having for some time conducted Chadijas affairs so much to her satisfaction, in spite of the great disparity of age[69] and the opposition of her father she at length determined to raise him from the position of her servant to that of her husband:[70] having made a feast Chadija helped her father so bountifully with wine, that becoming drunk he gave his consent to their marriage.

After this event Mohammed still continued trading, but soon lost all his fortune;[71] nevertheless his acknowledged honesty made him so respected that he was frequently called upon to act the part of umpire in matters of strife. In his thirty fifth year, when

prophet in the merchant: because he has red eyes and a cloud every-where overshadows him; and because a withered tree under which he sits begins to blossom, and bear fruit. He also cured two camels on the road. Chadija saw him on his return overshadowed by the wings of two angels.

[68] The Meccan people chiefly depended on commerce for support, and their habits strongly remind us of the company of Ishmaelites coming from Gilead, with their camels laden with spicery, balm and myrrh, going to carry it down to Egypt. Gen. XXXVII. 25.

[69] Chadija was forty, M. only a few months past twenty five. Other traditions make him twenty nine, thirty, or thirty seven, and Chad. twenty eight, thirty or thirty five.

[70] Chad. offered her hand through Nafisa, a female slave, and appointed the hour of meeting.

[71] Insan Aluyun says respecting M's stay in the cave of mount Hara: "He could not remain a month in it, because his circumstances were not so favourable as to provide a month's provision." It is also stated, that Abubeker had to advance his travelling expences at his emigration to Medina.

the chiefs of Mecca quarrelled, as to who should restore the black stone on the occasion of the rebuilding of the Kaaba, he settled the dispute to the satisfaction of the contending parties by laying the sacred stone on a carpet, and requesting the four pretenders to lift it up by the four corners, whilst he himself took the stone and put it in its place.[72] For the next five years Mohammed lived more and more in retirement; he frequently, especially during the sacred month of Ramadhan resorted to a cave in mount Hara, sometimes with Chadija, but generally alone. His grandfather Abdalmutalib was accustomed before him to ascend this mountain for religious exercises, and there to feed the poor.[73] It was doubtless during this period of seclusion that Mohammed projected his scheme of becoming the reformer of the religion of his people; there also he had leisure to digest his impressions of the Jewish and Christian religions.

3. In his fortieth year intending to avow his prophetical Mission[74] and "the night approaching which," according to Abulfeda "was to cover him

[72] "Er ließ den Stein auf einen großen ausgebreiteten Teppich legen, und diesen von den Prätendenten in die Höhe heben, bis an den Ort wo er hinkommen sollte. Hierauf nahm er alsdann selbst den Stein mit eigener Hand vom Teppich auf, und brachte ihn an den Ort, wo er liegen mußte." Wahl pag. 24. E.

[73] Thus Ali Halibi in his Insan Aluyun, who quotes Ebn Alathir. The same in Sirat Arrassul by Ibrahim Halibi, fol. 36. whose biography, compressed in sixty three lines of poetry was printed at Bulak 1248 of the Hedgra with a Turkish commentary.

[74] This period was no doubt fixed upon in accordance with an ancient Arabic tradition, that God never called a prophet before the fortieth year of his age.

with glory" Mohammed withdrew to the solitary cave in the recesses of mount Hara; and it worthy of notice that his pretended revelations here began with those spasmodic convulsions, to which he had been subject as a child, and which had frequently attacked him during the interval.

That Mohammed was subject to a species of epileptic fits has been recorded by Theophanes and other Christian writers who followed him; and though some learned critics, who might have been better informed, have accused these authors of slander,[75] yet the fact is established and placed beyond the shadow of a doubt by the oldest and most faithful Moslem biographers. As this subject is of the utmost importance for a just appreciation of the real nature of Islamism, we must be permitted to subjoin the testimony of those, whose interest it might have been to deny the matter.

Ali Halibi writes in his history of the prophet: "Ebn Ishak relates, what he has heard from his masters, viz., that Mohammed was subjected to the treatment of an exorcist, when in Mecca before the Koran was revealed to him.[76] On the coming down

---

[75] This was done by the learned Frenchman Gagnier in his work: "La vie de Mahomet; traduite et compilée de l'Alcoran des traditions authentiques de la Sonna et des meilleurs auteurs Arabes," A. D. 1732; which has become the foundation of almost every other European biography since his day; and it is not perhaps to be wondered that more modern authors should have followed his views on the subject in question. See also Ockley Hist. of the Saracens, Vol. 1. pag. 300.

[76] The word applied signifies: "Treated or cured by an exorcist." That this could not refer to the attacks which M. had as

of the Koran the same attacks returned which he had before. Prior to that period he was subject to fainting fits after violently trembling; with closed eyes he foamed, and roared like a young camel.[77] Chadija (God be gracious unto her) then said: I will fetch somebody to cure thee (an exorcist); but he replied. I want nobody at present."[78]

After the first alleged vision of the angel Gabriel Mohammed coming to Chadija trembling and damp with perspiration, exclaimed: "Cover me;[79] I fear for my soul." Chadija said: "rejoice: God will not put you to shame, thou art so kind to thy relations, sincere in thy words, afraid of no trouble to serve

a child is clear from the fact, that this was not in Mecca, but in the country; and then, the Moslem saw nothing in that attack but the effect of M's breast being opened by the angel.

[77] Ali Halibi adds to this term: "this is an attack which Mohammed sometimes had; referring especially to the *fainting* which was caused by demons, on which account M. said to his wife I fear for my soul."

[78] See the Arabic text: "Journal Asiatique, Juillet 1842."

[79] Sur. LXXIII. with an allusion to this fact, M. is called "the wrapped up," المزمل, the participial form, which is used per syncopen instead المتزمل; and Sur. LXXIV. 1. he is addressed: "O thou covered one": المدثر. "Es hat alle Vermuthung für sich, daß schon jener, Amme und Mutter in Schrecken setzende Anfall, welcher ihn in der frühesten Kindheit erschütterte, in welchem die Amme geradezu Satans Werke erblicken wollte (Abulf. Vit. Muh. cap. IV.), nichts anderes gewesen ist als was wir Jammer und Böses Wesen zu nennen pflegen. War M. ein Fallsüchtiger, so erklärt es sich hieraus am leichtesten, daß ihn seine ungläubigen Zeitgenossen einen Besessenen, daemoniacum, nannten....... Man hatte die Gewohnheit, solche zu Boden gestreckte, zitternde Fallsüchtige, während der krampfhaften schüttelnden Verzuckungen, um dem Auge den grausamen Anblick zu entziehen, oder um den übelberüchtigten Zufall zu vertuschen, mit Gewand zu bedecken oder in Kleider einzuhüllen." Wahl pag. 639. 643.

thy neighbour, supporting the poor, given to hospitality, and defending the truth." From these words it is clear that Mohammed was all but certain of being under the control of an evil spirit. According to Janabi, Chadija had the difficult task of consoling her husband, whilst in her own mind she was troubled as to the nature of the vision. She went with him to Waraka, a relation and a Christian priest, who told her that a holy angel would flee at the sight of an unveiled woman, but that an evil spirit could bear the sight.[80] Chadija was determined to apply the test,[81] and requested her husband to inform her when the vision should next appear; Mohammed did so; and on her removing the veil from her face he declared, the angel was gone; which circumstance convinced her that it was a holy angel and not the devil!

As it is of the utmost importance to establish the connection between the visions of Mohammed and these dreaded[82] attacks, we refer to other evidence derived from Ali Halibi, who records the ac-

[80] Probably an allusion to the words of St. Paul: διὰ τοῦτο ὀφείλει ἡ γυνὴ ἐξουσίαν ἔχειν ἐπὶ τῆς κεφαλῆς, διὰ τοὺς ἀγγέλους. 1 Cor. XI. 10.

[81] Ali Halibi records that Chadija made M. sit in different positions and that in each of them he declared, he saw the angel, till she removed the veil, when he saw him no more. "Then said she: "by God! it is true, it is true, it was an angel and no devil." To this tradition the author of the Hamzijah refers, when he writes: „She threw her veil away to know whether it was a true revelation or a fainting produced by demons."

[82] As a proof of Mohammed's misgiving as to the source, from which his revelations proceeded, may be added, that he used to tremble and shake violently, when the time of his visions drew near.

count given by Ayesha. We read in his Insan Aluyun: "A tradition, which is founded upon Ayesha's testimony, says: the prophet was exceedingly oppressed, as often as the angel appeared; the sweat fell from his forehead during the coldest weather, his eyes became red, and at times he roared like a young camel."[53] Zaid, an eyewitness adds: "As often as the prophet received a revelation, it was as if his soul was to be taken from him, he had a kind of fainting, and looked like a drunken man." Abu Hariri,[54] says: "when the revelation came down to Mohammed, none dared to look at him; according to another account, he was angry if any one looked at him: his face was covered with foam, his eyes were closed, and sometimes he roared like a camel."

Harith Ebn Hisham asked the Arab prophet: "In what manner dost thou receive the revelation? He answered: sometimes an angel appears in the form of a man[55] and speaks to me; sometimes I hear sounds[56] like those of a bell; then I become very bad, and when he (the angel) leaves me, I have received the revelations."[57]

From these facts we gather, that Mohammed

---

[83] Weil "Mohammed der Prophet," pag. 44. note 48. Zaid Ebn Thabit repeats the same, and adds that he was frequently attacked when riding on the camel.

[84] In "Moslem's Collection of traditions".

[85] Generally in that of his friend Dihja, the subsequent ambassador to the Persian Monarch.

[86] Noise in the ears is one of the well-known symptoms of epilepsy.

[87] See the MSS of Insan Aluyun and Chamis.

was subject to violent spasmodic attacks at various periods of his life; that he himself considered them the work of an evil spirit; that he put himself under the treatment of an exorcist; and that even after his alleged Mission he expressed his misgivings as to the nature of the demon which inspired him; and we can easily understand the reason why his countrymen constantly charged him with being possessed by a devil, even after he and his followers had persuaded themselves to the contrary.[88]

Waraka, Ebn Naufal, the cousin whom Chadija had consulted, was a learned priest, converted to Christianity from Judaism "in the time of ignorance," well read in the Old and New Testament,[89] and is said to have translated the Gospel into Arabic;[90] all this explains the influence which he had

---

[88] "Why will they not understand," he makes God complain "that there is no evil spirit in their fellow-man." Sur. VII. 183. Gagnier makes M. a hypochondriac and Noel des Vergers pag. 8 considers him mad; "atteint de folie." Others class him with Montanists, quakers and jumpers, and thus account for his alleged inspirations. Theophanes was of opinion that M. put forth the vision of an angel to hide his disease, but the disease no doubt was the cause of the vision, only in a different sense from what is commonly accepted, as will be shown towards the end of this chapter.

[89] وكان ورقه قد تنصر وقرا الكتب وسمع من اهل التوراة والانجيل فاخبرته بما اخبرها به رسول الله
Sirrat Arrusul fol. 36.

[90] وكان يكتب العربى وفى رواية العبرانى يكتب بالعربيه من الانجيل ما شاء الله ان يكتب وكان شيخا كبيرا قد عمى Chamis second leaf of the chapter "Of the events at the beginning of the prophetical mission." See also Mamizade pag. 53.

E *

with his cousin and Mohammed in removing the suspicion that his attacks were caused by satanic agency. That Mohammed held this man in great esteem and acquired from him much of his knowledge of Judaism and Christianity is sufficiently known to require any further corroboration: and this may account for the importance, which Mohammed attached to Waraka's testimony, that he was the great prophet, who had been prophesied in the Scriptures.

In the first three years of his Mission,[91] Mohammed required his friends and relatives only, to acknowledge him as a prophet; among the first who did so, were Abubeker, a man two years his junior, Zaid, Mohammed's slave and Ali, a youth whom Abu Talib adopted during the famine,[92] who afterwards became his son-in-law. It will be remembered when Mohammed asked, who would be his Vizier or assistant to share the burden of his office, and none ventured to answer that Ali, then a mere youth, rose and spake: "I, O prophet am the man, whom thou seekest, whoever he be that shall rise up against thee, I will knock out his teeth, will tear out his eyes, will throttle him and grind his bones. Let me O prophet be thy Vizier!" This

[91] Respecting the day and month of his mission, the traditions do not agree, and it is a disputed point whether the celebration of ليلة القدر, the night of power or destiny, which falls on the twenty seventh of Ramadhan, is correct. See Lane's Modern Egypt II. pag. 238. and Abulfeda ed. Noel des Vergers pag. 107.

[92] Ali was only from eight to eleven years old; some say fourteen years, at all events he was a mere lad.

shows the spirit of the youth, and explains, why Mohammed afterwards called him the "lion of God."

Among the first Moslemin may also be reckoned Arkam, — in whose house their meetings were held after having been surprised and maltreated in the cave, — the dwarf Abdallah Ebn Masud, and the brave Abu Ubeida. Among the women we have besides Chadija, Um Afdal, the wife of Abbas, Um Eiman or Baraka the Abyssinian, and Asma, the daughter of Abubeker. The total number of Mohammed's followers, during the first three years of his Mission, amounted scarcely to forty, mostly young people strangers and slaves, yet a beginning was made.

In the fourth, or as some state the fifth year, Mohammed resolved to go a step further and *openly* proclaim himself a prophet;[93] first combating the idea that he was possessed by a devil.[94] In this bold step, from which he evidently shrank for some time, he met with the most decided opposition. On one occasion when threatening his relatives with hell-fire, he was loaded in return with imprecations: and on denouncing their idols as impotent, and their fathers as having lived in a state of ignorance, he

---

[93] To this he received a special commission: "Wherefore publish that which thou hast been commanded and withdraw from the idolaters. We will surely take thy part against the scoffers." Sur. XV. 94—99.

[94] "The devils did not descend with the Koran (as the infidels give out) it is not for their purpose, neither are they able (to produce such a book) for they are far removed from hearing . . . . . Shall I declare unto you upon whom the devils descend? They descend upon every lying and wicked person." Sur. XXVI. 210. 211. 221. 222.

would have been strangled in the Kaaba, had not Abubeker come to his assistance.[95]

Equally dangerous became the position of his followers; Mohammed therefore advised them to leave the country; consequently eleven men and four women sailed for Abyssinia, where with others who followed, they found an asylum, till Islamism became established in the Peninsula.[96]

The next step taken by the enemies of Mohammed was to plot against his life, and a price of a hundred camels and 1000 ounces of silver was set upon his head: but Omar, who had undertaken to murder him,[97] when about to perpetrate the deed, relented and became a Moslem. Notwithstanding this escape Mohammed's position soon became untenable, and he was so cast down and discouraged, that either from fear or with a hope of conciliating his enemies, he made a most dangerous concession: that of restoring the idols of the Arabs to the rank of mediators between God and man. Subsequently however being reassured by the protection of his uncle he declared this concession to have been made at the instigation of Satan.[98]

[95] Abu Talib being no longer able to protect M. requested his connections to share the responsibility.

[96] These emigrants were pursued to the coast, but managed to escape in a ship. Nor did the bribe afterwards sent to the Abyssinian prince, induce him to give them up.

[97] Omar, afterwards one of the staunchest defenders of Islamism was then only twenty six years of age. On his way to murder M. he is told by a secret Moslem, that his sister Fatima was a convert; going to her he finds her learning the twentieth Sura, and the result is his own conversion.

[98] The concession is alluded to Sur. XXII. 51. where Satan is

Abu Talib fearing further attempts on the life of his nephew, removed him to his fortified castle in the country, whither he was followed by many adherents of the new creed, who during the space of three years shared Mohammed's privations.[99] The Koreishites exasperated at his escaping through the assistance of his uncle, resolved to outlaw him and his friends as enemies of the peace, which they did by affixing a document to that effect on the walls of the Kaaba. Whilst an exile from Mecca two instances of conversion are recorded, the first being that of a Christian caravan from Nadjran, the second that of an exorcist, who hearing that Mohammed was possessed, offered to cure him, instead of which, he himself caught the infection of Islamism.[1] When at the end of three years, the interdict was removed, Mohammed returned to Mecca, and shortly after

said to have put wrong things into all the prophets before him; and Sur. XVII. 75. 76: "It wanted little (but the unbelievers) had tempted thee to swerve from the instructions, which we had revealed unto thee, that thou shouldst devise concerning us a different thing, and then they would have taken thee for their friend, and unless we had confirmed thee thou hadst certainly been very near inclining to them a little."

[99] It was only during the sacred months that they were permitted to enter Mecca; for during the festivals (mausam) hostilities were still suppressed, according to the Chamis and Jannabi.

[1] These two conversions were brought to light by Weil, who refers to Insan Aluyun, where Ali Halibi quotes Ujun Alather. M. said to the exorcist; "Thou professest to be able to deliver men from demons? Only God we may intreat for help; whom he guideth no one can lead astray, but whom he leads into error, no one can deliver. Confess that there is one God, who has chosen me to be his apostle." In this period fell the revelation of Sura XXX. and the prediction of the conquest of the Persians by the Greeks.

sustained the loss of his uncle, who died as a Pagan, never having acknowledged the Mission of his nephew: for although he protected him from first to last, he like most of his contemporaries considered his visions to be nothing but the effect of satanic inspiration.[2] Within three days of his uncle's death Mohammed lost his wife Chadija, but was, it appears, less afflicted at this event; for although his consideration for her prevented his taking other wives during her life time, only a month elapsed before he married Sanda a refugee widow in Abyssinia, and shortly after he was betrothed to Ayesha, the daughter of Abubeker, who was then only seven years old.

After the death of his uncle Mohammed's enemies became more violent than ever and expelled him from Mecca. In Taif, two days journey east of his native town, whither he fled for safety, he received no protection, although connected with its inhabitants, but was hunted out of the place by slaves and children, and compelled to return to Mecca, where happily through the influence of Mutim, a respectable non-Koreishite citizen of the town, he was re-admitted.

In spite of all the misfortunes connected with this disastrous occurrence, the persecuted prophet re-

---

[2] The homage of the Genii is related Sur. LXXII. 1—14. The rapture to heaven is a traditional legend, which is recorded in extenso: Gagnier, "La Vie de Mahomet" II. pag. 195—251. and is looked upon by many Moslemin as a mere vision, whilst the night-journey to Jerusalem is admitted by them as real. See Sur. XVII. 61. where M. speaks of this also as a vision; compare verse 1.

entered Mecca greatly strengthened by the homage of the demons, and the celebrated journey to heaven, whither he had been carried by a winged horse, and where he was saluted by God as the most beloved of messengers, and most excellent of creatures. The relation of this marvel exposed him to fresh outbursts of ridicule and contempt, and many of the faithful left him in consequence.³ Yet during the ensuing festival, Mohammed found some willing ears among the pilgrims from Medina; his new disciples could not indeed alter his precarious position, but they could use their influence on returning to their country to circulate his doctrines. In this they prospered to such an extent, that we find in the following year A. D. 621 a double number of converts in Medina, able to afford protection to refugees from Mecca.⁴

On the occasion of the next annual festival, when Mohammed was fifty three lunar years old, no less than seventy three pilgrims came from Medina, all Moslemin; the meeting on Akaba was resumed, and a treaty offensive and defensive concluded between them, with the request that Mohammed should emigrate to Medina. The prophet however remained for the

---

³ His own aunt, Um Hani thought it so incredible, that she took hold of his garment and conjured him not to make himself more contemptible in the eyes of the Koreshites. Weil pag. 171.

⁴ The men first taught by M. on mount Akaba belonged to the tribe of Chazradj, with whom he was connected through his mother, and who had long been allies of the Jews at Medina; through the latter they must have heard of a great prophet, the expected Messiah.

time at Mecca, but in September 622, in consequence of a conspiracy to murder him, he fled to Medina;[5] meeting the tribe Beni Sahm on his way, he gained them as converts, and their chief Bureida taking off his turban and tying it to his lance for a flag, accompanied him to Medina.

Arrived at Yathrib the ancient name of Medina, the latter simply signifying "town", — Mohammed's first acts were these, to institute the religious rites, to give a new home to the emigrants, to build the first Mosque,[6] and to organise a fraternity between the Meccan and Medina believers, which extended even to mutual inheritance at the expence of their own relatives.

In the seventh month after his arrival he married Ayesha in her ninth year, the wedding breakfast consisted of a cup of milk, which Mohammed

---

[5] For three months Abubeker had two camels in readiness to carry them away at a moment's notice. After his followers had left, M. was exposed to imminent peril, for expecting he would follow, his enemies surrounded his house to murder him. M. having been acquainted with their design ordered Ali to be put into his bed, whilst he escaped on the other side of the house and retreated with Abubeker to a cave one mile East of Mecca; leaving it on the fourth day they went towards Medina by a less frequented road along the Red sea. From this flight or rather emigration, dates the era of the Mohammedans; هجرة, emigration; مهاجر, the emigrant. The flight is confirmed by Sur. VIII. 30.

[6] Date trees were cut down, the dead burried beneath them exhumed, and a simple structure was reared of five to seven yards high, and a 100 square. At night it was illuminated with burning pieces of wood, till oil lamps were provided by some generous Moslem. The Kaliphs transformed it into a gorgeous temple, which is to this day a place of pilgrimage. By the side of it was built a harem, for Mohammed's favourite wives.

obtained from Zaad, who with Asad alternately supplied him with food. His daughter was shortly after married to Ali; her outfit was two garments, a kohel-apparatus, two silver bracelets, a leathern pillow of palm-leaves, a cup and a few water jars. Her bridal bed was a sheep-skin; and a dish of dates and olives composed the wedding feast.

With a view to gain the Jews Mohammed made several concessions; such as the turning of the face towards Jerusalem, the retaining of the celebration of the Sabbath, and the adherence to other Mosaic ordinances; he even went so far as to command the observation of the fast, Yom Kipur, or the tenth day of the month Tishri, with which the Jewish year commences; but failing in his scheme, these concessions were subsequently rescinded.[7] His most important act during the first year of the Hedgra was the proclamation of war, as the heaven-ordained means of spreading the faith. He could not yet venture on open warfare, but contenting himself with the irregular exploits of a robber, he plundered the Meccan caravans, which passed near Medina on their way to and from Syria.[8]

As the Koreishites however, were too cautious to be entrapped, he resorted to the base and treacherous measure of attacking them during the four sacred

---

[7] The Jews desired to retain all their laws and rites; and rejected M's claim, mainly because he was not of the house of David.

[8] M. once issuing forth with seventy men against a caravan the expedition ended in a league; a second was attempted against 2500 camels, a third against 1000, but both failed.

months, when they considered themselves perfectly safe.[9]

The first actual engagement at *Beder* between the rival parties took place in the month of Ramadhan, in the second year of the Hedgra; this time also Mohammed set out against a richly laden caravan, returning from Syria. But its chief, Abu Sofian having received news of his movements, sent for troops from Mecca, which came forth to meet Mohammed, whilst the caravan safely passed another way. In this struggle between 314 Moslemin and 600 Meccans;[10] the latter lost seventy men on the spot, many being made prisoners. Mohammed took no active part in the battle, but was engaged in prayer, hence the victory was ascribed to the help of angels.[11] This success with its rich spoil so far increased his ranks, that he now felt strong enough to revenge himself upon the Jews.[12] After a few assassinations open war was made against the tribe of the Beni Keinukaa, some of whom lived in Medina; on their refusing to embrace Islamism they were made prisoners, and would have been masacred,

---

[9] Great scandal was occasioned by M. sending Abdallah against them with sealed orders and it required a divine sanction to justify his murderous attack. Sur. II. 217.

[10] Journal Asiatique VII. p. 97 etc. and Sur. III. 124. 125. VIII. 9. 10. 16.

[11] Sur. VIII. 41.

[12] The first victim was Asma, the daughter of Mervan who had written some satyres against him; the second a Jew who was 120 years old. Weil, p. 117. 118.

had not Mohammed been prevented from carrying out his purpose.[13]

For thirteen months Mohammed continued plundering the caravans of Mecca with impunity, until the Koreishites determining to revenge themselves sent 3000 men against Medina. The prophet was compelled to meet them and in the battle of *Ohod*, lost seventy of his best men, amongst whom was his uncle Hamza; he himself being wounded was for some time considered dead.[14]

Many other misfortunes followed the battle of Ohod, which fell specially upon the Missionaries of Islamism, several of whom were murdered. With a view therefore to indemnify his followers Mohammed attacked another Jewish tribe,[15] but being well fortified in their castles they held out for some time and he permitted them to emigrate with part of their substance. As the spoil was gained without the sword, Mohammed's followers were disappointed by his claiming it for himself. These and other successful depredations caused another army of 10,000 men to be raised against Mohammed; it was commanded by Abu Sofian the head of the Koreishites.[16] The

---

[13] They were put in fetters, that he might slay them the more easily, but Abdallah, under whose protection they were, prevented it; Sur. V. 59. 60. was revealed to rebuke him for his interference.

[14] He was found in a ditch, and had lost one of his front-teeth; had he not been recognised by Kaab through his armour and helmet, he would probably have perished on the field.

[15] The Beni Nadhir, see Weil p. 134 till 139. and Sur. LIX. 1—16.

[16] This was in the fifth year of the Hedgra, March A. D. 627.

prophet now dreading an open engagement, entrenched himself within the walls of Medina, working himself at the fortifications. But want of courage to storm the place, unfavourable weather, and discord among the besiegers induced them after twenty days to raise the siege. Mohammed however wishing to revenge the siege upon the Jewish tribe, Beni Koreiza, who on this trying occasion had joined the allied army against him, ordered a wholesale massacre of the men and the women to be sold as slaves or exchanged for horses;[17] one of them, Rihana was converted and added to the number of the prophet's wives.[18]

The humiliating siege of Medina, and the domestic affairs of Mohammed stirred up a party among his followers headed by Abdallah Ebn Ubej who had long looked upon his growing power with extreme jealousy; having uttered some severe remarks on the

[17] Respecting the siege of Medina and this infamous war with the Jews: see Weil, pag. 160—170. A description by M. is found Sur. XXXIII. 9—14. 20. 25. 26.

[18] Shortly before this M. had married the beautiful widow Um Salma, and Zeinab the wife of his liberated slave Zaid, whom he had persuaded to divorce. As it caused great offence to his followers he received a special licence from heaven. Sur. XXXIII. 4. 5. 37—39. Another wife he had lately taken was Barra, one of the 200 captives from the Beni Mustalik. We cannot be surprised that the faithfulness of Ayesha was called into question at this time, when so many rivals were added. To silence her accusers, Sur. XXIV. 11—20. appeared. The case of Rihana reminds us of the words of Homer:

Τὴς δ' ἔλαθ' εἰσελθὼν Πρίαμος μέγας ἄγχι δ' ἄρα σὰς
Χερσὶν Ἀχιλλῆος λάβε γήνατα, καὶ κύσε χεῖρας
Δειράς, ἀνδροφόρους, αἳ οἱ πολέας κτάνον υἷας.

Iliad. Ω L. 477.

prophet,—who had not then the power to resent the affront—Abdallah was requested by his tribe to seek Mohammed's pardon, to which he replied: "you asked me to become a believer, and I became one; you commanded me to pay taxes for religious purposes, and I paid them; now nothing is wanting but that I should worship Mohammed."[19]

The prophet having thus raised a powerful feeling against himself, felt it necessary in order to recover his position and revive the enthusiasm in his cause, to take a fresh public step, and therefore proclaimed a pilgrimage to Mecca, inviting both his followers and allies among the Pagan Arabs to join him. This scheme however partialy failed, for in spite of having mustered only 700 men, he was compelled to start at once for Mecca in consequence of a dream,[21] trusting that the Koreishites would forbear active hostilities during the sacred months. Changing his armour for the garment of a pilgrim and taking seventy camels, whom he had marked for a sacrifice,[22] he set out, and without molestation reached

---

[19] This produced the infallible Sura, called "the hypocrite," which came down during one of his so called epileptic fits. See Sur. LXIII 1. 2. 5. 7. 8.

[20] Great murmurring was also caused by his cruel destruction of the palm-trees, which served as a means of subsistence to the Jewish tribe, Ben Nadir, whom he afterwards drove into exile and the appropriation of the entire spoil, which the verses, Sur. LIX. 1—8. 11—16. could not allay.

[21] M. dreamed that he entered Mecca, and as his dreams were revelations from God, in order to be consistent, he was compelled to go.

[22] The mark consisted in a cut on the back of the animal, and a piece of leather or an old sandal round the neck. The first was called "ishar" the latter "taklid."

the vicinity of Mecca; failing however to gain admittance, the ceremonies of the Hadj or pilgrimage were performed at a distance; and a truce with the Meccans was made for ten years with the promise that at a future festival Mohammed might enter their city as a pilgrim and remain for three days.[23]

To divert the discontent of his fellow-pilgrims under these discouraging circumstances, he proposed war against the Jews of Cheibar and Fadak, who dwelt about four days journey north-east of Medina: some of their fortified places were stormed, and the rest submitted, engaging to pay half of their income as tribute.[24] Not satisfied with the fifth part of the spoil, which he always claimed as divine right, he appropriated an additional wife, in the captive Jewess Safia, whose husband he had killed on account of his hiding some of the treasures.[25] Zeinab another Jewess seeking to revenge the death of her relatives prepared a poisoned lamb, for the prophet, who did not however take sufficient of it to cause his immediate death; yet he believed his health to have been destroyed from that hour.[26] On his way back to

---

[23] Respecting this visit at Mecca see Sur. XLVIII. 1—27.

[24] Mohammed's progress resembled that ascribed to Caesar by the Roman poet:
    Acer et indomitus, quo spes, quoque ira vocasset,
    Ferre manum, et numquam temerando parcere ferro;
    Successus urgere suos — —
    — — Impellens, quidquid sibi summa petenti
    Ostaret; gaudensque viam fecisse ruina.
                                    Lucan. lib. I. 146.

[25] Gagnier "La vie de Mahomet" II. p. 57.

[26] When Zeinab was charged with the crime, she said: "Thou knowest how my people are treated by thee; I thought therefore:

Medina two other Jewish tribes were conquered and made tributary.

Just at this period, returned the exiled Moslemin from Abyssinia, bringing with them a report of the kind treatment, they had received from the Prince of that country,[27] and this circumstance probably emboldened Mohammed to send written demands to foreign potentates,[28] requiring them to acknowledge him as a divine prophet and to embrace Islamism. Some are said to have complied with this demand, others doubtless from fear of his marauding bands, treated the ambassadors with courtesy and respect; but Chosroes, the Persian king tore up the epistle before he had finished reading its contents, and Amru, the Ghassanide killed the ambassador. To revenge the murder, Mohammed sent 3000 men against Amru, but the latter, being supported by Greek troops, defeated them near Mutta, and thus for the first time were Moslem forces brought into contact with a Christian army.

After Mohammed had performed a pilgrimage to Mecca, staying only three days according to the treaty, the Meccans broke their faith with him by

art thou only a prince I shall obtain rest; art thou a prophet, thou wilt be instructed of it." Traditions do not agree whether she was executed or pardoned.

[27] Amongst them was the widow of a Christian, Um Halibi, to whom he was betrothed before her return to Arabia, and by whom he enriched his Harem.

[28] To the Persian king Chosroes II; the Abyssinian king; and the Emperor Heraclius; the Governor of Egypt and the heads of various Arab tribes.

rashly attacking a tribe under his protection. Rejecting an offer to renew the treaty, the pseudo-prophet advanced with 10,000 men against Mecca, and when he unexpectedly encamped before the town, the inhabitants were only able to save themselves by acknowledging him as a sovereign and a prophet.

Order being restored, Mohammed circumambulated the Kaaba seven times, each time kissing the sacred black stone. The 360 idols without and within the sanctuary were then destroyed, and these idolatrous remains being removed, the prophet commenced his prayer; after which he received the homage of men and women on mount Safa. Whilst Mohammed was occupied in consolidating his power in the town his generals went through the provinces, destroying idol temples, murdering priestesses and propagating Islamism.

Mohammed had not yet however subjected all the Arab tribes; a strong army was now arrayed against him in the valley of Honein which being too numerous for his troops, the Moslemin narrowly escaped a most disastrous defeat. Equally unsuccessful was Mohammed's attack upon the strongly fortified town, Taif: for after twenty days he was compelled to raise the siege; then having settled a violent dispute in his army, and ordered the affairs at Mecca, he returned to Medina.

The ninth year of the Hedgra bringing embassies from various tribes in Arabia, was therefore called "the year of the deputations." Mohammed now felt sufficiently strong to think of revenging his defeat at Mutta, and proclaimed a holy war against the Byzantine Empire; he perceived however but little enthusiasm among his troops, notwithstanding his promise of pardon for sins past and future to those, who should engage in it. Some dreaded the intense heat of the season, others were occupied with the date-harvest, or could not afford the necessary provisions, but the greater part doubtless feared to measure their strength with the Greeks a second time on the field of battle. Half the army returned the next day to Medina under the disaffected Abdallah Ebn Ubej, regardless of the menacing Suras, which were hurled against them. Mohammed then proceeded to Tabak, but his army being reduced and discontented, he could not venture further, and had the mortification of being obliged to return to Medina amidst the reproaches of his disappointed soldiers. Added to this vexation, a domestic occurrence at this juncture occasioned so much scandal that he deemed it unsafe to make a pilgrimage this year to Mecca, he therefore sent Ali to proclaim to the pilgrims there assembled, that no league between non-Mohammedans should be valid after the expiration of four months; that the sanctuary should hereafter be approached only by Moslemin; and finally Ali was to recite among them the ninth Sura. On the following year the tenth of the Hedgra, Mohammed made his pilgrimage to Mecca in perfect safety at the head of at least 40,000 pil-

F*

grims; it was his last visit, and of this he seemed to have a presentiment.

Some months after his return from Mecca to Medina, Mohammed prepared for a third expedition to Syria, which indeed was never carried out; owing to his sudden illness. Doubtless excited by fever, he rose up one night desiring his slave to accompany him to the burial-place of the town; on reaching the spot he saluted the dead, and said to Abu Munhaba: "To me is left the choice to remain in the world, whose treasures are opened to me till the last day or to meet my Lord earlier, and by God, I have chosen the latter." He then prayed for the dead saying, he was commanded to do so. On his return home Ayesha complaining of headache, he said; "let *me* rather complain, I feel in great pain."

From this moment his illness rapidly increased, he nevertheless continued his routine among his wives; when at last with Maimuna, he called them all together and requested, that he might be allowed to remain in Ayesha's house, which adjoined the mosque. Here his fever reached such a height, that seven skins of water were poured over his head; when relieved he said: "Now I feel that the poison I took at Cheibar tears the vein of my heart." He then went to the mosque to announce his end; and there commending Abubeker and Usuma, — the latter of whom he had appointed general of his army against the Greeks, — he concluded with this charge: "Whosoever among you has anything on his conscience, let him rise, that I may ask God's grace on his behalf." A man who was considered a good Moslem rose saying: "I was a hypocrite, a liar and an indolent Moslem." Omar vociforated: "Woe to thee, why revealest thou, what God has hidden!" Mohammed rejoined: "O son of Chattab, it is better to blush in this life than in the life to come;" and continued: "Have I beaten any of you, here is my back, let him smite me in return; have I injured the honour of any, let him attack my own; have I robbed any one of money, let him receive it back, and fear no anger on my part, for that is not my way." When a man came forward to claim three denars, he gave them, repeating: "better to blush in this world, than in the world to come."[29] Returning to Ayesha's house he fainted; Abbas caused them to give him some medicine; which so annoyed him, that on recovering his consciousness, he made all present take a dose.

During the last day of his life he appeared much better: but a fresh attack coming on, before losing his consciousness he granted liberty to his slaves, caused them to divide seven denars among the poor, and prayed: "God stand with me in the agony of death." He then expired A. D. 632. in the arms of Ayesha, his last words being: "to the highest companion in Paradise!" His body remained, contrary to all eastern custom, two or three days uninterred, whilst his friends and relations were occupied with the task of

[29] M. visited the mosque several times after, but with one exception, never took an active part in the worship. Abubeker generally acted for him, which doubtless favoured his subsequent election as Kaliph.

choosing a successor; when the contest was decided in favour of Abubeker, they at last agreed on his being buried in Ayesha's house, where he died, which was accordingly carried into effect at night.

4. Mohammed is said to have been of middle stature; to have had a large head, strong beard, round face, and reddish-brown cheeks. His biographers state, that his forehead was high, his mouth wide, his nose long, and somewhat of an aquiline shape; that he had large black eyes; that a vein which extended from his forehead to his eyebrows enlarged, when excited by anger; that his splendidly white teeth stood far apart; and upon his lower lip was a small mole. His hair hanging over his shoulders retained its dark colour to the day of his death: he sometimes dyed it brown but more frequently applied to it odoriferous oils. It was only at his last pilgrimage that he had his head shaven. He trimmed his moustache and his finger-nails every Friday before prayer. His neck, it is said, "rose like a silver bar upon his broad chest." Between his shoulders he had a large mole, which was looked upon as the prophetic seal. A physician once wishing to remove it, Mohammed objected, saying: "He who made it, shall also heal it." His hands and feet were very large, yet his step was so light, as "to leave no mark on the sand."

Mohammed spoke but little, yet occasionally permitted himself a joke. A woman once came to him, saying: "My husband is ill and begs thee to visit him;" upon which he enquired, "has not thy husband something white in his eye?" She returned in order to examine it; on her husband asking, what she was doing, she replied: „I must see, whether you have anything white in your eye, for the Apostle of God asked the question." Her husband at once recognising the joke convinced her, that this was common to all eyes. On one occasion when an old woman conjured him to pray for her, that she might enter paradise; he replied: "no *old* woman dares enter paradise!" As she began to weep, he reminded her of the verse in the Koran which declares that perpetual youth will be restored to women.

The Arab prophet was compassionate towards animals, and would wipe down his horse, when it perspired with his sleeve; but this was nothing extraordinary among his countrymen. His cat was lifted up to share his own dish; and a white cock, which he had, he called his friend, considering him a protection against devils, genii, witchcraft and the evil eye! What he could do for himself, he never allowed to be done for him by others. He bought his own victuals in the market, cleaned and mended his own clothes, milked his own goats, and often had no fire for cooking purposes for several days together. From the time he had tasted the poisoned lamb at Cheibar, he never received food from strangers, before they had themselves partaken of it. He was very superstitious and prognosticated good or evil from the most trivial incidents.

His dress was simple, usually consisting of a cotton shirt, and an upper linen garment of native manufacture, but on festive occasions he wore a yellow mantle. His woollen cap was sometimes turbaned with a white or black piece of cloth; to trowsers he only accustomed himself in after life.[30] He constantly used a tooth-pick, and even died with one in his hand. His sleeping apartments accorded with the general simplicity of his habits. He slept on straw-mats covered with a cloth; his pillow was a leathern cushion filled with the fibres of the palm. The prophet however displayed considerable vanity in his toilet: he always carried with him a mirror in which he loved to contemplate his person, also a comb, a pair of scissors, odoriferous oil and paint for the eyelashes. On the battle-field Mohammed was anything but brave, generally wearing a double shirt of mail and a helmet with a visor, which covered the whole face, the eyes only excepted.

After these preliminary remarks on the personal appearance, habits and manners of Mohammed, we arrive at the difficult task of defining his extraordinary *character*. No character has ever been painted in more varied and opposite colours than that of this remarkable individual; some authors applying to him every opprobrious term that could be invented; others representing him a pattern of greatness, power and

[30] „Bei außerordentlicher Veranlassung bestand sein größter Staat in einzelnen Stücken, welche er zum Geschenk erhalten hatte, in einem vom Kaiser Heraklius zum Geschenk erhaltenen tuchenen, mit Seide durchwebten und gestickten Gewande, einem Paar vom König von Abyssinien geschenkten schwarzen, buntgemalten Stiefeln, einem großen Kopfbund, und einem Gurt oder Wehrgehenk von Kupferblech mit silberner Schnalle, silbernen Haftspangen, drei silbernen Ringen und silbernem Gebräme. Die Farben seiner Kleidung waren seine Lieblingsfarben weiß, schwarz, grün, auch roth." Wahl pag. 73.

virtue. Nor can we be surprised at this contrariety of views, when we remember how one excess is generally followed by another, and re-action is the natural consequence where truth and justice have been outraged.[34]

It is indeed no easy matter to form a just estimate of a character composed of such consummate duplicity. If we regard Mohammed as acting the part of a conscious impostor or as a monster of cruelty and injustice, we shall find it hard to reconcile with our view the sparks of real devotion which here and there appear in his life, and to account for the moral and religious revolution which he accomplished among the nations of Asia and Africa in so wonderfully short a period. Again, if ambition alone is put forth as the main-spring of Mohammed's mind, we must remember that the love of power manifested in one party, is always opposed by the instinctive unwillingness of the other to be governed; if then there had been no admixture of truth in his work and character, or if a want had not been felt, to induce men to submit to his claims, his passion to rule would have met with but little result.

To judge from the manner in which Mohammed constantly alludes to his impression that the Jews and Christians had corrupted their Scriptures he

[34] Before the twelfth century it was hardly understood in the West, that M. was only a false prophet and not a pretended divinity; and still earlier he was known as Maphomet, Baphomet, Bafum (whence the French words bafumerie and momerie our English mawmetry and mummery, see M. Renan and Trench "on the study of words"), and believed to be a false god to whom human sacrifices were offered!

must *at one period of his life have believed*, that the ancient prophets wrote of him as the last prophet: never deeming it necessary to give an account of their dishonest transaction but always taking it for granted as a well-known fact. He accuses them [32] of having been bribed by their spiritual guides to suppress those prophecies, which referred to him. He censures the envy of the Jews [33] which would not allow them to admit, that any other nation, besides their own, could give a prophet to the world. Again he declares [34] that having killed their prophets, no one need be astonished that they should corrupt their Scriptures with a view to reject him. He also tells the Christians that in perusing their books, they might as certainly recognise his divine Mission, as a father would recognise the features of his son; but in the wickedness of their heart they denied him. [35] That Mohammed was strengthened in this faith by his friend Waraka, who was a Christian priest and acquainted with the Old and New Testament, has been already seen in this chapter.

Taking these and other matters into consideration, we cannot possibly side with those who consider Mohammed to have been a thoroughly self-conscious impostor *at the commencement* of his career. If the question therefore be raised whether we are to consider him as an impostor or a misguided fanatic,

---

[32] Sur. III. 185.   [33] See Sur. II. 89.   [34] Sur. III. 21. 103.

[35] He flatters them, especially the monks, to induce them to give up the writings they had secreted, and proceeds to threaten them and the Jews with awful judgments, if they would not deliver those prophecies, which they had so long withheld.

we answer, that he was neither wholly the one nor the other, and yet he was both. Mohammed in our opinion *commenced* his pseudo-prophetical career with honest intentions. Though Satan contrived to delude him with consummate craft, and even though there was in Mohammed's own heart the germ of all the evil of which he became the author, it still remains to be proved, that he was from the beginning an hopelessly wicked impostor. A man may be in error, and yet be sincere; those who killed prophets and apostles, thought that they were doing God service; nor can we ascribe want of sincerity to Saul the Pharisee, when raging against the Church and destroying her members.

We have seen in the previous biographical sketch of Mohammed, that in his infancy as well as in after life, he was afflicted with a kind of epileptic fit, which was considered both by himself and others to be the effect of demoniacal possession. He was treated by an exorcist with a view to the expulsion of the demon. When his alleged revelation commenced, it was accompanied with the same spasmodic convulsion which he had had before, and Mohammed himself, as well as his friends, was at first impressed with the idea, that it was an evil spirit, which influenced him. It was no doubt from a fear, of sanctioning this apparently superstitious view of the native Arabs,—whose testimony in the matter has been deemed too doubtful and unintelligent to be regarded by European savans — that these facts have been wholly disregarded in forming an estimate of Mohammed's character. But have we not a parallel case[36] in holy Scriptures, where a youth is described as being possessed of a devil, who was *precisely* affected in the way, in which we find Mohammed is represented to have been in the writings of his own followers? Mohammed's attacks are considered to be of an epileptic character: and no physician will fail to recognise the same type of disorder in the case brought before us in the Gospel. If in the latter instance the author of the evil was the devil, why should we not assume him to be the author in the case of the false prophet?[37]

Independently of Mohammed's own impression, the belief of Chadija, Abu Talib and the generality of their contemporaries in Arabia, we cannot resist expressing our conviction that the assumption of satanic influence can alone solve the mystery which envelops the origin of this fearful "delusion." Even supposing that no evidence existed of Mohammed's

[36] "And one of the multitude answered, and said: Master I have brought unto thee my son, which hath a dumb spirit, and wheresover he *taketh him* (καταλάβῃ cfr. the asabahu of M.) he *teareth* him, and he *foameth*, and gnasheth with his teeth, and *pineth away* (ξηραίνεται cfr. ighmaȧ in M's case). And they brought him unto him; and when he saw him, straight way the spirit *tare him* (ἐσπάραξεν), and he *fell on the ground* and *wallowed foaming* (M's face was covered with foam). And the *spirit cried* (M. roared like camel), and *rent him sore*, and came out of him; and he was *as one dead*, insomuch that many said *he is dead*." Mark IX. 17.

[37] It need scarcely be added that the ordinary cases of epilepsy present some of the most unaccountable and perplexing phenomena to medical science, since post mortem examinations entirely fail to discover the slightest trace of disease in any part of the body, a circumstance, we believe, without parallel. But, alas we have altogether swerved very far from Biblical views as regards maladies in general, their true source and the secret of healing!

having been afflicted with such a malady — one which was invariably ascribed to the immediate agency of the powers of darkness, — could we consider it possible, that so grand, comprehensive and lasting an apostacy as that of Islamism should have been conceived, and have obtained such a fearful dominion over nations, some of whom were polished and civilised, without the direct co-operation of the prince of darkness?

Mohammed the Arab prophet must be considered a type of Antichrist, if that last great enemy of the Church is to win his temporary power through the abounding of heresy among Christians, and is to claim that position in the world, which is due only to the Son of God.[38] If this be so, may we not assume, that his coming would be also "after the working of Satan with all power of signs and lying wonders, and with all deceivableness of unrighteousness in them that perish?"[39] How natural therefore that Satan should appear to Mohammed as an "angel of light;"[40] and if we assume, that he took the form and acted the part of the angel Gabriel, we account

---

[38] It can only be ascribed to the sceptical views of too many of our learned men, that they so carefully avoid this point of satanic agency at the commencement of Islamism. See 1 Chron. XXI. 1. John XIV. 30. Lu. XXII. 3. 31. Math. XIII. 25. 29.

[39] Ὄυ ἐστιν ἡ παρουσία κατ' ἐνέργειαν τοῦ σατανᾶ ἐν πάσῃ δυνάμει, καὶ σημείοις καὶ τέρασι ψεύδους, καὶ ἐν πάσῃ ἀγαπῇ τῆς ἀδικίας ἐν τοῖς ἀπολλυμένοις. 1 Thess. II. 9. 10.

[40] "For such are false Apostles (ψευδοαπόστολοι, cfr. رسول الله) deceitful workers, transforming themselves into the Apostles of Christ: And no marvel; for Satan himself is transformed (μετασχηματίζεται) into an *angel of light*." 2 Cor. XI. 13. 14.

not only for the mysterious origin of Islamism and its potent spell among the nations of the world, but also for the otherwise inexplicable contradictions in the character of the false prophet. If ever it has been fulfilled that: "God shall send them *strong — or energetic — delusion,* that they should believe a lie,"[41] it was in this instance.

Assuming then that Mohammed had the vision of an angel, or rather of a devil "transformed into an angel of light," we may take it for granted that he began his work of reformation with honest intentions, and not with the consciousness of acting the part of an impostor. If we consider the imposture as the master-piece of Satan, framed and carried out under the immediate co-operation of the powers of darkness; if we allow for the workings of Mohammed's natural fervent imagination, at a period when his nation expected a prophet; and if we regard the mature age, at which he announced his Mission; the convictions of Chadija, Abubeker, Omar and others, who had the opportunity of judging of his real state of mind; his endurance for twelve years, of every kind of insult, abuse and persecution; his rejection of all offers of riches and power, when made on the condition of abandoning his infatuation;[42] the simplicity of his mode of life to the day

---

[41] Καὶ διὰ τοῦτο πέμψει αὐτοῖς ὁ Θεὸς ἐνέργειαν πλάνης, εἰς τὸ πιστεῦσαι αὐτοὺς τῷ ψεύδει. 2 Thess. II. 11.

[42] According to the Sirat Arrassul a Koreishite said to him at the beginning of his Mission: "Resign thy faith, wilt thou money, beautiful women, or desirest thou for power? Say what thou wilt, it will be granted unto thee; seest thou a spirit from which thou

of his death:—taking these and other considerations into account we cannot believe that Mohammed *commenced* his work merely as an ambitious conqueror, or a base imposter, who had no faith. in himself or his Mission.

He was perhaps the unconscious instrument at first for originating an unparalleled delusion, which should maintain the most active and lasting antagonism to Christ's religion; and he was urged on in his work by some superhuman impetus which in the course of time he vainly persuaded himself to be the inspiration of Heaven. Thus having set his bark afloat, his zeal kindled, his work prospered and in his enthusiasm he may have interpreted this success as a mark of God's favour and support. His new religion was not therefore on his part a premediated scheme of deception, but was suggested to him as the most appropriate means of uniting the professors of the three creeds, then prevalent among his countrymen, and of thus satisfying an acknowledged want among them. Thus led on step by step, Mohammed soon came to act the part of a conscious and decided impostor: in whatever way, therefore the question as to his individual guilt at the beginning may be determined, there can be no doubt of that guilt as his scheme ripens. The following alleged revelations, incontrovertibly stamp Mohammed as a false prophet; first the Sura which had for its object to re-establish the innocence of Ayesha his

canst not free thyself, we will pay the exorcist with our own money." Sirat Arassul fol. 47. 48.

favourite wife ; then the authority to empower him to marry the wife of his adopted son Zaid, to enlarge his Harem at pleasure ; and to obtain a larger proportion of the spoils, made by his army.[43] The first drop of blood which was shed in his name by Abdallah during the sacred months, marked him as a man, who had now entered the path of deception, and wilful imposture.[44] He might possibly persuade himself that he was acting in the spirit of Moses, and following the steps of some sincere Christians, when he declared war against the unbelievers, and agreeably to the practice of his age and country he might justify single instances of murder ; but he could not desecrate the sacred months by plunder and bloodshed without having some real or pretended revelation to sanction the act : yet according to his most orthodox biographers, this sanction was not

[43] In Sur. VIII. 41, the fifth part is apportioned to the prophet. The Sura respecting the innocence of Ayesha is XXIV. 11—20. also 4—5. The answer to the murmurs which were caused by his marrying Zeinab, the wife of Zaid, is found Sur. XXXIII. 4. 5. 36. 30—39. No one will be surprised when Maraccius commences his "Refutationes" to this Sura with these words : "Inter alia quae manifeste demonstrant Alcorarum non esse a Deo, illud est praecipium, puod in eo Mahometus omnia fere ad commodum suum metitur." This will also aid us to define Mohammed's character.

[44] The letter which was given to Abdallah Ebn Djach contained these words : "In the name of the Most Merciful, the Most Gracious go with thy companions, God's blessing be upon thee, into the valley Nachala, and watch there the caravans of the Koreishites, perhaps thou canst bring me word about them." The last sentence seems a Moslem addition, to protect M's character. Sura II. 217. refers to this transaction. Weil, pag. 98—102.

given till a considerable time had elapsed *after the return* of Abdallah from his infamous expedition. The mystery with which he confides to him an ambiguously written letter to be opened only after he had travelled a few days from Medina, again stamps Mohammed as an impostor, who was conscious that he was committing an act of injustice and treachery.

Again the "Sura of Joseph",[45] composed by Mohammed in Mecca, before his flight, is given as a direct revelation from Heaven, and appealed to as a proof of his divine Mission, though it contains incontrovertible proof of having been partially borrowed from the Bible and still more largely from Rabbinical tradition. Here was no delusion, no deceivable vision or satanic inspiration, which could have been mistaken for divine revelation, but a wilful fraud, and palpable deception. But even granting the supposition that Mohammed justified base means by the good end he had in view, before his flight, we still find him acting with a crafty, inconsistent and shortsighted policy throughout his stay at Medina. He first flatters the Jews and makes surprising concessions in order to win them to his cause but being disappointed in his expectations, he rescinds all his former concessions in their favour and becomes their deadliest enemy. Some he pardons through fear of Abdallah, others he slaughters like a flock of

---

[45] Sur. XII. was written in a romantic style and was meant to attract the Arabs, whose taste for such compositions is notorious.

sheep. To day he limits the number of wives, to morrow he transgresses his own laws in the name of God.[46] The murderer may save his life by paying a ransom, but the thief is to have his hand cut off. In critical moments he seeks the advice of others, which he carries out against his own will.[47] His strange shortsightedness became apparent, in his neglecting to choose a successor.

It was comparatively easy for Mohammed to gain the assent of his Pagan contrymen to his prophetical dignity without any distinguished talent, for his creed was unquestionably of a higher order than their own; added to which his attractive manners, his eloquence, liberality and general uprightness were sufficient to secure him many admirers. At Medina, success was attributable rather to his good connections, the prospect of spoil, the disunion of the tribes, and his own powers of deception than to his personal bravery or talents as a general; he deemed no means too base to rid himself of an enemy, where he felt strength and courage to do so: his art consisted in first acquiring every possible information and then surprising the enemy; hence he preserved the greatest secresy on all occasions,

---

[46] Sur. XXXIII. 47. 48. 49. After mentioning various degrees of affinity, within which the prophet may marry it is added, "and any other believing woman, if she give herself unto the prophet, in case the prophet desireth to take her to wife. This is the peculiar privilege unto *thee above the rest of* the true believers."

[47] At Ohod he goes forth against his will; during the siege of Medina he wished to make a separate league, and at Taif he commands the storming, although he knew it would be fruitless.

and only in one instance did he inform his army beforehand of the plan and object of his expedition.[48]

In reviewing the character of Mohammed, we find that it decidedly deteriorates from the time that he had *assumed the office of a prophet,* and this most significant fact ought to be specially borne in mind. In his early days of religious reform he commenced as a sincere fanatic, mistaking dreamy visions and satanic influence for divine inspiration; but he completed his career as a licentious impostor, who brought forth his pseudo-revelations whenever he found it necessary to sanction the most unjustifiable acts. It now devolves upon us to examine the history and the general character of the document, containing those revelations bequeathed by Mohammed to the world.

CHAPTER IV.

HISTORY AND DOGMAS OF THE KORAN.

"They have seen vanity and lying divination saying: The Lord saith, and the Lord hath not sent them: and they have made others to hope that they would confirm the word. Have ye not seen a vain vision and have ye not spoken a lying divination, whereas ye say: The Lord saith it; albeit I have not spoken."
Ezek. XIII. 6. 7.

The Koran[49] purporting to be the work of Mohammed could not long remain an indifferent book

---

[48] This was the expedition against the Greeks to Tabak.

[49] القرآن Koran from قرأ legere; hence lectio, liber lectionis,

to the literary and religious world, hence we possess a considerable number of printed editions in the original;[50] various translations being also made into other languages. The first Latin version appeared in the days of St. Bernard A. D. 1143. When at the request of Peter, abbot of the Monastery at Clugni, the Koran was translated by Robert of Retina an Englishman, and Hermann of Dalmatia a German, but it remained hidden in the cloisters for nearly 400 years, when A. D. 1543 it was published at Basle by Theodor Bibliander[51]; and though scarcely deserving the name of a translation it was again rendered into Italian, German and Dutch.[52]

מִקְרָא in the same sense among the Jews: Another name فرقان, פֻּרְקָן, Foorkan; often only كتب, βίβλος, liber answering to סֵפֶר.

[50] The Koran was first *printed* in the original Arabic at Venice, at the beginning of the sixteenth century, under the short title: „Alcoranus Arabice. Venet." but no copy seems now to exist. Hinkelmann edited it in Hamburg 1694. In the year 1698 Maraccius followed with his edition: "Alcorani textus universus" etc. The next was by the Russian Emp. Catharina II: "Al Koran Arabice. Petropoli 1787." Anno 1829: "Muzihi-el-Koran in Calcutta; Arabic and Hindustani." The same in Serampore 1833; with an English version, Cawnpore 1834. Again at Calcutta in Arabic and Persian 1831; the same at Cawnpore 1835. G. Flügel edited it 1834 Lips. Another followed in Leipsic 1837. and in Calcutta appeared the same year an edition with two Pers. Com. and an interlin. Hindi translation.

[51] "Machumetis saracen. princ. ipseque Alcoran quae ante annos CCCC Petrus Abbas Cluniacensis ex Arab. lingua in Lat transferri curav. Haec omnia in un. Vol. red. sunt op. et st. Th. Bibliandri Eccles. Tigur. Ministri... Basil. 1543. Fol."

[52] The Italian appeared at Venice 1547. "L' Alcorano di Macometto nel qual si contie ne la dottrina, la vita, i costumi e i legge sue." The German version by Sal. Schweiger appeared 1616 and 1623 at Nurnberg, and the Dutch 1641 at Hamburg.

The learned Maraccio published his work, consisting of the Koran in Arabic, a Latin version, with notes and refutations A.D. 1644.[53] This Latin translation was published separately in Germany and rendered into the language of that country.[54] The oldest French version was executed by M. du Ryer, who had acquired a knowledge of Arabic at Constantinople and Alexandria;[55] and this version became the parent of several other translations into English, Dutch and German.[56] M. Savary gave a new version to the world in the year 1783;[57] and still more recently we received a fresh translation from M. Kasimirski.[58]

Of the English Translations of the Koran from the original we first name that of George Sale, so well and deservedly known to the British public; it was published in 1734 and is frequently quoted in this work

[53] "Alcorani texius universus ex correct. Arabum exempl. descriptus .. ex Arab. idiom. in. Lat. translat. appositis unicuique cap. notis atque refut. his omnibus praemiss. prodrom. Auct. Ludovico Maraccio. Patavii 1698. Fol."

[54] The German version by David Nerreter Nurnberg 1703. The Latin one was edited by Chr. Reineccius Lips. 1721.

[55] "L'Alcoran de Mahomet. Translaté d'Arabe en Français. Paris 1647."

[56] Alexander Ross turned it into English, Lond. 1649 and 1688. Glazemaker into Dutch 1698. Rotterd. and G. Lange published a a German version from the Dutch at Hamburg.

[57] Le Coran traduit de l'Arabe accomp. de not. et preced. d'un abrégé de la vie de Mahomet tiré des ecriv. orient. le plus estimés par M. Savary. Paris 1783.

[58] Pantheon littéraire, collect. univers. de chefs d'oeuvres de l'ésprit humain, les livres sacrès de l'orient. pag. 463—752: Civilisation musulmane, le Koran, traduction nouvelle faite sur le texte Arabe, par M. Kasimirski. Paris 1840. 2me edition 1841.

in spite of the great inconvenience which arises from his neglecting to divide the Suras into verses, which are invariably in the original and several of the foreign versions.[59] Sale's version was rendered into German by Theod. Arnold, who in translating it consulted other versions, especially that of Maraccio.[60] The first German version from the original was accomplished by Professor Megerlin; it has the advantage of being divided into verses.[61] In 1773 Boysen's new translation appeared in Germany, furnished with notes.[62] His version was revised and corrected from the original by Wahl in the present century, and is accompanied by a valuable introduction.[63] Two new versions from the Arabic have lately been added to the above by Ullmann in Germany, and Rodwell in this country.[64]

There are not wanting other auxiliary means to render the Koran more intelligible to the European student, such as concordances and indices specially compiled for this purpose.[65] The commentaries of

[59] The Koran commonly called the Alcoran of Mohammed by G. Sale. London 1734.

[60] Arnold's translation was published A.D. 1746. at Lemgo.

[61] Die Turkische Bibel, oder des Koran's allererste deutsche Uebersezung aus der Arabischen Urschrift von M. D. Fr. Megerlin, Frankfurt 1772.

[62] Der Koran oder das Gesetz für die Musselmänner durch Muhammed, unmittelbar aus dem Arabischen übersetzt mit Anmerkungen. Halle 1773 und 1775.

[63] Der Koran nach Boysen von Neuem übersetzt aus dem Arabischen mit einer historischen Einleitung c. c. von G. Wahl, 1828.

[64] Der Koran von Dr. L. Ullmann. Crefeld 1940. Rodwell's Koran, translated from the Arabic, with introduction, notes, and index 1865.

Moslem doctors are so numerous, that their names alone would fill entire volumes. There are not less than 20,000 of them in the library at Tripolis in Syria; but the best and most known are the works of Zamakshari, Bedawi, Mahalli and Sujuti.

1. The Koran, as we now have it, is confessedly not the work of Mohammed, but of his followers.[66] On his death, his alleged revelations were found scattered in fragments here and there, some in the hands of Hafsa, one of his numerous widows, others remained only in the memory of believers. Mohammed not only omitted to compile these written fragments, but with the exception of a few, he never encouraged their general circulation; this would have precluded the possibility of his adding, altering, modifying and recalling previous revelations, as occasion might require. That it was a common practice of the prophet to revoke and alter his phrenetic productions is proved by the Koran itself,[67] as well as by tradition.[68] On one occasion a verse having been

cutta 1811. and Concordantiae Corani arabicae ad literarum ordinem et verb. radices dilig. disp. Gust. Flügel. Lips. 1842.

[66] That M. employed secretaries to write down his visions is not called into question; less known is the fact, that he must have had the knowledge of writing during the latter part of his life. He required writing materials in his last moments. Again he said to Muawia, one of his secretaries: "Draw the ب straight, divide the س properly etc. etc." Note et extrait. des Manu. de la Biblio. Imper. tom. VIII. p. 357.

[67] "We recal none of our verses, or bring them to oblivion without supplying better ones or at least some equally good." Sur. II. 100. also Sur. XVI. 103. 104.

[68] When it was revealed that those who stay at home were not before God as those who go forth to war, Abdallah and Ebn Um

recited by Mohammed to a friend, who immediately wrote it down, it was the next morning discovered to have been effaced; the prophet on being told of the disappearance of the verse replied, that it had been taken back to heaven; in other words, that he himself had obliterated the writing.[69]

As Mohammed was not always able to destroy a condemned or recalled Sura, or any part of such, the many contradictions and abrogations which are to be met with in the Koran are easily accounted for. Commentators indeed seek to explain away many of these discrepancies, yet in spite of their ingenuity they are compelled to admit no less than 225 passages, containing laws and dogmas, which have been abrogated by subsequent Suras. Mohammed frequently made experiments with his heaven-sent commands, not scrupling to alter his inspired directions according to circumstances: thus we have seen that when his faith was greater in the Jews and Christians than in his Pagan countrymen, he fixed the Kebla at Jerusalem, and made other similar concessions; but when the former disappointed his expectations, he altered it for Mecca hoping to conciliate the latter. The law which Mohammed had made[70] on behalf of the Moslem fraternity of emigrants

---

Maktum exclaimed: "and what if we were blind"! The prophet asked for the shoulder-blade upon which it was written — then had a spasmodic convulsion and when recovered — made Zaid add: "not having a bodily infirmity." Sur. IV. 94. The secretary related long after: "I fancy, I see the words now on the shoulder-blade near a crack." Mem. de l'Accad. des inscrip. I. 308.

[69] Weil, Einleitung in den Koran, pag. 45.   [70] Weil pag. 355.

at Medina, excluding their kindred from inheritance, was repealed when they had acquired property and had taken root among the original inhabitants. Originally Mohammed required two believers as witnesses in special cases, but afterwards when his power increased, he declared one to be sufficient. Again, at an early period toleration was recommended towards non-Moslem communities, but it was abolished in Suras of a later date;[71] so long as his cause remains weak, the false prophet preaches gentleness and patience under persecution but no sooner does he obtain a firm footing, than he proclaims death and destruction to all non-conformists. Such being Mohammed's mode of enacting and revoking laws and precepts throughout his prophetical career, we can easily understand, that it would have been contrary to his uniform policy, to collect all the Manuscripts of his alleged revelations and to give them to the world.

The following circumstance will serve as a proof that the posthumous collection of the scattered

---

[71] Sur. V. 78. II. 61. where Jews, Christians and Sabians are assured of heaven, are in toto abolished by Sur. XLVIII. 13. LXIV. 11. III. 84. See Maracci Refut. ad Sur. II. pag. 33. The most remarkable contradiction concerning M's private life occurs Sur. XXXIII. 47—47. where he first receives an unlimited licence to marry, and in the latter part he is restricted to the wives he already possessed. As M. died betrothed to a fresh wife, commentators assume, he first received the restriction, and afterwards the broad licence; for it is added: "the verses do not follow in the Koran in the order they were revealed." It is however enough for our present purpose to prove that M. enacted and abolished laws in the name of God as it suited his personal convenience.

Suras, depended much upon the *memory* of Mohammed's followers. — In the engagement between the Moslem troops and the army of the rival prophet Moseilama, the most celebrated mnemonical reciters of the still uncollected Suras were slain, and Abubeker, fearing lest they should all be cut off, requested Zaid Ebn Thabat to compile the book, whose history we are now to consider.[72] Zaid therefore collected all the pseudo-revelations that could be found, written upon parchment, leather, palm-leaves, shoulder-blades of mutton, stones and other materials, and collated these with the Suras, which the survivors knew by heart.[73] It was not to be expected that this compilation would be acceptable to all parties, many of whom professed to be in possession of verses which were either altogether omitted or differently worded in the collection;[74] the consequent discord increased to such a degree under Kaliph Othman, that he determined to remedy it by a coup d'etât: Zaid was now charged to revise his former collection, to omit the "variae lectiones," which had been retained in the first, and to make several copies of this new edition; these were sent to the chief

---

[72] "I fear said Abubeker, the learned might all die out, and therefore advise the collection of the Koran." Weil pag. 348.

[73] Mem. de l'accad. des inscriptions. Tom. I. pag. 330. Alcoran ed. Maracci. pag. 38. etc. etc.

[74] Different editions of the same Suras were in existence during M's life-time. Once two men quarrelled as to the correctness of the twenty fifth Sura. Each being requested to read his own version before the prophet, he declared both to be correct, adding the Koran was revealed in seven different readings. Mem. de l'Accad. Tom. L. pag. 330.

cities of the Empire with a command to *burn* all others then existing.[75]

It will be seen that the object of Othman was to establish for future ages, the unity rather than the purity of the text, and in removing those discrepancies which Mohammed had suffered to exist, he not only compiled but reformed the Koran. As however the vowels and interpunctuations were not introduced before the second century of the Hedgra, when fresh differences had already crept into the Manuscripts, the unity enforced by Othman was of very short duration: we soon meet with seven different editions, possibly to accommodate Mohammed's assertion that the Koran was revealed in seven different readings.[77] The perplexity arising from these various

---

[75] It is however not quite certain whether Abubeker did more than collect the materials, whilst Othman caused copies to be made from them. M. Quatremere appealing to Mudjmil Attawarich says: Le Kaliphe Othman, troisième successeur de Mahomed, s'était occupé avec un soin infatigable à faire réunir en un seul corps les parties dispersées et incohérentes de l'Alcoran etc. Journal Asiatique de Paris, Juillet 1838. pag. 41.

[76] Othman's own copy of the Koran, which he read when he was assassinated, is said to have been brought to Antartus, and four leaves marked with his blood were preserved in the Mosque of Cordova. In Egypt too they professed to have a copy of his; the same in Marocco and Tiberias. Journal Asiatique de Paris tom. VII. pag. 41.

[77] Two editions originated in Medina, a third in Mecca, a fourth at Kufa, a fifth at Bussura, a sixth in Syria, the last was the "editio vulgaris." The first of the two in Medina counts 6000 verses; others as many as 6236. This will explain the difference which frequently occurs in the quotation of verses. All are said to contain an equal number of words, some say 99,464, others 77,639; and 323,915 letters. It has been also computed how many times each letter of the alphabet occurs in the Koran. Reland. p. 25.

editions is naturally heightened by the confusion prevailing in the Koran itself, and serves not only as an apple of discord among Moslem divines, but also baffles the most acute criticism of European savans.

The division of the entire book into 114 Suras[78] or chapters, was made upon most arbitrary principles and their succession wantonly defies all chronological sequence. Nor is this all; even verses which were revealed in one Sura are transposed and inserted into another which appeared at a different time and on a different occasion. A learned Moslem doctor declares:— [79] "Whosoever will give his opinion respecting the book of God, must know how the Suras appeared in succession, in Mecca as well as in Medina, and be acquainted with those, concerning the period of which the learned disagree; he must know what has been revealed twice; what appeared in Medina concerning the people at Mecca, and what appeared in Mecca belonging to the Suras of Medina, and what was made known in Djofa, Jerusalem, Taif and in Hudeibia. He must be able to discover which Mecca verses are mixed

---

[78] The word Sura occurs 9 times in the Koran. Sur. II. 23. IX. 66. 88. 126. 129. X. 38. XI. 14. XXIV. 1. XLVII. 21. Here it may signify verses; literally it implies a row, order or series; a rank of soldiers. Sowar being the plural of Sura, is now the term in India for horsemen. In Rabbinical Hebrew שׁוּרָה signifies also a row or line; and we conclude Sura to be of Hebrew origin as 3 names of the Koran correspond to Hebrew names:— القران, מִקְרָא; פָּרְקָן, الفرقان, Foorkan; כֶּתֶב, or كتب, Kitab. Each Sura is subdivided into verses, called Ayat أية, from the Hebrew אוֹת, a sign or wonder.

[79] Imam Abul Kasim Hasan Ebn Mohammed, in the introduction to the MS. "Chamis", quoted by Weil pag. 363.

up with Medina Suras, and which Medina verses were confounded with Mecca Suras; he must be likewise acquainted with those which were carried from Mecca to Medina, and from Medina to Mecca and Abyssinia; finally he must know which are the revoking and revoked verses."

In defining the chronological succession of those Suras, produced in Mecca before the Hedgra, there are three things which may serve as guides to our intricate path; first, the frequent *allusions to historical events* of that period; secondly, the *peculiar character* of the Suras, which became entirely, altered at Medina, where Mohammed assumed the character of a lawgiver and prince in addition to that of a prophet; lastly, the *style* of the Suras, which originally was rhythmical greatly resembling that of the Arabian soothsayers, but which Mohammed afterwards exchanged for prosaic diction, that he might not be considered possessed,[80] and also because he was spent and exhausted by his first effusions: for it is remarkable that the very subjects which kindled all his enthusiasm at the commencement of his so-called Mission, were subsequently treated in a most prosaic style.

It is generally agreed that Mohammed's first revelations were the sixtyninth and seventyfourth Suras, in which he refers to his alleged Mission and writing.[81] The CXI. chapter with its imprecations

---

[80] Soothsayers were generally considered to be possessed by an evil spirit.

[81] In assigning the Suras to their respective periods it must

against his uncle Abu Lahib, — who had cursed his nephew and lifted up a stone against him, when delivering his first sermon, — belongs to this period.[82] Then follow a series of chapters in which Mohammed is encouraged to persevere in his course, in spite of the opposition of his townsmen; the divine character of the Koran is proclaimed;[83] his own office as a prophet is defined, as distinguished from that of poets, soothsayers and possessed persons, and the doctrine of the Resurrection and Judgment to come is defended against the reviling attacks of his antagonists.[84] These chapters, produced during the first five years of his Mission bear the stamp of deep conviction, earnestness and sincerity, in which Mohammed appears rather as a misguided fanatic than as an impostor. The man evidently believes what he preaches and is carried away by his enthusiasm.

The second period of Mohammed's prophetical career at Mecca, still produces some very poetical Suras, but in these we discover more of the prophet and less of the dreamy visionary and enthusiast; more

not be forgotten, that sometimes verses or portions of them belong to a different period.

[82] The same may be said of the last 6 verses of Sur. XV. where M. is commanded to proclaim his Mission beyond the circle of his friends and connections.

[83] Although not yet completed; "Koran" here and in other places signifies any writing which is to be read. See Sur. XXXIII. 25.

[84] Sur. LXXXI. LXVIII. LXXX. LXXXIX. XCIII. XCIV. CIII. C. CVIII. CII. CVII. CV. CXIII. CXIV. CXII. XCVII. XCI. LXXXV. XC. XCV. CI. LXXV. CIV. LXXVII. LXXXVI. LXX. LXXVIII. LXXIX. LXXXII. LXXXIV. LVI. LXXXVIII. LII. LXIX. LXXXIII. XCIX.

effort is apparent in his teaching and less freshness in the outpourings of his supposed inspirations. His censures of the superstitious Meccans become more detailed; his doctrines assume a calmer tone; hell and Paradise are more minutely described;[85] and the attributes of God more clearly defined; legends touching the ancient prophets increase in number and variety, so as to excite the suspicion of his being materially assisted in his strange productions.[86] This suspicion among his sharp-sighted townsmen is alluded to in the Koran, and in no way satisfactorily repelled by the assertion that the persons suspected as his coadjutors, being foreigners, were not sufficiently acquainted with the Arabic tongue to be of use to him;[87] for,—admitting they were foreigners,—they might nevertheless supply him with materials, which he could easily work up into pseudo-revelations. The Suras produced during the last few years of Mohammed's life at Mecca, seldom rise above the the level of ordinary prose, the first glow of prophetic vision having entirely subsided. It would seem that at the outset of his career the false prophet was impelled by an unseen power, which gave his mind for a time an extraordinary zeal and impetus, but

---

[85] Promises of paradise and threatenings of hell together with their detailed descriptions occupy at least the 6th part of the Koran.

[86] The chapters for which we are indebted to this period are: Sur. I. LI. The first 23 verses may be older. XXXVI. L. LIV. XIX. XX. XXI. XXIII. XXV. LXVII. XXX. XXXVIII. XLIII. LXXI. XLIV.

[87] Sur. XXV. 4. 5. XLIV. 14. XVI. 105. لسان الذى يلحدون عليه اعجمى وهذا لسان عربى مبين

that he was subsequently left to carry out that system of delusion which, ere long, degraded him to an artful impostor.[88]

A new and strongly marked period in the history of the gradual production of the Suras commences after the Hedgra, when Mohammed's line of policy became entirely changed. It is generally received that the Sura of "the Cow" was the first revealed after his arrival at Medina; Mohammed's principal object now was to win the numerous and influential body of Jews, who lived in and around that city; that he entertained great hopes regarding them, may be gathered from previous Suras, in which he frequently appeals to their testimony;[89] he shows the Jews from their own history, that they had always been wanting in faith, even in the days of Moses, and enlarges generally on the history of their ancestors.

Religious, social and civil laws are now enacted for the community of believers.[90] From this period

---

[88] The portions produced before the approaching flight are the following: Sur. VII. LXXII. XXXV. XXVII. XXVIII. XVII. X. XI. XII. VI. XXXI. XXXIV. XXXIX. XL. XXXII. XLII. XLV. XLVI. XVIII. XVI. XIV. XLI. XXX. XXIX. XIII. Sur. XVII. verse 33. must have been given at Medina; also 77.

[89] "If thou art in a doubt concerning any part of that which we have sent down unto thee, فسل الذين يقرون الكتب قبلك ask them who have read the book of the law before thee." Sur. X. 94. "Was it not a sign unto them, that the wise men among the children of Israel knew it?" Sur. XXVI. 196. See also Sur. XXVIII. 53. 54. XXIX. 47. XLVI. 10. LXXXVII. 18—19.

[90] The Kebla is fixed and again altered; precepts for worship, fasting, pilgrimage, divorce and legal purifications are intermixed with directions for warfare, keeping Friday as a day of worship, making wills, dealing with thiefs, murderers, userers, and dividing the spoil.

Mohammed's character grows decidedly darker; he recals revelations previously communicated, shifts his course and alters his policy at every turn; enemies are murdered; oaths are broken; wickedness and treachery receive divine sanction; war and plunder become the means of spreading that creed, which he originated amidst discouragements and difficulties.[91] In the twenty three chapters which Mohammed produced at Medina,[92] a marked deterioration of character is observable; — "the path of the just is as a shining light, that shineth more and more unto the perfect day: the way of the wicked is as darkness: they know not at what they stumble."

2. In tracing the divinity of the Koran,[93] we shall at present as far as possible, confine ourselves to the distinctive doctrines of Islamism, intending hereafter more particularly to notice what has been derived from Judaism and Christianity. We are indeed aware that there is perhaps scarcely a page in the Koran in which a most determined plagiarism is not perceptible; yet as the real character of Mohammed's teaching can only be gathered from the manner in which he amalgamates those foreign elements with his peculiar system of religion, a concise view of the leading

---

[91] Sur. II. 116. 146. XXII. 53—55. II. 61. III. 8. XLVIII. 13. VLVII. 70. VIII. 4. LVII. 84. LXXIII. XXIV. XXXIII. V. 98. LXVI. 2.

[92] These are Sur. II. XCVIII. LXII. LXV. XXII. IV. VIII. XLVII. LVII. III. LIX. XXIV. LXIII. XXXIII. XLVIII. CX. LXI. LX. LXVIII. XLIX. IX. LXVI. LXXVI.

[93] See the excellent treatises: "Beiträge zu einer Theologie des Korans" von Dettinger in der Tübinger Zeitschrift für Theologie.

dogmas cannot be dispensed with at this point of our argument.

The Koran clings with the utmost tenacity to the primary article of faith, the Unity of the Godhead;—the words "there is but one God" repeatedly recur in it and indeed constitute the key-note of Islamism. The arguments brought forth for the Unity of the Godhead are not always conclusive; sometimes it is inferred from the works of creation and providence,[94] at other times it is maintained, that a plurality of Gods is against reason,[95] that two deities would of necessity counteract and destroy each other,[96] and that each would strive to overcome his rival.[97] The chief evidence however rests upon the united testimony of the prophets, who all preached the same doctrine.[98]

With this dogma the Koran protests not only against the Paganism of the Arabs,[99] whose idols are represented as nought and vanity;[1] but also against the Jews, who are accused of regarding Ezra as the Son of God, and of considering their Rabbis to be Lords besides God.[2] But especially violent is the opposition of the Koran to the Christian dogma of the Holy Trinity, which it represents as consisting

[94] Sur. II. 163. 166. VI. 96—100. XVI. 3—22. XXI. 31—36. XXVII. 60—65. XL. 64—70. XLI. 9. XXXI. 10. 11.
[95] Sur. XXIII. 119.   [96] XXI. 22.   [97] Sur. XXIII. 93.
[98] Sur. XXX. 35. XXI. 25. XXXIX. 65. LI. 50—52.
[99] Sur. LIII. 19. LXXI. 23. 24. XVI. 57. XVII. 4. XLIII. 16. LII. 39.
[1] Sur. X. 19. XVI. 20. 21. XL. 75. XXI. 74. XXXIV. 22. XL. 42—44.
[2] Sur. IX. 30.

of God, Jesus the son of Mary, and His mother![3] Yet in spite of the indignation justly expressed against this misconceived and blasphemous idea, the Virgin Mary is highly exalted and honoured;[4] and our Lord, notwithstanding that His *mere* human nature is asserted,[5] and His crucifixion denied,[6] is styled, the Word and the Spirit of God, and acknowledged as an Apostle and Prophet come from God.[7] The doctrine of the Trinity and the Divinity of Christ is combatted by considering the gross impropriety of the supposition "that God should have a wife and beget a son;"[8] by arguing that to have a son, would militate against the supreme independence and all-sufficiency of God,[9] and by showing that it might become dangerous to the sovereign power of God to have an offspring.[10] To believe therefore in the doctrine of the Trinity and in the Godhead of Jesus is a mark of infidelity and excludes from Paradise.[11]

The Majesty of God is described in the Koran in words of considerable power and beauty; Mohammedans frequently recite these words and carry them about their persons, engraved on agate or other precious stone: "God! there is no God but he, the living, the self-subsisting: neither slumber nor sleep seizeth him; to him belongeth whatsoever is in heaven and

---

[3] Sur. IX. 25. V. 82.   [4] Sur. XXI. 91. III. 42. XXIII. 52.
[5] Sur. XVI. 43. XXI. 8. XVIII. 110.   [6] Sur. IV. 156. 157.
[7] Sur. XIX. 32. IV. 169. III. 39. V. 119. VI. 58.
[8] Sur. XIX. 34. LXXII. 3. XIX. 87.
[9] Sur. IV. 169. XXV. 2. XXXIX. 5.   [10] Sur. XXIII. 93.
[11] Sur. V. 58. IX. 31. III. 78.

on earth. Who is he that can intercede with him, but through his good pleasure? He knoweth that which is past, and that which is to come unto men and they shall not comprehend anything of his knowledge but so far as he pleaseth. His throne is extended over heaven and earth and the preservation of both is no burden unto him; he is the high the mighty."[12] According to the Koran God is incomparably excellent and no similitude can possibly reach His perfection.[13] His indescribability is thus strangely expressed: "God is the self-sufficient, the praise-worthy. If whatever trees are in the earth were pens, and if he should after that swell the sea into seven seas of ink, the words of God would not be exhausted." Amongst the hundred names which Moslem divines ascribe to God, that of *Allah* is the nomen maximum.[14] The appellation of "Lord" never occurs in the Koran; Mohammed no doubt excluded it from its being invariably applied to the Lord Jesus Christ in the sacred books of the Christians.[15] That these "beautiful names," must be considered to indicate the incomparable Majesty of God, we may gather from the following passage: "Serve the Lord of heaven and earth and persevere in his service, for knowest thou one

---

[12] Sur. II. 256. XXIV. 36.   [13] Sur. XLII. 10. XVI. 74. XXX. 27.

[14] The 99 names are recorded: Fundgruben IV. p. 16 the last being not so much יְהֹוָה as الله, the standing name of God.

[15] الرب, dominus, is only used with personal pronouns: my Lord, ربى; thy Lord, ربك, their Lord, ربكم, or with the following Genitivus: رب العالمين, Lord of the worlds.

who has a name like his?"[16] This leads us to the worship which the Koran maintains is due to God. "All things in heaven and earth adore God voluntarily or involuntarily; their shadows also morning and evening" are said to "bow themselves right and left."[17] Not only is God to be glorified on rising up and lying down, — but his Majesty is considered so great and august, that little is said to be wanting to cause the heavens to rend asunder from a sense of his glory.[18] Allah is eternal, the living one, who never dieth, the first and the last,[19] and the omnipresent.[20]

The attribute of *Holiness* is utterly ignored in the Koran; all that is said of God might be asserted of any honest man.[21] This total negation of the Holiness of God may be considered the fundamental lie of Islamism, which marks its teaching as directly opposed to reason and revelation, and as false from beginning to end. The favourite attribute of the Koran seems to be the *Omnipotence* of God; who is there described, as Lord of the worlds; Lord of heaven and

[16] هل تعلم سميّا, knowest thou one named like him: or who comes up to him?

[17] Sur. XIII. 15. XXII. 18. XXIV. 42. XVI. 48. سجد الله, προσκυνοῦντες τῷ θεῷ.

[18] Sur. LII. 48. XLII. 4. [19] Sur. XXV. 58. LVII. 3. XV. 23.

[20] Sur. II. 187. 116. LVII. 3. LXXIII. 8. LXX. 40. II. 116.

[21] الله يحب المحسنين, God loves them that do well. Sur. II. 196. or "he loves the pure", مطّهرين Sur. II. 223. "them that deal justly" V. 49. II. 191. III. 140. V. 73. XV. 23. VII. 29. 34.

earth and of all that is between them;[22] it also adds: to Him belongs their government;[23] His word of command must be obeyed;[24] His are the treasures of heaven and earth, as well as the powers which are therein, and His energy is indefatigable.[25] All human events and deeds are to be ascribed to His irresistible Omnipotence. Hence the reason, why so much weight is given to the formula: "*so God will;*" which is constantly upon the lips of the Moslem.[26] As the most convincing demonstrations of God's omnipotent power, the creation of the world, and the future Resurrection of the dead, are instanced.[27]

The *Omniscience* of God is also mentioned in almost every Sura, and in the second chapter alone, we have at least twenty six expressions to the effect, that "God knows and sees all ye do;" He has the keys of knowledge and in the dark furrows of the earth, happens nothing which is not entered into the book of God; the secrets of the heart are known to Him.[28]

[22] Sur. XLIV. 7. II. 20. 106. 109. VI. 101. 102.
[23] Sur. II. 107. 256. 285. IV. 130. IX. 118.
[24] Sur. II. 118. III. 47. VI. 73. XIX. 30. XXXVI. 82. XL. 70. XXIII. 82. XL. 16.
[25] Sur LXIII. 7. XLVIII. 7. XXXI. 28.
[26] ان يشاء الله Deo volente. cfr. ἐὰν ὁ κύριος θελήσῃ καὶ ζήσομεν. James IV 13. 15. Act. XVIII. 21. 1 Cor. IV. 19. Hebr. VI 4. See also analogies in Classics: Schneckenburger Com. in Epi. Jac. ad locum. Sur. XVIII. 25.
[27] Creation: Sur. XIV. 11. III. 191. 192. XLV. 3—5. LI. 20—22. X. 6. 7. XXX. 20—25. XIII. 4. 5. XXIV. 44. 45. Resurrection: XVII 50. 51. 98. 99. XXIII. 12—14. 15. 16. XXXII. 7. XXI. 104. XXXVI. 78—81. II. 260.
[28] Sur. VI. 58. XXXIV. 2. XI. 6. 7. XXXIV. 2—4. II. 235. 236.

Next to the Omnipotence of God His *Mercy*, is most prominently set forth and to these two attributes all the rest are deemed subordinate.[29] As the Koran ignores God's holy will and purpose of love to save the world in righteousness, its conception of the divine Mercy could not fail to prove a most revolting carricature. The formula: "*In the name of the most merciful God*," has indeed become the Shibboleth of Islamism,[30] being the superscription to every chapter, with the exception only of the ninth Sura; and is to Mohammedans what the Lord's Prayer is to Christians. The application of the Bismillah is accompanied with the most magical effects; not only are all letters and public documents inscribed with it, but it is worn as a talisman against evil spirits; nor is meat considered eatable to this day except the animal has been killed "in the name of the most merciful God."[31]

To the Mercy of God are ascribed the comforts of life; such as rest at night, the services of brute beasts and the production of the earth.[32] Among

[29] كتب على نفسه الرحمة, scripsit super animam suam clementiam. Sur. VI. 12.

[30] بسم الله الرحمان الرحيم in the name of God the most merciful, is briefly called Bismillah.

[31] "When these words were first revealed," quotes Abu Zaid from a Moslem author "the clouds fled to the east, the winds were hushed, the sea roared, the animals pricked up their ears to listen, the demons were chased with fiery darts from heaven, God swore he would bless all upon whom his name was called, and whosoever should utter these words would enter Paradise." See also Sur. V. 5. II. 175. XVI. 115. VI. 21.

[32] Sur. XL. 63. XVI. 5—8. XXXIV. 6. XLII. 19. XXXV. 1—3. XL. 80—82. LVII. 25.

spiritual mercies are enumerated the Revelation of the true Religion; specially the sending down of the Koran.[33] The revelation of Islamism is called the perfection of divine Love and Mercy, and the Mission of Mohammed is said to have been granted out of compassion to all creatures.[34] The sin-forgiving Mercy of God is characterized as an act, altogether capricious and arbitrary, being overruled by His irresistible power. "He forgiveth whom he pleaseth;" is one of the standing phrases of the Koran. The Holiness of God being disowned the divine Mercy is consequently made dependent on the imperfect services of man. God is represented as willing to pardon sin upon man's repentance: "But as for those who repent and amend, and make known what they have concealed, I will be turned unto them, for I am easy to be reconciled and merciful."[35] But faith, that is the acknowledgement of Mohammed as the greatest of all Apostles, — is the most meritorious of all virtues; whosoever believes in the prophet and repents, receives pardon and a free admission into Paradise.[36] Thus no one need fear lest the standard of repentance and good works might be beyond his reach; and with such views of God's Holiness and Mercy the Koran is quite consistent in repeatedly declaring, that none need despair of obtaining Mercy.[37] As the Mercy of Allah is manifested by the arbitrary acts of a capri-

---

[33] Sur. XII. 39. II. 90. 105. 235.
[34] Sur. V. 4. XXI. 100.   [35] Sur. II. 155. 162.
[36] Sur. XXIX. 7. XXIII. 1. 59. XVIII. 31. 9. XIX. 95. XX. 71. XXI. 94. XXII. 14. 111. 135. 136.

cious potentate, so is his *Righteousness* by the working of an uncontrollable power. The Righteousness of God recompences and punishes in this life and in the life to come; and is termed the reward from Heaven, the wrath of God, the revenge of the Lord, who is powerful and swift in bringing man to account. He is Lord of the day of Judgment, and not indifferent to what we do.[38] But God is said to lay snares, deceive and mock in administering Righteousness.[39] The Justice of God is frequently alluded to under the figure of a balance. Good and evil of the size of the smallest atom shall meet with its just recompence; only with this difference, that good works will be rewarded two or tenfold whilst evil deeds will meet with simple punishment.[40]

3. That Mohammed should have received the biblical doctrine of the world having been created by God in the beginning of time, is neither astonishing nor meritorious. In some places the Koran assigns six days for the creation, in others only four.[41] Concerning man's formation, it states, — God made man from clay or earth, and endowed him with a beautiful form. That the woman was formed out of a rib is no where stated in the Koran, but the Sonna sup-

[37] A woman condemned to hell was pardoned, because on passing a well, she tied up her ass and gave water to a dog on the point of perishing from thirst. Fundgruben I. pag 278. quoted from the Sonna. Sur. XXXIX. 53. XII. 87. XV. 53. 54.
[38] Sur. II. 58. 61. III. 5. 11. XL. 3. II. 168. 221. I. 4. II. 74. 85.
[39] Sur. VIII. 29. III. 53. XXVII. 51. LXXXVI. 15. 16. IV. 14. 15. IX. 51.
[40] Sur. XCIX. 7. 8. XLII. 39. VI. 170. XVI. 88.
[41] Sur. X. 3. XI. 9. L. 37. LVII. 4. XLI. 8—11.

plies the omission:[42] "Treat women with consideration, for the wife was formed out of a *crooked* rib, and the best of them bears traces of the crooked rib; if thou seek to make it straight it will break, if thou leave it alone, it will continue to be crooked. Treat women with consideration."

The Koran teaches, that the *soul* of man is endowed with power for good and evil, and is known only to God; that God has implanted in man an inclination for good and *evil;* and in harmony with the doctrine of predestination, it affirms that man's moral liberty consists only in choosing the one or the other.[43] The external condition of Adam is described to have been one of great felicity; the place of his original abode to have been heaven — no distinction being made between an earthly and a heavenly Paradise, — and his knowledge to have surpassed that of the angels.[44] Adam and Eve were neither to hunger nor thirst, nor feel their nakedness, which the learned doctors explain by assuming that they were covered with hair![45] Of their *immortality,* nothing

---

[42] Sur. VII. 12. XV. 26. 27. XVII. 62. XXXVIII. 72. cfr. VI. 2. XX. 51. XXXVII. 11. XL. 65. LXV. 3. LXXXII. 7. 8. and Fundgruben I. No. 389. pag. 276.

[43] Sur. LV. 4. XVII. 86. and XCI. 8. it is said of God: الهمها فجورها وتقويها clandestino instincta docuit (s. inspiravit in) animam malitiam suam et pietatem suam; and it will be found difficult to explain it otherwise.

[44] Sur II. 30—36. 35. VII. 20. 13. 25.

[45] So Jahja expounds in Sur. XX. 116. 117. the "non eris nudus;" and he deserves the ironical note of Maraccius Prod. IV. 107. col. 1. and: Refut. in loco IV. p. 448: "Duos, scilicet *ursos*, non *homines*, creaverat Deus!"

is mentioned in the Koran; on the contrary it is the uniform opinion of this book, that mortality essentially belongs to human nature.[46] Much is said of the superior knowledge of man in his primal state but nothing of his moral perfection.

The history of man's fall is closely interwoven with that of Satan. "We created you and afterwards formed you, and then said unto the angels, worship Adam, and they all worshipped him, except Eblis who was not of those who worshipped;"[47] upon which Eblis was ejected from Paradise and "caused them to fall through deceit."[48] The fall of man therefore was brought about by the devil in order to revenge himself, by the destruction of the happiness of our first parents. The Koran making no difference between the tree of knowledge and the tree of life teaches, that the devil tempted man, to eat of the tree of immortality and the punishment which ensued was Adam's banishment from Paradise, and the enmity which should spring up between man and man, which to Mohammed's mind was the extreme point of human misery, The nature of sin appears to be such, as to cause the *earth* only, to be corrupted;[49] for a correct notion of it: as a *moral offence* against the Divine Majesty, we vainly seek in the Koran; nor is the

[46] Sur. LVI. 62. XXI. 36. III. 186. IV. 77. To obtain exemption from death the tempter entices them to eat of the forbidden tree. Sur. XX 218.
[47] Sur. VII. 10—26.
[48] Eblis, ابليس from διάβολος; Satan, شيطان from שָׂטָן
[49] Sur. VII. 25. cfr. II. 36. افسد فى الارض corrumpere in terra. II. 27. XIII. 27. XLVII. 22. XII. 73. LXXXIX. 11. 12.

fearful truth of original sin ever acknowledged. Hence it was sufficient, that Adam should be instructed,[50] and left with a promise of future direction from God.[51] This direction is to be looked for in the Koran; on receiving which, man is certain of eternal bliss; but its rejection is the sin which of all others is unpardonable. We here perceive the utter hollowness and falsity of the creed of the Koran, in which the denial of the Holiness of God and the moral depravity of man revenges itself: had both these fundamental doctrines been acknowledged, the need of Redemption would necessarily have been felt; as it now stands, a meaningless petition for mercy, is substituted for the teaching "*of salvation in righteousness,*" and the Koran presents merely the unauthenticated message of a pseudo-prophet, as a "direction."

4. The next point we shall notice among the doctrines of the Koran is the *Pneumatology* of Islamism, as forming an essential branch of its system. Among intelligent beings, angels occupy the highest rank; they were created before man and take a considerable part in the dispensation of God's providential government.[52] They are represented as having been created

---

[50] Adam was taught كلمات: words, which he was to repeat; Sur. II. 37. 38. Maraccio: "verba, quibus peteret veniam peccati sui."

[51] هدى: directio, which according to Jelladdin is none other but the كتاب ورسول, the Koran and the apostle, liber et legatus.

[52] ملاك messenger like the Hebrew מַלְאָךְ to be desired from לְ, اَلَّ IV. misit related with הָלַךְ. That the angels are superior to man may be gathered from Sur. XXXVII. 8. 11.

from fire,[53] and as possessing a subtle, penetrating, etherial nature.[54] As ministering servants they are near God, but that they are holy is nowhere stated in the Koran, the notion of sinless purity being foreign to the author of that book. The only allusion to the purity of angels is to be found in the Sonna, where we are told, that they never enter a house, in which a dog is to be found![55] Angels generally appear in human form; thus Gabriel showed himself both to Mohammed, and to Mary. Should infidels demand the appearance of an angel to convince them, it is stated, that God would have to clothe him as a man for their sake. Animals are capable of seeing angels or devils: "If you hear a cock crow, pray for mercy, for it has seen an angel; but when ye hear an ass bray, take refuge with God, for the ass has seen a devil,"[56] The Koran speaks also of an invisible presence at the battle of Honein, where the Moslem army trusting to their numerical strength were at first repelled, but at last gained the victory through the heavenly host, which they saw not.

[53] مِنْ نَار, Sur. VII. 12. XXX. VIII. 77. LV. 15. XV. 27. Hebrew Theology speaks of an angel אֲרִיאֵל, fire of God. Ode de angelis pag. 312. Origen describes the body of angels as ἀιθέρια and ἀυγοειδὲς ϛως, Tatian ascribes to them a πνευματικὴ συμπηξις ὡς πυρος, ὡς ἀἑρος. See also Sur. XV. 27.

[54] "Nous sommes tenus de croire, que ce sont des corps subtils, purs, formès de lumière, qui ne mangent, qui ne boivent, qui ne dorment et qui n'ont ni sexe, ni appetit charnel, ni pere ni mere." Moslem Confession of faith Reland. pag. 11.

[55] لَا تَدْخُلُ الْمَلَائِكَةُ بَيْتًا فِيهَا كَلْبٌ non entrant angeli domum in quo canis est. Ode de angelis p. 452. Fundgrub. I. p. 187. No. 354.

[56] Fundgrub. I. No. 383. pag. 278.

A belief in the existence of angels is an essential article of the creed of the Koran: "he is an infidel, who is an enemy of God, of his prophets and angels, especially of Gabriel and Michael."[57] The same teaching is maintained in the creed of Islamism as translated by Reland.[58] Gabriel is considered the most celebrated angel, to be prevailing in his intercessions, of great power and might, and chief mediator of divine revelations; he is called the Spirit, or the Spirit of holiness;[59] in order to magnify him the Koran invents a variety of fables.[60] Gabriel is *par excellence* the angel of Islamism; and the mention of Michael in the above quotation, is doubtless out of compliment to the Jews, as Mohammed considered him to be their guardian.

In several Suras Mohammed swears by the angels; in these they are described as ordering and settling affairs, as reading the counsels of God; abstracting the soul from the body in the agony of death; guiding the righteous into Paradise; running swiftly and fulfilling God's demands with diligence; spreading their wings; conveying admonition and bearing the burdens of prophecy.[61] Among their *heavenly* offices, are the contemplation and adoration of the divine Majesty,

---

[57] Sur. II. 98. 286. IV. 135.

[58] "C'est une des conditions absolues de la foi, de les anges, aimer tous; c'est une infidélité, de les haïr, ou d'en haïr un seul; et quiconque ne se soucie point de croire en eux, ni de les aimer — qu'il soit tenu pour infidèle. O Dieu, preserve nous d'infidélité." Reland Leç. IV. No. 4. pag. 12.

[59] Sur. LXXXI. 20. 19. LIII. 5. 6.   [60] Sur. XX. 94.

[61] Sur. XXXVII. 1. 3. LXXIX. 1. 2. 3. 4. 5. LXXVII. 1. 2. 3. 5. LI. 1. 2. 3. 4.

and making processions around the throne of God;[62] the consideration and the writing down of the mysteries of God; the act of intercession for the faithful is not however restricted to Gabriel.[63] Among their *earthly* offices are enumerated that of transmitting fresh revelations to those whom God has chosen; counting the days of men, and specially protecting, blessing, and comforting believers; at death they examine and pass a preliminary judgment upon the departed soul:[64] "How will it be with the unbelievers, when the angels shall make them die and beat their faces and backs."[65] If the departed soul, on being examined, disavow Mohammed, the two angels present on the occasion, will inflict such a blow on the head of the poor victim, as would be sufficient to crush and dislodge mountains.[66] Lastly, the angels are active in the day of Judgment, and have their appointed functions in hell and Paradise; eight of them will bear the throne of the Judge of the world, the rest will be filed in lines on each side; Judgment being passed, they will convey the just to Paradise and drive the wicked into hell.[67]

[62] Sur. XIII. 15. XLI. 37. XXI. 19. 20. XVI. 49. XXXIX. 75. XL. 8. XLII. 4.
[63] Sur LII. 37. XXXVII. 10. LXXX. 12—15. XXXIII. 41. II. 161. XL. 8—10.
[64] Sur. XLII. 50. XCVII. XXII. 76. XXI. 26—30. L. 16. XXIII. 114. VIII. 9. XLI. 30. XXXIII. 53. LXXXVI. 4. VI. 60. LXXII. 27. 28. XIII. 13. LXXXII 8—14. XXXII. 12. VII. 38. VI. 94. XLVII. 27. VIII. 53.
[65] Sur. XLIX. 27.
[66] Fundgr. I. No 468. p. 290. No. 173. p. 167. also Commenta. Maracc. Schol. Sur. II. 161. pag. 67.
[67] Sur. LXXXIX. 23. LXXVIII. 18. LXX. 4. 5. XXV. 23. XXXVII. 23. LXIX. 30. XLIV. 45.

Other angels open the gates of Paradise and welcome the faithful. The wicked are received into hell by nineteen tormenting angels, who are also called "*Lords of fire*," and preside over the place of punishment;[68] these are described as being very terrible and ferocious; the number nineteen is said by commentators to have been chosen, because that number was specified in the Scriptures of the Jews and Christians![69]

Eblis, as we have seen, fell from pride, having refused to worship the newly created man;[70] when questioned as to the cause of his disobedience, he urged his superiority to man, who was created from *dust*, whilst he was formed from *fire;* in spite of this difference God had honoured man more than him; hence Satan has received his cognomen of "envier." In consequence of pride and disobedience he is expelled from Paradise: God said "Get thee down therefore, for it is not fit, that thou shalt behave thyself proudly; get thee hence, and be thou one of the contemptible. He answered: give me respite until the day of Resurrection. God said: verily thou shalt be one of those who are respited."[71] Where the devil abides, until the execution of the sentence at the last day, is not stated in the Koran, but that his power

[68] Sur. XXXIX. 73. 71. XL. 50. LXVII. 8.

[69] Maraccio, who always sides with the commentators when they ascribe a folly to the Koran, exclaims here as usual: "impudenter mentitur."

[70] Sur. II. 34. XV. 31. XXXVIII. 75.

[71] Sur. VII. 12. 13. 14. XV. 34. XXXIII. 78. and 35 it is said: super te erit maledictio usque ad diem judicii.

in this world is in nowise circumscribed, and that he takes possession of certain individuals, is distinctly affirmed, as we have already seen. Eblis is declared to be the author of all bodily evils,[72] to be invisible but able to see men on all occasions; to betray, deceive and carry on his work with the fiercest malignity; to be false in his promises, whilst God remains true.[73] On the day of battle he is said to assure the unbelievers, that no one shall conquer them, but when the fight commences, he turns away and leaves them in disgrace.[74] Satan is also stated to be the author of all anti-Moslem feelings, sentiments and movements, but of sin, only in so far as it is not consistent with Islamism. Sin itself, as such, is not considered to be the peculiar work of the devil, and may be committed upon divine authority, as we have seen in the life of Mohammed.

The cardinal sin is *unbelief;* not to believe in the Koran is deemed equivalent to siding with Satan;[75] for as the Koran comes from God, so all error proceeds from the Evil One.[76] Idolatry is condemned as the special work of the devil; drinking wine, playing dice, divining with arrows, sowing discord and abstain-

[72] Sur. XXXVIII. 43. where Job is introduced.
[73] Sur. VII. 28. II. 170. 208. VI. 142. XVII. 53. XVIII. 15. XXXV. 6. XXXVI. 59. XLIII. 60. XLVII. 53.
[74] Sur. XV. 30. XXXI. 33. XXVIII. 15. IV. 116. XXII. 3. XXXI. 33. VII. 24. IV. 117. III. 156. IV. 117. XXXVI. 61. IV. 58. XXIX. 38. XIV. 22. LIX. 16. VIII. 50.
[75] Sur. II. 257. IV. 74. XIX. 42. II. 108. IV. 82. XXII. 3. II. 258. VII. 28. 31. IV. 118. XLIII. 33. IV. 37. XLVII. 25.
[76] Sur. XIII. 36. XIX. 3. XXXVI. 209.

ing from certain meats are also his works.[77] Prodigals are called the brethren of Satan; but he is said to be chiefly skilled in placing the sin of opposing Islamism in an alluring light;[78] and to these deceptions the prophets are particularly exposed. Divine revelations are alleged to be abstracted by the devil and his own falsehoods substituted; this is educed from Mohammed's own experience:[79] a poor comfort for his followers! who have the sad and perplexing task of separating in the Koran what is from God, and what from the Wicked One. To relieve the minds of the faithful from too much disquietude, it is added, that the power of Satan extends only so far as God permits.[80] The Koran however contains nothing which bears any comparison with the extravagant teaching of the Sonna upon this point of Moslem divinity.[81]

Genii,[82] a class of beings otherwise called demons,

[77] Sur. II. 160. IV. 118. VI. 141. 142. II. 171. IV. 117—119. V. 99. 100. V. 4. XVII. 53. XII. 100.

[78] Sur. XVII. 27. VIII. 50. XV. 38. XVI. 63. XXIX. 38. XXXV. 36. 8. XLI. 25.

[79] Sur. VI. 12 XXII. 53. 54. LIII. 18—23. VI. 67. Sur. XII. 42. forgetfulness is also the work of Satan.

[80] Sur. LVIII. 10. XXXIV. 35. IV. 47. XVI. 99. 100. XV. 38. XVII. 10. VII. 200. 201. CXIV. 4.

[81] Fundgruben No. 374. pag. 277.

[82] Three forms: الجان, الجن and الجنّة; the first signifies Genii more in the *abstract*, the second in *concreto*; third, in *collectivo*. The Greek νυμφαι, νομαδες και δαιμονες can only partially be compared with the Moslem Genii; the Rabbinical שֵׁדִים or שֵׁדִין are also different from their having come into existence after the human race, whilst the Genii of Islamism were thought to have

—the term being promiscuously applied to both angels and devils — are sometimes treated as a nondescript link between good and fallen angels: they, like the angels, are created of fire and partake of their general character; Mohammed took them under his pastoral charge, and read the Koran to them.[83] Some of the Genii seem to be of the fallen, others rank more among the pure angels; but much confusion respecting them prevails in the Koran. Idolaters are said to worship and believe in them.[84] As devils, they are described to be friends of the unbelievers, to whom they communicate what they occasionally pick up from the conversations of angels; but the Koran must not be considered to proceed from them.[85] The Genii or Djins are said to rove over hill and dale, displaying their sprite-like nature, especially at *night*;[86] none among men had so great a power over them as Solomon, for he had in his army, not only men and birds, but also Genii, who made

been created long before mankind. جَانٌ answers to the *Genius* of the Latins; *genere, gignere* or γεννάν, from which this word is generally derived, has been traced to the Sanscrit,—Wahl pag. 632. 633.—where dshan signifies to be produced, begotten, created, born. See Buxtorf lex. Talm. Rab. verb. שֵׁדִים

[83] Sur. LV. 14. 15. XXXVII. 158. LV. 31. LXXII. 1. XVIII. 51.

[84] Sur. XXXIV. 40. compare with this ἃ θύει τὰ ἔθνη, δαιμονίοις θύει, καὶ οὐ Θεῷ 1 Cor. X. 20.

[85] Sur. VII. 28. VI. 112. XIX. 82. XXXVII. 7—10. LXXII. 8. 9. XXVI. 219. M. guards himself verse 209.

[86] "Wenn die Nacht einbricht haltet eure Knaben zu Hause, denn die Teufel irren herum zu dieser Stunde; schließe dein Thor und rufe den Herrn an, lösche deine Lampe aus und rufe den Herrn an, besorge deine Milchschläuche und rufe den Herrn an, decke deine Gefässe zu und rufe den Herrn an." Fundgrub. I. No. 375. pag. 277.

for him, "whatever he pleased of palaces and statues, large dishes like fish-ponds and cauldrons, standing firm on their trevets."[87] Lest these skilful artificers should cease from work after Solomon's death, the event was concealed from them, but they at length discovered it on perceiving a worm eating the staff upon which the dead king was leaning: then the Genii declared, had they known the truth, they would not have continued at so degrading an occupation. As an instance of the swiftness of these Genii the Koran gravely relates, that one of them brought the throne of the queen of Sheba in the twinkling of an eye, and placed it before Solomon. The uncertainty which prevails in the Koran respecting the Genii, is less indeed than that regarding angels and devils; probably owing to the fluctuating sources from whence Mohammed derived his information.

5. The Resurrection of the dead and the Judgment to come are fully taught in the Koran, concerning which detailed descriptions are not wanting.[88] "Surely those who believe, Jews, Christians and Sabians, whosoever believeth in God and the *Last Day* and doeth that which is right they shall have their reward with their Lord."[89] Each man therefore will

---

[87] Sur. XXXVIII. 40. Others he kept in chains. XXVII. 18. 38. XXXIV. 12. 13.

[88] Sur. XVII. 50. 51. L. 40—43. LXXV. 3—15. XXIII. 102—115. L. 16—33. XXV. 12—21. LII. 13—16. LIV. 46—49. XLIV. 9—15. XLVII. 19.

[89] الذين هادوا ولنصارى والصبيون, Jews, Christians and Sabians. The latter here not the worshippers of צְבָא הַשָּׁמַיִם although they are also called الصابيين or الصابئين by Arab

be judged by the light he possesses; this is more plainly set forth, in another passage:—"On a certain day we will call all men to *Judgment* with their guides, every one with the book of his actions in his right hand, and they shall read it and they shall not be wronged a thread."[90] Here is clearly an allusion to the different religions existing before Mohammed's time. Every one, the Koran declares, will bear his own burden, and no satisfaction or substitute will be accepted;[91] nor will intercession from any be admissible on that day; not even Gabriel will be allowed to intercede: this privilege is reserved to Mohammed alone:[92] hence his cognomen among the prophets of "the intercessor."

Commentators inform us that the souls of prophets are at once admitted into Paradise, but those of martyrs abide in the crops of green birds, which

---

writers; but the "*Mendai Juchanan*," as the disciples of John the Baptist are called in Syriac; from *zaba*, baptise. Sur. II. 61.

[90] Sur. XVII. 72—73. فتيل signifies like the Hebrew פתיל, thread, "*Faden*" not, hair as Wahl and Sale give it.

[91] Sur. X. 41. XVII. 15. II. 135. 142. LIII. 38. XXXIX. 8. XLV. 15. XXXV. 18. XXIX. 12. 13. XVI. 25. III. 90.

[92] Sur. LIII. 28. LXXVIII. 37. XXI. 28. 29. In the last passage: "except him, whom God will;" الا لمن ارتضى cfr. XXXIV. 23. If doubts remain, they are removed by the Sonna. "Jedem Propheten wird von dem Herrn Erhörung einer Bitte bewilligt. Ich bat den Herrn, daß ich in dieser und in jener Welt Vertreter meines Volkes sein möchte." Again: "Ich bin der Herr der Menschen am Tage des Gerichts.... Ich werfe mich vor dem Throne Gottes nieder, und es erschallt die Stimme: Moh. hebe dein Haupt empor! Lege Fürsprache ein, und sie wird erhört, begehre, es wird dir verliehen werden." Wahl pag. 415. Note c. Here then is Antichrist!

eat the fruit and drink the water of Paradise; that other departed spirits remain near their sepulchres; some imagine them near the well of Zemzem, others place them in the lowest heaven with Adam; some hide them in the great trumpet which the archangel will sound at the Resurrection; and others again make them dwell in white birds beneath the throne of God! The souls of the wicked are confined in a dungeon under a green rock, or, according to a tradition from Mohammed, placed beneath the jaws of the devil to be tormented. One part of the body, the rump-bone, is preserved to serve as a base for the new body. The dead will appear from the grave in three classes, some walking on foot, some riding, others will come forth with their faces on the ground; each according to his merit.

Descriptions of hell and Paradise abound in the Koran; it has been computed that one sixth of it is filled with the details. He that is punished lightly will be shod with shoes of fire, the heat of which will make his skull boil like a cauldron. The happiness of the blessed is depicted in colours not less material and revolting: — gold and silver, precious stones, crowns of pearl, bracelets of gold, gardens of pleasure, pleasant fruits, sweet rivers, and arbours of delight, ravishing girls with large black eyes, beautiful youths and angels, enchanting songs and sweet sounding bells; all kinds of food and beverages; beasts for riding and litters, couches and pillows, silken carpets and other furniture embroidered with gold and gems, — in these and such like material enjoyments consist the glories of the Moslem heaven![93] According to Mohammed it will take 1000 years for the meanest dweller in Paradise to see his gardens, wives, servants, furniture and other possessions; the portion of the distinguished Moslemin may be guessed from this estimate.[94]

6. Among the *ceremonial injunctions* of the Koran, we first notice the precepts respecting *ablutions*, which however were in use among the Pagan Arabs,[95] having, it is said, been prescribed to Abraham by the angel Gabriel.[96] With a view of endowing them with a religious character, Mohammed styled these lustrations to be the "key of prayer." Lest so necessary a preparation for devotion should be omitted, either from want of water or from consideration of health, sand is permitted to be used instead. In this

---

[93] These descriptions strongly remind us of the savage ideas which the West Indian or Scandinavian warriors, entertained of the future existence, and Virgil thus describes the occupations and pleasures of his heroes in the world to come:

    Pars in gramineis exercent membra palaestris
    Contendunt ludo, et fulva luctantur arena.
    Pars pedibus plaudunt choreas, et carmina dicunt.
    —   —   —   —   quae gratia currum
    Armorumque fuit vivis, quae cura nitentes
    Pascere equos; eadem sequitur tellure repostos.
                                      Virg. Aeneid. VI.

[94] Sur. XIII. 35. XLVII. 16. LV. 54—77.

[95] Herodot lib. III. C. 198.

[96] Al Jannabi in Vita Abrah. Pocock. Spec. pag. 303. Compare with this the Spanish Gospel of St. Barnabas chap. XXIX. "Dixo Abraham: Que harè yo para servir al Dios de los sanctos y prophetas? Respondio el angel, Ve a aquella fuente y lavate, porque Dios quiere hablar contigo. Dixo Abraham, como tengo de lavarme? Luego el angel se le apparcciò como uno bello mancebo, y se lavò en la fuente, y le dixo, Abraham, haz como yo. Y Abraham se lavò etc. etc."

accommodation the Koran followed the Jews and Christians there being an instance on record in ecclesiastical history, of sand being used instead of water in the administration of holy Baptism, prior to Islamism.[97] Tertullian notices the observance of ablutions among the early Christians.

Prayer is to be offered up five times a day; at day-break, at noon, in the afternoon, at sun-set and one hour and a quarter after it. The prayer itself consists in the constant repetition of certain small Suras, the Moslem confession of faith, the salutation of Mohammed and of the angels.[98] Personal observation will convince the spectator that these acts of devotion are not performed with the solemnity which certain descriptions have represented to the European world as usual; they are rather the cold and mechanical performance of a meritorious duty, than the outpouring of the heart, real devotion therefore cannot be expected. A man may be frequently seen in the act of prostration, giving orders to his servant about his horse, coffee or pipe, and then continuing his devotions. The Mohammedan has no conception of prayer beyond his prescribed forms of vague and unmeaning repetitions, to recite which, he requires a string of beads, resembling the rosary of the Church of Rome. In the 10,000 verses of the Koran there are not so many petitions as in the Lord's prayer;[99] this book incul-

---

[97] Sur. III. 46. V. 8—9. Gemar. Berachoth cap. II. Pocock. not. ad Port. Mosis pag. 389. and as used in baptism, Cedren. p. 250.

[98] Sur. III. 188. II. 230. XXIII. 3. IV. 46.

[99] A thoughtful Hindoo lad about 19 years of age was overheard repeating the Lord's Prayer admidst his heathenish devotions;

cates a spirit too proud to ask any gifts even from heaven, hence the arrogant bearing of the Moslem; he wants nothing and asks nothing, self-sufficiency, self-righteousness and a blind confidence in his own merits constitute his entire character. These feelings are strengthened by the alms, fasting and pilgrimages which the Koran commands. *Alms* are called "an acceptable loan unto God" they deliver from hell and ensure a free entrance into Paradise.[1] Specially meritorious are contributions for the propagation of Islamism by holy warfare, and collections are still made among the faithful for the support of religious institutions in Mohammedan countries.

The Koran teaches that charities, to ensure an everlasting reward, are not to be distributed from ostentation, or with uncharitable feelings;—"for a fair speech and to forgive is better than alms followed by injustice."[2] There is however no precept enjoining deeds of charity towards any but the faithful; this is the more remarkable as kindness is frequently enforced towards brutes: nor ought it to be overlooked that notwithstanding Moslem charity claims heaven for its reward, Christian charity, admitting of no such motive, far exceeds it. *Fasting* was considered by Mohammed as "the gate of religion, and the breath of him that fasteth is more grateful to God than that

when taunted by his friends with being a Christian, he replied, he was no Christian, nor had he any desire of becoming such, but that he had learnt that prayer at School, and he never had heard or conceived language that expressed his wants or feelings so well, therefore he should continue to use it!

[1] Sur. LVII. 10—12. II. 255. 265—267. [2] Sur. II. 265. 266.

of musk." The month of Ramadhan is one continued fast, no one being allowed to eat, drink or smoke from sunrise to sunset. Exceptions are made in favour of the sick, women with child, old persons and travellers. After a day of rigorous fasting and sleeping, follows a night of feasting, revelry and excess. The month of Ramadhan is chosen for fasting because during that month the Koran began to be revealed.[3]

The Hadj, or *pilgrimage* to Mecca though a pre-Islamite rite is enforced by the Koran and made an imperative duty to all true believers;[4] it is to be performed during the anciently sacred months with the observance of various precepts, sacrifices, alms and processions. The pilgrim is allowed to trade, whilst performing this sacred rite.[5] We have seen that the second Sura, which first ordains the Hadj, was revealed on Mohammed's arrival at Medina, at a period when his plans were not sufficiently matured to proclaim a universal religion; for no other than a national religion can prescribe pilgrimages to any specific locality. The Israelite indeed was to perform a pilgrimage to the temple three times a year, and this was possible so long as divine revelation was confined to a single nation, but when the hour came, in which

---

[3] Sur. II. 179—186. Ramadhan is also called شهر الصبر, the month of patience.

[4] Sur. II. 191—195. V. 3. 104—106. CIX. 1—5. CVIII. 2. III. 90—92. XXII. 27—38.

[5] When at Jedda, the author observed an inconceivable variety of goods from all parts of the world being hawked about by Moslem pilgrims who shouted forth the sum of the highest bidder.

God was to be worshipped in Spirit and in truth, men were neither to worship in Jerusalem nor on a mountain in Samaria. Mohammed therefore in ordaining the Hadj proved to the world, that his creed was neither adapted to all nations, nor originally intended for any, but the native tribes of Arabia. If pilgrimage to Mecca be an essential article in the teaching of the Koran, and if its doctrines are expected to be embraced by all nations, it follows that all nations must visit the Kaaba;[6] if it be nonessential it was folly to ordain a vain and useless ceremony; if essential to salvation, it was unjust and inconsistent to institute a rite of such momentous import, when comparatively so few believers could possibly perform it. Such inconsistencies and miscalculations are however not surprising in a book like the one whose dogmas we are now reviewing.

Some European writers represent Islamism as destitute of *sacrifices,* but this is a palpable mistake. "O true believer violate not the holy rites of God nor the sacred month, nor the *offering,* nor the ornaments hung thereon."[7] During the Ramadhan 1846, a Moslem sacrifice of three sheep took place in Jerusalem on the occasion of three companies being discharged from military service. Mohammed himself set the

---

[6] Mohammed is said to have declared that he who dies without performing the Hadj, may as well die a Jew or a Christian.

[7] Sur. V. 104—106. Peace-offerings exist among the Arabs to this day. Two servants of the author having once quarelled, on the day they were reconciled, they sacrificed a sheep, declaring such was the usage of their countrymen.

example of sacrificing during his pilgrimages to Mecca.[8] To this may be added that every animal slaughtered for use, may be considered an *immolation*, being killed "in the name of the most merciful" God.[9] Most of the religious rites connected with the Hadj, the pilgrim garment, the shaving of the head, the throwing of stones at Djumrah, the circumambulation of the Kaaba, the kissing of the black stone, the sacrifices, and almost every other item too tedious to enumerate, were borrowed from the pre-Islamite religion of the Arabs.

Circumcision, though a part of the ritual of Islamism upon which no small stress is laid, is not so much as once mentioned in the Koran: if it be essential to Islamism, then the Koran is deficient, and if deficient cannot be a divine revelation; Baptism for instance is considered essential to Christianity, as the initiatory rite of admission, but if it were nowhere mentioned in the Bible, the Mohammedan might fairly object, that Baptism was not what we believed it to be; or that the Bible omitting to ordain a rite of such great importance was imperfect, and therefore not a true Revelation. If the rite of Circumcision was intended only as a sign of distinction from other religious communities, then it will appear singular that Mohammed should have chosen that already in

[8] His successors, the Saracen Kaliphs annually immolated a camel in their capacity as High-priest of the faithful. The Jewish traveller Benjamin of Tuleda witnessed the ceremony at Bossura in the 12th century.

[9] In Abyssinia therefore, Christians abstain from meat slaughtered by the Mohammedans, and these refuse, what has been killed by Christians in the name of the Holy Trinity.

use among the Jews, and one, which existed also among the Pagan Arabs! In omitting to notice its existence, we infer that Mohammed possibly disapproved of the rite, or did not consider it of a religious import, or, that he passed it over as the self-understood and natural mode of initiating into the religion of Abraham: the latter assumption seems at variance with the fact that Mohammed admitted his first converts by the rite of baptism, corresponding to the baptism of Jewish proselytes. Among the forty kinds of ablutions, given by Reland, one is the baptism of Kaffers on their becoming Moslemin: we here discover one of those singular vacillations which so frequently appear in Mohammed's mind and practice, and find the national custom eventually restored to its primitive character as a religious ordinance, one moreover to which his countrymen were already reconciled. Circumcision is not administered by the Mohammedans in the thirteenth year as among the ancient Arabs, but generally as soon as the candidate can say the confession of the Moslem creed: "There is no God, but God, and Mohammed is his prophet," or whenever a convenient time occurs between the ages of six and sixteen. These few remarks on the history and leading dogmas of the Koran may suffice for the present; other doctrines will be brought forward in later chapters of this work; in the two following, it will be our object to notice those portions of the Koran which were more particularly borrowed from Judaism and Christianity.

CHAPTER V.

WHAT MOHAMMED BORROWED FROM JUDAISM.

"I am a prophet also as thou art; and *an angel* spake unto me by the word of the Lord, but he lied unto him." 1 Kings XIII. 18.

1. The Koran frequently assumes a polemical bearing towards the Jews and the Jewish religion, and Arab writers frankly admit that Mohammed now and then made alterations in his plan to diminish, as far as possible, the analogy which his creed bore to that of the Jews.[10] The Jews are styled the enemies of Moslemin because they killed the Prophets, are bigotted, proud and self-conceited, consider Ezra to be the Son of God, believe Paradise to be created only for themselves, trust to the intercession of their pious ancestors and corrupt their sacred Scriptures.[11] Hence the Koran is not scrupulous in opposing Judaism in its laws of divorce,[12] in abolishing certain laws concerning particular kinds of meat,[13] and in the laws of retaliation.[14] Yet in spite of this opposition, Mo-

---

[10] كراهة لموافقة النفى التشبيه باليهود "from necessity to abolish the analogy with the Jews." Pocock. not. miscell. cap. IX. pag. 369.

[11] Sur. V. 85. II. 58. V. 74. 21. II. 88. LXII. 6. IX. 30. II. 128. 135. II. 73.

[12] Sur. II. 229. 230. with Deut. XXIV. 1.

[13] Sur. IV. 158. III. 44. 86. IV. 158. V. 89. 90. V. 4. VI. 146. XVI. 116. VI. 47. cfr. Leo. XI. 3. VII. 27. III. 9.

[14] Sur. V. 94. with Exod. XXI. 23—25. M. admits of expiation by money, only where the offended parties agree; but the Rabbis, whom he calls "unjust" extend it to all cases: סמא את עינו קטע את ידו שבר את רגלו רואין אותו כאלו הוא עבד נמכר בשוק ושמין כמה היה יפה וכמה הוא יפה Mishnah Baba Kamma VIII. 1.

hammed borrowed so largely from Judaism, that his creed could not exist without it. This gross plagiarism has long been universally acknowledged, but few have taken the trouble to point out in what it consists.[15]

We have already noticed the frequent collisions between Mohammed and the Jews, who were at that time numerous and powerful, dreading them both in argument and on the battle-field, the shrewd Arab prophet found it expedient to conciliate their deep-rooted prejudices on various occasions[16] and also to advise his followers to deal gently with them.[17] There was cause therefore, why Mohammed should desire to adopt as much of Judaism as he possibly could without sacrificing any of the distinctive doctrines of Islamism; he had every opportunity of becoming acquainted with Jewish divinity and practises:[18] but that this knowledge was neither very correct nor profound is abundantly shown in the Koran![19] His igno-

[15] Much may be gleaned from Eisenmenger, Pococke, Sale, Maraccio, Wahl, Hottinger and others, but pre-eminent still remains the Prize-essay of a Jewish Rabbi, Abraham Geiger, in answer to the question put by the University at Bonn: "Inquiratur in fontes Alcorani seu legis Mohammedicae eos, qui ex Judaeismo derivandi sunt." We shall follow in this chapter the *published* translation: "Was hat Mohammed aus dem Judenthume aufgenommen?" Bonn 1833.
[16] Sur. II. 38. XVI. 119. XXVII. 78. XXXII. 25. XLV. 15. II. 136.
[17] Sur. XXIX. 45. ولا تجادلوا أهل الكتاب الا بالتى
[18] His intercourse with Jews on his travels, with Abdallah, Waraka and Habib Ebn Malek are well known.
[19] His *order* of enumerating the prophets: Job, Jonas, Aaron, Solomon, David, Sur. IV. 161. Still more ridiculous: Sur. VI. 84. 85. 86: David, Solomon, Job, Joseph, Moses, Aaron, Zacharias, John, Jesus, Elijah, Jonas, Lot!

rance of Jewish history is proved for instance by his solemnly declaring that before John the Baptist, no one bore that name at any time.[20] To return to our subject, it was perfectly consistent with Mohammed's avowed principles to adopt freely from Judaism, since he professed to reveal nothing but what was in harmony with all that had come down before him. At other times he plainly styles it a "repetition:" "God sent down the most beautiful news, a *repetition* similar to other Scriptures:"[21] with this distinction however, that he desired to be considered the "seal of the prophets," whose book was so "clear and perspicuous" that no occasion could arise to make any other prophet necessary after him.[22]

The contemporaries of Mohammed not only recognised in some of his prophetic communications a reproduction of what had previously been considered divine revelation, but suspected that he was assisted by a certain man, or men of Jewish or Christian be-

---

[20] John, يحيى, יוֹחָנָן, Ἰωάννης, in the name of which we read Sur. XIX. 8. لم نجعل له من قبل سميا. Mohammed however knew nothing of 1 Chron. III. 15. 24. V. 36. 36. 2 King XXV. 23. Ezra VIII. 12. Jer. XL. 8. 1 Macc. II. 1. 2. It arose evidently from misunderstanding Lu. I. 61.

[21] The peculiar charm of the Koran was, that it was مصدق لما معهم: in accordance with what they already possessed. Sur. II. 89. XLVI. 11. and Sur. XXXIX. 24. add: الله نزل أحسن الحديث كتابا متشابها مثاني

[22] M. is said to be the seal of the prophets: خاتم نبيين, Sur. XXXIII. 4. and his book, كتاب مبين; so clear as not to be doubted or liable to be disputed.

lief.²³ If these coadjutors were Jews, as doubtless were some of them, we can thus account for the Hebrew ideas and expressions we meet with in the Koran, which cannot be explained from analogy of language or idiom, but are considered to be directly imported from Judaism. The word *"Ark"* as used in the history of Moses and in connection with the *"ark of the covenant"* is applied in the Koran exactly in the same way as in the old Testament.²⁴ Again Torah²⁵ the law, is made to signify the entire Old Testament as it is in the New Testament, and the term clearly dates its origin from the Hebrew; again, the *Hebrew name* for Paradise was also adopted by Mohammed, as well as the Rabbinical description of the place itself.²⁶ The same may be said of the Hebrew term for hell.²⁷ Gehinnom was originally nothing but

²³ Sur. VIII. 31. XVI. 26. XXIII. 85. XXV. 5. 6. XXVII. 70. XLVI. 10. 16. LXVIII. 15. LXXXIII. 13.

²⁴ Sur. XX. 39. Exod. II. 3. Sur. II. 249. The word, تابوت is not Arabic in its termination, ـوت, and answers to תֵּבָה or the Rabbinical תֵּיבְתָא.

²⁵ تورية, תּוֹרָה, the law, is always used in a sense analogous to ὁ νόμος in the New Test.

²⁶ "Das Paradies ist ein Ort, wo man ohne alle körperliche Anstrengung ißt und trinkt, und wo die Edelsteine zu Haufe sind, seidene Betten, Ströme von Wein, wohlriechende Oele, und anderes der Art." Again: "Eden ist ein Ort der Wonne, das fruchtbarste Land, wo sehr viele Bäche und Fruchtbäume sind, welche Gott künftig den Menschen zeigen wird, um dort erfreut zu werden." Maimonides apud Sanhed. XI. 1. جنات عدن from גַּן עֵדֶן is the usual name of Paradise, seldom جنات الفردوس from παραδεῖσος.

²⁷ Gehenna, جهنّم, גֵּיהִנֹּם; in the New Test γέεννα. The term occurs Sur. II. 201. III. 10. 198. IV. 58. 95. 99. 115. 120. That جهنم was adopted direct from the Jews is proved by the final letter م.

K

the valley of Hinnom near Jerusalem, which being at one time so notorious and detested for its idolatries, its name was applied in the Talmud and the New Testament to hell. Again, among the Pharisees or Separatists who formed themselves into a distinct community, holding the traditions of the elders and studying to excel by exterior sanctity, was a party distinguished for learning and intelligence whose members were called Chaberim or "fellows;" thus the term became identical with teachers; and this usus loquendi in Rabbinical language, was adopted by the Koran.[28] The words "Rabaan" another term signifying teacher, "Sabbath" the seventh day of the week, "Shekinah" implying God's peculiar presence, "Foorkan" signifying redemption, and "Mathani" meaning *repetition*, are all terms of Hebrew origin introduced into the Koran.[29]

2. It would be irrelevant to our purpose to wade through all the incongruous matter of the Koran in order to discover every trace of Judaism, but we shall glance at some peculiarly Jewish *ideas*, which

---

[28] אַחְבַּאר, חֲבֵרִים; חָבֵר, socius was the term of a member of a party among the פְּרוּשִׁים, claiming peculiar knowledge. Thus חֲבֵרִים acquired the sense of teachers. Sur. V. 48. 68. IX. 31. 34.

[29] Compare Sur. III. 73. V. 48. 68. 80. IX. 31. 34. رباني and רַבָּן. Respecting سبت, שַׁבָּת Sur. II. 61. VII. 163. XVI. 125; and about سَاكِينَة, שְׁכִינָה see Exod. XXV. 8. Deut. XXXIII, 12. 16. Sur. II. 249. IX. 26. 40. XLVIII. 4. 18. 26. فرقان, פֻּרְקָן, help, salvation: Sur. VIII. 29. 42. 181. مثاني or מִשְׁנָה, repetition. Moh. put his book in the place of the entire Jewish teaching called it: قُرْأن, מִקְרָא as well as مثاني, מִשְׁנָה.

ought to be noticed. Passing over the creation, we remark that the seven heavens and the seven earths which are held in the Talmud, have found their way into the Koran.[30] During the creation, God's glorious throne was placed in the air upon the water.[31] "The world is the sixtieth part of the garden, the garden is the sixtieth part of Eden" according to the Talmud; and Mohammed states that the breadth of the garden is that of heaven and earth.[32] Both in the Koran and Talmud we find seven hells as the appointed abode for the damned, and each hell has seven gates, in both documents.[33] The entrance of the Gehinnom is marked by two date-trees, between which, smoke issues, and the Koran speaks of a tree in hell, of which the damned are to eat and of which many terrible things are related.[34]

In the Talmud the prince of hell demands supply for his domain, and a similar request is made in the Koran.[35] Between the seven heavens and the seven hells is an intermediate place, for those who are too good to be cast into hell, and too imperfect to be

---

[30] Chagiga IX. 2. שִׁבְעָה רְקִיעִים "there are seven heavens." Emek Hammelech Eisenmenger I. pag. 459. and Sur. II. 27. XVII. 46. 88. XLI. 11. LXV. 12. LXVII. 3. LXXI. 14. سبع السموات.

[31] Sur. XI. 9. XXVII. 26. XXIII. 117. LXXXV. 15. and Rashi to Gen. I. 2. עֲמֹד בָּאֲוִיר מְרַחֶפֶת עַל פְּנֵי הַמָּיִם

[32] Taanith X. Pesahim XCIV. כְּעוֹלָם אֶחָד מִשִּׁשִּׁים בַּגַּן גַּן אֶחָד מִשִּׁשִּׁים בְּעֵדֶן and Sur. III. 127.

[33] Talmud Erubin XIX. 1. Midrash at the end of Psalm XI. Sohar II. pag. 150. Sur. XV. 44.

[34] Sukkah XXXVII. and Sur. XXXVII. 60 XLIV. 43.

[35] Othioth by Rabbi Akiba VIII. 1. and Sur. L. 29.

admitted into heaven.³⁶ This intermediate abode is however so narrow that the conversations of the blessed and the damned on either side may be overheard. The happiness of Paradise is similarly depicted in both Talmud and Koran;³⁷ and the difficulty of attaining it is equally set forth; the Talmud declaring that it is as easy for an elephant to enter through the eye of a needle, the Koran merely substituting a camel for an elephant.³⁸ That the dead live in the sight of God is stated in both documents in the same terms, and that the admission to the actual presence of the Almighty is not to be expected before the day of Judgment and the Resurrection of the dead.³⁹ The signs of the last day, as given in the Koran, are borrowed equally from the Scriptures and the Talmud.⁴⁰

The lengthened descriptions in the Koran of the future Resurrection and Judgment are also decidedly tinged with a Talmudical colouring. That the several members of the human body shall bear witness against the damned, and that idols shall share in the punishment of the worshippers is stated both in the Talmud

---

³⁶ Midrash to Eccles. VII. 14. Sur. VII. 44. 45. 46. 47.

³⁷ Mishnah Aboth IV. 17. Sur. IX. 38. XIII. 26.

³⁸ Compare the Talmudic: בְּמָא דְמְעַיֵל פִּילָא בְּקוּפָא דְמַחֲטָא with حتى يلج الجمل فى سمّ الخياط in Sur. VII. 38.

³⁹ The pious "enjoy the glory of the Shechinah:" נֶהֱנִין מִזִּיו הַשְּׁכִינָה Sur. LXXV. 23. الى ربها ناظرة "their Lord contemplating". Also Sur. LXXXIX. 27.

⁴⁰ Sur. XXI. 104. XXXIX. 67. XLIV. 9. XVII. 60. XXII. 2. XXVII. 89. Isa. XXXIV. 4. Ezek. XXXVIII. XXXIX. Sur. XXI. 96.

and Koran.⁴¹ The time of the last Judgment Mohammed declined to fix, resting upon the Jewish or Scriptural sentence that "one day with God is like a thousand."⁴² The Jews in speaking of the Resurrection of the dead allude to the sending down of rain; the Koran also affirms that this means of quickening the dead will be employed;⁴³ and the Talmudical idea that the dead will rise in the garments in which they were buried has likewise been adopted into Moslem tradition.⁴⁴ The Jewish opinion that "all the Prophets saw in a dark, but Moses in a clear mirror"⁴⁵ is modified in the Koran by the addition that God sends down his angelic messenger Gabriel, as "the Holy Ghost" with revelations; this extraordinary notion of Gabriel being considered the Spirit of God is also imported from the teaching of the Jews.⁴⁶

Again, the *Demonology* of the Koran is chiefly borrowed from the Talmud. "Three of the properties of demons are in common with angels, and three

---

⁴¹ Chagiga XVI. Thaanith XI. and Sur. XXIV. 24. XXXVI. 65. XLI. 19. Sukkah XXIX. and Sur. XXI. 98.

⁴² Psa. XCIV. Sanhedr. 96, 2. and Sur. XXII. 46. XXXII. 4. Ezek. XXXVII. 13. and Sur. C. 9.

⁴³ מוֹרִיד הַגֶּשֶׁם "who sends down the rain" is introduced: Thaanith at the beginning. Sur. VI. 95. XXX. 49. XXXVI. 33. XLI. 39. XLIII. 10.

⁴⁴ Sanhed. XC. 2. Khethubhoth CXI. 2. See also VI. 95. and Pocock. not. misc. cap. VII. p. 271. ان الميت ببعت فى ثيابه التى يموت فيها

⁴⁵ Jebamoth XLIX. with Sur. XLII. 50.

⁴⁶ 1 King XXII. 21. נְבִיא הָרוּחַ; and רוּחַ סַפְקָנִית "the clearly speaking spirit" is also taken as Gabriel: Sanhedrin XLIV. and Sur. LXXVIII. 38. XCVII. 4: XVII. 87.

with men; they have wings like angels, can fly from one end of the world to the other, and know things to come. But do they know future events? No, but they listen behind the veil. The three properties in common with men are: they eat and drink, indulge in physical love and die."[47] This was adopted in the Koran and spun out ad libitum; for instance, whilst listening once to the angelic conversations they were hunted away with stones! Their presence in places of worship is admitted both in the Talmud and the Koran: "when the servant of God stood up to invoke him, the Djins all but pressed on him in the crowd."[48]

Amongst the *moral precepts* which are borrowed from the Talmud, we may mention, that children are not to obey their parents, when the latter demand that which is evil;[49] prayer is to be performed standing, walking, or even riding;[50] devotions may be

---

[47] שִׁשָּׁה דְבָרִים אֶמְרוּ בַּשֵּׁדִים שְׁלֹשָׁה בְּמַלְאֲכֵי הַשָּׁרֵת יְשַׁלֵּשָׁה בִּבְנֵי אָדָם שְׁלֹשָׁה בְּמַלְאֲכֵי הַשָּׁרֵת יֵשׁ לָהֶם כְּנָפַיִם וְטָסִין מִסּוֹף הָעוֹלָם וְעַד סוֹפוֹ וְיוֹדְעִין מַה שֶּׁעָתִין לִהְיוֹת אֶלָּא דְקָא בָעְקַף אָבָּא שׁוֹמְעִין מֵאֲחוֹרֵי הַפַּרְגּוּד וּשְׁלֹשָׁה בִּבְנֵי אָדָם אוֹכְלִין וְשׁוֹתִין פָּרִין וְרָבִין יְמֵיתִין׃ Chagiga XVI. 1. and Sur. XV. 17. 34. XXXVIII. 78. LXXXI. 24. LXVII. 5. XXXVII. 7. LXXII. Hence the appellative رجيم, the stoned one.

[48] Compare the Talmud: הִי דְּדָחֲקָא רַבִּי כָּלָּה מִפְּנֵיהּ הִיא and Sur. LXXII. 19.

[49] "Saith the father to his son being a Priest, defile thyself, or return not that which is found, should he in this obey him?" Jebhamoth VI. cfr. Sur. XXIX. 7.

[50] Sur. II. 239. III. 188. X. 13. The Jews, Berachoth X. תְּפִלָּה מִצְוָה, pray standing; may be done riding on an ass. Mishnah Berachoth IV. 5.

shortened in urgent cases, without committing sin;[51] drunken persons are not to engage in acts of worship;[52] ablutions before prayer are in special cases enforced, but generally required both in the Talmud and the Koran;[53] each permit the use of sand instead of water, when the latter is not to be procured.[54] The Talmud prohibits loud and noisy prayers, and Mohammed gives this short injunction:—"cry not in your prayers;"[55] in addition to this secret prayer, public worship is equally commended.[56] The Shema-prayer of the Jews is to be performed, "when one is able to distinguish a *blue* from a *white thread;*" and *this,* is precisely the criterion of the commencement of the fast in the Koran.[57] The following social precepts are likewise copied from Judaism,—a divorced woman must wait three months before marrying again;[58] mothers are to nurse their children two full years; and the degrees of affinity within which mariages are lawful.[59]

[51] Sur. IV. 102. and Mishnah Berachoth IV. 4.
[52] Sur. IV. 46. and Berachoth XXXI. 2. Erubin LXIV.
[53] Sur. IV. 46. V. 9. Mishnah Berachoth III. 4.
[54] Sur. V. 8. and Berachoth XLVI. מְקַנֵּחַ בִּצְרוֹר וְדַי he purifies himself with sand and has done enough.
[55] لا تجهر بصلوتك Sur. XVII. 110. with Berachoth XXXI. 2. מֹבֶן בְּלִבּוֹ שֶׁלֹּא יַשְׁמִיעַ קוֹלוֹ that he do not lift up his voice.
[56] Sonna LXXXVI. LXXXVII. LXXXVIII. and the תְּפִלָּה בְּצִבּוּר of the Jews.
[57] Mishnah Berach. 1. 2. Sur. II. 183.
[58] Sur. II. 228. Mish. Jabhamoth IV. 10.
[59] Sur. II. 233. XXXI. 13. The Talmud: Kethuboth LX. 1. where it is added, that beyond that period it was like suckling a worm; and Sur. XXIV. 31.

3. The *historical incidents*, which Mohammed borrowed from Judaism, are recorded with the most grotesque and fabulous admixtures; regardless of the sources from which he gleaned them he is indifferent to all order or system. Ignorant of the general features of Jewish history, Mohammed appropriates none of the historical waymarks which determine the great epochs recorded in the Old Testament, but confines himself to certain occurrences in the lives of single individuals; we shall review these in chronological order, noticing the flagrant anachronisms as they arise in the Koran.

At the head of the line of *Patriarchs* prior to the flood, stands the primogenitor of the human race. Even before the formation of man, the jealousy of the angels existed to such a degree, as to cause them to oppose his creation; but God revenged it by endowing Adam with superior knowledge:— "When thy Lord said to the angels, I am going to place a substitute on earth, they said: wilt thou place there one who will do evil therein and shed blood? but we celebrate thy praise and sanctify thee; God answered: Verily I know that which ye know not; and he taught Adam the names of all things, and then proposed them to the angels, and said: Declare unto me the names of these things, if ye say truth; they answered: Praise be unto thee, we have no knowledge but what thou teachest us, for thou art knowing and wise. God said: O Adam tell them their names. And when he had told them their names, God said: Did I not tell you that I know the secrets of heaven and earth, and

CHAP. V.]   THE PATRIARCHS BEFORE THE FLOOD.   153

know that which ye discover, and that which ye conceal."[60] Let us examine whence the Koran obtained this occult information: "When God intended to create man, He advised with the angels and said unto them we will make man in our own image, Gen. 1, 26. then said they, What is man that Thou rememberest him, Psalm VIII. 5. what shall be his peculiarity? He answered his wisdom is superior to yours. Then brought He before them, cattle, animals and birds, and asked for their names but they knew it not. After man was created He caused them to pass before him and asked for their names, and He answered: this is an ox, that an ass, this a horse and that a camel. — What is *thy* name? To me it becomes to be called "earthy," for from "earth" I am created. — And *I?* "Lord," for Thou rulest over all thy creatures."[61]

To this may be added the fable that God *commanded* the angels to worship Adam;[62] which is likewise appropriated with certain modifications from

---

[60] Sur. II 28—33.

[61] בְּשָׁעָה שֶׁבָּא הַקָּדוֹשׁ בָּרוּךְ הוּא לִבְרֹאת אֶת הָאָדָם נִמְלַךְ בְּמַלְאֲכֵי הַשָּׁרֵת אָמַר לָהֶן נַעֲשֶׂה אָדָם בְּצַלְמֵנוּ אָמְרוּ לְפָנָיו מָה אֱנוֹשׁ כִּי תִזְכְּרֶנּוּ אָדָם זֶה מָה זֶה טִיבוֹ אָמַר חָכְמָתוֹ מְרֻבָּה מִשֶּׁלָּכֶם הֵבִיא לִפְנֵיהֶם אֶת הַבְּהֵמָה וְאֶת הַחַיָּה וְאֶת הָעוֹף אָמַר לָהֶן זֶה מַה שְּׁמוֹ וְלֹא הָיוּ יוֹדְעִין כֵּיוָן שֶׁבָּרָא אָדָם הֶעֱבִירָן לְפָנָיו אָמַר לוֹ זֶה מַה שְּׁמוֹ אָמַר זֶה שׁוֹר זֶה חֲמוֹר זֶה סוּס וְזֶה גָמָל וְאַתָּה שִׁמְךָ אָמַר לוֹ אֲנִי נָאֶה לְהִקָּרֵא אָדָם שֶׁנִּבְרֵאתִי מִן הָאֲדָמָה וַאֲנִי מַה שְּׁמִי אָמַר לְךָ נָאֶה לְהִקָּרֵא אֲדֹנָי שֶׁאַתָּה אָדוֹן לְכָל בְּרִיּוֹתֶיךָ: Midrash Rabbah to Leviticus Parashah XIX. and Genesis Parashah VIII. and Sanhedrin XXXVIII.

[62] Sur. VII. 10—26. XV. 28—44. XVII. 63—68. XVIII. 48. XX. 115. XXXVIII. 71—86.

Talmudical writings. Some Jewish fables record, that the angels contemplated worshipping man, but were prevented by God;[63] others precisely agree with the Koran,[64] that God commanded the angels to worship man, and that they obeyed with the exception of Satan. The Sonna informs us that Adam was sixty yards high, and Rabbinical fables make him extend from one end of the world to the other, but upon the angels esteeming him a second Deity, God put his hand upon him and reduced him to a thousand yards![65] Jewish writings thus record the intention of the creatures to worship Adam: — "When the creatures saw Adam, they were afraid thinking him to be the Creator and came to worship him, but he said to them: Ye come to worship me, but come with me, and we

---

[63] There are signs of great veneration for Adam, but when about to worship him, God prevented it: אָדָם הָרִאשׁוֹן יָשַׁב בְּגַן עֵדֶן וְהָיוּ מַלְאֲכֵי הַשָּׁרֵת צוֹלִין לוֹ בָּשָׂר וּמְצַנְּנִין לוֹ יַיִן Sanhedrin XXIX. Again: בְּשָׁעָה שֶׁבָּרָא הַקָּדוֹשׁ בָּרוּךְ הוּא אֶת הָאָדָם טָעוּ בּוֹ מַלְאֲכֵי הַשָּׁרֵת וּבִקְשׁוּ לוֹמַר לְפָנָיו קָדוֹשׁ מֶה עָשָׂה הַקָּדוֹשׁ בָּרוּךְ הוּא הִפִּיל עָלָיו תַּרְדֵּמָה וְיָדְעוּ הַכֹּל שֶׁהוּא אָדָם: Midrash Rabbah ad Genesis Parash. VIII

[64] The Midrash of Rabbi Moses Haddarshan examined by Zunz "Die gottesdienstlichen Vorträge der Juden" pag. 296. "Locutus est Deus angelis ministerii, ut supplicarent Adae. Venerunt angeli ministerii ad beneplacitum Dei. Satan vero erat major omnibus angelis in coelo. Locutus est igitur Deo sancto et benedicto, et ait: Domine mundi, nos creasti ex splendore Schechinae et tu dicis nobis, ut supplicemus ei, vel ut adoremus eum quem de limo terrae formasti. Dixit ei Deus sanctus et benedictus, in isto, qui est de limo terrae, est plus sapientiae et intelligentiae, quam in te. Factum est itaque, cum nollet supplicare ei, nec obedire voci Dei sancti et benedicti, expellit illum de coelis et factus est Satan, et de eo dicit Jasaj. XIV. 12. quomodo cecidisti de coelo, splendor, fili aurorae!" cfr. Raymund Martini Pugio fidei edit. Carpzov. pag. 563. 564. from Bereshit Rabba to Gen. V. 5.

[65] Fundgrub. I. p. 278. and Eisenmenger's Judenthum I. p. 365.

will take *Him* as our king who has created us."[66] The account given in the Koran of Cain's murder of his brother, is borrowed from the Bible; his conversation with Abel before he slew him,[67] is the same as that in the Targum of Jerusalem. After the murder, Cain sees a raven burying another, and from this sight gains the idea of interring Abel. Jewish fable differs only in ascribing the interment to the parents: — Adam and his wife sat weeping and lamenting him, not knowing what to do with the body, as they were unacquainted with burying. Then came a raven whose fellow was dead, he took and buried it in the earth hiding it before their eyes; then said Adam, I shall do like this raven, and taking Abel's corpse, he dug in the earth and hid it."[68] The sentence following in the Koran: — "wherefore we commanded the children of Israel that he who slayeth a soul not by way of retaliation, or because he doeth corruptly in the earth, *shall be as if he had slain all mankind; but he who saveth a soul alive, shall be as*

---

[66] Eisenmenger's Judenthum I. pag. 367. quoted from the Pirke Rabbi Elieser. To prove Adam's extraordinary knowledge, the Talmud and Koran relate that the angels brought down from the higher worlds a book fullof mighty things beyond their comprehension, in order to learn from Adam the mysteries it contained.

[67] Sura V. 30—33. "I will certainly kill thee; Abel answered. God only accepteth the offerings of the pious; if thou stretchest forth thy hand against me to slay me, I will not stretch forth my hand against thee to slay, for I fear God, the Lord of all creatures."

[68] הָיָה אָדָם וְעֶזְרוֹ יֹשְׁבִים וּבוֹכִים יִמְתְאַבְּלִים עָלָיו וְלֹא הָיָה יָדְעִים מַה לַעֲשׂוֹת לְהֶבֶל שֶׁלֹּא הָיוּ בְּקִבְיָרָה בָּא עוֹרֵב אֶחָד שֶׁמֵּת לוֹ אֶחָד מֵחֲבֵרָיו לָקַח אוֹתוֹ וְחָפַר בָּאָרֶץ וּטְמָנָה לְעֵינֵיהֶם אָמַר אָדָם כָּעוֹרֵב אֲנִי עוֹשֶׂה מִיָּד לָקַח נִבְלָתוֹ שֶׁל הֶבֶל וְחָפַר בָּאָרֶץ וּטְמָנָה

Pirke Rabbi Elieser cap. XXI. Compare with this: Sur. V. 34. 35.

if he saved all souls alive," — would have no connection with what precedes or follows, were it not for the Targum of Onkelos in the paraphrase of Gen. IV. 10. where it is said that the "bloods" of Cain's brother cried to God from the earth, thus implying that Abel's posterity were also cut off: and in the Mishnah Sanhedrin, we find the very words which the Koran attaches to the narration of the murder without sense or connection.[69]

4. *Noah* stands forth as the preacher of righteousness, builds the ark and is saved with his family whilst the whole of mankind perish:[70] his character is however drawn more from Rabbinical than Biblical sources. The conversations of Noah with the people and the words with which they mocked him whilst building the ark,[71] are the same in Talmudical writings as in the Koran: the former declare that the waters of the flood were heated, and the latter that the generation of the flood was punished with boiling water.[72]

[69] מְצִינוּ בְּקַיִן שֶׁהָרַג אֶת אָחִיו שֶׁנֶּאֱמַר קוֹל דְּמֵי אָחִיךָ צֹעֲקִים אֵינוֹ אוֹמֵר דַּם אָחִיךָ אֶלָּא דְּמֵי אָחִיךָ דָּמוֹ וְדַם זַרְעִיּוֹתָיו לְפִיכָךְ נִבְרָא אָדָם יְחִידִי לְלַמֶּדְךָ שֶׁכָּל הַמְאַבֵּד נֶפֶשׁ אַחַת מִיִּשְׂרָאֵל מַעֲלֶה עָלָיו הַכָּתוּב כְּאִלּוּ אִבֵּד עוֹלָם מָלֵא וְכָל הַמְקַיֵּם נֶפֶשׁ אַחַת מִיִּשְׂרָאֵל מַעֲלֶה עָלָיו הַכָּתוּב כְּאִלּוּ קִיֵּם עוֹלָם מָלֵא Misnah Sanhedrin IV. 5.

[70] Sur. VII. 57—63. X. 72—75. XI. 27—50. XXII. 43. XXIII. 23—32. XXV. 39. XXVI. 105—121. XXIX. 13. 14, XXXVII. 73—81. LIV. 9—18. LXXI. 1—29.

[71] אָמְרוּ לוֹ זָקֵן תֵּיבָה זוֹ לָמָּה: Old one, wherefore this ark? Sanhedrin CVIII. cfr. Midrash Rabbah ad Gen. Parash. XXX. and XXXIII. ad Eccles. IX. 14. Midrash Tanchuma adds: הָיוּ מַשְׂחָקִין מִמֶּנּוּ וּמַלְעִיגִין בִּדְבָרִים they mocked and annoyed him with words.

[72] وفار التنور the oven poured forth boiling water. Sur. XI.

The next Patriarch after the flood is *Hud*, who is none other than *Eber*; another sample of the ignorance of Mohammed.[73] In the days of Hud[74] the tower is constructed; the *"obstinate hero,"*[75] — probably Nimrod, takes the lead; the sin of idolatry abounding, an idol is contemplated as the crowning of the tower; but the building is overthrown, the tribes are dispersed and punished in this world and in the world to come:[76] these particulars are evidently borrowed from Scripture and Rabbinical writings; in the Koran however the dispersion is caused by a poisonous wind and not by the confusion of tongues. The significance which the Koran gives to Hud is again in perfect accordance with Rabbinical Judaism. "Eber was a great prophet, for he prophetically called his son Peleg (dispersion), by the help of the Holy Ghost, because the earth was to be dispersed."[77]

42. XXIII. 27. בְּרִיתְחִין דְּהוֹנֵי דּוֹר הַמַּבּוּל the race of the flood was punished with hot water. Rosh Hashanah XVI. 2. Sanhedrin CVIII.

[73] هود, Hud. עֵבֶר hence עִבְרִי, Hebrews. This original name was forgotten and יְהוּדִי, Jews or يهود sometimes هود became common among the Arabs.

[74] Sur. VII. 63—71. XI. 52—64. XXII. 43. XXIII. 33—44. XXV. 4. XXVI 123—141. XXIX. 37. XXXVIII. 11. XL. 32. XLI. 12—16. XLVI. 20—25. L. 13. LI. 41. 42. LIII. 50. LIV. 18—20. LXIX. 4—9. LXXXIX. 5—9. XVI. 28.

[75] جبار عنيد see Nimrod's cognomen of גִבֹּר Gen. X. 7. 8.

[76] Sur. XI. 63. and Mishnah Sanhedr. X. 3. where we read: "The generation of the dispersion has no part in the world to come."

[77] נָבִיא גָדוֹל הָיָה עֵבֶר שֶׁקָּרָא אֶת שֵׁם בְּנוֹ פֶּלֶג בְּרוּחַ הַקֹּדֶשׁ שֶׁבְּיָמָיו נִפְלְגָה הָאָרֶץ Seder Olam quoted Midrash Jalkut cap. LXII.

5. Among all the Patriarchs, Abraham[78] was the most esteemed by Mohammed, as being neither Jew nor Christian but a Moslem![79] That he wrote books according to the Koran, is also the belief of the Jewish doctors.[80] His attaining the knowledge of the true faith; his zeal to convert his generation, his destruction of the idols; his placing the staff in the hand of the largest idol and ascribing to it the deed; his effort to persuade the people of the impotence of their gods; the fury of the people; their insisting on his being burned, and his marvellous deliverance; all these particulars in the life of Abraham, as given by the Koran,[81] are minutely copied from Jewish fictions. We confine ourselves to one passage; "Terah was an idolater,[82] and idol-maker. — Once he went a journey and left Abraham to sell the idols; who, when a purchaser came, asked his age: if the person replied

[78] ابراهيم, Ibrahim; אַבְרָהָם, called خليل الله, friend of God.

[79] Sur. XVI. 124. II. 129. III. 60. VI. 79. XVI. 121. 124. II. 134. IV. 124.

[80] The Jews ascribe to him the cabbalistical Sepher Jezirah, which is certainly very old.

[81] Sur. VI. 74—82. XIX. 42—51. XXI. 52—69. XXII. 43. XXVI. 69—105. XXIX. 15—23. XXXVII. 81—95 XLIII. 25—28. LX. 4—6. IX. 115. XXVI. 86—104. Sonna 395. Sur. II. 260. XXI 69—74. XXIX. 23—27. XXXVII. 95—99.

[82] תֶּרַח called آزر, Asar by M. Sur. VI. 74. Eusebius in his Church History calls him ᾿Αθαρ which may have arisen from Θαρα and the Greek ᾿Αθαρ was turned into آزر, Asar. The later Arabs however know the proper name تارخ, See Elpherar to Sur. VII. 78. According to Tarikh Montekheb Asar was the father of Terah. The words תֶּרַח עֹבֵד בִּצְלָמִים הָיָה according to the context must imply also a seller of images.

fifty or sixty years, Abraham said to him: Woe to a man of sixty who will worship the work of one day; so that purchaser went away ashamed.[83] Once a woman came with a dish of flour and said: here, put this before them! but he took a stick, broke all the idols and placed the stick in the hand of the largest of them. When his father returned, he asked, who has done this? whereupon Abraham said, — "why shall I deny it? a woman came with a dish of flour, telling me to place it before them; scarcely had I done this when each was determined to eat first, and the largest of them beat the others to pieces with the stick he has in his hand. But Terah said, why dost thou impose upon me, have they any knowledge? Abraham replied, do not thy ears hear what thy mouth speaketh? Then Terah seized his son and handed him over to Nimrod, who said to Abraham: we will worship the fire! Abraham:—Rather the water, which extinguishes the fire! Nimrod:—then the water! Abraham:—Rather the cloud which carries the water. Nimrod:—then the cloud! Abraham:—Rather the wind, which disperses the cloud. Nimrod:—then the wind! Abraham:—rather man who resists the wind. Nimrod:—Thou art talking vain things; I worship the fire and cast thee into the midst of it, may the God whom thou worshippest come and save thee out of it. Abraham was then cast into a burning lime-

[83] وكان ازر ابو ابراهيم يصنع الاصنام ويطيعها
وخعل ابراهيم ليبيعا فكان أبارهيم يقول من يشتري
ما يضره ولا بنفعه. Abulfeda histor. ante Islam. pag. 20.

pit and was saved."[84] The Koran states that the angels whom Abraham received, appeared as *ordinary Arabs*, and he was astonished when they declined to eat.[85] According to the Talmud, they also "appeared to him no more than *Arabs*;"[86] but another passage adds: "The angels descended and did eat, are they then said to have really eaten? No! but they appeared as if they did eat and drink."[87] As a proof of Mohammed's uncertainty respecting the history of Abraham we add, that the doubt regarding their having a son in their old age, is expressed in the Koran by *Abraham* instead of *Sarah*, and she is made to laugh at the promise of a son, before it was given;[88] again, the command to offer his son, is given to Abraham before *Isaac* is born or promised, so that the son who was to be offered up could be none other than *Ishmael*,[89] who was spoken of immediately before as the *"meek youth!"* Mohammedan divines are however not agreed whether *Ishmael* was to be offered up although it is reported by some, that the horns

---

[84] Midrash Rabbah ad Genesis Parash. XVII.

[85] Sur. XI. 72—79. XV. 51—61. XXIX. 30—32. LI. 24—38.

[86] לֹא נִדְמוּ לוֹ אֶלָּא לְעַרְבִיִּים Kiddushin LII.

[87] מַלְאֲכֵי הַשָּׁרֵת יָרְדוּ לְמַטָּה וְאָכְלוּ בָּשָׂר אָכְלוּ סָלְקָא דַעְתָּךְ אֶלָּא אֵימָא נִרְאֶה כְּמִי שֶׁאָכְלוּ וְשָׁתוּ Baba Mezia LXXXVI. 2.

[88] Sur. XV. 54. XI. 74. This caused the most absurd explanations.

[89] Sur. XXXVII. 99—114. explains what II. 118. is only hinted at, viz. the son Ishmael was to be sacrificed but was "ransomed with a noble victim"; and after that 112. وبشرناه باسحق نبيا من الصالحين and we rejoiced him with the promise of Isaac.

of the ram which was sacrificed in his stead, were preserved at Mecca his dwelling-place![90] We may perhaps account for Mohammed's speaking of Ishmael as a pious man and reckoning him among the prophets and patriarchs,[91] from the fact, that he was considered the patriarch of the Arabs and the founder of the Kaaba,[92] yet nothing but ignorance could betray him into the mistake of counting Ishmael among the forefathers of Jacob;[93] not less surprising is the assertion that the *latter* was the son of Abraham![94] The dying charge of Jacob, as related in the Koran, is in perfect accordance with what is found in Jewish writings: "When Jacob was dying he called his sons together and said unto them: hear ye sons of Israel, is there perhaps a doubt in your hearts concerning God? they replied: hear Israel our father, as there is no doubt in thy heart concerning God, so is there none in ours; but the Lord is our God, the one Lord only."[95]

Among the sons of Jacob, *Joseph* occupies the pre-eminence. His history is mainly the same as in

---

[90] Geiger pag. 133. 134. 135.

[91] Sur. XIX. 55—56. XXI. 85. 86. II. 130. 134. VI. 86. XXXVIII. 48. XIV. 41. The Talmud records that Ishmael repented: יִשְׁמָעֵאל עָשָׂה תְּשׁוּבָה בְּחַיֵּי אָבִיו Ishmael repented during the life-time of his father. Baba Bathra XVI.

[92] Sur. II. 119.   [93] Sur. II. 127.

[94] Sur. XI 74. VI. 84. XIX. 50. XXI 72. XXIX. 26. Sonna 398 and 400, Joseph is called the grandson of Abraham, and Jacob his son.

[95] Sur. II. 126. 127. and Midrash Rabhah to Gen. Parash. 98. and to Deut. Parash. II. Also Targum Hierosolym. to Deut. VI. 4. Tractat. Pesachim pag. 56.

the Bible, embellished with fabulous traditions of the Jews. Among these is the assumption that Joseph "would have resolved to sin, had he not seen the evident demonstration of his Lord;"[96] that this is borrowed from the following fable none can fail to admit. "Rabbi Jochanan saith: both intended to commit sin; seizing him by the garment she said: lie with me ... Then appeared to him the form of his father at the window, who called to him: Joseph! Joseph! the names of thy brothers shall be engraven upon the stones of the Ephod, also thine own, wilt thou that it shall be erased?"[97] This is almost literally repeated by a Moslem commentary to the Koran.[98] The fable of Potiphar's wife inviting the Egyptian ladies to a feast, to see Joseph, because they laughed at her being so charmed with him and of their being so overcome with admiration of Joseph[99] that they accidentally cut their hands in eating fruit, is exactly so related in a very ancient Hebrew book from which Mohammed doubtless derived it. The story about the garment being rent, and the setting up of an evidence of guilt or innocence respecting it, is also.

[96] Sur. XII. 24. وهم بها لولا ان راى برهان ربه

[97] אָמַר רַבִּי יוֹחָנָן שְׁנֵיהֶם לְדָבָר עֲבֵרָה נִתְכַּוְּנוּ וַתִּתְפְּשֵׂהוּ בְּבִגְדוֹ לֵאמֹר שְׁכָבָה עִמִּי מְלַמֵּד שֶׁשְּׁנֵיהֶם לַעֲבֵרָה בָּאוּ אִישׁ כְּאִישׁ בְּאוֹתָהּ שָׁעָה בָּאתָה דְּיוֹקְנוֹ שֶׁל אָבִיו וְנִרְאֵית לוֹ בַּחַלּוֹן אָמַר לוֹ יוֹסֵף יוֹסֵף עֲתִידִין אַחֶיךָ שֶׁיִּכָּתְבוּ עַל אַבְנֵי אֵפוֹד וְאַתָּה בֵּינֵיהֶם רְצוֹנְךָ שֶׁיִּמָּחֶה שִׁמְךָ מִבֵּינֵיהֶם Sotah XXXVI. 2.

[98] Elpherar to Sur. XII. 24. Geiger pag. 142.

[99] Sur. XII. 26. 31. 50. and the commentary of Elpherar to the passage.

borrowed to the very letter from the same source.[1]
In this Sura it is also stated that "the devil made
him (Joseph) forget the remembrance of his Lord,"[2]
in perfect harmony with the Jewish tradition: "Vain
speech tendeth to destruction; though Joseph twice
urged the chief butler to remember him yet he had
to remain two years longer in prison."[3] The seeking
protection from man is here represented as the instigation of Satan. The Koran causes Jacob to tell
his sons to enter at different gates; and the same
injunction is given by the Patriarch in the Jewish
writings: "Jacob said to them enter not through one
and the same gate."[4] The exclamation of the sons
of Israel, when they found the cup in Benjamin's sack:
"has he stolen, so has his brother also;" are clearly
a perversion of the words which the Jewish traditions
put into their mouths: "Behold a thief, son of a female thief," referring to the stealing of the Teraphim
by Rachel.[5] Mohammed again acquaints us that
Jacob knew by divine revelation that his son Joseph

---

[1] The ספר הישר Sepher Hajjashar, quoted in the Midrash Jalkut by the name דברי הימים הארוך and existing in a Jewish—
German version with the title ויישר ות. cfr also the intimation in
the Midrash Abhkir quoted in Mid. Jalhut cap. CXLVI.

[2] فَأَنْسَاهُ ٱلشَّيْطَانُ ذِكْرَ رَبِّهِ This is falsely applied to
the chief butler; the translators were betrayed by the previous
verse. Sur XII. 42.

[3] Midrash Rabbah to Gen. XL 14. Geiger pag. 146. Sur. XII.
42 "wherefore he remained in the prison some years."

[4] Sur. XII. 67. and אָמַר לָהֶם יַעֲקֹב אַל תִּכָּנְסוּ בְּפֶתַח אֶחָד בְּבַת אַחַת
Mid. Rabbah to Genesis Parash XCI.

[5] Sur. XII. 77. and הָא גַנָּבָא בַּר גַּנַּבְתָּא Midrash Rabbah Parash.
XCII. Gen. XXXI. 19.

was still alive,[6] and Jewish tradition enables us to point out whence he obtained the information. "An unbeliever asked our master: do the dead continue to live? your parents did not believe it, and will ye receive it? Of Jacob it is said, he refused to be comforted; had he believed that the dead still lived, would he not have been comforted? But he answered, fool, he knew by the Holy Ghost that he still really lived, and about a living person, people need no comfort."[7]

6. Mohammed made but scanty allusions to the early patriarchs, Joseph only excepted; but concerning *Moses* it was his interest to be more liberal and definite in his communications,—possibly from the desire to be considered like him, as he is generally thought to have taken that prophet as his model— whose character as lawgiver and whose personally eventful life, furnished him with abundant materials which he wove together as follows. Among the oppressions which Pharaoh exercised towards the Jews are named, his ordering their children to be cast into the water. Moses the son of Amran[8] was put into an ark by his mother; Pharaoh's *wife* observing the child, rescues him from death, and gives him

---

[6] Sur. XII. 86. 97. and Midrash Tanchuma quoted in Midrash Yalkut cap. CXLIII. The Koran also makes Joseph tell Benjamin first, that he was his brother XII. 69. in harmony with the Sepher Hajjashar.

[7] Of the contradictions and inconsistencies with which the "Sura Joseph" abounds, we only mention that Joseph interprets the dream in Sur. XII. 47. and in 50. he is fetched from prison.

[8] Moses is introduced as: מֹשֶׁה בֶּן עַמְרָם, or موسى بن عمران Gen. VI. 20.

back to his mother to nurse. When Moses was grown up he sought to assist his oppressed brethren, and kills an Egyptian; being the next day reminded of this deed by an Hebrew, he flees to Midian, and marries the daughter of an inhabitant of that country.[9] When about to leave Midian he sees a burning bush, and approaching it, receives a call to go to Egypt, to exhort Pharaoh[10] and perform miracles; he accepts the mission but requests the aid of his brother Aaron.[11] Pharaoh however remains an infidel and gathers his sorcerers together, who perform only inferior miracles, and in spite of Pharaoh's threats they become believers.[12] Judgment falls upon the Egyptians, they are drowned whilst the Israelites are saved.[13] A rock yields water; Moses receives the law[14] and desires to see the glory of God.[15] During Moses' absence, the Israelites make a golden calf, which he destroys, and reducing it

---

[9] Sur. XX. 37—44. XXVIII. 2—29.

[10] فرعون פַּרְעֹה Pharaoh, title of Egyptian kings.

[11] هرون, Aaron. Sur. XX. 8—37. 44—52. XXVI. 9—17. XXXVIII. 29—36. LXXIX. 15—20.

[12] Sur. VII. 101—125. X. 76—90. XI. 99—102. XX. 50—79. XXIII. 47—51. XXVI. 15—52. XXVII. 13—15. XXXVIII. 36—40. XL. 24—49. XLIII. 45—54. LXXIX. 20—27.

[13] Sur. II. 46. 47. VII. 127—135. X. 90—93. XX. 79—82. XXVI. 52—69. XXVIII. 40—43. XLIII. 55.

[14] الالواح, הַלֻּחֹת Sur. VII. 143. 150. Elpherar says to the first passage: "Ben Abbas says, he means the Torah by Alwach;" and more correctly to the last: التى فيها التوراة wherein the Torah is.

[15] Sur. VII. 135—147. 170. II. 52—55. 60. 87. IV. 152.

to powder, makes them drink it;[16] after this, Moses chooses seventy men as assistants.[17] The spies sent to Canaan are all wicked with the exception of two; the people being deceived by them must wander forty years in the desert.[18] Korah, on quarrelling with Moses, is swallowed up by the earth.[19] The marvellous journey of Moses with his servant is an addition which should not be omitted in this summary of events.[20]

Among the details, deserve to be mentioned that Haman and Korah were counsellors of Pharaoh.[21] It is not surprising that Mohammed should associate Haman with Pharaoh, as an enemy of the Jews; since he cared little, *when* individuals lived provided they could be introduced with advantage. Korah, according to Jewish tradition, was chief agent or treasurer to Pharaoh.[22] The Ante-Exodus-persecution of the Jews is ascribed to a dream of Pharaoh;[23] this is in exact accordance with Jewish fable: "The sorcerers said to Pharaoh, a boy shall be born who will lead the Israelites out of Egypt; then thought he, — cast all male children into the river and he will be cast in among them."[24] The words, Exod. 11. 7.

[16] Sur. II. 48—52. 87. VII. 147—155 XX. 82—99.
[17] Sur. VII. 155.   [18] Sur. V. 23—30.
[19] Sur. XXVIII. 76—83.   [20] Sur. XVIII. 59—82.
[21] هامان and قارون Sur. XXVIII. 57. 38. XXIX. 38. XL. 25.
[22] קֹרַח הָיָה קַתִּ־לִיקוֹם לְבֵיתוֹ שֶׁל פַּרְעֹה Midrash to Numbers Parash. XIV.
[23] Sur. XXVIII. 5.
[24] אָמְרִי הַחַרְטֻמִּים לְפַרְעֹה נַעַר עָתִיד לְהִוָּלֵד וְהוּא יוֹצִיא אֶת יִשְׂרָאֵל מִמִּצְרַיִם וְהָשַׁב וְאָמַר בְּלִבּוֹ הַשְׁלִיכוּ כָּל הַיְלָדִים הָעִבְרִים אֶל הַיְאוֹר וְהוּא יֻשְׁלַךְ עִמָּהֶם Pirke Rab. Elieser cap. XLVIII.

"I will call one of the Hebrew women" produced the Rabbinical fiction: "why just a Hebrew-woman? This shows that he was handed to all the Egyptian women, but he would not drink; for God said: the mouth which shall once speak with *Me*, should it drink what is unclean?"[25] This was too valuable for Mohammed to omit in his Koran.[26] Although it is nowhere said in the Bible, that the sign of the leprous hand was wrought in the presence of Pharaoh,[27] yet the Koran relates it as having there taken place,[28] and in this also it was preceded by Jewish tradition: "He put his hand into his bosom and withdrew it leprous white as snow; they also put their hands into their bosom and withdrew them leprous white as snow."[29] Again among Moses' own people none but his own tribe believed him;[30] this Mohammed doubtless inferred from the statement of the Rabbis: "the tribe of Levi was exempted from hard labour."[31] Among the sorcerers of Egypt who first asked for their wages and then became believers when their

---

[25] מִי שָׁנָא עִבְרִיוֹת מִלַּמֵּר שֶׁהֶחֱזִירוּהוּ עַל כָּל הַמִּצְרִיּוֹת בָּפָן וְלֹא יָנַק אָמַר הַקָּדוֹשׁ בָּרוּךְ הוּא פֶּה שֶׁעָתִיד לְדַבֵּר עִמִּי יִינַק דָּבָר טָמֵא Sotah XII. 2.

[26] Sur. XXVIII. 11.

[27] It was wrought in the wilderness on the occasion of Moses being called; but as to its being repeated before Pharaoh, Scripture is silent.

[28] Sur. VII. 105. XXVI. 32.

[29] הִכְנִיס יָדוֹ לְחֵיקוֹ וְהוֹצִיאָהּ מְצֹרַעַת כַּשֶּׁלֶג וְגַם הֵם הִכְנִיסוּ יָדָם לְחֵיקָם וְהוֹצִיאוּם מְצֹרַעַת כַּשֶּׁלֶג Pirke Rabbi Elieser cap. XLVIII.

[30] Sur. X. 83.

[31] שֶׁבְּטוּ שֶׁל לֵוִי הָיָה פָטוּר מֵעֲבוֹדַת פֶּרֶךְ Midrash Rab. to Exod. Parash. V.

serpents were swallowed by that of Moses,[32] Pharaoh himself was chief;[33] here again Mohammed is indebted to Judaism. "Pharaoh who lived in the days of Moses was a great sorcerer."[34] In other places of the Koran he ascribes divinity to Pharaoh;[35] and Jewish tradition makes him declare: "Already from the beginning ye speak falsehood, for I am the Lord of the world, I have made myself as well as the Nile; as it is said of him Ezek. XXIX. 3. "mine is the river and I have made it."[36] The prophet seems to have been much confused with regard to the plagues; in some places he enumerates nine,[37] in others only five, the first of which, is said to be the Flood![38] As the drowning in the Red Sea, happened after the plagues, he can only allude to the Deluge.

The following somewhat dark and uncertain passage[39] concerning Pharaoh, has caused commentators great perplexity; it is stated that Pharaoh pursued the Israelites until actually drowning, when confessing himself a Moslem he was saved alive from the bottom of the sea, to be a "witness for ages to come,"[40] but

[32] Sur. VII. 110. XXVI. 140.   [33] Sur. XX. 74. XXVI. 48.

[34] פַּרְעֹה שֶׁהָיָה בִּימֵי מֹשֶׁה אַמְגּוּשִׁי גָדוֹל הָיָה Midrash Yalkut cap. CLXXXII.

[35] Sur. XXVI. 128. XXVIII. 38. XLIII. 50.

[36] אָמַר לָהֶם מִתְּחִלָּה שֶׁקֶר אַתֶּם אוֹמְרִים כִּי אֲנִי הוּא אָדוֹן הָעוֹלָם וַאֲנִי בְּרָאתִי עַצְמִי וְאֶת נִילוֹס שֶׁנֶּאֱמַר לִי יְאֹרִי וַאֲנִי עֲשִׂיתִנִי Midrash Rab. to Exod. Par. V.

[37] Sur. XVII. 103. XXVII. 112.   [38] Sur. VII. 130.

[39] Sur. X. 90.

[40] Bedawi, see Henzii frag. Arab. pag. 201. alone keeps to the literal sense of the text: فاليوم ننجّيك ببدنك لتكون لمن خلفك آية

we find that it is merely a Mohammedan version of a Jewish fable: — "Perceive the great power of repentance! Pharaoh king of Egypt uttered very wicked words: who is the God whose voice I shall obey? Exod. v. 2. yet as he repented saying, who is like unto thee among the gods, XV. 11. God saved him from death; for it saith, — almost had I stretched out my hands and destroyed, — but God let him live that he might declare his power and strength."[41] As Jewish commentators add to Exod. XV. 27. — where we read of twelve fountains being found near Elim, — that each of the tribes had a well,[42] so Mohammed transposes the statement and declares, that twelve fountains sprang from the rock which had been smitten by Moses at Rephidim. The Rabbinical fable that God covered the Israelites with mount Sinai on the occasion of the lawgiving[43] is thus amplified in the Koran: "We shook the mountain over them as though it had been a covering, and they imagined that it was falling upon them; and we said: receive the law which we have brought unto you, with reverence."[44] The Koran adds, that the Israelites now demanding to see God, die, and are raised again.[45] It will not be difficult to trace the origin of this figment: —

[41] כִּי עַתָּה שָׁלַחְתִּי אֶת יָדִי נאָה א'תְךָ וְהַאֲמִירוֹ הֲקָ׳ בְּ׳ ה׳ מִבְּיָן הֵמִיתִים לְסַפֵּר כֹּחִ׳ וּגְבִירָתִי׳ הִמְּנוֹ שֶׁהֶאֱמִירוֹ שֵׁבַ׳ וְאִלָּם בַּעֲבִיר זֹאת הֶעֱמַדְתִּיךָ Pirke Rabbi Elieser cap. XLIII. cfr. Mid. to Psalm CVI. Mid. Jalkut cap. CCXXXVIII.

[42] כְּנֶגֶד שְׁנֵים עָשָׂר שְׁפָטִים נִזְדַּמְּנוּ לָהֶם Rashi to Exod. XV. 27. cfr. also Targum Hierolym.

[43] כָּפָה אֲנִי עֲלֵיכֶם אֶת הָהָר כְּגִיגִית Aboda Tarah II. 2.

[44] Sur. VII. 170. 171. [45] Sur. II. 52. 53. IV. 152.

"Two things demanded the Israelites from God; that they might see his glory, and hear his voice, and both were granted to them, as it is said: Behold the Lord our God has shown to us His glory and greatness and His voice we heard out of the midst of the fire. Deut. v. 21. These things however they had no power to resist; as they came to mount Sinai and He appeared unto them their souls escaped by His speaking, as it is said: 'my soul escaped as He spake'. The Torah however interceded for them, saying: 'does a king give his daughter to marriage and kill his household? The whole world rejoices (at my appearance) and thy children (the Israelites) shall they die?'— At once their soul returned, therefore it is said: 'the doctrine of God is perfect and brings back the soul."[46]

The history of the *golden calf* afforded a favourable subject for the Koran which follows as usual, the fabulous account of the Rabbinical traditions relating to it. Both represent Aaron as having been nearly killed when at first resisting the entreaty of the people to make it. The Sanhedrin relates: "Aaron saw Chur slaughtered before his eyes, (who opposed them) and he thought, if I do not yield to them they will deal with me as they dealt with Chur."[47] According to another passage in the Koran, an Israelite by the

---

[46] ולא היה בהם כח בם בעמוד כיון שבאו לסיני ונגלה להם פרחה נשמתם שלשדבר עמהם שנ׳ נפשי יצאה בדברו אבל התורה בקשתה עליהם רחמים מאבני הקב״ה יש מלך משיא בתו והרג אנשי ביתו כל ה עולם כלו שמחים ובניך מתים מיד חזרה נשמתן ש״נ תורת ה׳ תמימה משיבת נפש Abodah Sarah II. 2.

[47] Sur. VII. 150. and אהרון ראה חור שזבוחים לפניו אמר אי בא שמעינא דהי השתא יעבדי לי כדעבדו בחור Sanhedrin V.

name of Samari enticed them and made the calf.⁴⁸ Like the wandering Jew in the Christian fable, Samari is punished by Moses with endless wandering, and he is compelled to repeat the words "touch me not."⁴⁹ Jewish traditions make Micah assist in manufacturing the idol calf;⁵⁰ but Mohammed either derived Samari from Samael; or as the Samaritans are stated by the Arab writers to have said: "touch me not," he may have considered Samari as the author of the sect of the Samaritans.⁵¹

That the calf thus produced by Samari from the ornaments of the people, *lowed* on being finished,⁵² is evidently a Koran repetition of the following Jewish tradition: "The calf came forth Exod. XXII. 24. *roaring*, and the Israelites saw it. Rabbi Jehuda says: Samael entered the calf and roared to deceive the Israelites." The addition that the tribe of Levi remained faithful to God, is both Scriptural and Rab-

---

⁴⁸ Sur. XX. 87. 90. 96. The name السامري, Samari, may have arisen from סַמָּאֵל who is said to have assisted in making the calf.

⁴⁹ Sur. XX. 97. the words he has to repeat, are: لا مساس, no touch!

⁵⁰ Rashi to Sanhedrin CI. 2. The Micah the same as Judg. XVII. hence Arab writers consider Micah and Samari identical Achmed ben Idris in Hotting. hist. orient. pag. 84.

⁵¹ It may also have arisen from a Pharisaical sect called by the Talmud: פְּרִישׁ: אַל תְּמִשֵׁנִי: "the separated one: touch me not!" The fable is clearly a composition from various elements.

⁵² Sur. VII. 147. XX. 90. and וַיֵּצֵא הָעֵגֶל הַזֶּה גֹּעֶה וְרָאוּ אוֹתוֹ יִשְׂרָאֵל רַבִּי יְהוּדָה אוֹמֵר סַמָּאֵל נִכְנַס בְּתוֹכוֹ וְהָיָה גֹעֶה לְהַטְעוֹת אֶת יִשְׂרָאֵל Pirke Rabbi Elieser cap. CLIX.

binical.⁵³ In the following events we have abbreviations, but no alterations or additions, except in the "matter of Korah" which is honoured with singular embellishments; for instance, Korah had such riches, that from ten to forty strong men were required to carry the keys of his treasures.⁵⁴ Moslem *traditions* go much further; Abulfeda says forty *mules* were required to convey the keys. Nevertheless *Jewish* tradition, whence it is taken, is still more extravagant.—"Joseph buried three treasures in Egypt, one of which became known to Korah. Riches are turned to destruction to him that possesses them, Eccles. V. 12. and this may well be applied to Korah. The keys to the treasures of Korah made a burden for 300 white mules,"⁵⁵ The accusation from which God cleared his servant Moses, of which the Koran makes mention, was according to the best commentators, occasioned by Korah. "Abu Aliah says: it refers to Korah hiring a harlot to reproach Moses before all the people, upon which God struck her dumb, and destroyed Korah, which cleared Moses from the charge."⁵⁶ This is unquestionably an amplification of the following

⁵³ Sur. VII. 159. Exod. XXXII. 26. Pirke Rabbi Elieser cap. XLV.
⁵⁴ Sur. XXVIII. 76. The words by Sale: "many strong men" signify a general number from 10—40.
⁵⁵ זֶה עָשְׁרוֹ שֶׁל קֹרַח מַשּׂוֹי שְׁלֹשׁ מֵאוֹת פְּרָדוֹת לְבָנוֹת הָיָה מַפְתְּחוֹת בֵּית גְּנָזָיו שֶׁל קֹרַח Pirke Rabbi Elieser cap. XLV.
⁵⁶ Sur. XXXIII. 69. LXI. 5. وقال لبو للعالة هو ان قارون استاجر بغية تقذف موسى بنفسها على راس لملا فعصمها الله وابرا موسى من ذلك واهلك قارون Elpharer to Sur. XXXIII. 69.

passage. "Moses heard and fell on his face. What was it he heard? That they accused him of having to do with another man's wife.⁵⁷ Other commentators of the Koran conceive the unjust charge from which Moses was cleared, to have been that of murdering Aaron on mount Hor, because he and Eleazar only were present when Aaron died!⁵⁸ That they have again had recourse to Jewish tradition will appear from the subjoined extract: — "The whole congregation saw that Aaron was dead; and when Moses and Eleazer came down from the mountain, the whole congregation gathered together asking: where is Aaron? But they said, he is dead. — How can the Angel of death touch a man, by whom he was resisted and restrained, as it is said: he stood between the dead and the living and the plague was stayed; if ye bring him, it is well, if not we will stone you. Moses prayed: Lord of the world, remove from me this suspicion! Then God opened and showed them Aaron's body, and to this the passage applies: the whole congregation saw etc. etc. Numb. xx. 29."⁵⁹

7. The time of the Judges is passed over unnoticed, and from the manner in which the election

---

⁵⁷ וַיִּשְׁמַע מֹשֶׁה וַיִּפֹּל עַל פָּנָיו מָה שָׁמְעָה שְׁמוּעָה מְכֻעָר שֶׁחֲשָׁדוּהוּ בְּאֵשֶׁת אִישׁ Pirk. R. Elieser cap. XLV. M. speaks of the unjust charge against Moses in the very Sura in which he strives to clear himself from just imputations!

⁵⁸ According to Elpharer and Abulfeda, the angels showed the dead body of Aaron.

⁵⁹ Midrash Tanchuma to Numb. XX. 29. The fabulous expedition of Moses, Sur. XVIII. 59—82. is likewise of Jewish origin. Zunz: Die gottesdienstlichen Vorträge der Juden, historisch entwickelt. The hero of the tale is however a certain Rabbi Jushua.

of a king is introduced Sur. II. 247. 253. it would appear that Mohammed was ignorant of the long interval between Moses and Saul.[60] Of David's history only his victory over Goliath and his fall through Bathsheba are recorded. The Sonna makes mention of the brevity of his slumbers, and commentators of the Koran affirm the same: "The apostle of God said: David slept half the night, he then rose for a third part and slept again a sixth part."[61] This the Koran derived from the Rabbis, who assert that the king slept only for the term of "sixty breathings."[62] Of the wisdom of Solomon the Koran makes particular mention; and to support the statement, adds, that he understood the language of birds; this was also the opinion of the Jewish doctors. The winds, or more probable *spirits* obeyed him;[63] and demons birds and beasts formed part of his standing army.[64] Jewish commentators record that "demons of various kinds and evil spirits were subject to him."[65] The story of the queen of Sheba and the adventures of

[60] M ascribes to Saul what Scripture relates of Gideon. Judg. VII. 5—6.

[61] Sonna CXLVIII. Elpharer to Sur. XXXVIII. 16: قل رسول الله صلعم كان داود ينام نصف الليل ويقوم ثلثه وينام سدسه

[62] שִׁתִּים נְשִׁימֵי. Berachoth. In his days the Sabbath-breaking Jews are metamorphised into apes. Sur. II. 61. IV. 50. V. 65. VII. 166.

[63] ريح like רוּחוֹת the Spirits. Sur. XXVII. 15. 16.

[64] Sur. XXI. 81. 82. XXXIV. 11. 12. XXXVIII. 35—40.

[65] לֵהּ וְלָשַׁמְּשִׁין שֵׁדִין וּפִגְעִין וְסִחִין וְרוּחִין בִּישִׁין אֲתִמְסָרִי בִּידֵהּ The second Targum to Esther I. 2.

the lapwing,[66] are only abridgements from Jewish traditions. As the original is less accessible and more important to the student of the Koran we shall insert a version of this ridiculous fable.—"The wild cock was once sought for among the birds, and not being found the king angrily commanded that he should be brought in, intending to kill him. Then said the wild cock to the king: My Lord king, give heed and hear my words! Already for three months I weighed in my mind, and flew about in the whole world in search for a town, which does not obey thee. I saw then a city in the East, of the name of *Kitor*, in which are many people, and a woman governs them all, she is called queen of Sheba. If it please thee, my Lord king, I shall go to that city, bind their kings in chains and their rulers with iron fetters, and bring them hither. As it pleased the king, writers were called, who wrote letters and bound them to the wings of the wild cock. He came to the queen who observing the letter tied to the wing, loosened it and read the following contents:—From me king Solomon, greeting to thee and to thy princes! Thou knowest well that God has made me king over the beasts of the field, over the birds of heaven, over demons, spirits and goblins, the kings from all regions of the earth approach me with homage; wilt thou do this, thou shalt have great honour, if not, I will send upon thee kings, legions and horsemen. The kings are the beasts of the field, the horsemen the birds of heaven

---

[66] The sagacious bird هدهد forms a conspicuous part in the fable of the queen of Sheba: Sur. XXVII. 20—46.

the hosts, demons and spirits; the goblins are the legions who shall strangle you in your beds." When the queen had read this, she rent her garments and called for the elders and lords, saying: know ye what king Solomon has sent to me? They answered, we neither know nor esteem him. The queen however trusting them not, called for sailors and sent presents to the king, and after three years she came herself, The king on hearing of her arrival sat in a crystal hall to receive her, which made her fancy that he was sitting in water, she therefore uncovered her feet to pass through. On seeing his glory she said: may the Lord thy God be praised who has found pleasure in thee and made thee sit on the throne to exercise mercy and justice.[67]

With regard to the fable before alluded to, that demons assisted Solomon in the building of the temple, and being deceived, continued it after his death, we may here add that Mohammed borrowed it directly from the Jews.[68] When Solomon became haughty, one of his many demons ruled in his stead till he repented.[69] The Sanhedrin also refers to this degradation: "In the beginning Solomon reigned also over the upper worlds;" as it is said: "Solomon sat on the throne of God," after that only over his staff, as it is said: "what profit hath a man of all his

[67] Targum II. to the book of Esther.
[68] Sur. XXXIV. 13. and Gittin LXVIII.
[69] Compare Talmud עין יעקב Psa. II. Tract. גיטין et ילקוט in lib. Reg. pag. 182 with Sur. XXXVIII. 33—35. Sale, 374. Wahl pag. 451 not. b.

labour," and still later: this is my portion of all my labour."[70] On repenting he maimed his horses considering them a useless luxury. In the Talmud and the Scriptures we find allusion to his obtaining them as well as to their being prohibited.[71]

Among the few characters which Mohammed notices after Solomon, *Elijah* the prophet takes the precedence; nothing is mentioned of his rapture to heaven, yet he is considered a most remarkable prophet.[72] Among the Jews, Elijah is deemed an intermediate person between heaven and earth; he appears in human form to the pious on earth, visits them in their places of worship and communicates revelations from God to eminent Rabbis. In this character Elijah also appears in Moslem divinity. *Jonah* "the man of the fish"[73] is not forgotten; Mohammed relates his story in his usual style, not omitting his journey to Nineveh or the gourd which afforded him shade.[74] Job too, with his suffering and cure is noticed;[75] also

---

[70] בְּהִתְחִלָּה מֶלֶךְ שְׁלֹמֹה עַל הָעֶלְיוֹנִים שֶׁנֶּאֱמַר יֵשֵׁב שְׁלֹמֹה עַל כִּסֵּא ה׳
וּלְבַסּוֹף לֹא מָלַךְ אֶלָּא עַל מַקְלוֹ שֶׁנֶּאֱמַר מַה יִּתְרוֹן לָאָדָם בְּכָל עֲמָלוֹ
וּלְבַסּוֹף זֶה חֶלְקִי מִכָּל עֲמָלִי. כְּתִיב Sanhedrin XX. also Mid. Rabh. to Numb. Parash. XI.

[71] Sur. XXXVIII. 29—33. Sanhedrin XXI. and Deut. XVI. 16. 1 King X. 29. Wahl pag. 451. The fable of the ants Sur. XXVII. 18—20. arose probably from Prov. VI. 6. Compare Talmud, Chullin LVII. 7.

[72] Sur. VI. 85. XXXVII. 123. 130. الياس; among the Jews: אֵלִיָּהוּ הַנָּבִיא, Elijah the prophet.

[73] يونس, Jonah, also صاحب الحوت, the man of the fish, Sur. VI. 85. X. 98. XXXVII. 139. XXI. 87. LXVIII. 48.

[74] The whole very briefly Sur. X. 72. XXI. 87. 88. XXXVII. 139—149. LXVIII. 48—51.

[75] Sur. XXI. 83. XXXVIII. 40—45.

the three men who were cast into a burning fiery furnace,[76] the turning back of the shadow of degrees on the occasion of Hezekiah's recovery,[77] and the excessive veneration of the Jews for the memory of Ezra,[78] may be added as instances of the most flagrant plagiarism.

On reviewing the contents of this chapter, we find the assertion that Mohammed borrowed largely from the Judaism of his age—encumbered as it was by fabulous traditions—has been fully established. It would seem that Mohammed drew his knowledge of Jewish history and religion only from these impure fountains which long before his day had been placed on a par with the Word of God. Many more fables and teachings of the Koran might doubtless be traced back to same source, but let those already adduced, suffice to prove to Moslemin, whence the alleged revelations of their prophet date their real origin. We shall now see what the false prophet adopted from Christianity and examine the relation of the Koran to the New Testament.

[76] Sur. LXXXV. 4. etc. Dan. III. 8.
[77] Sur. XXV. 47. 47. 2 King XX. 9—12.
[78] רָאוּי הָיָה עֶזְרָא שֶׁתִּנָּתֵן תּוֹרָה עַל יָדוֹ אִלְמָלֵא לֹא קְדָמוֹ מֹשֶׁה
Ezra would have been worthy to have given the law, if it had not already come by Moses. Sanhedrin XXI. 2. and Sur. IX. 30.

CHAPTER VI.

WHAT MOHAMMED BORROWED FROM CHRISTIANITY.

"It was *needful* for me to write unto you, and exhort you that ye should earnestly *contend* for *the faith* which was once delivered unto the saints. For there are certain men crept in unawares, who were before of old ordained to this condemnation; ungodly men, *turning the grace of our God* into lasciviousness, and *denying* the only Lord God and our *Lord Jesus Christ.*" Jude 3. 4.[79]

It will appear in the course of this chapter that Mohammed was better acquainted with the *traditions*, than with the canonical Scriptures of the Christians, just as he was more versed in the Rabbinical writings than in the Old Testament; hence we may expect to find most of those parts of our Lord's life, on which the apocryphal writings chiefly treat. The Koran however going beyond the favourite subject of the childhood of Jesus, begins with the *fore-runner* of Christ; Zacharias his father dwells in the temple, and asking for a son and heir, is promised one by the angels, or according to another account, by God Himself. Although the New Testament relates nothing of the parents of the Virgin *Mary*, the apocryphal Gospels invariably call them Joachim and Anna; the Koran however designates her family, the family of Amran or Imran.[80] From her being called the sister

---

[79] This will only be fully understood, when we remember, that St. Jude was one of the founders of the *Arabian* Church, and probably addressed these prophetic words to it in particular.

[80] *Evang. de nativitate Mariae* and *Protevang. Jacobi* cap. I. and II. Also Euseb. Hist. eccl. lib. I. cap. VI. and Sur. III. 33. 35. LXVI. 12.

of Aaron, and the daughter of Amran[81] it has been fairly concluded that Mohammed considered the Virgin Mary, and Miriam the sister of Moses and Aaron, as identical; and no sophistry on the part of Mohammedan divines or European writers can remove this impression.[82] The birth and childhood of Mary are related in these words, "The wife of Imran prayed, Lord verily I have vowed unto thee that which is in my womb to be dedicated to thy service. Accept it therefore of me, for thou art he, who heareth and knoweth. And when she was delivered of it, she said Lord verily I have brought forth a female;—Allah knew what she had brought forth;—and a male is not as a female. I have called her Mary, and I commend her and her issue to thy protection against Satan driven away with stones. Therefore the Lord accepted her with a gracious acceptance and caused her to bear an excellent offspring. And Zacharias took care of the child, whenever he went into the chamber to her, he found she had provisions with her, and he said, O Mary whence hast thou these? She answered, this is from God, for God provideth for whom he pleaseth without measure."[83] Again,

[81] עַמְרָם, the father of Moses and Aaron, also of מִרְיָם, Μαρίαμ: مريم ابنت عمران اخت هرون, Mary, daughter of Amran and sister of Aaron.

[82] It is assumed that Miriam was kept alive to become the mother of Jesus: in this they have partly the Rabbis on their side: מִרְיָם כֹּא אַלָּא שֶׁבַט בָּהּ מַלְאַךְ הַמָּוֶת אֶלָּא בִּנְשִׁיקָה מִיתָה וְלֹא שָׁלַט בָּהּ רִמָּה וְתוֹלֵעָה "Over Miriam the angel of death had no power, but she died by the divine breath, and no worms molested her." Babha Bathra XVII. Geiger pag. 173.

[83] Sur. III. 35—37.

"The angels said, O Mary, verily God hath chosen thee and hath purified thee and hath chosen thee above all women of the world, O Mary be devout towards thy Lord and bow thy knees with them that bow their knees. This is one of the secret histories; we reveal it unto thee (Mohammed) because thou wert not with them, when they threw in their rods to cast lots which of them should have the education of Mary, neither wast thou with them when they strove among themselves."[84] This is faithfully borrowed from Christian apocryphas.[85] We here perceive the same pretensions of Mohammed to having received by revelation "a secret history,"—though in reality, one which was in the mouth of most oriental Christians at that period,—as in the history of Joseph, which he pretended to divulge as one utterly unknown till

[84] Sur. III. 42—44.

[85] Εἶπε δὲ "Αννα· ζῇ κύριος ὁ θεός μου, ἐὰν γεννήσω εἴτε ἄρρεν εἴτε θῆλυ, προσάξω αὐτὸ δῶρον κυρίῳ τῷ θεῷ μου, καὶ ἔσται λειτουργοῦν αὐτῷ πάσας τὰς ἡμέρας τῆς ζωῆς αὐτοῦ. *Protevang. Jacobi* cap. IV. In the Gospel of the Nativity of Mary we read "voverunt tamen (Mariae parentes) si forte Deus donaret eis sobolem, eam re domini servitio mancipaturos." *Evang. de nativ. Mariae* cap. I. Again cap. VII: "Quotidie ab angelis frequentabatur, quotidie divina visione fruebatur, quae eam a malis omnibus custodiebat et bonis omnibus redundare faciebat." Again Protevang. Jacobi cap. VIII: "ἦν δὲ Μαριὰμ ὡσεὶ περιστερὰ νεμομένη ἐν τῷ ναῷ κυρίου, καὶ ἐλάμβανε τροφὴν ἐκ χειρὸς ἀγγέλου." Again in "Historia de nativitate Mariae et de infantia Salvatoris," cap. IV: "Abierunt simul Joachim et Anna, uxor ejus, ad templum domini, et offerentes hostias domino tradiderunt infantulam suam Mariam in contubernio virginum, quae die noctuque in Dei laudibus manebant." Cap. VI: "Quotidie esca, quam de manu angeli accipiebat, ipsa tantum reficiebatur; escam vero, quam a pontificibus templi consequebatur, pauperibus dividebat. Frequenter videbantur cum ea angeli loqui et quasi carissime obtemperabant ei."

then. The casting of lots as to who should have the care of the infant Mary, who was probably left an orphan at a very early age, is fully described in the apocryphal books, and Mohammed, although "none of the party who cast the lots," could have read it there in all its minutest and most circumstantial details.[66] It may be added that the Koran omits all mention of Joseph, Mary's relation to him being never once alluded to; but the apocryphas assert that she vowed perpetual virginity when the subject of marriage was on one occasion brought before her.[87]

3. The *birth of Jesus* is thus recorded by Mohammed in Sur. XIX. 16—21: "Remember to notice in the book concerning Mary, when she retired from her family to a place towards the East, and took a veil to conceal herself from them; and we sent our Spirit[88] unto her, and he appeared unto her in the shape of a perfect man; she said I fly for refuge unto the merciful God to defend me against thee, if thou fearest God: he answered, I am sent to give thee a holy son; she replied, how shall I have a son, seeing a man has not touched me, and I am no harlot; he answered, so shall it be; thy Lord said, this is easy with me, and we shall ordain him for a sign unto men and a mercy from us, for it is a thing decreed." In another passage, the annunciation is made not by

---

[66] *Evang. de nativit. Mariae* cap. VI—VIII. *Protevang. Jacobi* cap. VIII. IX.

[87] *Evang. de nativitate Mariae* cap. VII.

[88] רוּחַ, رُوح, πνεῦμα is here not the Holy Ghost in the Christian acceptation of the word, but the angel Gabriel.

one, but by several angels; which is the more authentic of the two versions of the story we must leave to Mohammedans to decide. "The angels said, O Mary, verily God sendeth thee good tidings of the *word* from him, his name shall be Christ Jesus the son of Mary, honourable in this world and in the world to come, and one of those who approach God, and he shall speak to men in the cradle and be righteous in his old age; she answered, Lord how shall I have a son, since a man hath not touched me? he answered, so shall it be, God createth what he pleaseth, and when he decreeth a thing, he only says unto it, *be,* and *it is.*"[89]

When Mary was overtaken by the pains of childbirth "near the trunk of a *palm-tree,* she said, would to God I had died before this and were forgotten and lost in oblivion;[90] and he who was beneath her[91] said, be not grieved, now hath God provided a rivulet under thee, and do thou shake the palm-tree and it shall let fall ripe dates unto thee, ready gathered; eat and drink and calm thy mind. Shouldest thou meet any one who should question thee (on account of the child) say, I have vowed a fast unto the most merciful God, wherefore I will by no means

---

[89] Sur. III. 45—48.

[90] "Historia de Nativitate Mariae et de infantia Salvatoris' probably gave rise to this statement, when it relates cap. XX. that on their flight to Egypt, Jesus commanded the branches of a palmtree, under which they rested, to bend down to refresh the travellers by their fruit, after this the infant Saviour causes a fountain to bubble up from between the roots of the tree.

[91] من تحتها, refers to the new born babe.

speak to any man this day."⁹² We find in consequence, that Mary answers the inquiries of her relatives only by signs, as if to say: the birth of this child is a subject concerning which, I have only to answer to God and need not justify myself before men.⁹³ The fear which Mary expresses in the Koran leaves no doubt as to the manner in which the conception was thought to have been accomplished; hence we may account for the accusation which the Jews are said by Mohammed, to have brought against her, and which seems to be intimated by the apocryphal writings, when they declare that Mary "hid herself from the sons of Israel."⁹⁴

Throughout the Koran, Jesus is called the son of Mary; in accordance with the New Testament he is also styled the "word from God" and "the word of truth."⁹⁵ It also adds, "To Jesus the son of Mary gave we proofs of his divine Mission, and strengthened him by the spirit of holiness."⁹⁶ In another place

⁹² Sur. XIX. 22—25. As regards the dates and the fountain: Hist. de nat. Mariae et de inf. Salvat. cap. XX.

⁹³ Gerock's Versuch einer Darstellung der Christologie des Koran, pag. 36. We make free use of this work; but would caution others who may consult it after us, of its singular partiality to Mohammed.

⁹⁴ Sur. IV. 155. In the Protevang. Jacobi cap. XII. we read: καὶ ἔκρυβεν ἑαυτὴν ἀπὸ τῶν υἱῶν Ἰσραήλ.

⁹⁵ Jesus Sur. XIX. 32. is called قول, קֹדֶשׁ, whilst otherwise قول الحق ;كلمة or كلمة الله: word of truth. The Arab translation of the Bible gives John I. 1. by كلمة.

⁹⁶ ايدناه بروح القدس Sur. II. 87. 254. V. 119.

He is called the Spirit from God,[97] Again, we are to "remember her who preserved her virginity, and into whom we breathed of our Spirit, ordaining her and her son for a sign unto all creatures."[98] As the same is said of Adam, Mohammed finds a strong analogy between him and Jesus, as regards their respective entrance into the world.[99] After the *birth of Jesus* under the palm-tree, the Koran thus continues: "She brought the child back to her people, carrying him in her arms, and they said unto her, O Mary, now hast thou done a strange thing, O sister of Aaron, thy father was not a bad man, neither was thy mother a harlot. But she made signs unto the child to answer them; and they said, how shall we speak to him who is an infant in the cradle? Whereupon the child said, verily I am the servant of God, he hath given me the book of the gospel, and hath appointed me a prophet; and he hath made me blessed, wherever I shall be, and hath commanded me to observe prayer, and to give alms, so long as I shall live, and he hath made me dutiful towards my mother and hath not made me proud or unhappy; and peace be on me the day whereon I was born, and the day whereon I shall die, and the day whereon I shall be raised to life."[1]

[97] مِنْهُ رُوحٌ, the Spirit from him. Sur. IV. 169.
[98] Sur. XXI. 91. LXVI. 13. cfr. XXXVIII. 72.
[99] Sur. III. 58. Bedawi adds to Sur. V. 84. "God created Jesus without father, Adam without co-operation of father and mother, which is a greater miracle."
[1] Sur. XIX. 26—32. Of this reproach of Mary by her friends, nothing is said in the Apocryphas; but the friends of Mary say to

That the child spoke in the cradle, Mohammed borrowed from the Arabic Gospel of the infancy.[2] During his childhood, Christ performed various miracles which are recorded in the apocryphal books of the early Christians. From them therefore the following details of the Koran are copied: "Verily I come unto you with a sign from your Lord; for I will make before you, of clay, as it were the figure of a bird, then I will breathe thereon, and it shall become a bird by the permission of God; and I will heal him that hath been blind from his birth, and I will heal the leper and raise the dead by the permission of God."[3] Again: "I taught thee the Scripture and wisdom and the law and the Gospel; and when thou didst create of clay, as it were the figure of a bird, by my permission, and didst breathe thereon and it became a bird by my permission, and thou didst heal one blind from his birth, and the

---

her mourning husband: "Quotidie cum ea angelus domini loquitur, quotidie escam de manu angeli accipit. Quomodo fieri potest, ut si aliquod peccatum in ea? Nam si suspicionem nostram tibi vis ut pandamus, istam gravidam non fecit nisi angelus Dei." Joseph replies: "Utquid seducitis me, ut credam vobis, quia angelus domini impraegnasset eam? Potest enim fieri, ut quisquam finxerit se esse angelum domini, ut deciperet eam." *Historia de nativitate Mariae et de infantia Salvat.* cap. X.

[2] Compare Sur. III. 46. XIX. 27. V. 119. with the following: "Invenimus in libro Josephi pontificis, qui vixit tempore Christi, Jesum locutum esse, et quidem cum in cunis jaceret dixisseque matri suae Mariae: Ego, quem peperisti, sum Jesus, filius Dei, verbum, quemadmodum annunciavit tibi angelus Gabriel, misitque me pater meus ad salutem mundi." *Evangel. infantiae,* cap. I.

[3] Sur. III. 48. The last part of the passage may likewise refer to the infancy of Jesus, for the apocryphal books relate many such miracles performed by the infant Saviour.

leper by my permission, and didst bring forth the dead by my permission, and when I withheld the children of Israel from killing thee, when thou didst come to them with evident signs, and such of them as believed not said, This is nothing but manifest sorcery."[4] Again,—Jesus being seven years old and at play with several children of his age, they made several figures of birds and beasts of clay, for their diversion; and each preferring his own workmanship, Jesus told them that he would make his, walk and leap; which accordingly at his command they did. He also made several figures of sparrows and other birds, which flew about or stood on his hands as he ordered them, and also ate and drank when he offered them meat and drink. The children telling this to their parents, were forbidden to play any more with Jesus, whom they held to be a sorcerer![5]

4. What the Koran relates of the miracles of Christ, has already been noticed. All he did, is said to have been done *by the permission* of God to prove his being an apostle of God." "I come unto you with a sign from your Lord, therefore serve him, this is the right way."[6] But Jesus perceiving their unbelief,

[4] Sur. V. 119. 120. Respecting these marvels see: *Thomae Evang. Infantiae* cap. II.; and: *Evang. Infantiae Arab.* cap. XXXVI. XLVI.

[5] *Evang. Infantiae* pag. III. etc. etc. The apocryphal books as well as the New Test. have nothing to say of the life of Jesus between his 12th and 30th year. Yea the "Arab. Evang. Infantiae" says expressly, cap. LIV. that Jesus performed no miracles after his 12th year till the commencement of his public ministry. Nor is the Koran more communicative respecting the 18 years of retirement.

[6] Sur. III. 49.

asked who would be his helpers, when the *Apostles* offered their services, confessed their belief in God, and desired to be acknowledged true believers by Christ.[7] He, like David, cursed his unbelieving generation, which ascribed all he did and said to sorcery.[8] The believers in Jesus are generally called Nazarenes; the Apostles are nowhere mentioned by name, nor is their number specified, but three are said to have been shamefully treated by the inhabitants of a certain town.[9] No intimation is given in the Koran as to how the disciples of Jesus were made, or when they were called, but it gives a strange misrepresentation of the institution of the Lord's Supper, in the following conversation between Jesus and his Apostles. — "When I commanded the apostles of Jesus saying, Believe in me and in my messenger; they answered, we do believe and do thou bear witness that we are Moslemin. When the apostles said, O Jesus son of Mary is thy Lord able to cause a table to descend unto us from heaven? He answered, fear God, if ye be true believers. They said, we desire to eat thereof, that our hearts may rest at ease, that we may know that thou hast told us the truth and that we may witness thereof. Jesus the son of Mary said, O Lord our God, cause a table to descend unto us

---

[7] Sur. III. 50. 51.   [8] Sur. V, 87. LXI. 6. 14. 119.

[9] Sur. XXXVI. 13—26. Apostles or as they are called الحواريون, which signifies the white, pure, *candidi;* then friends, assistants, Ansarier. In the transitive sense the word signifies also: *lotor, dealbator vestium,* whence some commentators thought the Apostles were engaged in the trade of bleaching; others assume they wore white garments: *candidati!*

from heaven, that it become a festival day unto us, unto the first of us and unto the last of us and a sign from thee, and do thou provide food for us, for thou art the best provider. God said, verily I will cause it to descend unto you. But whosoever shall disbelieve hereafter, I will surely punish him with a punishment wherewith I will not punish any other creature."[10] The concluding denunciation reminds us of the words which St. Paul subjoins to his account of the institution of the Lord's supper.[11]

5. The last events of our Lord's life are singularly perverted in the Koran. It has been already noticed, in the summary of its dogmas, that Mohammed emphatically denied the death of Jesus to have been caused by violent means; hence he was consistent in disguising the nature of the Lord's Supper. The son of Mary, he alleges, was miraculously saved from death on the cross. "The Jews devised a stratagem against *him*, but God devised a stratagem against *them*, and God is the best deviser of stratagems. Allah spake thus, O Jesus verily I will cause thee to die, and I will take thee unto me, and I will deliver thee from the unbelievers, and I will place those who will follow

[10] Sur. V. 121—124. Maraccio Refut. pag. 241. VII. assumes, that the feeding of the 5000, and the parable of the wedding feast had been here thrown together by M., but we can easily recognise the τραπεζα κυριου, or the δειπνον κυριακον of the Christian Church. The Sura is itself called: المائدة: the table. Nor was it likely M. should have overlooked so essential an institution, which was retained by the Christians, even in the most corrupt ages of the Church.

[11] 1 Cor. XI. 27. Commentators liberally supply the table with fish and fruit. See L. Warner, Compend. histor. pag. 25. etc. and Maracc. Prodrom. pars IV. p. 89. also Refut. to Sur. V. p. 238. 239.

thee, above the unbelievers, until the day of the Resurrection, then unto me shall ye return, and I will judge between you of that, concerning which ye disagree." "The Jews have said, we have slain Christ Jesus, the son of Mary, the apostle of God; yet they slew him not neither crucified him, but he was represented by one in his likeness; and verily they who disagreed with him, were in doubt as to this matter, nor know they anything but opinions about him, but they have not really killed him, but God hath taken him up." Again, "I withheld the children of Israel from killing thee when thou hadst come unto them with evident signs."[12]

The Moslem divines severally agree in the denial of Christ's death upon the cross;[13] but they differ as to the person crucified in his stead. Some record that a person similar to Jesus was crucified, whose body was taken down, after six hours, by the carpenter Joseph, to bury it in his own grave, having obtained the permission from king Herod, whose name was also Pilate. In the mean-time, the son of Mary was sent down to his mother to assure her of his happiness and safety. Others inform us: that Jesus, when pre-

---

[12] لاقتلوه ولا صلبوه they slew him not, nor crucified him. Sur. IV. 156. 157. III. 53. 53. V. 119.

[13] The death of Christ is not in itself denied. Christ to M. was a mere man; and every man tastes death: كل نفس ذائقة الموت Sur. XXI. 36 LVI 62. III. 186. IV. 77. The necessity of all men dying is spoken of in the apocryphal books in the same terms. See "*Historia Josephi*" cap. XXII. pag. 42. cap. XVIII. XXVIII. XXXI. Maracc. Refut. pag. 113. 114. Prodrom. pars III. pag. 63—67. supplies copious extracts from Moslem writers, as to the person crucified in his stead.

dicting his being taken to heaven, asked, who among his disciples would assume his form and be crucified in his stead, with a view to a reward at the day of the Resurrection. One offered to comply with the proposition, whilst Jesus was taken to heaven. Ebn Abbas adds: Jesus was brought into a certain house through the window, and thence taken to heaven through a sky-light. Titianus, persuaded by Judas, got into a side window to murder Jesus; on entering the room, Titianus being suddenly changed into the form of the son of Mary, was himself crucified by the Jews.

That this is not an original invention of Mohammed may be gathered, from the history of the early heresies of the Christian Church. The Basilidians denied that Christ suffered, and held that *Simon* from Cyrene was crucified in his stead.[14] The Cerinthians and Carpocratians believed that one of his disciples suffered death upon the cross in his stead.[15] The Gospel of St. Barnabas represents Christ to have been snatched to heaven, when the Jews were on the point of apprehending him in the garden, and that Judas being transformed into the form of his master was taken, delivered to Pilate and crucified.[16] Others

---

[14] Iraen. lib. I. 1. cap. XXIII. Eiph. Haeres. XXIV. 3.

[15] In the "Περίοδοι ἀποστόλων" Photius discovered the same error: πολλὰς δὲ καὶ τοῦ σταυροῦ κενολογίας καὶ ἀτοπίας ἀναπλάττει καὶ τὸν Χριστὸν μὴ σταυρωθῆναι ἀλλ᾽ ἕτερον ἀντ᾽ αὐτοῦ. See Photius Biblioth. Cod. CXIV. pag. 192. Jesus then is made to laugh at those who thought they had crucified him. Toland's Nazarenus pag. 17.

[16] Menagiana tom. IV. p. 326.

again taught, that the prince of darkness was crucified in the place of the Saviour of the world![17] It would seem that Mohammed revenged himself upon the *vicarious atonement* of Christ, by adopting these heretical opinions, which represent other persons as having suffered in His stead.

From the various passages referring to the death and exaltation of Christ,[18] we gather, that Jesus must have been dead and removed to Paradise at the time Mohammed compiled his Koran; if this be the case, it must be considered a special mark of divine favour, for even Abraham is spoken of, as one who would *hereafter* have his place among the blessed ones in the world to come, thus making it a future event.[19] The Christian Apocryphas speak of the Virgin's assumption without death, and Mohammed in ascribing this honour to her, as well as her Son, doubtless borrowed from them.[20]

6. Of the *Ascension* of Christ, in the Christian acceptation of the word, the Koran knows nothing, nor was it possible that Mohammed should admit the royal dignity of the Redeemer at the right hand of

[17] Mani, Epist. fundamenti, ap. Evodium: Princeps itaque tenebrarum cruci est affixus, idemque spineam coronam portavit. *Joh. Damascenus* de Haeres. pag. 466. ed. Bas. states it to be Moslem belief: "Judaeos contra legem cum in crucem agere voluisse; et cum eum tenuissent ejus quidem umbram egisse in crucem, Christum autem nec in crucem actum fuisse, nec mortuum. Deum enim cum ad se in coelum transtulisse, quod ei esset carissimus."

[18] Sur. XIX. 32. III. 54. V. 126. IV. 156. 157. XXIII. 52.

[19] Sur. II. 131. XVI. 122. XXIX 27. Wahl pag. 303. Note.

[20] "Et posuimus filium Mariae et matrem ejus in miraculum, et recepimus utrumque in locum sublimum." Sur. XXIII. 52.

God; since this would militate against the leading doctrine of the divine *Unity*, as taught in the Koran. The *second Advent of Christ* was received as a formal article into the creed of Mohammed, but there are only scanty allusions to it in the Koran. "He shall be a sign of the approach of the last hour, wherefore doubt not thereof."[21] The second advent of Christ is differently described by Moslem divines; some say that he will appear near the white tower, east of Damascus; others that he will descend on a rock on mount Moriah, confess Islamism, destroy Christianity and every other creed, kill all swine, break every cross, pierce Antichrist with his lance at Ludd or Lydda, near Jaffa; after this he will marry, beget children, die after forty or forty-five years and be lamented by Moslemin, who will bury him by the side of Mohammed. After this he will appear again at the Resurrection as Judge.[22] The Koran, however ascribes no such honours to the son of Mary; instead of acting as Judge, it teaches that Christ himself will be required to give an account of his doings upon earth, like all the other prophets.[23]

[21] Sur. XLIII. 59. وانّه لعلم للساعة literally, et ille est cognitio horae. The expounders make it: His advent is the sign of the approaching Judgment. In the: "Carmen Arabicum, *Amali* dictum" edited by Bohlen 1825 we read verse 31: "Jesus aliquando reveniet contra Antichristum miserum astutumque, quem tunc perdet." When the Kaliphate was restored to the Abbassides, Abdallah I. was told by his uncle David that the Kaliphate would remain in his family, till it would be transferred into the hands of Jesus Christ, the son of Mary. M. d'Ohsson I. 139.

[22] M. d'Ohsson I. pag. 138.

[23] We have thus an account of the birth of Mary, her parents,

7. We now come to the consideration of those Christian dogmas, which the Koran represents as blasphemous. The doctrine of the blessed Trinity was either not known to Mohammed, or maliciously perverted into a Tritheism, with which he reproaches the Christians from beginning to end:— "Say not, there are three gods, forbear this, it will be better for you. God is but one God. Far be it from him that He should have a son." Again; "They are certainly infidels who say, God is the third of three, for there is no God beside one God."[24] The *Tritheism* against which the Koran so strongly protests, consists of God, Jesus Christ and Mary His mother. The first and highest of these, is *Allah*.[25] That Allah however should be considered Father and have a son is a doctrine which rouses the highest indignation of Mohammed.[26] It is unworthy of Allah to have a son;

her guardian and intercourse with angels: Sur. III. 33—37. 42—44; promise of the birth of John the Baptist, XIX. 1—15. XXI. 89. 90. III. 38—41. Jesus announced to Mary: III. 45—48. XIX. 16—21. His birth: XIX 22—28. Speeches of the newborn babe: XIX. 29—32. His miracles: III. 48. V. 119. Description of his prophetical work: V. 87. XXXIII. 7. XLIII. 56—63. LXI. 6. Choice of the Apostles: III. 51. 52. LXI. 14. The Lord's table: V. 121—124. Mistake of the Jews in crucifying another in His stead: III. 53. 54. IV. 156—158. V. 119. Miraculous removal of Christ: XIX. 32. III. 54. Assumption with Mary into Paradise: XXIII. 52. Christ's second advent the signal to Judgment: XLIII. 59. Lastly His giving an account of Himself: XXXIII. 7. 8. V. 118. 119. 125—127. IV. 158.

[24] Sur. IV. 169. V. 82.

[25] Allah الله, from אֱלֹהַּ, אֱלֹהִים; the expression: God the Father is therefore never used in the Koran.

[26] "They say, Allah hath begotten a son, God forbid." Sur. X. 67. cfr. Ps. II. 7. Act. XIII. 33. Hebr. I. 5. and the Nicene formula: γεννηθέντα ἐκ τοῦ πατρός.

he has neither a son nor a partner.²⁷ He hath begotten no issue, neither is there any besides Allah. The idea appeared to Mohammed so impious that he says, "it wanted but little, that the heavens should rend and the earth cleave asunder and the mountains be overthrown and fall."²⁸ How should Allah have a son, having no partner? They are certainly liars, who maintain that he has offspring. He provides for all things, and is Lord over all; he speaks and it is done."²⁹ The Koran therefore, classes Christians among Polytheists as they associate two other Gods with Allah.³⁰ The second person of the alleged Tritheism of the Christians, is *Mary*, who was both mother and goddess. She is, as we have already seen, highly exalted by the Koran and considered the most distinguished among her sex, beloved of God, honoured by angels and praised as a miracle.³¹ God breathed into her of His Spirit and she was favoured to be the mother of Christ. Yet she was no more than a human being, which is proved by the fact that both she and her son ate food!³² Jesus being asked at the day of Judgment, whether he told men

²⁷ Sur. XIX. 34. 91. VI. 101. LXXII. 3.
²⁸ Sur. XXIII. 93. XIX. 87.
²⁹ Sur. XXI 26. XVII. 110. X. 67 XXV. 2. XIX. 34.
³⁰ The standing name for Pagans and Christians is المشركين, associantes. Sur. VI. 14. IX. 34.
³¹ Mariam, مريم, מִרְיָם, Μαριάμ. Sur. XXI. 91. III. 42. 47. XXII. 52. XIX. 20.
³² كانا ياكلان الطعام they both ate food. Sur. V. 84. "His mother was a woman of a truth;" وامه صديقة, or a real woman. V. 125.

to receive him and his mother as Gods besides Allah, is made to answer: "Praise be unto thee, it is not for me to say that which I ought not, if I had said so, thou wouldest surely have known, thou knowest what is in me, but I know not what is in thee for thou art the knower of secrets. I have not spoken to them any other, than what thou didst command me, viz. worship God, my Lord and your Lord."[33]

The question arises, whence has Mohammed derived the blasphemous notion, that Christians worshipped the Virgin Mary as a goddess, and considered her a member of that Tritheism which the Koran asserts to be an article of their creed? We have already noticed that Epiphanius speaks of a sect, called the Collyridians which arose in Thracia towards the end of the fourth century and afterwards spread in Arabia and other parts of the East.[34] But there is no need to fix upon any particular heresy as the source, whence Mohammed obtained the idea that the worship of the Virgin was the practice of Christians *in general;* for on referring to the History of the Church in those corrupt ages, we cannot fail to notice the persecutions which fell upon those of her members,

---

[33] "Hoc enim commemorat, Christum cum in coelum pervenisset, a Deo interrogatum fuisse: an Dei filium se esse dixisset, eumque facit hoc modo respondentem: in me Domine sis placato animo. Scis, hanc meam orationem non fuisse, meque tuam non fastidire servitutem; homines sunt isti, qui contra leges hoc me dixisse arguerunt, falsoque me circumvenerunt crimine, et vehementer errarunt. Tum Deum haec ei vult respondisse: Scio, hanc tuam non fuisse orationem." Joan. Damascenus de haeres. pag. 466.

[34] Epiphan. Tom. I. Haeres. LXXVIII. lib. III. cap. 1. Haeres. LXXIX. cap. 23. Opp. edit. Petav. Colon. pag. 1054—1057. Anakephalaeos Tom. II. pag. 128—130. 150. Also this work p. 52. 53.

who resisted the appellation of "Mother of God" as applied to the Virgin. It was therefore at that period by no means a difficult step, to *transfer the divinity* of the person of the Holy Ghost to the much honoured and highly favoured Mother of Jesus. Hence we find attempts among Christian writers to represent the Holy Ghost as of the *feminine gender;* and this being done, it required no very great stride of erroneous teaching to transfer the honour direct to the Virgin Mary.[35] The Gnostic sects looked upon the words spoken on the occasion of our Lord's baptism, "This is my beloved son," as spoken by the Holy Ghost, who descended upon Christ.[36] Simon Magus is declared to have considered his wife Helena the third person of the Trinity.[37] Epiphanius speaks of a Jewish sect of the Ossenes, who held the Holy Ghost to be of the feminine gender.[38]

In other apocryphal writings of which fragments are preserved, the Holy Ghost is invoked as the mother

---

[35] Long before M. we discover traces of the Holy Ghost as δεύτερος θεός being of feminine gender; רוּחַ being sometimes considered so, but חָכְמָה always. Σοφία appears personified already in the canonical books of the Old Test. Prov. VIII. 22—32. but is frequently synonymous with πνεῦμα ἅγιον in the Apocryphas. Wisd. Sol. IX. 9. Sirach I. 1. 4. 9. XXIV. 14. Wisd. Sol. I. 4. 5. VII. 7. 22.

[36] "Descendit fons omnis spiritus sancti et requievit super eum (Jesum) et dixit illi: Fili me etc."; quoted by St. Jerome from the Gospel to the Hebrews. The same with Epiphanius: "Me fili in omnibus prophetis exspectavi te, ut venires."

[37] Gerock's Christologie des Korans, pag. 77.

[38] The chief passage is however: Origen. in Joan. Vol. IV. pag. 63. already quoted note 47. pag. 53.

of the believers.[39] The author of the apostolical constitutions compares the Bishop with God the Father, the Deacon with the Son, and the *Deaconess* with the Holy Ghost; which shows at least a tendency in the same direction. The Arabic Gospel of Christ's infancy, — which if not existing in the days of Mohammed has at least drawn from the same fountains as he did, — invariably speaks of the mother of Jesus as "*the exalted divine Mary.*" She is always there set forth, as the object of the highest veneration, nay of formal adoration, in consequence of the miracles which she wrought upon her own authority. Under the circumstances now stated, what was more natural, than that the Virgin Mary should assume the position of the Holy Ghost in the alleged Tritheism, just as the angel Gabriel is invariably styled, Spirit or Holy Spirit in the Koran.[40]

8. The third member of the Christian Tritheism, according to the Koran, is *Jesus Christ the son of Mary*.[41] "The Christians say, *Christ* is the son of God.... may God suppress them. How are they infatuated! They take their priests and monks for their Lords besides God, and Christ the son of Mary, although they are commanded to worship one God only, there is no God but he. The curse be on those

---

[39] Valentinus styles him μήτηρ τῶν ζώντων. The πνεῦμα, σοφία was also sometimes looked upon by heretics as the sister or spouse of Χριστός.

[40] Sur. LXX. 5. LXXVIII. 37. XCVII. 4. XV. 29. XLII. 52. روح or روح القدس. XVI. 102. XXVI. 192.

[41] المسيح عيسى بن مريم, Mesich Isa ben Mariam.

whom they associate with him in his worship."[42] Christ's omnipotence and omniscience is denied as a matter of course; and to worship him is idolatry. Christ himself is made to declare that he is not more than any other man or prophet;[43] he is only a servant and need not be ashamed of it.[44] Jesus and Mary had bodies which, requiring to be sustained by food, were thus proved mortal, consequently they are not Gods; nor could any one prevent God from destroying Christ, his mother and all the inhabitants of the earth. Again to suppose that Allah should beget children is highly irreverent nor does his all-sufficiency admit of any increase to his happiness; for his are all things in heaven and earth.[45] Nor has he need of an assistant in his government of the world; and to associate any one with Allah is an unpardonable crime.[46]

Whilst however Mohammed insisted upon the mere human personality of our blessed Redeemer, he suffered him to be endowed with all the power and authority of a divinely accredited messenger.[47] It was however not without imminent danger to his

[42] Sur. IX. 31. 32, to believe Christ to be God, is the mark of an infidel. V. 19.
[43] Sur. V. 125. 85. XLIII. 80. III. 78. V. 81. 125. 126.
[44] Sur. XLIII. 58. IV. 170. XVI. 43. XXI. 7.
[45] Sur. XXI 8. V. 19. 84. X. 67. XIX. 91. II. 117. LXXII. 3. XXV. 2. XXXIX. 5. IV. 169.
[46] Sur. IV. 169. V. 85. XVII. 110. XXV. 1—3. IV. 46. 169. V. 81.
[47] He was a Nabi نبى, נְבִיא, and رسول, who commenced his office in the cradle. Sur. XIX. 29. IV. 169.

system, that Mohammed admitted certain names and titles to Christ, which he borrowed from the New Testament. He is called the Messiah,[48] but the Jews and Christians associated very different ideas with the name from what the Koran could possibly admit. Again, Jesus is called "the word of truth;"[49] the word of God; "the word, who is called the Messiah."[50] This is evidently an allusion to St. John's Gospel; and we might expect that it would bear the same meaning in the Koran which it does in the New Testament, whence it was borrowed. As this appellation of Christ points distinctly to an extraordinary and Divine nature, we need not be surprised to find that its application has caused no small perplexity to Moslem divines. Again the Koran speaks of our Lord as *the Spirit of God;* and of His having been *strengthened* with the Spirit of holiness.[51] All these terms, if they have any meaning at all, imply that there was something in the person of Christ, which no other prophet could claim; we must however remember that the false prophet adopted titles from

---

[48] عيسى, יֵשׁוּעַ, Jesus, *Saviour*: المسيح, מָשִׁיחַ, from מָשַׁח, مسح, to annoint, is "the *Annointed One*," ὁ Χριστός; and both the Old and New Test. plainly assert His Divine character.

[49] "This is Jesus, the son of Mary," the word of truth, قول الحق, concerning which they doubt." Sur. XIX. 33.

[50] "And his word, وكلمته, which he planted into Mary. Sur. IV. 169. Again: يبشرك بكلمة منه اسمه المسيح Sur. III. 45.

[51] منه روح, the Spirit from Him, viz., الله. Sur. IV. 169. ايدناه بروح القدس Sur. II. 87. 254. V. 119.

the Christians and their Scriptures without retaining the original sense. The Koran admits one of the mysteries of Christianity, in stating, that God sent His word into the Virgin Mary, and yet paradoxically denies that the word was made flesh; whilst therefore the son of Mary is said to be conspicuous in this world and in the world to come, and to be one of those, who *approach* God to intercede, there is not one passage in the Koran, which alludes to the sinlessness of His nature without which He could not effectually perform the office of intercessor. It will therefore be seen that the clear and unequivocal abnegations of the Divinity and assertions of the mere humanity of the son of Mary, prevent our ascribing to the above titles of distinction, any other than a common and general meaning, very different from that which they bear in the New Testament. Mohammed's own dignity being then by no means affected by these admissions of the Koran concerning Christ, he could well admit Jesus to be the greatest prophet before him, and to be endowed with extraordinary power, without prejudice to himself; nay he might even flatter himself with the idea of crowning and of perfecting the work which Jesus had commenced.[52] Mohammed, in spite of his usual inconsistency, was cautious to give no honour to Christ which might endanger his own position, though perilous indeed was the admission that Christ was "*the word of God;*" hence the anxiety of the Moslem di-

---

[52] Compare the blasphemous assumption of M. that Christ prophesied him as the Comforter.

vines to confer the like honour on their prophet[53] and on his Koran.[54] The supernatural events, attending the birth of Christ, which distinguished Him from the rest of mankind, are carefully supplied by a host of miracles which are said to have accompanied the birth of the Arab prophet.

9. Christ is throughout represented as the Author of the *Gospel,* including the entire body of the books of the New Testament, which God revealed to Him from heaven.[55] This Gospel or Ingeel was a confirmation of the Torah. "We also caused Jesus the son of Mary to follow the footsteps of the prophets, confirming the law which was sent down before him, and we gave him the Gospel, containing direction and light; confirming also the law which was given before it, and a direction and admonition unto those who fear God: that they who have received the Gos-

---

[53] God decreed 50,000 years before hand that M. was to be the greatest prophet. Adam had the surname of اب المكند, father of Mohammed; the latter was in existence before Adam and his name was read by him in the empyreum before the throne of God; surrounded by prophetic light. M. d'Ohsson pag. 64. In the Pend-Namêh a poem in praise of M. we have this passage: "le prince du monde présent et du monde futur; les prophétes, et les Saints ont eu recours á son intercession; la création de ce prophête a été le salut de l'univers, l'extrémité de son doigt a séparé en deux parties l'astre de la nuit; que chaque instant de notre vie soit consacré á honorer et á benir mille fois sa mémoire et celle de ses enfans et de sa race." Fundgrub. des Orients II. pag. 15.

[54] Que le Courann est la parole de Dieu incréée; qu'il est écrit dans nos libres, gravé dans nos coeurs, articulé par nos langues et entendu par nos oreilles, dans lesquelles est reçu le son de la parole, et non la parole elle-même qui est éternelle et existante par soi." M. d'Ohsson pag. 29.

[55] Sur. V. 119. III. 48. XIX. 29. الانجيل being a corruption from Evangelium, ἐυαγγέλιον.

pel might judge according to what God hath revealed therein; and whoso judgeth not according to what God hath revealed, they are transgressors. We have also sent down to thee the book of the Koran with truth, confirming that scripture which was revealed before it, and preserving the same safe from corruption."[56]

There are but few allusions in the Koran to the *doctrinal* parts of the New Testament, these being unsuited to Mohammed's purpose in the compilation of his spurious creed.[57] In the passage, "How many beasts are there, which provide not their food? It is God who provideth for them and for you, and he both heareth and knoweth," we recognise a mere imitation of the sentiments expressed. Matt. VI. 26. Lu. XII. 24. Again, "Say not of a thing, I will do it to morrow, except thou addest, if God will," reproduces the admonition of St. James in his general Epistle.[58] An allusion to St. Paul's words as to a man reaping what he sowed, is found in the following passage, "Whoso chooseth the tillage of the life to come, unto him will we give increase in his tillage, and whoso chooseth the tillage of this world, we will give him the fruit thereof, but he shall have no part in the life to come."[59]

---

[56] Sur. V. 54—56. III. 3.

[57] Sur. II. 104. "Pray without ceasing," seems to refer to 1 Thess. V. 17. ἀδιαλείπτως προσεύχεσθε. Also Sur. III. 58. which contains a comparison of Adam and Christ, might allude to 1 Cor. XV. 45. 57.

[58] ولا تقولن لشىءٍ انى فاعل ذلك غدًا الا ان يشاء الله
Sur. XVIII. 25. and James IV. 13. 15.

[59] Gal. VI. 6—8. with Sur. XLII. 41.

It is doubtful, as we have seen in the previous chapter whether the words, "Neither shall they enter Paradise until a camel pass through the eye of a needle," are borrowed from the Rabbinical writings or from the New Testament; the latter however is more probable, partly on account of the more striking resemblance,— the Gospels having also the image of the *camel*,— partly because it is more frequent, occurring three times in the New Testament and but once in the Talmudical writings where it is considerably altered.[60] When Mohammed enjoins his followers not to give alms "to appear unto men" we at once detect a borrowing of our Lord's words on the same subject.[61] Again among the descriptions of hell, we find the following passage, "and the inhabitants of hell-fire shall call unto the inhabitants of Paradise, saying, pour upon us some water," which strongly reminds us of the rich man's request, when in torment.[62]

10. According to the Koran, Christ was exclusively sent to the children of Israel: "I come," the

---

[60] Sur. VII. 41. with Matt. XIX. 24. Mark. X. 25. Lu. XVIII. 24. جَمَل, جَمْل, גָּמָל, camelus, κάμηλος; if the reading were κάμιλος, جُمَّل, funis rudens, חֶבֶל, cable, the sense is altered, but the fact of M. borrowing from the Gospel still remains.

[61] Sur. II. 272. with Matt. VI. 3. 4. ὅπως ᾖ σου ἡ ἐλευμοσύνη ἐν τῷ κρυπτῷ.

[62] Sur. VII. 272. with Lu. XVI. 24. Compare also Sur. LVII. 13: "On that day the hypocritical men and women shall say unto those who believe, stay for us that we may borrow some of your light. It shall be answered, Return back into the world and seek light;"— an evident allusion to Matt. XXV. 8. 9.

Messiah is made to say,—after He was declared 'the apostle to the children of Israel,' to confirm the law which was revealed before me and to allow you as lawful, part of that which hath been forbidden you, and I come unto you with a sign from your Lord, therefore fear God and obey me." This then clearly shows the object of Christ's Mission to the Jews, who are said to have broken the covenant and put the Scriptures away from them.[63] The Jews throughout the Koran are represented as frivolous transgressors of the law of their fathers, who had killed their prophets, and were cursed by David and Jesus the son of Mary;[64] as might be expected, it declares, that Christ taught all the leading dogmas of Islamism, specially the Unity of the Godhead; also that the children of Israel were to serve his God and their God, and those who associate any other with him are excluded from Paradise and threatened with hellfire.[65] Mohammed speaks of Christ as a favoured servant and prophet of God;[66] yea he cedes to the son of Mary the honour of being the chief of all the prophets who appeared prior to Mohammed, but to the latter *alone* belongs the prerogative of being the greatest of all divine messengers, since Abraham is said to have prayed for him, and he was prophesied in the Torah and the Gospel.[67]

---

[63] Sur. III. 48. 49. Also V. 54. LXI. 6. XLIII. 61. V. 14. 17.
[64] Sur. VI. 92. II. 91. IV. 154. 155. V. 97. 87. cfr. 1 Thess. II. 15.
[65] Sur. XLIII. 62. III. 50. V. 121. 126. V. 81.
[66] Sur. XLIII. 30. XIX. 4. 30. III. 46. XVII. 55. II. 254.
[67] Sur. II. 129. 130. LXI. 6.

Convenient it is for the Moslem doctors to find a distinct prophecy of Mohammed in the Arabic Gospel of St. Barnabas, where Jesus predicts the coming of the Arab prophet, who would free the world from all error.[68] The interpolation of this spurious Gospel by a Moslem hand, is too palpable to deserve a word of comment or argument. Still more so, is it to conjecture how the false prophet came to claim the honour of being predicted in the Gospel of St. John as the Comforter;[69] it is not improbable that he derived it from his early proselytes, who, knowing of the promise of the Holy Ghost may possibly have flattered their newly-acquired prophet by declaring it to be fulfilled in his person; hence the idea that Mohammed was taught by the Holy Ghost, sent down upon him. As however this prophecy does not stand in the New Testament as Mohammed has quoted and applied it, commentators on the Koran maintain, that the Christians had maliciously expunged it from their Gospel; the same charge is boldly made against the Christians respec-

---

[68] "Ego vero, quantumque innocentem vitam in mundo transegi, tamen, cum homines me Deum et filium Dei vocaverint, Deus, ne in die judicii olim daemonum essem ludibrium, voluit in mundo ignominia me affici ab hominibus per mortem Judae, persuasis omnibus, me in cruce mortem obiisse. Unde ista ignominia durabit usque ad adventum Mohamedis, qui, cum in mundum venerit, omnes legi Dei credentes ab hoc errore liberavit." Fabricii Codex apocryph. N. Test. tom. II. pag. 378. 384.

[69] Sur. LXI. 6. it is stated that Jesus prophesied of Achmed, أحمد, Mohammed, محمّد, laudabilis, multa dignus; παρίκλητος John XIV. 16. XV. 26. being turned into περικλυτός, inclytus, the object was gained.

ting other prophecies, said to have been extant in their sacred Scriptures. The parable of the labourers, it seems, has been overlooked by Christians, though considered particularly applicable to Mohammed's followers![70] Again the true worshippers, who neither worship in Jerusalem nor on Samaria's mountain are none others than the Mohammedans! The boldest and shrewdest of all the mis-applications of Scripture by Moslem divines, is that of their finding a most flattering allusion to Mohammed in a passage which more than any other marks him as one of the truest types of Antichrist: — Mohammed is said to be the Spirit from God who confesseth that Jesus Christ appeared in the flesh, that is, as a *mere man*, and not as God![71]

11. Having seen what Mohammed taught concerning Christ and what he borrowed from the canonical and apocryphal writings of the New Testament, it remains yet to show, what sentiments he entertained towards Christians. It has been satisfactorily proved,[72] that there are two distinct systems of teaching in the Koran; the one assuming a thoroughly peaceful, the other a perfectly inimical relation to Judaism and Christianity, as well as to all pre-existing creeds; the former being an act of compromise on the part of Mohammed, the latter, a violation of the pacific principle

---

[70] Mishcat-ul-Masabih, or a collection of the most authentic traditions regarding Mohammed; from the Arabic by Capt. A. N. Matthews, Calcutta 1809. Vol. II. pag. 814.

[71] 1 John IV. 1—3.

[72] In the article by Dr. J. A. Möhler: "Ueber das Verhältniss des Islam's zum Evangelium." 1839.

just laid down, inculcating instead, the rankest bigotry and exclusiveness, and enforcing a sanguinary system of propagandism. Mohammed, on several occasions put forth the following statements: that it evidences a spirit of pride to assume that only one religion is of a saving character to the exclusion of all others, such an assertion implying that all nations were not equally the object of Divine favour; that the cause of the existence of various beliefs must be sought for in the decrees of Allah, and that it will only be discovered in the world to come, where truth alone is to be found; and he adds, that it was sufficient for Jews, Christians and Moslemin to live in accordance with the laws of God, respectively revealed to them, and to be prepared to give an account on the day of Judgment.

Mohammed accuses the Christians and Jews [73] of considering themselves exclusively the people of God, whilst they might easily gather from the judgments which had fallen upon them, that they were no better than other people. It would have been easy for God to unite all men in one religion, but as he did otherwise, it naturally followed that each nation would be judged according to its particular religious law; and that it would be better for all nations to strive to excel each other in doing good than for unconditional superiority. All would return to God, who would explain the real cause of their differences.[74] From

[73] "The Jews and Christians say, we are the children of God and his beloved. Answer, why therefore doth he punish you for your sins." Sur. V. 21.

[74] "Unto every one of you have we given a law and an open

these premises it naturally follows, that Jews and Christians will be judged according to the law, they severally possess; the Sabians also are included in the same class of religionists, who need fear no evil, provided only they believe in God, the last day, and act justly.[75] According to the Koran then, the plurality of creeds has its origin in a divine decree, and each party has a right to prefer his own: a certain delusion on the subject being now suffered to prevail, which will be removed in the world to come.

These views however being not only modified, but actually abrogated by other passages, we cannot possibly determine the relation between Christianity and Islamism through any conclusions which might be drawn from them. There are numerous passages in which Christianity is totally set aside, and which assert that all unbelievers of whatever persuasion are to be destroyed:[76] no league is to be made with the

---

path; and if God had pleased, he had surely made you one people, but he hath given you different laws, that he might try you in that which he hath severally given you. Therefore strive to excel each other in good works. Unto God ye shall return and then will he declare unto you concerning which ye have disagreed." Sur. V. 56.

[75] "Verily they who believe, and the Jews, Sabians and Christians, whosoever of them believeth in God and the last day, and doth that which is right, there shall come no fear on them, neither shall they be grieved." Sur. V. 73. And Sur. XXIX. 46: "Dispute not with those who have received the Scriptures (اهل الكتاب) unless in the mildest manner, except against such as behave injuriously, say: we believe in the revelation, sent down unto us and unto you; our God and your God is one, and unto him we are resigned."

[76] "Kill the associating ones (Pagans and Christians) wherever you find them." Sur. IX. 5.

Scripturalists and unbelievers. The question therefore is, which of these two antagonistic views expresses Mohammed's real meaning; incompatible as they are, they yet claim some attention from us, for even in contradictions an internal connection may often be discovered, by which they may be rendered intelligible. Certain Arabian Theologians maintain, that the *majority* of passages is to determine the real views of Mohammed; and as those occur more frequently, which equalize all religions, they declare that Judaism, Christianity and Islamism differ only in external laws and ceremonies! As this opinion however assumes that Mohammed's real views may be obtained by a mere casting up of numbers, others prefer to ascertain which were the prophet's views in the latter part of his life, judging those to be the most orthodox; and this is certainly the more rational method of solving the difficulty.[77] As the dates of the respective Suras cannot be *positively* determined, some of the Christian apologists aver, that so long as Mohammed was in straitened circumstances, he feigned the greatest reverence for the Jewish and Christian religion, but as soon as his power became established, and his cause free from danger, he enunciated those mandates which condemn all other creeds and supplant his own.

Had Mohammed *from the beginning* been a consummate and ambitious impostor, this reasoning would

---

[77] "Abul Kasam Habat Alla bemerkt in biesem Sinne ganz kurz, durch Sura IX. 5. seien 124 andere Verse des Coran entkräftet worden." Möhler's Gesammelte Schriften pag. 365.

be completely convincing, but as we have shown that he set out with honest intentions, we must attribute the contradictions in the Koran to his vacillating state of mind at different periods of his life. The Arab prophet, at first, directed his attention solely to national objects, seeking to establish for his countrymen a *national* Deism; he therefore only tolerated Christianity, as a religion not unsuitable to other nations; but, carried away by enthusiasm on meeting with unexpected success, his views enlarged beyond his own city, tribe and nation, and he began at length to entertain the idea that Monotheism must of necessity, be the religion of the whole world.[78] Embracing the doctrine of the divine Unity as distinctly as Mohammed ultimately did, he was led to change his position from a national, to that of a universal prophet, and having comprehended this new and enlarged scheme, he felt that Christianity could no longer be co-ordinate with his own creed, but must necessarily take a *subordinate* relation to Islamism.[79]

In accordance with all *national* creeds, Mohammed mixed *political* elements to such an extent with his system of belief, that national and religious institutions became scarcely distinguishable; and as in most national creeds there is but one head for both

---

[78] In describing the process by which Mohammed's future system was developed, we merely illustrate a well known psychological law, that the speculations regarding a future project begin with broad generalities and gradually take a more concise view.

[79] M. was an idolater up to the 40th year of his age. The religion of his nation was a mixture of Monotheism and idolatry and it was not without many a hard struggle, that he confessed the unity of the Godhead as clearly as he does in the Koran.

religion and state, so he made himself at once, the executive of *spiritual* and *civil* power.[80] Again, the fact that Islamism was spread by the *sword*, can only be explained by its being of a national character, mixing religion with politics; as these were not kept distinct, internal conviction by argument was superseded by external force. Hence to submit to Mohammed's political power, was equivalent to acknowledging him as a prophet; and when his religion became universal, his monarchy assumed the like pretensions, war being proclaimed against all states as well as against every other system of belief. Thus the Mohammedans in passing over the frontier of the Peninsula to propagate their religion, with it, invariably imposed their national manners and customs upon the conquered and converted nations, destroying their national peculiarities.[81] Christianity on the contrary, when it passed the boundaries of Palestine, appeared at once as a universal religion, throwing off its national character and leaving its Jewish rites behind.[82]

---

[80] In this double capacity he appealed for a precedent to Moses.

[81] The rite of circumcision, fasting in the manner required, being in many places, e. g. the polar regions, impracticable, and the Hadj to Mecca are all proofs that Islamism was calculated to be only a *national* religion.

[82] It started as the religion of *Spirit and truth*, and claimed to be universal. Depending on its own spiritual power, it permitted the kingdoms of the earth to stand, leaving the national peculiar characteristics undestroyed, only refining and purifying them. Christ being Himself the Truth, had not to work out His way by experiments like fallible men, but saw the whole scope and object of His divine mission from the beginning; M. on the contrary, began not knowing where he was to end; Möhler pag. 375. he fell into mis-

Another proof of the exclusively national character of Islamism, is founded in its peculiar *system of ethics* and morality; universal philanthropy is not inculcated in the Koran; love or charity in its widest sense, is among Moslemin, strictly circumscribed to their own community, their prophet having utterly ignored the law of universal kindness.[83] Again, the national custom of the "lex talionis," and the institution of polygamy with power to divorce at pleasure, involve principles, totally adverse to the spirit of a universal religion. In Mohammed's personal life, those moral requisitions only were fulfilled, which would answer to a prophet of Arabia; for although he must be condemned as a false prophet, if brought before the tribunal of pure ethics, yet according to the ethics of Arabia, his very faults would be deemed virtues,[84] thus it becomes intelligible why his claims to the dignity of a prophet were not rejected, notwithstanding those flagrant immoralities, which the Koran records to his shame.

Lastly, it does not appear from Mohammed's personal history, that he originally desired to establish a catholic religion; for it will be remembered that

takes and was driven from one extreme to the other, without after all finding the truth.

[83] The fact that Moslemin are the chief promoters of slavery and that from among them, no voice was ever raised against it, proves that they do not recognise the common brotherhood of the human race.

[84] Mankind first became acquainted with pure ethics through the only perfect character of Christ, in whom, the ideal of a spotless morality is represented to the world at large; since as the Son of man He belonged to the whole of mankind, and not to any one nation in particular.

a few years after he had asserted his pretensions as a prophet, a number of his followers were obliged to flee to Abyssinia, when it would naturally be expected that,—like the primitive Christians, who under similar circumstances were driven from Jerusalem—the persecuted Moslemin would be zealous in propagating their faith; but as no effort of the kind was then made, we may infer that Mohammed had *not yet* given injunctions to his followers to proselytize among foreigners.[85] It was not till the twentieth year of his Mission that we discover any trace of Mohammed's enlarged plans, when he sent those embassies to foreign potentates, to which we have previously adverted.

Thus we see that Mohammed did not originally intend framing a religion for all nations, and therefore looked so favourably upon Christianity that he even received his *first converts* by the rite *baptism*, which mode of admission, he subsequently discontinued. Most of the distinctive features of the Moslem ceremonial, date as we have seen, from the latter years of the Arab prophet; the same may be said of the most prominent doctrines of his new creed.[86]

[85] Very different was the conduct of Katris, an officer of rank, when obliged to leave Arabia after the death of M. Scarcely had the ruler of Mazenderam assured the refugee of his protection, than the latter boldly desired his protector, either to confess Islamism, or to pay tribute. Möhler pag. 380.

[86] When Assad of Yathrab asked M. before his flight, in what his religion consisted, M. replied, that he taught men to worship one God, to requite kindness to parents, not to kill children nor any other person, to shun every crime, not to touch the goods of orphans and to keep promises. M. added no more and Assad at once acknowledged him as a prophet. Möhler pag. 382.

During the early stages, Mohammed saw no reason to exalt Islam above Christianity, but when he ultimately adopted the Christian doctrine of the atonement and asserted, that only those, for whom he should intercede with God, could obtain remission of sins, and that none who believed in Mohammed could absolutely be condemned, then it became necessary to subordinate Christianity to Islam.[87] As soon as he claimed to be the only mediator between God and man, he was compelled to make his creed universal and to deny all further authority to Christianity: those passages therefore which declare it to be of equal authority with Islam, refer to that period of Mohammed's life, when he was as yet undecided as to his own influence or the full extent of his alleged Mission; those which annul Christianity and every other creed, belong to the more matured form of his system.[88]

12. Christians in their efforts to win the Mohammedans will do well to insist upon the more original and more favourable views expressed in the Koran of their religion and their persons. One of the first objects in dealing with Moslems ought ever be to sever the traditional elements which Mohammed derived from the early Christians from what he em-

---

[87] It became then a principle: "La foi et l'Islamism sont une seule et même chose." M. d'Ohsson I. 54.

[88] When M. felt persuaded that his external position was more exalted than that of the Founder of the Church of God, he foolishly, though quite logically asserted, that the internal worth of his tidings was likewise of far greater value, and therefore that Christianity ought to make way for Islam.

bodied from the historical Scriptures of the New Testament.

There can scarcely be any doubt that Mohammed would never have felt the strong inward call to avow himself to be a prophet to his people, had it not been for the very gross corruptions of the Christians around him both in doctrine and practice. The undisguised deification of the virgin Mary was in itself enough to fire the fierce indignation of the Arabian reformer. The virulence against the divine Sonship of Christ was equally intelligible from the most gross and revolting notions which prevailed in Arabia on the subject.

Yet we must hold Mohammed responsible for following the early heresies and apocryphal Gospels, rather than the New Testament Scriptures, which were accessible to him, and a copy of which we know was on Mount Sinai.

Equally vain is the effort to explain away the fierce injunctions in Sura viii. 3, 1, 47, ii. 216, iii. 82, xlviii. 29, by which Moslems are commanded to fight against unbelievers, "until there be no more opposition and the religion be wholly God's." In Sura xlvii. 4, we read: "When ye encounter the unbelievers, strike off their heads until ye have made a great slaughter amongst them and bind them in bonds." See also ix. 4, 6.

When philo-mohammedan writers endeavour to modify these fierce denunciations of the Koran, alleging that they were intended to be humane and temporary, we can only reply that such an explanation is opposed to the entire spirit of Islam, and has at least never yet been carried out.⁹⁰ The same spirit of hatred to Christians and their religion, which inspired the author of Islam and those propagators who immediately succeeded him, has been transmitted with all its pristine zeal and fanaticism to the present generation.

Scarcely a month passes in which some outrages, against the followers of Christ, are not recorded in the public journals of Christian Europe; and the greater part of the cruelties and barbarities which are committed against our brethren, never reach the ear of their fellow-christians who live under European protection. Those concessions and mitigations which Christians of the Turkish Empire have in later times acquired, have only been wrung from the Porte by the influence of Christian power.

If any doubt had remained as to the sentiments of Mohammedans towards Christians, the recent occurrences in India, Arabia, Syria and Morocco must have removed it for ever. Yet we should greatly mistake, were we to regard these occasional outbursts as symptoms of a hopeless antagonism to Christianity.

The furious outbreaks and rancorous animosities against Christians, which now and then vent themselves, to our dismay, are prompted more by an utter misconception of our dogmas, than by an honest disavowal on our part of the claims of Mo-

---

⁹⁰ Tychsen: Com. soc. reg. Gott. tom. XV. pag. 156. may here be consulted.

hammed. There is something noble in an honest opposition, however mistaken in itself. Saul of Tarsus, even when most virulent against Christ, engages our sympathy. The Mohammedans, like him, do it "ignorantly," being "zealous towards God," and "thinking of doing Him service." When most violent in "breathing out threatenings and slaughter against the disciples of the Lord," Saul was nearest his marvellous conversion.

CHAPTER VII.

SPREAD AND SUCCESS OF ISLAM.

"Loose the four angels which are bound in the great river Euphrates; and the four angels were loosed, which were prepared for an hour, and a day, and a month and a year for to slay the third part of men. And the number of the army of the horsemen were *two myriads of myriads:* and I heard the number of them."
Rev. IX. 14—21.

The rapidity of the spread of Mohammed's creed is without parallel in the annals of propagandism. In the twenty-first year of the Hegira, the crescent floated over an extent of territory as wide as that of the Roman eagle; and the Saracen empire may be said to have extended its dominion over more kingdoms and countries in eighty years than the Roman, in 800.⁹⁶ In Syria, Palestine, Egypt, Asia Minor, North-Africa and other countries, the Koran was introduced at the point of the sword. Thence its contents were promulgated eastward to the frontiers of India and China; westward to the shores of the Atlantic ocean; and northward to the banks of the Oxus and Jaxartes, reaching to the frozen borders of the Caspian Sea, in an incredibly short space of time.

1. In twelve years the whole of Arabia had embraced Islamism; there was indeed some opposition yet to overcome, but the chief work was accomplished. The Koreishites, who at one time contemplated returning to the religion of their ancestors, were dissuaded by *Sohael;* ⁹⁷ and the rest of the discontented Arabs, who had been tempted to rebellion by the rival prophet Moseilama, and roused by the recollection of that much-loved independance which now seemed lost for ever, were speedily subjected by the sword of the ferocious Khaled. With a view to divert the minds of the people, Abubeker, the first Kaliph, declared war against all nations, especially against the Emperor of Constantinople and the "great

---

[96] "Wie eine verzehrende Flamme brach plötzlich die neue Glaubensform mit unwiderstehlicher, Alles vernichtender Gewalt hervor aus den Wüsten Arabiens, und in zehenfach geringerer Zeit, als die Römer vordem zur Aufrichtung ihres Weltreiches bedurft hatten, waren die Völker von der chinesischen Mauer bis zu den Säulen des Herkules, vom Caspischen Meere bis zum Niger der Herrschaft des Islam oder doch der Gewalt seiner Bekenner unterworfen," Prof. Döllinger's "Muhammed's Religion", pag. 5. Ockley, Hist. of the Sarac. Vol. I. pag. 315.

[97] Sohael addressed them in these words: "Ye men of Mecca, will ye be the last to embrace Islamism, and the first to abandon it?"

king of Persia," at that time the two most powerful monarchs of the East.

Abubeker published a proclamation to the Arab tribes, encouraging them to join the army which he proposed sending to Syria, to free that country from infidel dominion.[98] Accompanying the assembled host on foot for a considerable distance from Medina, the Kaliph gave them a few parting injunctions[99] and dismissed them with his blessing. The assault was impetuous, but Sergius the Byzantine commander resolutely maintained his ground in Syria, till the country was opened to the Arabs by the conquest of Bostra. Another division of Greek troops was conquered near Gaza, and amidst the treachery and inability of the Greek generals, the cowardice of the soldiers and the discontent of the inhabitants, the Moslem army made rapid progress in the conquest of the country. During this expedition Abubeker died, and Omar who was with the army, was nominated his successor. One of his first acts was the conquest of Damascus, in after ages, one of the three

[98] "In the name of the most merciful God, to the rest of the true believers: peace and happiness, grace and blessing from God upon you. I laud the Most High God, and pray for his prophet Mohammed. It is known to you that I intend sending the true believers to Syria to take that land from the hands of the unbelievers, and I make known to you that it is an act of obedience to God to fight for religion."

[99] "Keep yourselves from injustice and oppression, said he to his generals, in conducting the battles of the Lord; fight like men without wavering, but defile not the victory by the blood of women and children. Destroy no palm-tree, burn no corn-fields; what ye have promised keep faithfully; spare all except the shorn crowns, (the monks) for they belong to the kingdom of Satan."

holy cities of the Mohammedans. But the battle which decided the fate of Syria, was fought near the lake of Genezareth, whilst Khaled shouted to his soldiers, "Paradise is before, and death and hell are behind you!" Three times the Arabs gave way before the enemy, and three times they were driven back into the fight amidst the reproaches and castigations of their wives, who, being armed with bows and arrows, fought in the rear with desperate courage; and the result was the utter defeat of the Byzantine army.[1]

Jerusalem capitulated upon easy terms, yielding her neck to the yoke of Mohammedan tyranny which she has born to the present hour; and *Omar*, whose name has been handed down by a Mosque, called after him, and built upon the very site of the ancient temple of Jehovah, entered the holy city, riding on a camel in mean attire, a wooden drinking-vessel being fastened to his side, a bag of dates before and one of barley behind him: such was the stern simplicity of the first Kaliphs; such also the just retribution upon the sacred city of the Jews, whose corrupt teaching had furnished the false prophet with so large an amount of error in the compilation of the Koran!

2. From Jerusalem, Omar wrote to *Amru*, one of his generals, who was on his way to Egypt, that if still in Syria, he should return at once on the receipt of the letter, but if he had crossed the boundary he

---

[1] The proclamation of the Moslem army was to this effect: "150,000 enemies are killed, 40,000 are made prisoners, and of the faithful 4030 have perished, to whom God had decreed the honour of martyrdom. Allah has made us the lords of their country, their riches and their children."

should proceed depending on the help of Allah and his brethren. Amru received this epistle whilst encamping near Gaza, but in spite of its contents, proceeded towards Egypt until the tents were fairly pitched beyond the boundary of Palestine, when, collecting his officers, he inquired the name of the station and reading his instructions aloud to them, added that he was ready to comply with the commands of Omar. After a siege of thirty days, the army carried *Pelusium*, the key of Egypt. Amru then marched against the ancient *Memphis*, and after a seven months siege, the Moslem army stormed *Babylon* which was situated in the suburbs of Memphis. *Bishop Benjamin* submitted to the invaders with the whole community of the Coptic Church, and paying poll-tax, secured to themselves their property and liberty of conscience. *Alexandria* was most bravely defended during fourteen months by the Melchites, but the noble city surrendered A. D. 640 after 23,000 Arabs had fallen before her walls. Amru was made prisoner, but owing to an artifice of his slave was not recognised and so escaped.

Upon the fall of Alexandria, Amru wrote to Omar his master: "I have conquered the great city of the West; it is impossible to specify its manifold riches, and I must be satisfied to mention, that it contains 4000 palaces, 4000 baths, 400 places of pleasure and amusement 12,000 shops, selling victuals, and 40,000 Jews paying tribute." When the general asked Omar, at the request of the philosopher, John Philoponus, whether he would consent to his sparing the Library, the Kaliph is said to have replied, "If the books of the Greeks agree with the Koran, then they are superfluous and need not be preserved, if not, they are dangerous and must be destroyed."[2] The conquest of *northern Africa* was fairly commenced by Amru. In *Cyrenaica* or *Cyrene*, and indeed on the whole of the southern shores of the Mediterranean sea, the Arabs met with but little resistance, for recognising in the inhabitants, people of the same stock, the introduction of the religion and power of the Saracens, was greatly facilitated. Amru sent an embassy of the natives to Omar who received them kindly and acknowledged them as brethren.

Nor was the scheme of subjugating *Persia* abandoned by the successors of Mohammed; whilst Amru was engaged in the West of Arabia, *Khaled* turned to the East and made fearful progress; Omar however did not live to see the result of the enterprise as regards Persia itself, being assassinated by a Persian in a mosque at Medina, A. D. 644.[3] At this period

---

[2] This cruel loss of some of the best treasures of the world by Moslem fanaticism cannot be sufficiently deplored; especially as regards Manuscripts of the Holy Scriptures and the writings of the early Church. It is not however likely that much was left of the celebrated Library of the Ptolemys. The 400,000 volumes in the Museum in that part of the city, called Bruchion, were burned when Julius Caesar besieged Alexandria, but this loss was partially restored by Antoninus, who presented Cleopatra with a library of parchment. The 300,000 vols in the temple of Serapion, were destroyed in the 4th century under the Emperor Theodosius, when a fanatical mob of Christians stormed the temple.

[3] During his Kaliphate the foundation of the Saracen empire was laid upon a broad basis: 36,000 cities were taken and 4000 churches and temples destroyed!

innumerable Christians apostatised, many from fear, others from ignorance and some embraced Islamism voluntarily;[4] those who remained faithful were exposed to shame and persecution. When Khaled entered Persia he said to his warriors, "If we wished not to fight for the cause of God, and were only bent upon seeking our own interest, we should still be anxious to conquer these provinces, leaving distress and hunger henceforth to others."[5] Irak or *Assyria* was subdued and plundered, Bussora occupied, the *Euphrates* together with the Gulph of Persia fell into the hands of the Arabs; *Ktesiphon* or Madayu with *Faristan*, whither the king of Persia had fled, were placed under Saracen domination.[6]

3. The successor of Omar was the weak and aged *Othoman*, but his career was cut short being assassinated soon after his accession to the Kaliphate. The *Ommayades*, who were the chief promoters of the rebellion and the murder of the Kaliph, being headed by *Moavyia* or *Movia*, now accused *Ali* of the crime. In spite of this accusation Ali was appointed to the Kaliphate,[7] but is said to have accepted it with reluctance, doubtless fearing so powerful a rival

[4] The Christian writer Elmacin states: that there was also a voluntary influx of Pagans, Magians, Jews and Christians.

[5] Taberistanensis Annales regum atque legatorum Dei. (Ed. Kosegarten, Gryphisvald. 1833.) II. p. 25.

[6] In Ktesiphon a booty was raised which has been estimated by Arab historians to have amounted to some 3000 millions of pure metal. This naturally kindled the zeal of Moslem propagandism.

[7] Three times he had been passed over, and even now Ayesha sought to prevent his election.

as Movia. The latter, who happened to have Ayesha's influence on his side, took possession of most of the Persian provinces, but notwithstanding he was completely defeated in a fearful battle with Ali,—in which Ayesha was made prisoner, and magnanimously given up,—Movia gained the ascendency, and was made Kaliph though destitute of all claim to the dignity. Ali was assassinated at Kufa, and his eldest son, Hassan died of poison at Medina, given to him by his own wife at the instigation of Movia;[8] not long after, his brother Hossein also fell before his enemy, being pierced with three and thirty wounds. But neither the fame, nor yet the house of Ali was extinguished by the death of his two sons; for although the Omeyades were victorious for the time and numbered fourteen rulers, many of the faithful were attached to the original line of succession. Amongst those who acknowledge Ali, as the legitimate successor of the prophet, the Persians stand foremost, and we notice it as one of the chief points' of difference between the Shiites and Sonnites.

To avoid needlessly wearying the reader with details of horror and bloodshed, connected with the further propagation of Islamism, we hasten to its introduction into *Europe*. It was during the twenty years reign of Movia, the usurper, that Sicily was completely subdued, and Constantinople endured one of its long and heavy sieges; but the hostile fleet of

---

[8] Hossein his brother swore to revenge his death, but the dying man replied, "O brother, life in this world consists only of transitory nights, let him go till he and I meet before Allah."

P

the Saracens being destroyed by the celebrated Greek fire, the siege was raised for some time. More fortunate was Movia's army in Africa than before the walls of the Byzantine capital; one of his generals [9] marching through the desert of Barke and passing victoriously through the country of the Moors, hoisted the standard of Islamism and there established Moslem supremacy. From the year A. D. 697. under Movia's successors, we may consider North-Africa the home of Islamism;—Christianity, which once flourished in that country, having, alas been completely uprooted.

4. The Saracen empire obtained its greatest extension under the Kaliph *Walid*, who succeeded his father Abdelmalek A.D. 705. In his efforts to propagate the Koran in the West, Walid derived the greatest assistance from *Musa*, the Governor of North-Africa. Tarik, one of Musa's subordinate officers, being invited by count Julian to assist him against Roderich, king of the western Goths, readily complied, and landed on the rock of Gibraltar, or Gebel el Tarik. Roderich met Tarik near Cadiz with a host of about 100,000 strong, but after a battle of a week's duration, this immense army was dispersed and Roderich himself drowned in the Guadalquivir. [10] One province of Spain after another

---

[9] Akbo Ben Nafi beholding the Atlantic Ocean in the harbour of Asfi and elated by a succession of victories, urged his horse into the surging waves, exclaiming, "Great God if my power was not limited by this sea, I should proceed to unknown empires of the West to preach the unity of thy holy name and to exterminate with the sword those rebel nations, that worship other Gods beside thee!"

[10] The Saracen host consisted of 12,000 men. "How should one

now became speedily subdued, and for 800 years the country remained under the dominion of the Saracens. Meanwhile, Musa, who had previously obtained permission from the Kaliph to conquer Andalusia, followed Tarik, and instead of rewarding him for his glorious achievements, actuated by jealousy, called him to account, caused him to be scourged and cast into prison. Musa now conceived the idea of destroying the new kingdoms of the *Franks* and *Longobardians*, of passing through *Germany*, taking *Constantinople* by land and then retiring to Mecca for the rest of his days: but whilst one day mustering his army, a message arrived from Damascus to request his return to Syria. On his arrival, he was publicly scourged like a criminal by command of Kaliph *Soloman*, Walid's newly appointed successor, and sent to Mecca, where he died of a broken heart. Brave Tarik ended his days among the slaves, which crowded the effeminate court of the Kaliphs at Damascus. How different *their* luxury from the austere simplicity of the first Kaliph Omar, whose daily fare was barley bread, a few dates and water, whose royal robe consisted of an old cloak, and who was not seldom discovered by his generals sleeping upon the steps of a Mosque among beggars! Solomon least of all seems to have followed the abstemious habits of Omar; whilst preparing for a fresh attack on Constantinople he died suddenly of a fit of indigestion.[11]

chase a thousand to flight, except their Rock had sold them, and the Lord had shut them up!" Deut. XXXII. 30.

[11] According to Abulfeda he ate two baskets of eggs and figs,

Although deprived of Musa's counsel and energy, the Saracen army did not abandon the plan of subduing the whole of Europe; crossing the *Pyrenees*, it entered *Gaul* under Abderrachman with a force of 400,000 men, spreading consternation throughout the woods of Allemania. Here everything gave way before it; having crossed the Rhone it wasted the country, burned houses and Churches, and carried the women into slavery. In this emergency, *Charles Martel*, son of Pepin, gathered together the scattered forces of the empire, and between Tours and Poitiers the great question was to be decided, whether the *Koran* or the *Bible* was to be the future rule and portion of Europe. After the two armies had faced each other for seven days, one Saturday evening the Saracen host rushed upon the army of Christian warriors, as if sure of victory; but steady like a wall stood the iron-harnessed forces of the Franks. After much fearful bloodshed, which led to no decision, the giant-like Austrasian warriors rushed forward; their large battle-swords doing terrible execution, and Abderrachman himself, falling before them, the fate of the invading army was decided. Some 375,000 Arabs remained slain on the field, and from that time, A. D. 732 the wave of Saracen conquest appeared to be broken and steadily to retire from Europe.

5. Whilst these mighty efforts were being made by the Saracens to establish and maintain their re-

concluding his repast with marrow and sugar. On one of his pilgrimages to Mecca he consumed at one meal, 70 pomegranates, a kid, 6 fowls and a large quantity of grapes from Tayef!

ligion and political supremacy in the West, another army penetrated eastward into Asia, pushing forward as far as *China;* but here their progress was stayed by means of bribes from the Emperor. Returning to India they founded vast empires on the shores of the Indus and Ganges, which for a long period were strongholds of Islamism. As a fresh success, deserves to be mentioned the restoration of the Kaliphate to the house of Ali;[12] and with the accession of the legitimate line, a period commenced in which literature was cultivated among the Saracens to a considerable degree. The empire was however unable long to support its colossal weight, and gradually became like a "house divided against itself:" the governors of the provinces in Africa, Spain and the East assuming the rank of independent princes, their respective feuds and jealousies so weakened the Moslem dominion, that had not the Christian powers been utterly destitute of vigour, they might then have given it a fatal blow.[13]

Fresh energy however was infused into the Moslem community by the accession of the Turks.[14] After this very ancient tribe had descended from

---

[12] The Abbassides re-assumed the Kaliphate A. D. 750, and the Omayades lost, on one occasion, during the struggle 600,000 men.

[13] The Kaliphate being now split in two, one of the contending Kaliphs resided at Bagdad, the other at Cairo.

[14] The Turcomans or Turks derive their name from a certain founder called *Turk*, which reminds us of the *Targitus* or Targitaos of Herodotus IV. 5. and תֹּגַרְמָה, Togarmah Gen. X. 3. In Ezek. XXVII. 14. XXXVIII. 6. the name of this northerly tribe is written תֹּגַרְמָה. The Armenians also call themselves: "the house Torgum".

Altai, they inhabited the fruitful steppes of the highlands of Asia, between Thibet, Siberia and the Aral Sea, which are still known by the name of Turkistan.[15] *Oghus-Khan*, the founder of the nation, originated three great dynasties, the *Oghuses*, the *Seltschuks* and the *Osmans*. The Turks are however historically celebrious only since the sixth century, when they appear as the enemies of the Parthians, Saracens and Romans, by whom they were alternately opposed and flattered. Mohammed Ebn Inbriel having sought their aid against the Indians and Babylonians, they accordingly seized upon Persia, made themselves masters of the Grecian empire, and established the seat of their government at Iconium or Nice.[16] The Turks, in their turn, were overrun by *Mongol* and *Tartar* tribes, also of Scythian origin, who coming from the shores of the Caspian Sea, passed over Persia, Armenia and Asia Minor, laying the foundation of the empire of the *Ottomans* or *Turks*, properly so called.[17] It is remarkable that both the

---

[15] "Uralt ist das Volk der Türken, deren noch herrschender Zweig der Osmanen. Vom Altai, ihrem Ursitz, herabgestiegen, bewohnten sie das fruchtbare Steppenland Hochasien zwischen Tübet, Sibirien und dem Aralsee, das nach ihnen den Namen Turkistan führt." v. Hammers Geschichte des Osmanischen Reiches.

[16] Mosheim Vol. II. pag. 51. 52. also: Venemac Institut. Hist. Eccl. tom. V. pag. 156. 157.

[17] Othman, Osman or Ottoman is the founder of it. The first of those barbarous deeds, which for 500 years were perpetrated against the *Christians*, was that of Osman, when he commanded the brother of Kelanus to be eviscerated. v. Hammer adds: "Noch jetzt heißt die Stelle das stinkende Feld des ausgeweideten Hundes." He also killed his uncle, who contradicted him. The Ottoman empire was founded 1307.

Turks, and their successors, the Mongols and Tartars, voluntarily embraced Islamism, from the very people whom they conquered.[18] The Mongols and Tartars had slaughtered in Irak alone, 24,000 Moslem doctors,[19] and destroyed the Kaliphate; but after their conversion, they founded the Ottoman empire, which for so long a period constituted the right arm of Islamism.

The end of the Byzantine empire was now fast approaching; *Amurath*, who came across to Europe extended his conquests and made Adrianople his capital. *Bajesid*, who commenced his reign with fratricide, obtained a signal victory over the emperor Sigismund, who, at the instigation of the Pope, had undertaken a crusade against the Turks. Whilst the enterprizing Sultan was rejoicing over his success, and threatening shortly to feed his horses on the high altar in the Church of St. Peter's at Rome, he was suddenly recalled into Asia, to oppose Timur or Tamerlin, who had appeared against the Turks with 800,000 men, with the intent of re-establishing the Mongolian empire. Bajesid was overthrown and had to follow Timur's army in a portable iron cage. Yet the Turks recovered under Mohammed, and Amurath II. left nothing to the Greek Emperor but Constantinople, the capital, which was not long destined to remain in his hands: for Mohammed II, a wild

---

[18] Here also it was true: "Graccia capta ferum victorem cepit." Seneca declared respecting the influence of the Jews upon the Romans: "Victoribus victi leges dederunt." See, True and false Relig. Vol. I. pag. 140.

[19] Ebn Batuta's travels by Lee pag. 89.

and passionate young man of twenty-one years of age, resolving to conquer it, besieged the city by land and sea, and took it after a few months.[20] The Mohammedan empire now became the terror of Italy, Hungary and Germany for many centuries. Meanwhile, *Timur* extended his conquests to India; and the Mohammedans in that country have recently proved themselves worthy sons of this monster tyrant, to whom they are indebted for the Koran. In order to quell a revolution Timur piled up 2000 living human beings with mortar, in layers like bricks, in order to construct a tower of human bodies. He caused the inhabitants of a Christian town to have their heads tied between their feet and to be buried alive in graves, which, to prolong the torture, were first only covered with boards. When Bagdad was taken, he struck off 90,000 heads and heaped them up in a tower-like shape. He died A. D. 1405, seventy-one years old, leaving as monuments of shame, devastated countries, smoking cities and skull-pyramids.

6. We have now seen that Islamism, as a rule, never extended its boundaries by means of instruction and conviction. The heretical sects indeed, which rose in the second century, had recourse to this *peaceable* and *rational* method of conversion, and their Missionaries or *Daï's* sought to win the orthodox members with indefatigable zeal and perseverance.

---

[20] The inhabitants met the assault with desperate resistance; a chain, drawn across the harbour, was of good service to the Greeks; but the storming of the city, in which the Emperor was killed, decided its fate: the public buildings were spared and the beautiful Church of St. Sophia was turned into a Mosque.

In the conversion of *Kaffers* however, this was an exception, which only proves the rule; for instance it is related that the inhabitants of the *Maldive* islands were converted by an Arab of Magharib,[21] but this man not being a Missionary, merely took advantage of the readiness of the king and the favourable circumstances in which he was placed, to introduce his creed. It was always considered sufficient in the eyes of Moslemin to send a demand requiring a town or an army to embrace Islamism, if this was not complied with, the disobedient were forthwith treated as infidels, whose hearts were hardened by divine decree.[22] Those peaceful conversions which occurred among the Turks and Mongol tribes, it must be remembered, took place only after the warlike zeal of the Saracens had spent itself.

The same exception to the general practice may be traced in the peaceful conversions which were effected in the interior of Africa. *Ebn Batuta* traversed the great desert and found Islamism widely propagated in *Sudan* and *Melli*.[23] In *Bornu* the creed of Mohammed reigns in its most bigotted form: whosoever breaks the fast of Ramadhan by taking a drop of water is scourged to death and women of lewd

---

[21] Travels of Ebn Batula (1352) transl. by Lee pag. 180.

[22] Evidences are never thought of except those arising from the beauty of the Koran, which is inappreciable to foreigners. "In den Ländern, in welchen der Moslemische Fanatismus noch am wenigsten geschwächt ist, wird es sogar für ein Verbrechen gehalten, einen Christen Arabisch zu lehren, und wollte ein Fremder eine Moschee betreten, um sich durch die dort stattfindenden Gebete und religiösen Vorträge zu belehren, so würde er das Leben verwirken." Döttinger pag. 17.

[23] Ebn Batuta by Lee pag. 233—241.

character were hung.[24] In *Sudan* and *Hussa* the great kingdom of the Felatahs, and in the kingdoms of *Ghana, Tokrur Bussa, Berissa, Wawa* and *Kiama* we have likewise Mohammedan religion and customs prevailing.[25] It is also the established religion in *Timbuctu*.[26] A remarkable instance is found in the history of the *Mandingo*-land, north east of Sierra-Leone. A century ago, a few Mohammedans settled in that country, they established schools in which Arabic and the Koran were taught, a community was formed which increased, and after some time the whole country fell into their power.[27] Nor is this a singular instance: none but those who have witnessed the missionary zeal of the modern Arab merchant, would believe what efforts are still being made to proselytize the Pagans in the interior of Africa; every year fresh tribes are added to the Moslem community.[28] The Galla tribes are converted one by one; and in Malabar, the Mohammedans purchase or procure children of the lower classes to bring them up in the "true faith". War and bloodshed then are the means by which the Koran is generally propagated, but when power is wanting or policy dictates

---

[24] Narrative of travels and discoveries in North and Central Africa, by Denham, Clapperton and Oudney, pag. 103.

[25] Journal of an expedition to explore the course of the Niger, by Richard and John Lander.

[26] Park's Travels into the Interior of Africa. 1817. Chap. II.

[27] See Report of the directors of the Sierra Leone Comp. in Winterbottom's account of the native Africans near Sierra-Leone. 1810. Vol. 1.

[28] This the author may confidently assert from his own observation on the African coast.

another method, it is peaceably effected in opposition to its avowed principles and character.

7. The success then of Islamism, was great and beyond all measure surprising. With the exception of Spain, it has never yet been suppressed in any country where it had taken root; on the contrary, as it is almost the only creed besides Christianity, which proselytizes, it makes perhaps more converts than all the others put together. There are at this day, at least three Mohammedan empires, Turkey, Persia and Morocco. In India, the Pagans are in proportion to the Mohammedans, as eight to one. *If not in numbers, yet certainly in territory it preponderates over Christianity.* To give anything like a correct estimate of the *numbers* of its professors seems to be impossible. One thing only appears certain from more recent calculations, viz. that the statistical tables which have been carefully constructed from the materials, which were formerly accessible, are far below the truth. Considering the great progress which Islamism has made in the interior of Africa, and the mystery which still hangs upon that unhappy continent we cannot assume a smaller number than from 140 to 180 millions of Moslemin. In India alone we have 15,000,000 of Mohammedans, so that it may well be said, that the Queen of Great Britain has more Moslem subjects than the Sultan of Constantinople. Here then is an immense body of fellow-men and fellow-subjects, little thought of, and only remembered, when they become a thorn in our side!

8. We shall now briefly examine the *causes* of

this rapid *success*, as well as of the *permanence* of the Mohammedan creed. It may first be noticed that the disciples of Mohammed appeal to the startling success of this imposture, as the grand evidence of its truth, and the enemies of Christianity have taken advantage of this circumstance to depreciate the evidence arising in its favour from the marvellous success of the Gospel. With this view no pains have been spared to render the analogy, which partially exists between them complete, by a laboured comparison of all the points touching their origin and promulgation.[29] The folly of the attempt and the weakness of such a comparison could only be overlooked by dishonest and disingenuous minds. Some have represented the success of Islamism as the fulfilment of the blessing, promised to Abraham for Ishmaels seed.[30] This line of argument is pursued by the Mohammedans themselves, who thus seek to establish their creed upon the foundation of a divine promise, and this alone ought to have prevented Christian men from adopting it. Where no *spiritual promise* was given, there can be no fulfilment of a *spiritual* character. The *promise* to Ishmael implied a numerous posterity, including twelve princes, which was a mere temporal blessing;[31] whilst the *prophecy*

---

[29] The obscure rise, the irresistible progress, the rapid and wide diffusion of both creeds have been adduced and dwelt upon, in order to level the claims of the Gospel and the gratuitous assumptions of the Koran to the same standard.

[30] This is the perverted scope of Mr. Forster's large work: "Mohammedanism unveiled." Vol. II.

[31] וּלְיִשְׁמָעֵאל שְׁמַעְתִּיךָ הִנֵּה בֵּרַכְתִּי אֹתוֹ וְהִפְרֵיתִי אֹתוֹ וְהִרְבֵּיתִי אֹתוֹ בִּמְאֹד מְאֹד שְׁנֵים עָשָׂר נְשִׂיאִם יוֹלִיד וּנְתַתִּיו לְגוֹי גָּדוֹל Gen. XVII. 20.

concerning him defined his character and that of his descendants.[32] To acknowledge the fulfilment of a promised blessing in Islamism, is to admit it to be a true religion; it may be the fulfilment of *prophecy*, but that is essentially different from the fulfilment of a *promise*. Is the creed of Mohammed the actual fulfilment of a promise to Abraham, then it is of necessity a divinely revealed religion. But to recognise more than the temporal fulfilment of a temporal promise is to confound the *flesh* with the *Spirit*, and prosperity in this world with the blessings of the life to come.

Whilst we repudiate the notion of the success of Islamism being the fulfilment of *a divine promise*, we do not deny that it was permitted to grow and flourish, in order to accomplish the mysterious designs of *Divine Providence;* since God often permits the success of those actions and the spread of those opinions, which it is contrary to His holy nature to approve. *Success* therefore in the propagation of a creed is not necessarily demonstrative of its being of divine origin. In God's providential administration one evil is frequently the antidote of another. Islamism belongs to the class of means, which Divine Providence employs to counteract the greater of two evils, until the final triumph of good is achieved, and the ultimate separation of good and

[32] It was implied in Abraham's prayer, that Ishmael should partake of God's mercy and blessing, but this could only be granted through Isaac and his seed, in whom all the families of the earth were to be blessed; for if *all nations* were to be blessed in the seed of Isaac, why should Ishmael be excluded?

evil can be safely effected; it being a fixed principle of God's dealings to let the tares and the wheat grow together till the harvest.[33] In this case, a smaller evil is tolerated for a time, to prevent a greater. In a period and in places where pure and undefiled religion could not through unbelief and darkness yet be received, a mixture of good and evil was suffered to prevail.

There is clearly much inconsistency in the anxiety of Christian writers to escape from the recognition of a providential interference in the rise and progress of Islamism. All commentators seem to agree, that its rise had been predicted in Holy Scripture; to deny therefore the overruling providence of God in bringing about an event which has been the subject of prophecy, and to ascribe it solely to the independent operation of human causes, is to take the government of the world out of the hands of God.[34] When Daniel e. g. foretells the fate of the four great empires of the world, or when Isaiah speaks of Cyrus, as the servant of God, we do not hesitate to admit the actual guidance of Divine Providence in shaping the career of those empires, or the special act of raising up instruments to execute His judgments. To account for the efforts made to explain Islamism from mere

---

[33] Ἄφετε συναυξάνεσθαι ἀμφότερα μέχρι τοῦ θερισμοῦ· καὶ ἐν τῷ καιρῷ τοῦ θερισμοῦ ἐρῶ τοῖς θερισταῖς κ. τ. λ. Matt. XIII. 30. Tum erit perfecta separatio.

[34] This view could not have been entertained, had it been considered that if carried to the extreme it would impugn prophecy itself, making the word of God a predictor of events, over which the Author of that word had no special control.

natural causes, we must take it for granted that those who make them, deem it essential to the interests of Christianity to ignore the notion of Divine interposition in the production of any results independent of revealed religion.

9. After the Nicene Council, the Eastern Church was engaged in perpetual controversies, which gave rise to the most bitter feelings between those who were commanded to love each other as brethren. Constantius[37] made himself notorious by confounding pure and undefiled religion with anile superstition, and in exciting disputes upon intricate and abstruse subjects. Arabia and Africa were polluted by schism and heresy of the worst description,[38] and were ripe for judgment. The European Church was corrupt in practice, but still retained an amount of sound catholic doctrine, especially on the Divinity of our Lord, which served as an antidote to the false teaching of the Koran, and prevented this

[37] "Eratque super his adimere facilis, quae donabat, Christianam religionem absolutam et simplicem anili superstitione confundens: in quo scutunda perplexius, quam componenda gravius, excitavit dissidia plurima: quae progressa fusius aluit concertatione verborum, ut catervis antistitum, jumentis publicis ultro citroque discurrentibus per Synodos, quas appellant, dum ritum omnem ad suum trahere conatur arbitrium, rei vehiculariae succideret nervos." Ammian. Mercellin. lib. XXI. de Constantio.

[38] The Archbishop of Toledo describes the state of religion thus in the 7th sec. "Cum Arabian et Africa inter fidem Catholicam et herein Arianam, et perfidiam Judaicam et idolatrum, diversis studiis traheretur." Hist. Arab. pag. 2. ad calc. Elmac. Hist. Sa.

judgment from falling so severely upon the Western, as upon the Eastern Church.[39] Europe did not indeed altogether escape the plague of Islam, because it had partly adopted the false teaching of the Eastern Church.[40] Spain in which the Arian leaven still lingered was overwhelmed in a manner, which clearly showed the finger of God.[40] The Spanish army melted away before a handful of

[39] "Non dissimulavit Deus haec populi sui vitia: quin ex ultimo Scythiae ac Germaniae recessu immensa agmina, quasi diluvio, effudit in orbem Christianum; et cum datae ab his strages maximae non satis profecissent ad corrigendos superstites, justo Dei permissu, in Arabia Mahumetis novam sevit religionem, pugnantem eam directa fronte cum Christiana relinione, sed quae verbis quodamodo exprimeret vitam magnae partis Christianorum." Grotius de verit. Relig. Christ. pag. 277.

[40] The author dare not follow the "Guardian" when in reference to this notice of Arianism in Spain the reviewer either ignores or forgets the undoubted fact that in the year 581 the Swevi in Spain partially relapsed into the Arian heresy which they had previously abjured in 559.
As a further proof of reckless criticism in the same periodical I should here point to pag. 107, note 76, where it is stated on the authority of Weil, Einleitung in den Koran pag. 51, that the copy of the Koran which Othman was reading when assassinated, was "said to have been brought to *Antartus.*" This *town* on the coast of Syria was transformed by the same reviewer into a *person*, it being added by the "Guardian," that this said place was a "*person of whom we never before heard.*" It is well known to every scholar, and certainly ought to have been known to any person assuming the dignity of reviewer that *Antartus* is the Arabic and Eastern name for the Syrian *Ortoso*, which so frequently occurs in the history of the Crusades. The Eastern and European name are both placed together in Weil's large and learned work: *Geschichte der Chalifen* Band IV. p. 70.

Saracen soldiers; the Godhead of the Redeemer being already denied, there was nothing to resist or to prevent an occupation of the country for the space of 800 years! But the Mohammedan invasion was effectually repelled by the glorious victory of Charles Martel.[41] In the seventeenth century, when Europe was once more assailed on her eastern frontier, God raised up Sobieski, to set bounds for ever to the Turkish empire, and the creed of Mohammed. "Hitherto shalt thou come and no further; and here shall thy proud waves be stayed!" In all these things we trace a remarkable *Providence* controlling the spread of Islamism. Nor can we fail to adore the wise and gracious choice of the instruments, by which God chastised the fallen Churches! The Western Church was first punished by the influx of Pagan hordes from the North, and had God chosen idolaters for the correction of the Eastern Church, there might have been cause to apprehend danger for the very existence of Christianity, more especially as Western Europe was already overrun by Pagan nations; but the enemy whom God chose to administer judgment in His name was one, who was as greatly opposed to idolatry as the fallen Church could be in her better days. Islamism made common cause with the Church in protesting against Paganism, and precluded the possibility of Pagan powers uniting against Christianity. We may therefore consider Mohammed, the servant of God in the same sense

---

[41] Calcutta Review No. VIII. December, 1845. to which the author is indebted for some of these remarks.

Q

in which Pagan Cyrus was called the servant of Jehovah.

Islamism was thus made subservient to great and important ends in the dispensation of the justice and holiness of God. It does not however follow, that this admission must necessarily place the Koran and the Bible upon the same footing: Mohammedanism, in its *providential aspect,* was the result of the natural course of events; Christianity, on the contrary, was introduced by a miraculous deviation from that course.[42] If we refer to Holy Scripture for guidance in this matter, we notice God's interposition in cases as unlikely in our estimation as that of Islamism. The lying spirit for instance, which was put into the mouth of false prophets, purporting to prophesy the truth, may serve as an illustration.[43] The special interference here, is unquestionable, and one peculiarly to the point; God, for purposes only known to Himself, might as easily have put a lying spirit into the mouth of Mohammed.[44] The action of the instrumentality being employed upon a greater or lesser scale, makes no difference as to the establishing of the principle of providential interference. The just distinction between Islamism and Christianity seems to

---

[42] The principle of an overruling Providence, working without a miracle, has been ably set forth by Mr. Davidson: Discourses on Prophecy. pag. 76. 77. 247. 248.

[43] 1 King. XXII. 19—23. "Now therefore behold, the Lord hath put a lying Spirit in the mouth of all these thy prophets:" וְעַתָּה הִנֵּה נָתַן יְהֹוָה רוּחַ שֶׁקֶר בְּפִי כָּל־נְבִיאֶיךָ

[44] Καὶ διὰ τοῦτο πέμψει αὐτοῖς Θεὸς ἐνέργειαν πλάνης, εἰς τὸ πιστεῦσαι αὐτοὺς τῷ ψεύδει· 2 Thess. II. 9—11.

be this: the phenomena of the spread of Christianity prove that it came from God, but those of Islamism show only that it sprang from an overruled agency of natural events, and that as to its permanence, it is still upheld by their providential concurrence.

At the very period when the Lombards were destroying the last vestiges of the Roman empire, God raised up an obscure people to a sudden greatness in order to correct His erring Churches, and to remove the candlestick from such as were past correction. The salt having lost its savour was cast out and trodden under foot of men.[45] This explains without comment, the cause of the success of Islamism. Our Lord indicated the characteristics of those devouring eagles, which were sent forth into the world by the false prophet who arose "in the desert", to prey upon the dead members of His Church. As the eagle does good service by consuming carcases, which otherwise would be left to poison the atmosphere, so Islamism benefited the Church, by consuming those dead members, which had become offensive in the sight of God, and if allowed to remain, would have endangered the very life of the body. It is remarkable that our Lord's words literally occur, in Alwakidi's description of the primitive Moslemin, "The Saracens he says, fell upon them like eagles upon a carcase."[46]

---

[45] "Ueber dieses christliche Morgenland, in welchem das Christenthum seit langer Zeit in der Stickluft des Despotismus, und unter dem todten Formelwesen, durch das feine Ideen verkümmerten und verkamen, todtkrank war, kam der Herr plötzlich und sein Gericht." Zimmermanns Lebensgeschichte der Kirche Jesu Christi, Vol. II. 518.

[46] Ockley's History of the Saracens, Vol. I. pag. 220.

The black eagle was moreover the ensign of the first Saracen conquerors, and that affords an additional reason for applying the prediction to them, as well as to the Romans, by whom the Jewish Church was devoured.[47] Nor is it against the principle of germinant interpretation of prophecy, to make it include both visitations upon the Old and the New Church, which had alike sunk into decay.

10. An *auxiliary* cause of the success of Islamism, was the *time* in which it appeared; for we may safely say, that in no former or subsequent period of the world could Mohammed have met with equal success. All the circumstances of that period, plainly and undeniably concurred to favour the rise and progress of the new religion. The heresies which divided and the corruptions which then degraded the Church, presented an open field for Mohammed. The *political* state of the world was likewise propitious. Islamism being a religion of conquest, the union of nations under compact and vigorous governments, would have opposed insuperable obstacles. Its success obviously depended, not on the strength and stability, but on the decay of the kingdoms of the earth; and its establishment could only be promoted by the divisions and distractions of mankind.[48] At a later or an earlier date, that of Trajan, of Constantine or Charlemagne, the assault of the half-naked

---

[47] Ockley Hist. of the Sarac. Vol. I. 172. Wahl pag. 73. E.

[48] "It has been observed by a great politician Machiavelli, that it is impossible a person should make himself a prince and found a state, *without opportunities.*" Sale, Prelem. Disc. pag. 25.

Saracens would soon have been repelled, and their religious fanaticism extinguished. This most favourable concurrence of a diversity of circumstances, both *ecclesiastical* and *political*, at once so contrary and so harmonious, cannot fail to strike every candid observer of the age in which Islamism made its appearance.

11. Another cause of the rapid spread and permanent establishment of Islamism, is to be looked for in the means which were used in its propagation. The appeal to the sword is natural to a politico-religious system, and in prescribing both moral and civil laws to the state, it decides every question of life or property.[49] In almost every Mohammedan country, so intimate is the connection and so absolute the dependence of the religious, upon the civil government, that in propagating the tenets of religion, an appeal to the civil force would be unavoidable. With few exceptions, this maxim of the Koran:—"Fight against them, until there be no opposition in favour of idolatry and the religion be wholly God's," has ever been strictly carried out. No alternative was allowed to the Pagan, he had to choose between an immediate recantation of his opinions and a cruel death. The Christian was permitted the privilege of compounding for the preservation of his life and property, by the payment of a heavy tribute. To men who had lost

---

[49] The recent appointment of a Minister of justice by the Sultan of Constantinople, is an innovation; inasmuch as this duty was till that time, incumbent upon their spiritual head of religion, the Mufti, who was the locum tenens of the Sultan himself, in his character of Kaliph.

almost every thing but the name of their religion, this mode of conversion was irresistible. Nor can we wonder that in many such cases, the voice of conscience was unheard amidst the cries of interest. Temporal ease and security under the banners of the pseudo-prophet, were to them, preferable to the distress of the despised and persecuted Christians.

We should however be much mistaken, were we to look upon the enthusiasm of the first propagators of Islamism, as springing merely from religious zeal.[50] The *hope of gain* and the prospect of plunder gathered hosts to Mohammed's standard, even in his life-time; and the national pride of the Arabs felt flattered by following a prophet who had risen from amongst themselves:[51] then Mohammed's rank, his personal influence, his consummate art and prudence, his fervent enthusiasm, which in the first instance, resulted from a sincere conviction that he was a chosen messenger of God,—all gave strength and solidity to each step in the early propagation of Islamism.

12. Mohammed's appeal to the Patriarchal faith and the Ishmaelitish descent of the Arabs, was like-

[50] Khaled who was termed "the sword of the swords of Allah," well described the mixture of power and persuasion by which he and the Koreishites were converted, when he said, that Allah seized them by their *hearts* and by the *locks* of their *hair* to lead them to the prophet. Taberistanensis Annales regum atque legatorum Dei. Edit. Kosegarten. II. pag. 103.

[51] The Arab general said to the Christian Arabs of Hira, who declined to receive Islamism: "Ye fools, will you wander to and fro in the wilderness of error; when two guides offer themselves to you, a foreigner and an Arab, will ye follow the first and forsake the latter?" Taberistanensis Annal. II. pag. 39.

wise highly favourable to a sudden spread of his creed. There was an artful accommodation to the divers classes of his countrymen, by which he drew the Jew, the Christian and the idolater into his net. A certain writer brings forward fifty pages of coincidences between Judaism and Islamism:— Each professes to derive a politico-religious economy from a prophet who united in his person the political and spiritual administration of the affairs of the nation. Each came to be possessed of a sacred book, composed by their respective lawgivers. In both cases we have a people in arms, professing to go forth by divine command to conquer, and so far as their respective conquests should extend, to extirpate the religion of the subdued countries and to substitute their own. The Jews, as far as their commission went, were to cut off the idolatrous inhabitants from the land of promise; the Mohammedans, according to the terms of their extended commission, demanded either conversion or death. Each nation left the same desert. Again Moses and Mohammed descended from Abraham, both commenced their office at the age of forty; the former received the law in Arabia, the latter the Koran. Both prophets are exiled, commune with God, and die in the desert before their followers leave the country; and no one will fail to perceive that in several points, Mohammed artfully accommodated himself to the history of Moses to give weight and effect to his pretensions.

We have noticed on a former occasion, with what skill Mohammed accommodated himself to the *Chris-*

tian religion, at the commencement of his career. The immaculate and wonderful conception of Christ was acknowledged, His miracles were admitted, His prophetical character was asserted, and certain titles were ascribed to Christ, which the Christians affirmed belonged to Him. It did its work and favoured Mohammed's cause among the Christians for a time. Then how well the national superstitions of the *Arabs* were blended with Islamism, to conciliate their love for ancient institutions! *Mecca*, the centre of the national worship, was chosen to become the sanctuary of the new creed; pilgrimage with all its Pagan rites was continued; circumcision and other national usages were adopted and incorporated into the system of Mohammed's religion. There was a compilation of heterogeneous religious elements, which proved acceptable to all parties, each finding in it, dogmas which were held by their respective ancestors.

13. The yoke which Islamism imposed upon the first believers, was by no means oppressive. It was presented as the religion of Abraham, a name revered by all parties; the Unity of God was a dogma which was held in common by Jews, Christians and Arabs. The rest of the teaching of the Koran was simple, — consisting mainly of precepts and maledictions. There was an absence of those holy and blessed mysteries of our faith, which are at all times humiliating to human reason. That which is most needful, but at the same time most opposed to the depraved taste of the natural man, is carefully excluded. Islamism, as a false creed, offers no Redemp-

tion, no means of grace; insists on no repentance, no self-denial and no mortification of the flesh, and where there exists no love of the truth, it can reckon upon a more ready reception than Christianity can expect. The mixture of truth and falsehood, the simplicity of its formula, the mechanism of its devotions, washings and fastings, combined with an unbridled licentiousness, renders it more acceptable than the Gospel of Christ, with its free mercy to lost sinners, with its rigid morality and elevating hope of glory; for the world will love its own in religion, not less than in other things.[52]

The *permanency* of Islamism, which is another of its striking features, may in some measure be attributed to its close connection with the existing Governments. Any attempt to alter or reform the religion, necessarily involved the ruin and overthrow of the Government of the land. Every case of religious apostacy is therefore punished by the state as a capital crime. It was solely owing to the external pressure of the European powers of late years that an alteration has been made in the Turkish empire. Again, the permanence of Islamism is in no way surprising, when

[52] "Entsagung, Aufgebung der liebsten Neigungen wurde nicht gefordert; die Leidenschaften sollten nicht sowohl gebändigt und in strenge Zucht genommen werden, als nur auf einen Gegenstand, den Kampf für die Ausbreitung des neuen Glaubens concentrirt werden ... Das Verbot des Weines konnte nicht lästig sein in einem Lande, wo die Frucht der Rebe nicht gedeiht, das periodische Fasten nicht da, wo Unfruchtbarkeit des Bodens oft auch den Wohlhabenden Entbehrungen auferlegt, und schon das Klima zur größten Mäßigung im Genusse der Nahrung einladet. Das Drückende war am Anfang die Religionssteuer, die aber bald durch die reiche Beute hundertfältig vergütet wurde; für so geringe Opfer erkauften die Gläubigen die Aussicht auf enbloses Schwelgen im Paradise sinnlicher Lüste." Döllinger pag. 4. 5.

we remember that each child swells the ranks of the community; for according to Moslem teaching, every child is born a *Moslem*, and it is only the parents who make him a Jew or a Christian! Not so with Christianity; for according to its teaching, every child is born in sin; and as by nature, all are children of wrath, the Gospel has to struggle against the whole course of nature, and when it has prevailed with one generation of professed Christians, it has to renew the struggle in the next.[53]

These then are *some* of the principal causes, the joint agency of which, sufficiently accounts for the *success* and *permanent character* of Islamism. We protest against the dangerous and fallacious assumption, that there is in it any fulfilment of a divine *promise*, but willingly admit a *providential control* of this heaven-sent scourge.[54] How often did God raise up instruments of His wrath to chastise the Jewish Church, and these after having served as the rod of correction, were invariably cast into the fire! Let only the cause of the scourge be remedied, let the Eastern Churches be cleansed from their dross; let the Church of Christ in the West fulfil her duty towards both the Christian and the Mohammedan community, and the scourge itself will be removed;

[53] The Church in extending her Missionary operations has to contend with these natural obstacles which impede her progress, whilst Islamism in propagating its tenets and in maintaining its ground, only flatters the natural *pride* and indulges the *passions* of man.

[54] Success alone, can afford no absolute proof of divine favour; for we observe, how God permits error to prevail upon earth and that, not seldom, to a far greater extent then truth itself.

let Paganism also be abolished, and Islamism, which in God's purpose has served as a barrier to the abomination of idolatry, will be destroyed.

14. Thus we have seen how the sword has been the chief instrumentality in propagating Islamism; but God, who brings good out of evil, life out of death, peace and order out of strife and confusion, evidently assigned certain functions to this apostacy, which in the end should work together for good. At a period when the nations of the East had reduced Christianity to a miserable caricature, Islamism, being armed against all teaching except its own, seemed to be the less fatal of two evils.[55] Whilst it spread the Koran, and assumed an attitude of inveterate hostility, it acted at the same time, as an antidote to the poison of *heretical* teaching in the Church. As regards the Western Church, Islamism roused her from her slumber, served as a correction of her abuses and corruptions, and called forth new life and energy among the stagnant masses of her professors. When this object was attained, God withdrew the rod, and showed mercy to His Church, which could not be

---

[55] "Islam diente als die geistige Quarantaine, in welcher die Völker gegen das Contagium einer solchen Corruption abgesperrt, besserer Zeiten und des Wehens reinerer Lüfte harren. Daß jene Gefahr wirklich vorhanden und dringend gewesen, das bezeugt nicht nur der Hang zum häretischen Sektenwesen, der unter den orientalischen Christen jener Zeit schon überwiegend war; es bezeugt es auch der große Erfolg, welche die giftige, alle Sittlichkeit zerfressende Lehre der Paulicianer und Bogomilen unter den Christen, so wie der mit diesen nahe verwandten Bateni's und Islameli's unter den Moslemen hatte. War doch selbst die abendländische Kirche der von dieser drohenden Gefahr in so hohem Grade bloßgestellt, daß im Beginne des 13. Seculums bereits ganze Provinzen von der pestartig um sich greifenden Lehre angesteckt waren." Döllinger pag. 140.

destroyed in this terrible earthquake.[56] Moslem historians maintain, that the locust armies carried on their wings the Arabic inscription: "We are the host of Allah, every one of us carries ninety-nine eggs, and if we had a hundred, we would destroy the world with all that is therein." The Moslemin themselves are these locust armies, and more than once, the want of the hundreth egg alone has prevented their utterly destroying the noblest powers of Christendom. Such an epoch was the Kaliphate of *Othman;* when in the course of the seventh century, the whole of the weak Byzantine empire would probably have fallen, and by its fall would have opened the door to central Europe, had not the best powers of the Moslem empire been consumed by those intestine feuds which succeeded the assassination of the Kaliph. *Another crisis* occurred, after the occupation of the south of France by Moslem troops, when the fate of Europe was suspended on that memorable battle won by Charles Martel. The *third* critical period, at which the hundreth egg was wanting, occurred in the third century of the Hedgra, when the Aglabites, having already subjugated Sicily, threatened to establish themselves in lower Italy: for had not the Moslem power at that period, succumbed to the Fatamites in Africa, Italy, as well as Spain, would have been overrun by the Moors, especially as it was in a defenceless condition, and France in a state of disturbance. Again, in the fourth century of the Mohammedan era, after the restoration of the Kaliphate to its legitimate line, the

[56] Ousley's Travels II. 149.

Saracen power, having recovered its pristine vigour and threatening to penetrate to the very heart of Christian Europe, was signally checked:—the Selchuk Turks under Soleiman A. D. 1084 had united the whole tract of country between the Euphrates and the Hellespont into one kingdom, and stood before Constantinople, prepared to march into Europe; when, the Emperor of Constantinople sending letters to the Christian princes imploring their assistance, Peter the Hermit with the assembly at Clermont, brought the whole of Europe to arms; and for the first time the religious enthusiasm of the Christians proved itself stronger than the fanatical zeal of the Moslem conquerors.

CHAPTER VIII.

CHARACTER AND INFLUENCE OF ISLAMISM.

"Ye shall know them by their fruits. Do men gather grapes from thorns or figs from thistles? Even so every good tree bringeth forth good fruit, but a *corrupt tree bringeth forth evil fruit.*"
Matt. VII. 16.

1. Mohammed, assuming to be a prophet rather of the type and character of Moses than that of Jesus, took upon himself to legislate on moral, civil and religious matters. The divine authority ascribed to his precepts on religion, was necessarily extended to those regarding the civil and social relations of life, and being thus endowed with a character of stability, an insurmountable barrier was placed to the free

development of Islamism in future ages.⁵⁷ Hence the rude, simple and in some instances, barbarous, customs of the Arabs of that age,—which Mohammed had tolerated by way of accommodation to their national prejudices,—became the *fixed law* for all future generations. Among these we may mention the *"lex talionis"*, which in subsequent ages, was introduced and adopted by all Mohammedan states.⁵⁸ The entire administration of the Moslem code of law may be fairly reduced to the precepts of the Koran, which also in this particular, adopted the traditional practice of the Arabs. That the adoption of this system could not fail to cause many crying abuses when applied to a semi-civilised people, may be easily imagined. That brief and simple mode of conducting trials previously used by the armed and roving Beduins of the Peninsula, is still maintained among all Moslem nations; this total absence of the legal forms and courtesies of European courts of justice, together with the non-acceptance of written documents to serve as evidence, produce a host of *false witnesses*, who in large towns, make a systematic trade of their infamous perjuries at the courts of law. On the other hand, the prophet blessing those "who cast the mantle

---

⁵⁷ "Die Gewänder, welche dem Knaben gepaßt hatten, sollte auch der Mann, der ihnen längst entwachsen war, nicht ablegen dürfen." From the valuable treatise by Prof. Döllinger: Muhammed's Religion nach ihrer inneren Entwicklung und ihrem Einflusse auf das Leben der Völker. 1838. pag. 7.

⁵⁸ "Noch jetzt werden daher Mörder den gesetzlichen Erben oder Verwandten des Ermordeten überliefert, um mit ihnen nach Willkür zu verfahren, ja selbst unmündige Kinder werden mit Messern bewaffnet, um ihre Hände in das Blut des Mörders ihres Vaters zu tauchen." Döllinger pag. 8.

over the crimes of their brethren," created an abuse in the opposite direction; evidence to convict the guilty party in criminal cases being scarcely procurable among Moslemin.[59]

The nefarious practice of wantonly making and breaking an oath, was enforced by the example of the prophet himself. Mohammed swore on the most frivolous occasions. At the beginning of Sura XXXVIII. he swears "by the Koran full of admonition", but no commentator has yet discovered for what reason. He swears in Sura XLIV. "by the perspicuous book" that it came down on the blessed night. In Sura LI. he makes oath by the winds, clouds, ships and angels, that the day of Judgment will surely come; also by the ways of heaven, that the Meccans quarrel about him; in Sura LXVIII. by "the pen and writer" that he is not possessed by a demon; in Sura LXIX. 34 by things "visible and invisible" that the Koran is not a poetical figment or a magical production. In Sura LXXV. he swears "by the day of the Resurrection and the soul that accuseth itself", but for what purpose, it is difficult to guess. God is made to swear by the planets, by night and day-break, that the Koran was revealed by Gabriel, and that Mohammed was not possessed.[60] In Sura XC. Allah is said to swear that he created man in toil, sorrow, and affliction; but in

[59] As the courts of justice take cognizance only of crimes committed against religion and the head of the state, offences which would be severely punished in Christian lands, are generally allowed to pass unnoticed. Correspondence d'Orient par Michaud et Poujoulat. Paris 1833. III. pag. 288.

[60] Sur. LXXXI. 15. cfr. with this Hebr. VI. 14—16.

Sura XCV. he makes oath by the fig-tree, the olive, mount Sinai and Mecca, that he "created man of a most excellent fabric, and afterwards we rendered him the vilest of the vile." In Sura XCII. we are assured by a double oath that men have different opinions!

From these examples of swearing on the part of Allah, it is not surprising that the Koran solemnly teaches, that oaths made precipitately, may be broken.[61] Mohammed himself broke his oath on several occasions; and taught his followers (Sura II. 225.) that after, or within four months, they may fairly break their vows, "for God is gracious and merciful." The expiation of an inconsiderate oath (Sur. V. 90—95), is "to feed ten men with moderate food, or clothe them; or else to deliver a captive, or if unable to fulfil these things, to fast for three days."

How greatly this contempt for the sanctity of an oath must tend to demoralise a people, can scarcely be conceived; we would challenge any traveller to find such, even amongst Pagans. Triple oaths, on the most trivial occurrences, are constantly on the lips of the Arabs. No Pagan nation deals so wantonly with the names of their gods, as the Moslem does with the sacred name of Allah. Oaths are affixed to the most outrageous falsehoods, and this being done from mere habit, such thoughtless and vain oaths are according to the Koran, unpunishable, "for God is gracious and merciful." The perjury committed at

---

[61] "God will not punish you for an inconsiderate word in your oaths." Sur. II. 224.

courts of justice, is therefore only one link in that chain of lying and falsehood, which Islamism has thrown around the entire community of its professors.

2. In spite however of the conscientious adherence of Moslemin to a system of legislation, which was considered unchangeable, the strictly literal sense of this heaven-sent theory was in some cases modified, where its application to the stern realities of practical life was found to be absolutely impossible. It was with this view partially, that the *Sonna* was added to the Koran.[62] The Sonna, or *traditions,* embody the expressions, occasional remarks and acts of Mohammed, which are traced back to his companions, his wives and the first Kaliphs;[63] and the doctrines as well as religious rites and ceremonies of the Mohammedans, are fixed and regulated according to these received traditions. On them, the true sense of the Koran depends, for the Koran can only be explained and its meaning understood, as it is given or hinted at by the Sonna. Regarding them, there is great uncertainty among Moslemin; as these traditions are neither all collected into one book nor are all approved by the whole body of their renowned divines. Collections indeed, have been made with great labour by learned men, but as they do not agree in all cases, latitude enough has been left to any

---

[62] سنة, Sonna mos receptus, traditio, regula; from سن formavit; secutus fuit regulam.

[63] Wüstenfeld's D'ahabi: liber classium virorum, qui Corani et traditionorum cognitione excelluerunt. Götting. 1834.

writer of reputation to add or to reject at his own choice.⁶⁴ To tell a lie for a good purpose, especially to add by it something to the glory of their prophet, is considered by Moslemin and particularly by the Shiites, quite right and proper. But whatever be the merits or demerits of these traditions, they widened the narrow limits of the legislature of the Koran and afforded some elasticity to the cramped and narrow-minded precepts of Mohammed.

The real character of Islamism may be better ascertained from these traditions, in which we see how the contemporaries of Mohammed and his immediate followers understood his teaching, than from the monotonous repetitions of the Koran.⁶⁵ What

⁶⁴ "Bukhári, one of the first of the collectors of the traditions, and esteemed the highest in point of authority, had, as is said, collected 200,000, or according to another statement, 630,000 traditions, of which he regarded but 100,000 as somewhat to be relied upon, and only 7275 as actually authentic and true. He died A. H. 256. Another collector has received only 5266, and the author of the Musábih only 4484 as authentic. The writers of the Shiás differ still more than those of the Sunnís about the number of the traditions to be regarded as actually to be relied upon; for since the Shiás regard as canonical also the sayings of their Imáms, they have a much greater number of traditions than the Sunnís, and consequently it is still more difficult for them to fix their number, or to distinguish between an authentic and an unauthentic tradition." Dr. C. G. Pfander's Remarks on the nature of Mohammedan tradition, pag. 30.

⁶⁵ "One of the most acknowledged collections of the Hadiths or *traditions* approved of "by the Sonnis is, *Mishcat ul Masabih*," which has been translated into English and published by H. N. Mathews, Calcutta 1810; and most of the traditions received by the Shias are contained in the books of "*Hayat ul Kulub*, *Huq ul Yaquin*," and "*Ain ul Hayat*," written by Mullah Muhammed Bakir Májlisi, a famous Persian divine, who lived about 200 years ago, and which were printed in Teheran in 4 folio Volumes." Pfander's

the prophet taught concerning divine truths, apart from a few practical injunctions, seems to be considered of little importance compared with the more attractive legends of the Koran which are over-laden with mythical embellishments. Let any one read what has been rendered accessible to Europeans, and they will find wearisome commentaries upon legal washings, ceremonial attitudes and histrionic positions at prayer, the physical relations of women, matrimony and divorce, buying and selling, salutations and the most ordinary transactions of life, intermixed with the most outrageous and wildly extravagant fables concerning the visible and invisible world. Ignorant of the real discipline of the soul, Islamism, in its traditions, beats out a path of vain and useless ceremonial, the fulfilment of which, produces a delusive sense of security; and the very irksomeness of the ceremonial enhances the feeling of its meritorious character. As regards the absurd and marvellous stories contained in them, it has been justly remarked that they exercise even a greater influence on the minds of the Mohammedans than the doctrines contained in the Koran, and this explains why they are so indifferent to the plain and unvarnished truths of the Gospel. These extravagant fables have so destroyed and vitiated their taste, that they have little relish for sober truth and look down

---

Remarks on the nature of Muh. pag. 8. See also Harrington's "Remarks upon the authorities of Moselman law" Asiatic Researches Vol. X. pag. 478. where he mentions 4 collections of traditions, which the Shiites consider authentic.

R*

with contempt on the simple but sublime doctrines of Christianity.[66]

3. In considering the *warlike fanaticism* which the Mohammedans manifested in propagating their faith, we recognise the fruits of the much enforced doctrine, that the *blood of infidels* is the best *sacrifice* which can be made to God. The means of conversion by sword and conquest soon assumed a cruel and sanguinary character. Thousands of prisoners were usually massacred after a victory; not in the heat of contest, but in cold blood and as a matter of principle,[67] and the law which assigned the wives and children of the slain to the conquerors greatly tended to inflame their zeal and increase the number of victims. Lest it might be thought, to be only the fresh-kindled enthusiasm of the first Moslem warriors which led to such excesses, we must add, that the same thirst for blood distinguished all subsequent conquests on the part of Mohammedans. This was evinced for a number of centuries, during which religious wars devastated the countries of *India;* and we may consider it but one instance out of many, when Mohammed

[66] The demoralising influence of these traditions may be seen from the fact, that some of the tortures which they ascribe to the Moslem hell, were applied to Christians during the recent mutiny in India. "With hooks they tear their bodies and with iron maces they are beaten; angels stout and fierce torture them, showing no mercy." Again: "There are such in hell of whose sides the angels cut off the flesh with scissors, and throw it into their mouths." Hayat ul Kulub Vol. II. leaf 174.

[67] Khaled, who was once M.'s right hand, vowed in a heavy engagement against Christian Arabs and Pagan Persians, that if God would grant him the victory, he would dye the waters of the stream with the blood of the slain. Taberist. Annal. reg. II. p. 29.

Shah Bahnum, king of the Deccan, fulfilled his vow 1368, that he would not sheathe his sword, till he had slain 100,000 infidel Hindoos, in order to revenge the defeat of a detachment of Moslem troops.[68] When Reinald from Châtillon attempted an expedition against Medina and Mecca, Saladin the celebrated hero of Islamism, declared it to be his sacred duty to cleanse the earth from these men, and to kill every Christian who should fall into his hands. Thereupon part of the captive Christians were dragged to the valley of Mina, where the pilgrims slaughtered them, instead of the accustomed sheep or lambs; the rest were brought to Egypt, where the Moslem ascetics considered it a meritorious work, to kill these "Christian dogs" with their own hand.[69] That demoniacal blood-thirsty hatred entertained by Moslemin towards all who disbelieve the Koran, imbibed from their very infancy, has ever operated so powerfully among them, that even their noblest characters have been tarnished by it:[70] thus the abomination of human sacrifices came to be revived by those, who prided themselves in having destroyed Paganism, as far as their arm of power could reach!

4. This flame of *hatred* towards all other reli-

---

[68] Ferishta, history of the Mohammedan power in India, trans. by Briggs. 1829. Vol. II. pag. 311.

[69] After the battle near Hittin, Saladin caused the captured knights and hospitallers to be killed by the pious fanatics, who followed his army. Reinaud Journal Asiatique V. pag. 237. 290.

[70] It is well known that Saladin has frequently been compared and preferred to his Christian contemporary, the Emperor of Constantinople.

gionists which is indeed the very element of Islamism,[71] is continually nourished by the reading of the Koran, replete as it is with threatenings and curses against unbelievers; it is also the necessary consequence of a doctrine, which teaches that the sword is the sanctified means of conversion,—and which inculcates warfare against all unsubdued Kaffers of every shade of opinion; warfare, interrupted only by a longer or shorter armistice, as necessity may demand. In this sense Mohammed's assertion, — that "the infidels are all one people,"—must doubtless be understood; and hence believers are destined to convert them by force of arms; if this be impossible, to exterminate, or make them tributary. Mohammed and the first Kaliphs, as we have seen, occasionally pretended to recommend milder measures towards the Scripturalists, but in proportion as their followers became conscious of the gulph, which separates the Moslem from all others, and the more the two parties became entangled in mutual hostilities, the more decided became their animosity towards Christians, and consequently the more oppressive the yoke which they laid upon them. Christians were not unfrequently dealt with on the same principle as Pagans; their holding the doctrine of the Holy Trinity was alone sufficient to place them on a level with Polytheists,

[71] "Haß gegen die Bekenner anderer Religion ist zu allen Zeiten das Lebenselement des Islamismus gewesen, und darf man von dem Vergangenen auf das Zukünftige schließen, so möchte man behaupten, daß, wenn einmal dieser Haß abgestumpft sein wird, auch der Verfall des ganzen Systems unaufhaltsam hereinbrechen, oder daß duldsame Gesinnung gegen Andersgläubige und religiöse Indifferenz bei den Mohammedanern Hand in Hand gehen werden." Döllinger pag. 14.

for, so early as the beginning of the Moslem era, were they branded by Abu Sofian with that opprobrious terms.[72] Kaliph Motawakkel A. D. 850. added bitter mockery and indescribable tortures to their already heavy afflictions, and in the bloody persecutions of the Fatamite Hakem, many lost their lives. Even common intercourse was interdicted between Moslemin and Christians,[73] and a Moslem to this day, is not permitted either to eat with a Christian or to partake of the same meal.[74]

If we come to more recent times, we find the notorious Sultan of Mysore, *Tippo Sahib*, perpetrating acts of persecution for the sake of religion which appear the more hateful, for being accompanied by the most brutal lust. The majority of his subjects being Hindoos, his object was to convert the whole population of the Malabar provinces to the faith of the Koran; in this he was assisted by the Moplays, descendants of an Arab colony, who, falling like wild beasts upon the defenceless Hindoos forcibly circumcised many; others, robbed of their wives, children

---

[72] Julal-Addin Al Siuti, history of the temple of Jerusalem; translated by Reynolds. 1836. pag. 197. 240. Encouraging the Arabs before a battle against the Greeks, Abu Sofian says: "Vos quidem propugnatores Arabum estis, atque Islamismi adjuvatores; illi vero propugnatores Graecorum atque adjutores polytheismi sunt." Taberist. II. pag. 101.

[73] Mohammed Ebn Ishmael, the king of Granada, was assassinated A. D. 1333 by the Moors because he had eaten with Christians and wore a garment which he received from the king of Castilia. Conde, Geschichte der Herrschaft der Mauren in Spanien. III. pag. 134.

[74] The author speaks from his own experience. See also: Fraser, Narrative of a journey into Khorasan. 1825. pag. 182.

and property, were driven back to the jungles. Tippoo Sahib took away the daughters of the Brahmins and having dishonoured them sent them back to their parents, who refused to receive them since they had lost their cast. Tippoo then compelled the Brahmins themselves to marry these outcasts, by which *they* also losing their cast, were expelled from their community.[75] Can we be surprised that such fearful outrages, which acknowledged no other than the unconditional right of the stronger party, should, as opportunity occurred, produce the most bloody reactions? Hence it is, that the Kaffers north of Badshur, the neighbours of the Moslem *Afghans*, deem no action more meritorious than that of killing a Moslem. But few comparatively of the deeds of darkness, committed in India by the Moslem conquerors, have ever come to light, since the only account we have of their rule in that country, was written by themselves.[76] The only exception to this bloodthirsty and oppressive rule, was made by the Mongol emperor *Akbar*, who

---

[75] It will be remembered that the loss of cast is ten times worse to a Brahmin than the cruelest death. The cruelties of Tippoo Sahib are recorded by Buchanan, "Journey from Madras through Mysore and Malabar." 1807. I. pag 56. II. 550.

[76] Ferishta, History of the Mohammedan power in India, trans. by Briggs. 1829. As late as Sept. 1849 we had an instance of this fanaticism; 64 Moslemin entered a temple in a town near Calicut, murdered every devotee then present, and then shut the doors, expecting to be slain and sent to Paradise. A small detachment of Sepoys, sent against them, was repulsed and the commanding European officer killed; a European detachment next forced an entrance, and as the fanatics declined to submit, they were cut down, and in the belief of themselves and their brethren, they went straight to Paradise!

adopted a more peaceable policy. As "the shadow of God upon earth," he said, it became him to suffer other religions, after the example of Allah, else it would be his duty to destroy five sixths of his subjects. Lest we should however ascribe such clemency to *Islamism*, we are informed by his son, that his father had become an apostate, having been persuaded by his Vizier Abulfadhel, that Mohammed was no more than an Arab gifted with extraordinary eloquence, and that the Koran was an invention![77]

5. In examining the influence of Islamism upon the *social* and *domestic relations of life* we touch upon one of the darkest sides of that pernicious creed. It is perhaps not too much to say, that everywhere beyond the precincts of Christianity a special curse rests upon one half of mankind,—the female portion,—but that this is nowhere so conspicuous as under the domination of the Koran.[78] Its detailed legislation respecting women in general, is founded upon the erroneous idea, that they are an inferior grade of rational beings, whose sole destiny is to bring forth children and to serve their husbands. Hence the Koran places the entire body of the fair sex in a condition of perpetual imprisonment, and encourages the jealousy and suspicion of the men, at the expence of the freedom and dignity of the women.

---

[77] Memoirs of the emperor Jahangueir written by himself, translated by Price. 1829. pag. 54.

[78] "Hier begegnet uns eine der dunkelsten Seiten dieser Religion, und ein sprechender Beweis, welch einen verderblichen Einfluß die persönlichen Leidenschaften und die nationale Befangenheit eines selbsterkornen Religions= stifters fort und fort üben muß." Döllinger pag. 20.

To the husband is extended by the heaven-sent Koran, the right of inflicting corporeal punishment upon his wife, and unfaithfulness on her part is punished with death or the most degrading and painful chastisements. Islamism, in short, lowers matrimony beneath the standard of Roman Paganism. The wife, not being the companion of the life and partaker of the joys and sorrows of the husband, entertains for him feelings of fear, rather than of affection, and recognises in him only the lord who decides her fate just as his capricious mood may dictate.[79] However low the standard may be which Moslemin take of the matrimonial alliance, they nevertheless consider it the duty of every woman to live in the marriage estate; to lead a single or widowed life, before she has reached old age, is regarded as wilfully transgressing a divine law. But this also arises from the idea that women are incapable of self-control, and incompetent to maintain a moral position without due supervision and guardianship; it also implies the deplorable impotence of Islamism, which despairs of effectually disciplining the heart of a woman, and resigns the task of controlling her passions as one hopelessly beyond its power.[80]

[79] Perfectly consistent with this view the prophet never elevated the solemnization of matrimony to a religious rite, the Imam, Molla or Sheich being only present in his civil capacity, at the execution of the marriage contract. Chardin voyages en Perse, ed. de Langle's II. pag. 230. D'Ohsson l'Empire Othoman II. 362.

[80] Though women are not directly excluded from future happiness, yet it is a disputed point in the schools of Moslem divinity, whether they are to have a separate Paradise, with pleasures corresponding to that of the men. Döllinger pag. 21.

The religious education of the Moslem women is limited to their being drilled into a mechanical repetition of certain forms of prayer, in which the spirit of true devotion never breathes. The innate suspicion and utter want of confidence with which Moslemin regard their religious teachers, forbids their women obtaining the shadow of religious instruction from the Sheichs,—the legitimate fountains of authoritative teaching;[81] Moslemin indeed discourage their wives from strict adherence to their religious duties, lest they should fancy themselves on an equality with their husbands and kick against their authority.[82] Under such circumstances it is not to be wondered, that a total destitution of religious feeling should exist among the females of the Moslem community. An Arab writer alludes to an exception in the case of Rabia,[83] but this isolated case, such as it, only renders the general darkness of female ignorance and degradation the more perceptible.

6. *Polygamy* has been defended with considerable ingenuity by Moslem writers but as might naturally be expected, with little success. The Koran itself admits the difficulty, in expressing Mohammed's own experience in the matter: "Ye cannot carry yourselves

---

[81] Admission to the Mosques is only granted to the more aged females, and that only at times.

[82] Burkhardt's Travels in Arabia. 1829. II. pag. 196.

[83] She lived in the 2ᵈ century of the Hedgra, but the account given by Ebn Chalikan implies that the Koran rather damped than nourished her flame of devotion; she considered herself divinely punished by sickness for having contemplated the pleasures of Paradise, as she had learned them from the Koran! Tholuck's Blüthensammlung aus der Morgenländischen Mystik, pag. 31.

equally between women in all respects." Sur. IV. 3. It has proved a curse in the education of the children; the sons are separated from each other from their childhood, and initiated into the revengeful plots of their intriguing mothers.[84] Hence it happens, especially in royal harems, that brothers only recognise in each other dangerous rivals and threatening usurpers. In one Moslem dynasty only, viz. that of the Ottoman empire, have we an undisputed line of succession; but how dearly was it purchased! The crime of *fratricide* was duly legalised and raised to an imperial statute by Mohammed II[85] after he and his great grandfather Bajesid had given the precedent for the perpetration of this atrocious crime;[86] not only were brothers of the Sultan thus cleared out of the way but also uncles and nephews. The *Fetwa* or sanction of the Moslem divines, is given upon the authority of the Koran: "Disquietude is worse than murder." Thus the successor of that prophet, who condemned the exposure of new-born children as a Pagan abomination legally becomes the murderer of his brother, nephews and uncles! The Persian custom of the

[84] See the excellent remarks on Polygamy Möhler: Ueber das Verhältniß des Islams zum Evangelium. Gesammelte Schriften p. 399—402. The article was translated into English by Mr. Menge.

[85] The Historian Raima records the murder of 19 brothers of *Mohammed* III. with a calmness, which is truely characteristic: "In a tumult which arose on the occasion of the funeral of the Sultan, 19 brothers of the emperor, all *innocent* and guiltless, were strangled and added to the company of Martyrs." Annals of the Turkish Empire, translated by Fraser 1829. I. pag. 41.

[86] Mouradgea D'Ohsson III. pag. 315. Hammer's Geschichte des Osmanischen Reiches.

Sofi-dynasty, of blinding those princes not destined to succession, appears merciful, in comparison with this barbarity.[87] In addition to these pernicious and terrible consequences of Polygamy which, besides four lawful wives, permits an unlimited number of concubines, we need scarcely mention the glowing revenge and the hot-burning jealousies of the incarcerated inmates of the harems, which are transformed into nurseries of unnatural vices, assassinations and secret poisonings. These crimes are committed with the greater impunity, as these hidingplaces are closed to the surveillance of the organs of justice. Not in vain have Moslem historians remarked, that certain princes have understood the difficult task of keeping order and peace in the several departments of their respective harems. Thus it is stated in praise of the Spanish king Aben Alahmar, that his consummate skill succeeded in restoring and maintaining peaceful relations among his wives.[88]

It is one of the laws of divine providence that every offence against the natural order of things is sure to be revenged; that polygamy is recompensed in its prejudicial effects, no one will deny; but it remains yet to be shown, that the institution has no foundation in the natural or psychological organisation

[87] Chardin V. pag. 242. Malcolm's History of Persia. II. pag. 431. Fraser in his Journey into Khorasan pag. 204. records, that he found a young prince in his room with his eyes closed, groping about with his hands. Upon inquiring what he was doing, the prince replied, "I practise myself in being blind, for thou knowest, when my father dies, they will either kill us, or put out our eyes."

[88] Conde III. pag. 29. The late Mohammed Ali, Pasha of Egypt is said to have met with equal success. Michaud VII. pag. 92.

of either sex. It is in the first place, morally impossible for a man to treat each of his wives with the like affection and confidence; and before it can be assumed to be desirable for men to have more than one wife, it must be proved, that the female heart is of such an organisation, as will enable it cheerfully to divide the affection of one husband. This we know is impossible; nor dare we suppose that here *alone* was an oversight in the wise providence of God, which caused Him to create wants in the nature of man, which He did not alike create in the constitution of woman.[89] Matrimonial love surrenders itself entirely and requires a similar return; but this cannot exist under the baneful influence of Islamism; that the wife is here but a slave and a commodity is proved by the fact, that the poor man has only one wife, just as he may happen to possess but one camel or one tent, whilst the rich man may have many; if it can be proved that man's constitution demands a plurality of wives, it is then unjust to withhold it from the less wealthy of the community.[90]

7, Being considered as a piece of property, which the thief hides in a dark corner of the house and removes from society, the woman can be disposed of at any moment by her lord and husband. *Divorce*[91]

---

[89] Polygamy obviously destroys all spiritual affection in matrimony; the spiritual element which should predominate, — since a mere physical union is not one of a matrimonial character in the Scripture term and signification, — is utterly unknown to the Moslem believer.

[90] Journal Asiatique 1836. II. pag. 420. Möhler pag. 401.

[91] The prescribed words need only be pronounced to make it effectual. Hedaya I. pag. 201.

makes it easy for Mohammedans to change their wives at any time; they have moreover the powerful example of the prophet: who, to enable him to marry Zaids wife, with whom he had fallen in love, persuaded him to divorce her![92] That divorce is not so common among the better classes of society, is not to be ascribed to a deeper sense of the responsibility of such a step, but to the law which requires the husband to restore to the divorced woman her *dowry;* also to the husband's jealousy which makes the thought intolerable that his wife should be ever seen by another man.[93] Among the poorer classes, separation is of daily occurrence. As Seneca could say of the Roman ladies of his day that they counted the years no more after the Consuls, but after their husbands, so Mohammedans mark the events of their age by the number of their wives. A French traveller having asked an aged Egyptian, whether he remembered the campaign of Napoleon, he answered, that he had his *seventeenth wife* at that time![94] Even among the simple Beduins, the cooling down of the husband's affection is sufficient reason for a divorce.[95]

---

[92] Sur. XXXIII. 4—6. 37. 38. 39.

[93] The difficulty of restoring the dowry is avoided, by compelling the poor woman through harsh treatment to sue for divorce, as in this case, she can claim nothing. Qanoon-e-Islam: or the customs of the Moosulmans of India by Jaffure Shureef, translated by Herklots. 1832. pag. 146. Malcolm's Hist. of Persia II. p. 592.

[94] Michaud VII. pag. 84. He also relates that a man once rejected his wife, casting her out into the street, because the day before she gave birth to a daughter, instead of a son, as he had wished.

[95] An Arab 45 years of age was found to have had 50 wives in succession. Burkhardt's Notes on the Bedouins and Wahabys. 1839. pag. 64.

In the face of so deep and prevalent a corruption, which gnaws at the very roots of social life, dissolves all family ties, and poisons the most sacred relations, it cannot be deemed exaggerated to aver, that Islamism hypocritically presents only the external appearance, instead of the reality of truth. Thus, it glories in maintaining the fundamental doctrine of the Divine Unity, but in its denial of the Divine Trinity, possesses only the abstract form without the substance of the truth; it surrounds itself with the external show of conscientious devotion, but as its ritual is destitute of the living breath of true and fervent prayer, it can only represent the semblance of communion with God. It enjoins fasting and requires abstinence from certain meats and drinks, but in letting loose those appetites, which *most* require spiritual restraint, it affords only another instance of the pharisaical straining at a gnat and swallowing a camel. What, it may be asked, is the careful veiling and the complete separation from men, which the Koran imposes upon women, but a revolting caricature of purity; since the practical contempt for women and the sanctity of matrimony, together with the extraordinary facility of divorce, stand directly opposed to the preservation of female morality. Not satisfied with this looseness of the matrimonial tie, Mohammed, after the conquest of Mecca, introduced a kind of *temporary marriage*,[96] which consisted in hiring

---

[96] The *Mota* or Matu was repeatedly sanctioned by Mohammed; on some occasions, e. g. during the campaign to Cheibar it was interdicted. Weil's "Mohammed der Prophet", pag. 228.

a wife for any definite term, at the expiration of which, she might be dismissed without any formality. Omar is said to have abolished it, but Kalip Mamun was only prevented from again legalising it by the persuasion of Moslem divines.[97] It is condemned by the Sonnites, but is practised among the Persian Shiites to the present day.[98] The condition of morals among the men, who so degrade the position of woman, may easily be imagined. It would be an offence to European, not to say, Christian refinement, to drag to light those heathenish and unnatural vices which are perpetrated under the sanction of the religion of the Koran.[99] This doubtless has hitherto been one of the main causes of the general failure of Missionary enterprise among Mohammedans: for the Moslem is naturally averse to abandon a creed which makes such extraordinary concessions to his most depraved and viscious appetites.[1] It is true that Christianity met with equal opposition among Pagans

[97] Abulfeda Annales Muslemici II. p. 197.

[98] Malcolm's History of Persia, II. p. 591. A parallel case in Arabia. Burkhartd's Travels in Arabia II. p. 378.

[99] Whoever may desire information upon these dark subjects, will find it in the "Memoirs of Basber" p. 29. Mouradgea d'Ohsson III. p. 270. Michaud VII. 86. Fraser's Journey into Khorasan p. 519.

[1] "La secte est trop libertine et trop attrayante pour la quitter, c'est une peste de loi, qui s'est introduite par les armes et par la force, et qui va toujours avançant de même (1680) je ne vois guère d' autres moyans que ceux-là mêmes qui soient capables de commencer à l'ébranler et à la déraciner, si ce n'est donc qu'il survienne de ces grands et extraordinaires coups du ciel, et que Dieu, par cette toute-puissante et toute particulière providence n'y mette la main." Demier, Voyages Amsterd. 1699. II. p. 86.

at the commencement of our era; but Paganism was not supported in its vices by a religious *system* like that of Islamism, the shaking and uprooting of which, will finally constitute one of the noblest triumphs of the Gospel of Christ.

8. To a somewhat more favourable result leads the examination of the domestic and national institution of *slavery*, as it exists among the Moslem community. The legislation of the Koran is on the whole, less cruel and degrading respecting slaves than it is concerning women. Although the female slaves who enrich the harem, share, as a matter of necessity, the degradation of the entire sex, yet Mohammed inculcates the mild treatment of slaves in general,[2] and to give them their liberty is deemed by him a meritorious work; Sura xxiv. 33. A female slave is not to be separated from her child, and if it be the child of the master, she is to be free at his death.[3] As the power of the Saracens became extended, and the number of slaves were multiplied, their lot consequently became more embittered, and the Moslem divines declared the murder of a slave to be a legal act.[4] As acts of opposition are generally revenged by rebellion and bloodshed, so it was in this case; the Zengi slaves at Bussora rose A.D. 868 against their masters, and acknowledging Ali, the Fatamite, as their ruler, a revolution followed which is stated to have cost 100,000 human lives, and could only be suppressed after nine

---

[2] Mathews' Translation of the Mishcat-ul-Masabih II. p. 139—141, 601.

[3] Hedaya I. 479.   [4] Hedaya II. 414.

years of bloodshed.[5] A notorious enemy of the Syrian Christians, Imad-ed-Deen, was likewise murdered in 1145 by a rebellious host of slaves, and not seldom it happened that fugitive slaves fought bloody battles at the head of an army of insurgents. But when rulers surrounded their persons with hosts of slaves, upon whose protection they mainly depended for personal safety, and began to entrust them with some of the most important offices of state, these slaves ultimately became lords of their masters, and the result was, that in Egypt, the unheard-of institution of a *Dulocratical Government* came to be established. The Circassian slaves were first introduced into Egypt by Sultan *Almansor Kelaun*, and they were soon powerful enough to possess themselves for 128 years of the government of the land, and to place thirty-two princes of the Circassian dynasty of Mamelukes on the throne.[6]

9. It is part of the character of Islamism, as a politico-religious system of faith, to put forth the

---

[5] Price's Mohammedan History II. pag. 162.

[6] Edebali, the Vizier of Urchan, proposed the horrible plan of forming the *Jeni Tjerry*, Janissaries or the "*New Army*", of Christian *children;* and for nearly 500 years, boys, all born Christians, were enlisted into a body of at first 12,000, at last 40,000 strong, torn away, year by year from their parents, circumcised, trained, corrupted to the faith and morals of their masters; thus producing a threefold apostacy from parents, religion and native country in at least *half a million* of instances. On the place where both the Nicomedian and Caesarian Eusebius were once forced to abjure their errors and to subscribe to the Nicene creed, there, these Christian youths were compelled to abjure their faith, and the walls of the Church of the holy Synod were written over with the Moslem creed! Hammer's Geschichte des Osmanischen Reiches.

most extravagant and illimitable claims. As successors of the Imams, the government of the universe belonged to the kings of Persia, and the like pretensions lie dormant in the Sultan of Turkey, as the alleged successor of the ancient Kaliphate. Ever since Selim I. was acknowledged by the Meccan sherifs, titular Kaliph of Cairo, as the successor of the last Abasside, the Sultan of Constantinople has been acknowledged as the spiritual head of the Sonnite section of the Mohammedans; and all Moslem princes with their dependencies consider themselves only members of the Osmanic Autocrat; even the Emperor of Morocco acknowledges the spiritual supremacy of the Sultan.[7]

According to the claims of the Kaliphate as a political and spiritual supremacy, no other than a Moslem ruler can demand obedience from Mohammedans; a point which statesmen at the present day would do well to bear in mind, in dealing with the refractory Mohammedans of India. The precept that the subject is bound to pay homage to "the powers that be," is not to be found in the Koran; Mohammed, never imagining that the true believers could ever fall under the dominion of any foreign power, made no provision for such an event; and so long as breath remains in the body of the Moslem community, they

---

[7] "Daraus entsprangen die Schwierigkeiten, welche die Forderung Rußlands bei den Friedensverhandlungen des Jahres 1772, daß die Unabhängigkeit der Tartaren von Seiten der Pforte anerkannt werden solle, erregte; die Türkischen Bevollmächtigten erklärten, daß der Sultan als Kaliphe der geistliche Oberherr aller Sonnis, also auch der Tartaren sei, daß der Tartaren Chan daher die Investitur durch den Sultan bedürfe, und daß dieser seine höchste Gewalt über Indien, Bothara und Marokko nur wegen der zu großen Entfernung nicht ausübe." Döllinger pag. 36.

will never, except from dire necessity, submit to any other than Moslem rule and government. They can only feel allegiance to be due, where they conceive Allah demands it from them; that is to say, only towards the government which derives its power, in some way or other, from the prophet himself, and this power, of course, could be delegated to no other than a Moslem sovereign. The rulers of Persia, if Shiites, or the Sultans of Constantinople, if Sonnites, can alone claim their obedience, for in them, they recognise the legitimate heads of the Shiite or Sonnite Mohammedans, both in a spiritual and political point of view.[8]

As the right of government belongs only to a Moslem representative and successor of Mohammed, — who is "the shadow of God upon earth" — the Mohammedans of India, being accidentally placed under a Christian power, feel themselves bound to consider it only as usurped for a time, and that they are in duty authorised to take the first favourable opportunity of shaking it off, and of transferring their allegiance, to a Moslem ruler. The Moslem divines of India, at one time, were prepared to consider that resistance to the Government of the East-India Company should be dealt with as a crime;[9] but their readiness to sup-

---

[8] As long therefore as Mohammedans remain, such it is not wise or prudent to trust to any loyal expressions, which they may utter when they feel *compelled* to submit to another, than that which they consider their divinely appointed government. Rebellion is not only a dominant natural instinct in Moslemin, but with them, it is *religion and a matter of conscience* to throw off a foreign yoke, at the very first opportunity.

[9] See Edinburgh Review L. pag. 473.

port the pretensions of the king of Delhi, in recent times, has proved their hypocrisy.[10] As the confession of Islamism is the indispensible prerequisite to legitimatize a government, a Christian power ruling over a Mohammedan community, can only be looked upon as an insufferable anomaly.

When Ferdinand of Spain expelled the Moors from his dominion, the measure was not merely prompted by a blind religious fanaticism, as has been thought by some, but was dictated by a deep-sighted policy.[11] The Spanish Mohammedans from the beginning were always well-armed and ready for action; and after their subjugation cast longing eyes towards their African brethren, with whom they sustained a secret intercourse; so long therefore as they remained, a threatening thunder-cloud hung over the Peninsula; since, the first landing of a Moslem army on its shores would have brought every Moslem under arms.[12]

[10] With wonderful precision Döllinger predicted this event as far back as 1838. "Zwar sind die Gesetzesgelehrten in Hindostan sehr bereitwillig, den Moslemischen Begriff strafbarer Empörung auf jeden Widerstand gegen die Herrschaft der Ost. Compagnie anzuwenden; aber dieselben würden, wenn man von dem Verfahren ihrer Collegen im Türkischen Reiche eventuell auf das ihrige schließen darf, bei der ersten günstigen Aussicht die Ansprüche eines Moslemischen Prätendenten mit Freuden durch ihre Fetwas unterstützen." Döllinger pag. 36. note 64.

[11] The Moors were expelled from Spain and driven back to Africa in the 15th century.

[12] Hence the Moslem rulers treated Christian princes simply as usurpers, who, as infidels, could not receive their power from God, or act as his vice-regents upon earth. Hence also the Arab word, Targhi, rebel-chief, *usurpator*, which the Moslemin already applied to the Byzantine Emperors; and after them to other Christian sovereigns. Louis XVI. caused a complaint to be lodged at the court of Morocco, requiring the Emperor to apply the title of Sultan to the kings of France; the reply was: "None knew who

Moslemin and Christians can never be fused into one political body; the former must ever remain a clog in the machinery of a commonwealth, owing to their singular pretensions and their peculiarly obstinate views and customs, which, from their heterogeneous character, resist every process of assimilation: on the other hand, Christians must ever remain strangers or passive members in a religious polity, which is administered upon the principles of the Koran. This has long since been exemplified in the Turkish Empire.

10. The absolutely *despotic form* of Moslem government has been sometimes considered as the general type of Asiatic rule, but erroneously so, as is evident from the fact of the sovereign power being limited in the non-Moslemite states of Asia. No Hindoo monarch e. g. could interfere with the immunities of the Brahmins or with the institution of caste. The Emperor of China, although the son of heaven, and approached by his subjects with profound reverence, yet can only fill up the offices of the state from a list of candidates which is prepared for him by a learned body of his subjects. Different is it with "the princes of the faithful;" here, the union of the civil and spiritual power, and a military rule, founded

should deserve this title in the life to come; those whom God would crown in paradise, were the true Sultans, and not those who were to be cast into hell-fire; the court could therefore never give that title to the monarchs of France; yea it would rather give it up, and though Turkey had given that title, it was done only by the Vizier, for the Sultan could never have sanctioned it." Sacy Chrestomathie Arabe III. pag. 318. Agrell's Reise nach Marokko. 1790. pag. 282.

upon the prestige of conquest, produce the most unqualified form of a despotic government. In Persia, the *military*, and in Turkey, the *theocratical* element of the Kaliphate predominate; hence we have less brutal tyranny, less convulsions of dynastic changes in the latter, than in the former.[13] To show that the despotic rule of the Sultan originates in the religion of which he is the head, we may add, that his acts of tyranny are all looked upon as proceeding from a kind of divine inspiration, which none ventures to question. The Moslem divines assert that the Sultan may kill fourteen people every day without owing an explanation to any one. The official holiness of his person is in nowise destroyed by any vicious deeds, he may commit as a private individual.[14]

The Sultan who is generally styled by his mother, "my Lion," or "my Tiger," is chiefly dreaded by those who are in his immediate presence. The higher the dignity and the greater the confidence, the greater has always been the danger; this is proved by the history of the ministers of the Porte. From 1370 to 1789, 168 of these dignitaries have occupied the highest post in the realm; few of them have retained it so long as two years, and many have died by the hand of the executioner. Soleiman caused most of

---

[13] The Persian proverb, "the presence of the Shah is a consuming fire"; and the Turkish titles of the Sultan, "the shedder of blood", "the murderer" *Chunkar* or *Kan-Idishi*, mark the character of both Governments. Chardin V. 220. Thornton's present state of Turkey 1809. I. 112.

[14] The same may be said of the Sultan of Morocco: "Alles hängt von seiner Willkür ab, er macht die Gesetze, ändert, zerstört sie, stellt sie wieder her, und wechselt damit gemäß seiner Laune, Convenienz oder seinem Interesse.

his prime ministers to be executed one after the other; but an instinctive obedience and inclination to submit to what is deemed the heaven-ordained power, so strongly influence the Moslem, that he considers any barbarity tolerable, and the most perverted deeds wise and natural; even to die by the hand of the Sultan or at his command, has been looked upon as a sure pledge of eternal salvation, and a martyrdom worthy to be desired.[15]

11. The question arises, whether amidst such tyrannical oppression, these despotic princes ever attempted to alter the religion of the country. The history of Islamism replies in the negative. There are but few instances in which Mohammedan princes have ventured to make any alterations in their creed; for they well knew, that were they to attempt such a thing, they would cease to be the organ of the Godhead in the eyes of the people, and the foundation of their own power and security would be fatally undermined.[16] The creed in question, had rooted too deeply in the hearts and lives of the people for any prince ever to succeed in accomplishing the task. The Mos-

---

Es gibt weder ein Corps der Ulema's, noch einen mit vom Herrscher unabhängiger Gewalt bekleideten Mufti, weder Divan noch Collegien und ministerielle Departements; Alles geschieht nach dem alleinigen Gebot des Herrschers." Graberg von Hemso's Kaiserthum, Morokko 1833, pag. 138.

[15] Döllinger pag. 39.

[16] The king of Delhi, Allah-Uddin-Chilshi 1830 conceived the idea, but was dissuaded from carrying it out. Ferishta 1. pag. 339. The Emperor Akbar under the title of خليفة الله, Vice-regent of God, attempted to originate a new form of Deism, but with his death it fell to the ground. Vans Kennedy's account in the Transactions of the Liter. Society of Bombay Vol. II. 1820.

lem seldom cares to fight for his native country, his home or liberty, but should his *religion* be endangered, he zealously takes his stand beneath the banner of the crescent. For the last 300 years, the defence and spread of the Shiite principles was the pretext for every battle which was fought by the Persians.[17]

More fortunate were Moslem monarchs as reformers of abuses, suppressors of heresies, defenders of orthodox doctrines and revivers of religious zeal; and so long as the head of the nation was satisfied, the subjects considered all to be right. "The power of religion is too weak without the authority," said Akhun Dervezeh, and he explained his failure in bringing back the sect of the Rosheniah to the orthodox faith, by the fact of there having been no monarch at hand to strike off the heads of the heretics.[18] This, indeed, was the usual method of settling disputes and suppressing abuses. Mir Zaid Sherif gave it as his opinion, and he was considered the prince of doctors, that Timur had been called by Allah to destroy infidels and heretics; which he did by saturating the earth with the blood of nations, and by causing the inhabitants of Damascus to be cut to pieces, in order to revenge the death of Ali, 800 years after the murder was committed.[19]

12. That the cause of Islamism should have been

[17] Malcolm's History of Persia II. pag. 339.

[18] Leyden's Memoir on the Rosheniah sect, Asiat. Researches Vol. XI. pag. 386.

[19] Instituts politiques et militaires de Tamerlan, proprement appellé Timour, écrits par lui-même et traduits par Langlès 1887. pag. 17. 120.

supported by such fearful destruction and bloodshed, is to be traced, not so much to the personal character of its protectors and reformers, as to the *nature* of Islamism itself, which teaches that religion is a system of compulsion, and maintains that it is the duty of God's vice-gerents upon earth, to punish transgression as a civil offence by physical power.[20] Offences against the precepts of the Koran, such as the ordinance of fasting or the prohibition of wine, are therefore, invariably punished with pecuniary fines or corporeal chastisements. Ebn Butata relates, with peculiar satisfaction, that in each Mosque in China, a whip was hanging, for the spiritual benefit of those who were not at their places during prayers, the castigation being performed by the presiding Imam.[21] Burnes found the same practice prevailing in Bokhara, where he saw persons publicly scourged because they had slept during prayer, or smoked on a Friday.[22] In times of extreme severity, an order of spies was regularly formed, who penetrated private families in order to betray the secrets of domestic life.[23] As the legislation of the Koran and the Sonna extend over private and public life, it is considered the duty of the organs

---

[20] Döllinger pag. 47 says: "Diese Religion ist nämlich ihrer Anlage nach eine polizeiliche Zwangsanstalt, ein strenges, mit einem Zaun von Pönalsanctionen umgebenes Gesetz, und die Pflicht der Stellvertreter Gottes auf Erden ist es, die Uebertretungen zu strafen."

[21] Travels of Ebn Butata (1325) translated by Lee 1829.

[22] Burne's Travels in Bokhara 1834. I. pag. 313.

[23] Kaliph Omar sanctioned this odious practice by his example, but Dhaher Billah, after it had risen to a scandelous pitch under his father, suppressed it. Price's Mohammedan History II. 211.

of its administration to inspect both departments and to punish offences in each.

It cannot therefore surprise us to learn, that the Fatamite, Moeslidin-Allah, who was by no means one of the most blood-thirsty and cruel, caused every person who was seen in the streets of his capital after the last evening prayer, to be beheaded.[24] This compulsory system of religious police attained its greatest height under *Hakem Biamar-Allah* from 996 to 1021; he prohibited the cultivation of certain plants, because they were favourites with the opponents of Ali, and the brewing and selling of beer, because Ali disliked it; dogs and swine were destroyed as impure animals, and the fishing and selling of eels was visited with capital punishment; people with whom were found resins, honey, or dates were executed, because these products were used for the preparation of spirituous liquors; chess was interdicted; women were no more allowed to look out of their windows nor to go into the streets, and shoemakers were forbidden to supply them with shoes.[25] This man, who committed innumerable cruelties against the Sonnites, Jews and Christians, and treated his subjects with such consummate tyranny, is still worshipped by a numerous sect, as an incarnation of the Deity! Religious zeal has rarely been carried to such an extreme, but the pseudo-theocratical principle, which points out the

[24] Quatremère, Vie du Khalife Moëzz Journal Asiatique 1837. pag. 44. He resided at Kairowan A. D. 959.

[25] The consequence of these prohibitions was, that many died from starvation in their houses. Sylv. de Sacy, vie du Khalife Hakem Biamar-Allah. Exposé de la religion des Druzes 1838. Tom. I.

despotic ruler as the person "to whom vengeance belongeth," could not fail to lead to tyrannical oppression.

13. This leads to the low estimation of human life, and that lust of abusing and mutilating the human body, of which the history of Islamism furnishes such numerous and unparalleled instances.[26] The Koran is not responsible for *all* the atrocious crimes committed in its name, but it is powerless to check or control the terrible satisfaction which its followers feel, not only in executions *en masse*, but especially in inflicting the most ingenious and unheard-of tortures. It cannot be said that the Koran directly advocates a cruel legislation; yet we must look for the cause of the inhuman atrocities committed by its followers, partly in the licentious excesses which it sanctions and which are generally accompanied with cruelty, and partly in its teaching that war and destruction are the legitimate means of propagating the faith. The Koran thus directly excites and sanctifies the worst passions of human nature. Weapons at first used against infidels, were soon turned against each other, and never perhaps were cruelties more fully revenged on the perpetrators, than when the Moslem parties executed vengeance upon each other.[27]

[26] Christianity in holding that the body is the temple of the Holy Spirit, protests, not indeed against capital punishment when lawful, but against any profanation of it by wanton and cruel mutilations: whenever these have been perpetrated, it was against the spirit of the Gospel.

[27] The reader will remember that more of the friends and companions of the prophet fell by the hand of co-religionists than by that of the enemy. In the battle between Ali and Moviah 70,000

In addition to the terrible struggle which ensued when the Omayades usurped the Kaliphate, we may refer to the equally cruel strife when they were defeated, and the Abassides, as the legitimate line of succession, resumed the power.[28]

Not less ferocious was the subsequent struggle between the Shiites and the ruling Kaliphs: in order to revenge the death of Hossein, Mochtar executes 48,000 Moslemin, and the great Sonnite Hadshadsha sacrifices in return 120,000 Shiites, leaving 30,000 men and 20,000 women in prison when he died. Another tyrant, who seeks for the Kaliphate, massacres 17,000 innocent inhabitants in Chorasan, only as a measure of precaution lest they might go over to Abu Moslem. What a revenge upon the doctrine of the Koran, that all true believers are brothers! If it be objected that this seed of Cain has been also at work among Christians, we may add, that wherever this was the case, they had rejected the precepts and denied the character of their Master. Moslem monarchs have not hesitated, in their dying moments, to give orders for unjust executions and even for putting their nearest relatives to death.[29] The Christian custom of granting condemned persons time and opportunity for repentance and preparation for death,

---

Moslemin fell. Quatremère, Memoires sur la dynastie des Khalifes Abassides, Journal Asiatique XVI. pag. 301.

[28] Price's Mohammedan Hist. I. pag. 571. II. 12.

[29] As soon as Mohammed VII, king of Granada, was sure of his death he wrote, "Alcayde of Xalubonia, thou my servant, on receiving this letter, kill my brother Zeid Jusef and send his head by the bearer." Conde III. 187.

is of course unknown among Mohammedans. Had such a humane law existed, many a life might have been spared, as time would have thus been given for the cooling down of the wrath of the despot, who had ordered the execution.[30]

14. The dogma of *predestination,* or rather fatalism, as taught in the Koran, produces a feeling of apathy and indifference on the part of the people which tends greatly to strengthen Moslem despotism. Mohammedan divines have indeed sought to modify the dogma by limiting it to religious matters, but the people indifferent to these metaphysical distinctions, have ever believed, that the minutest incidents of human life are pre-ordained and unalterably fixed by a Divine decree, and that no effort on the part of man can possibly alter or avert that which is written in the book of decrees;[31] nor can it be overlooked, that this belief, allied as it was with religious enthusiasm and warlike fanaticism, rendered most essential service to Islamism in its rise. As a moral opiate it served a variety of purposes, by calming the mind in disappointment, stimulating it to exertion in difficulties or presenting an excuse for incompetence and apathy. When Kaliph Hasham contemplated taking

[30] "The English Governors, said the ex-king of Ceylon, have an advantage over the kings of Candy; they are surrounded by counsellors who do not permit them to do anything in the heat of passion; and this is the cause why ye have so few capital punishments; unfortunately however for us the offending person is already dead before our anger is cooled down." Events, in the Island of Ceylon, written by a gentleman on the spot. 1815. pag. 31.

[31] So it is written إن مقتوب, the Moslem says on every occasion. Chardin III. p. 406.

measures against the Abassides, who sought for the Kaliphate, he was dissuaded by being told, that if it was decreed that the Abassides should recover the Kaliphate, all his efforts would avail nothing, and if it was not decreed, he need not resist their efforts to obtain it.[32] When a general sustains a defeat, he consoles himself by the reflection that such was his unavoidable fate written in Allah's book of decrees.[33] As evil, as well as good is pre-ordained, the dogma produces a most listless apathy in resisting temptation; nor need we enlarge on its prejudicial effects in times of calamity; when active measures might arrest an evil, all efforts are paralysed, and every vicissitude of life is borne with a morbid resignation. This doctrine has undoubtedly proved one of the most effective causes of the deep moral and political decay of the Moslem community.

Closely connected with the Moslem view of predestination is the eagerness with which Mohammedans pursue the baneful art of reading the fate of man in the stars. Astrology has become to them one of the most necessary and *practical* sciences of life. As the heavenly bodies are said to indicate the otherwise hidden decrees of Allah, the influence of this spurious science upon the acts of individuals has been immeasurably great. The mightiest monarchs made their greatest enterprizes dependent upon the predictions of astrologers: generals, governors and even relatives were suddenly murdered because it was read

---

[32] Quatremère, Journal Asiatique XVI. 331.
[33] Quatremère, Journal Asiatique 1837. p. 72.

in the heavens, that they meditated rebellion; and rebels again succeeded in dethroning a despot and in raising a creature of their own to the throne, because it was ascertained that the stars were favourable.[34] Each day and hour being placed under the favourable or unfavourable influences of the constellations, every undertaking, from the waging of a battle to the putting on of a new suit of clothes, requires the happy moment to be astrologically determined.[35]

15. Although heterodox teaching was in most cases summarily suppressed, by sending heretics to the rack and thence to the place of execution,[36] yet there was perhaps no religion more distracted by sects and heresies than Islamism; and as they afford a deeper insight into the character and influence of this creed, they may fitly be noticed in this chapter. The prediction of Mohammed that the world would

[34] Kaliph Moëss shut himself up in a subterraneous vault, which was constructed for that purpose, for a whole year, because the astrologers predicted, that only by so doing, he could escape a fearful calamity. Quatremère, Journal Asiatique 1837. p. 207.

[35] Bernier I. pag. 113. says respecting their decisions: "ce qui est une gêne incroyable, et une coûtume qui traîne avec soi des conséquences si importantes, que je ne sais comment elle peut subsister si long tems. Car enfin il faut que l'Astrologue ait connaisance de tout ce qui s'entreprend depuis les plus grandes affaires jusqu'aux plus petites." See also Malcolm II. 576.

[36] Such measures were already sanctioned by the example of Kaliph Omar; when a man was brought before him, who doubted the divinity of the Koran, he cut him completely in two, and thus earned the honourable cognomen of "*decider*". See other instances Abulfeda Annales II. 51. 641. Hammer, Geschichte des Osman. Reiches I. 499. 663. Herbelot p. 397. d'Ohsson. I. 156—159. Price's Moham. Hist. II. 464. Chronique d'Abou Djafar Tabari, traduite par L. Dubeux 1836. I. 255.

not come to an end, until one of his family and name should appear upon earth to assert his divine mission, and perfect the conversion of mankind to Islamism, was so direct an invitation to imposture, that even in his life-time, no less than three pretenders arose in Arabia. In a few years after his death, eight others sprang up, giving rise to endless schisms, sects and heresies. We will not recur to Mohammed's prediction, that his followers should be divided into seventy-three sects,[37] for its falsity is proved by the Moslem doctors themselves who so long ago filled up that number that they ceased to count them. Remarkable however as it might seem, that a creed without mysteries which may fairly be *inscribed on the nail of a finger*, should produce any dissent, yet in the fourth century of the Hedgra, there were no large towns or provinces, where hosts of sectaries were not found.[38]

At this rapid increase of heresy we may perhaps be the less surprised, if we consider that Islamism itself is but an arch-heresy; and it may be added that some of the sectarian offshoots of the creed in question, approximated nearer to Christianity. Christian heresies generally differ from the orthodox creed touching the mysteries of Redemption, the Incarnation of the Son of God, the dogma of the Holy Trinity, and the means of grace; but Islamism, being ignorant

---

[37] Sharestani speaks of 71 Jewish, 72 Christian, and 73 Moslem sects. One alone of the latter is said to attain salvation. Pocock Spec. hist. Arabum, pag. 213.

[38] Sacy, Exposé de la religion des Druses, Introd. pag. 25.

of anything higher than their prophet and his successors, could yield no other pretext for dissent than the question, who was the legitimate head of religion and the state. The rejection of the *God-man* Jesus Christ, has been justly pointed out, as the reason, why most of the Moslem sects thrust themselves, we might almost say *instinctively*, on some precarious substitute, veneration for whom, absorbs their religious feeling, and from whom they expect their salvation.[39] We can only explain this fact from the instinctive longing of the human heart after an approachable mediator between God and man, which, Islamism, in denying the incarnation of the Son of God, leaves unsatisfied. The principal cause for faction in the Moslem camp was connected with the Kaliphate, which was intended to unite the body of the believers. From the very earliest period questions arose as to whether Abubeker, Omar and Othman were legally chosen, or whether they were to be considered intruders and usurpers; whether Ali, as the relation and son-in-law of Mohammed, was the legitimate heir and successor; whether the Ommayades, or the Abassides—who successively assumed the power of the Kaliphate after the murder of Ali—were to be acknowledged; and

---

[39] "Das tiefe, durch den Islam unbefriedigt gelassene Bedürfniß des menschlichen Geistes, sich der Gottheit durch einen göttlich-menschlichen Mittler zu nahen, mußte jene Lehren und Sekten hervorrufen, nach denen eine Inwohnung der Gottheit in einzelnen Lehrern und Häuptern der Religion stattfindet... Ueberhaupt aber erkennt man in dem Mangel des Glaubens an den Gottmenschen den Grund, warum die Moslemischen Sekten großentheils fast instinktmäßig sich an einzelne Menschen anklammerten, deren Verehrung all ihr religiöses Gefühl absorbirte, und von denen sie ihr Heil erwarteten." Döllinger pag. 85.

whether the twelve Imams who succeeded Ali were the lawful and only successors. To these, other points of dispute were added, such as, whether the Kaliphate was at all hereditary and confined to one family, or whether the choice of a successor was not left to the faithful at large; whether only one Imam could reign at a time, or whether two might not reign at the same period;[40] whether in times of division there was a true Kaliph at all, or whether only he could be considered such, who was universally acknowledged.[41] Several sects insisted upon the sinless nature of the Kaliphs, and consequently upon their infallibility. Allah was thought to have united himself with Ali and his successors, or as the Hatibis understood it, the spirit of Allah became incarnate in the successors of the prophet. The different sects of the Rafedhis believed, that the Kaliphate was only reserved to a few chosen individuals; whilst their fierce opponents, the *Karedshis*, held it lawful to take up arms against any Kaliph who committed sin;[42] and these again were opposed by the *Kamelis*, who taught that Ali himself became an unbeliever, when he declined to fight out his rights with the sword. The *Mohakkims*, a branch of the latter sect, rejected Ali, because at Safein, he placed the decision as to the right of succession in the hands of the Harawris,

---

[40] The first opinion held, الهشامية, the Hashemis; السليمانية, the Soleimanis, الديروبية, or the Djaboris, the latter that of the followers of Hamssa, الحكمية. Ishmael Shachinshah apud Abrah. Echellensis Eutychius vindicatus. Rom. 1661. II. pag. 384 etc.

[41] Sacy Exposé introd. pag. 41.   [42] Makrissi apud Sacy p. 13.

who neither acknowledged Ali nor Moviah;[43] and the Shebibis, who admitted that even a woman was not excluded from exercising the functions of a Kaliph.[44] The *Ali-Illahis*, a sect which exists to this day in Persia, Arabia and Hindostan, receive the widely spread notion, that Allah united himself with the several Imams; only with this difference, that Adam was the first and Ali the last of these incarnations of the godhead. Ali is worshipped as such, his seat is supposed to be that of the sun, and the Koran, as it now stands, is considered to be the forgery of the first three Kaliphs.[45] That Ali-Allah or Ali-Murteza ranks above Mohammed can be easily inferred from this; and indeed, it is taught by this sect, that Allah assumed the form of Ali, on perceiving the incompetency and the defects of Mohammed as a prophet.[46] The Garabis, in the same spirit maintained, that the angel Gabriel was sent to Ali, but being misled by a great family-likeness, turned to Mohammed by mistake;[47] whilst the Halbanis and Dhemmis openly declare, that Mohammed usurped the prophetical office, which by right belonged to Ali. Others were more liberal and ascribed a divine character to Mohammed, Ali and Fatima, and their two sons Hasan and Hossein.[48]

[43] Quatremère, Nouv. Journ. Asiatique, IX. p. 400.

[44] Hazala, the mother of the author of this sect acted as Kaliph, in the Mosque at Kufa. Döllinger pag. 86.

[45] So the Dabistan apud Colebrooke on the origin and peculiar tenets of certain Mohammedan sects. Asiat. Researches VII. p. 338.

[46] Fraser's Journey into Khorassan pag. 286.

[47] Abulfeda II. 758.

[48] Ishmael Shachinshah apud Abrah. Eschellens. pag. 432.

16. One of the most fertile causes of various sects among the *Shiite* section, was doubtless the uncertainty as to the real successor of Ali; for at one time it was this, at another, that member of his family; and sometimes a stranger was fixed upon as Imam. The *Kissanis* at a very early period fastened their veneration upon Mohammed Ebn Hanefieh, one of the sons of Ali, but not by Fatima.[49] The *Baslemis* looked upon Abu-Selma as Kaliph; and Hakem Ebn Hashem or Mokana, the *veiled prophet* with the golden mask, who lived at Moravalnahar and Khorassan A. D. 779—many of whose followers are still found in the provinces of the Oxus — maintained, that the divine spirit of the assassinated Abu-Selma had descended upon him.[50] The *Bajanis* offered divine honours to their master, Bajan, who was supposed to have inherited the Kaliphate from Ali. The prophecy of Mohammed, according to which, the true guide or *Mahdi*, should come after a period of trouble and oppression to rear up a kingdom of peace and happiness, was naturally one of the most productive sources of heresy.[51] The Shiites transfer the idea of the Mahdi to the last of the twelve Imams, the young Abul-Kasem Mohammed, who disappeared A. D. 879. in the twelfth year of his age; they believe that he is now concealed in some secret place, and will reappear on some great emergency, to resume the spiritual

---

[49] Quatremère, Nouv. Journ. Asiat. X. 41.

[50] Abulfeda II. 47. Price II. 25. Sacy Exposé pag. 61.

[51] He is only to live 8 or 9 years among the faithful. Siuti, History of the temple of Jerusalem pag. 296.

and temporal power of the Moslem community.[52] The kings of the Sofi-dynasty with reference to him, bore the title: "servant of the king of the land." Ebn Batuta found a mosque at Hilla in Mesopotamia, the entrance of which was veiled with a silk curtain, and the building called the mosque of "the Lord of ages." The inhabitants appeared day by day before the gate in full armour with a saddled horse, calling for the Mahdi, and imploring his appearance to suppress tyranny and to separate truth from error.[53] We can easily conceive that where such fervent expectation existed, it could be no difficult task for any descendant of Ali to claim the dignity of the promised Mahdi.

17. The doctrine of the *divine attributes* being a point which comes next in importance to that of the succession, we should naturally expect that a diversity of views and opinions would spring up, wherever an interest in metaphysical questions happened to be excited. The schools of Moslem Theology have ever been distracted by religious controversies but particularly since the second century. In its earliest period, Islamism needed no other weapon than the sword; but when Kaliph Mamun caused the writings of the Grecian philosophers to be translated into Arabic, a leaven was introduced which, according to Makriss, produced incalculable mischief. The contradictions in the teaching of the Koran became now

---

[52] At Ispahan two saddled horses were always kept in readiness, one for the *Imam Mahdi*, the other for his vice-regent, Jesus. Chardin VII. 456. IX. 144. Pfander's Remarks. pag. 6.

[53] Ibn-Batuta's Travels pag. 109.

more and more apparent, sects arose in multitudes, and each fled to the newly acquired armoury of Grecian philosophy, appropriating such definitions and reasonings as best suited their particular views and tastes.[54] The orthodox Moslem divines being alarmed at such an influx of heretical teaching, resolved to use the poison itself as an antidote. Hence the memorable resolution of a theological assembly at Bossura: "Religion is so defiled and mixed with error, that only by the aid of the Grecian philosophy can it be purified."[55]

It will not be out of place to notice the difference between Islamism and Christianity under the pressure of Heathen Philosophy. Islamism, more than any other creed, was destitute of those elements which could be amalgamated with the speculations of classic antiquity; it was therefore rather for the benefit of the heretical sects that they were introduced. The most celebrated men among the orthodox party, who attempted to introduce these elements of Grecian philosophy into the body of Moslem divinity, openly avowed that their religious views had nothing in common with that of the masses;[56] hence, they were

[54] "Alors se produisirent au grand jour différentes sectes, telles que les Kadris, les Djahmis, les Motazales, les Kéramis, les Kharédjis, les Rafedhis, les Karmates, les Baténis, et la terre fut remplie. Il n'y eut aucune de ces sectes, dont les partisans n'étudiassent la philosophie, et n'embrassassent parmi les doctrines des différentes sectes de philosophes celle, qui leur agréait davantage." Makrissi apud Sacy cap. I. p. 25.

[55] Greg. Abul-Pharaji historia Dynastiarum Oxon. 1663. p. 218.

[56] This was done by Al Gazal, the author of a philosophical Romance. Tholuck comment. de vi, quam Graeca philosophia in theologiam Muhammed. exercuerit. 1835. p. 15.

suspected of heterodoxy.[57] Christianity on the contrary, has always possessed sufficient power to admit a free and honest inquiry into its teaching on the one hand, and on the other it has never lacked strength to repel the infusion of heterogeneous elements into its system. It preserved its distinctive doctrines for instance, in the third and fourth century against the Platonic errors of Origen, and when the philosophy of Aristoteles assayed to strike up an alliance with Christianity in the thirteenth century, it was confined to a few subtle schoolmen. Indeed the difference between an exoteric and esoteric religion, as held by the philosophical Moslemin, remained happily unknown to Christianity, being a creed essentially suited to the mass of the people.[58]

Several expressions in the Koran, and others ascribed by *tradition* to Mohammed, such as, "God making man in his own form," and the prophet feeling "the cold finger of Allah on his shoulder," produced certain anthropomorphistic conceptions of the divine nature, and gave rise to the sects of the *Moshabites* or "the assimilating ones." The *Keramites* ascribed a body and members to Allah; the *Beyanites*, upon the authority of a passage in the Koran, maintained that Allah had a human face, which alone should remain for ever; and the *Mogarites* ascribed to him

[57] This happened to Gazal, Ebn Sina and Alkendi, the three greatest men of Moslem science. Takieddin asserted: that God must revenge the damage done to piety by Mamun when he introduced Greek learning among the Arabs.

[58] Φιλοσοφειν... το πληθος αδυνατον ειναι, was already said by Plato de Republic. lib. VI. pag. 89.

a luminary body with human outlines. On the other hand, the orthodox believers being at a loss how to reconcile the spirituality of Allah with the infallible authority of the Koran, warned men against a too literal acceptation of its expressions.[59]

18. To avoid the distinction of persons in the Holy Trinity, the *Djamis* and the powerful sect of the *Motazalites*, which again split into twenty conflicting parties, denied the divine attributes, asserting that to ascribe eternal attributes to Allah, is to assume so many personalities and to fall into the error of the Christians.[60] Thus the Koran dogma of the *abstract Unity* led to a complete denial of the glorious character of God, and an utter negation of His divine perfections! The *Sefatians* or attributists rushed to the opposite extreme of a gross Anthropomorphism.[61]

It was to be expected that the dogma of the unconditional predestination of all events and deeds without respect to their moral or immoral nature, would be opposed by many a thoughtful Moslem; for according to the prevalent belief of the orthodox party, the bad as well as the good works of men were predetermined by the irrevocable decree of the Almighty. This doctrine was opposed by the Motazalites, and especially by the *Kadris*,[62] who taught that Allah did

---

[59] Pococke spec. hist. Arab. pag. 172. Sharistani apud Pococke pag. 226. 228. 231. المشبهة, Mashabites, Assimilantes; الكرمية, Caramitae; البيانية, Bajanitae; and المغيرية, Mogheiritae.

[60] المعتزلة, the Motazalitae. See Maracc. Prodrom. Pars III. 74.

[61] الصفاتية, Saphatitae. Ishmael Shachinsha pag. 396.

[62] القدرية, Kadritae so called from قدر power, or moral liberty to act.

not decree beforehand the deeds and inclinations of his creatures. Maabad, the leader of this party, was put to the rack and then executed at Bussora A. D. 699. by the command of the Kaliph Abdelmalek. The antipodes of the Kadris, were the *Tjabaris*,[63] who denied in toto that man has any power or liberty of his own, but that Allah compels him to perform all his deeds; also the Rayatis, who maintained that evil actions must be acceptable to Allah; and the Djamis, who taught that man is merely a dead instrument in all he performs; the Kalfis consistently added, that to punish man for his deeds would be unjust on the part of Allah. The *Heshamis* on the contrary, rejected several passages of the Koran, especially those, in which it is said that "Allah leads into error whomsoever he will," lest the moral liberty of man should be endangered: whilst the Maimunites and Basharites denied that God had any connection with human actions, hence excluding also the cooperation of his grace.[64]

19. Some of the Moslem sects ventured to approximate considerably closer to the truths of Christianity than Islamism; but even the *Hayetis* and Hadathites, who ascribed a divine character to the

---

[63] Vox Arabica الجبر est negatio actionis verae in homine, tribuendo illam Deo. Maracc. Prod. III. 75. hence their name الجبرية, Gebaritae.

[64] Respecting the Chalphitae, الخلفية, or Kalfis see, True and false Relig. I. pag. 367—377. upon Brahmanism. The Maimunitae, الميمونية, belong likewise to the many antinomistical sects, whose respective names we pass over on account of the licentious character of their views.

"son of Mary" can scarcely be said to have raised themselves above the level of Arianism, inasmuch as they recognised in Christ only a secondary, created divinity, who was to judge the world at the end of days.[65] The true character and influence of Islamism will be better understood from the comparatively new-born sect of the *Wahabees*, than from any other; since they not only profess to restore Islamism to its primitive form, but remind us in many respects of the days of Mohammed.[66]

Wahab, the author of this sect, destroyed the religious veneration with which Mohammed was regarded as the intercessor of the faithful, as well as that which was extended to a host of Moslem saints. The precepts of the Koran were again enforced at the point of the sword. His first disciples, Ebn Sehud and Abd el Assis, the son of the latter, revived Mohammed's original plan of restoring the religious and political unity of the Peninsula under one head. All Moslemin who had departed from the primitive creed, and other unbelievers were to be converted and reformed by compulsion; pilgrims and caravans, towns and mosques were plundered; thousands were slain, and the most desperate havoc was made of the sepulchral monuments and chapels of the Moslem saints. The successor of Sehud mustered an army of 120,000

[65] الحايطية والحدثية, Hajetitae et Hadathitae; they also asserted μετεμψύχωσις.

[66] Its author was Mohammed Abd el Wahab; A.D. 1729. They are only known since 1750 in Europe. See also: Burkhardt's notes on the Bedouins and Wahaby's. 1830. pag. 282.

and about thirty tribes of the Arabs were subdued by these sectarians. It was reserved to the late *Mohammed Ali* of Egypt, to break up their power, Abdallah their last head was taken to Constantinople and executed, notwithstanding which, the sect survived.

20. A very important link in the chain of Moslem sectarianism is found in the mystical *Sufiism*[67] which chiefly prevails among the Shiites. The feeling of animosity against the sect was always very bitter, and Gazal declared it to be a more meritorious work to kill a Sufi than to save ten human lives.[68] The whole structure of Sufiism is based upon these two ideas: first, *besides God all is deception and vanity and nothing really exists;* secondly, *union with God is the highest scope and object of human effort.* The means to obtain this highest degree of perfection is self-denial, total abstraction of the mind from earthly pursuits, and entire devotion to mental contemplation of the Deity and the human soul, by which all practical modes of religious worship, such as fasts and feasts, stated periods of prayer, ablutions and pilgrimages are rendered superfluous. It need scarcely be observed, that this religious mystical philosophy has been grafted upon Islamism from the religious systems of Paganism in the East. The Indian Yogee, the contemplative Buddha, and the philosophic Sufi are of the same type of religious error, and the way to perfection is alike with each.

---

[67] صوفى, Sufi, derived from ساف, Arabic, Hindustani and Persian, pure, clear, sincere.

[68] Pococke, spec. hist. Arab. pag 263.

To obtain the final beatitude of these philosophic dreamers, we have to pass through four different stages of probation; in the first, the candidate for the state of perfection is bound to a strict adherence to the religion of the Koran and the observance of all its rites and precepts;[69] when duly disciplined by these, he enters upon the second stage of mental worship, in which he is at liberty to throw off all external rites and ceremonies. In the third stage, the mind is rendered capable of diving into the essence of truth itself in its logical acceptation, and of receiving immediate inspirations from the Deity; and in the fourth and last stage the union of the soul with Allah is fully realised; the symptoms however of this state are generally those of delirium and madness. The "*confession of the Unity*" appears in the conviction, that nothing exists beside Allah, "the garment of self-existence is thrown off," and with a view "to be freed from the burden of existence the soul dives into the ocean of *nothingness*."[70] It will appear that this sect destroys the very foundation of all religious faith and practice; since "the *unbelief* of the perfected Sufi is in comparison with the *faith* of other people, what a costly garment is to filthy rags;"[71] and as the yoke of precept is broken, we may expect but a very low

---

[69] Graham's Treatise upon Sufiism in the Transactions of the Lit. Soc. of Bombay 1. 94.

[70] Djami in Notices et extraits. XII. pag. 339.

[71] The mystical book Gushenrass says, "When there is no more "*I*" and no more "thou" (when man is no longer a different *individuum* from God), what is there any more in the Kaaba of the Moslem, the synagogue of the Jews or the cloister of the Christian?"

standard of morality; we have in addition, the extraordinary custom of the Sufis of describing their religious exstacies under the most sensual and lascivious images; such as oriental depravity alone could supply. Some of the sects of the Sufis in Persia and India, abandon themselves to intoxicating drinks, music and dancing in order to kindle the flame of devotion.[72] There is little indeed to move the popular mind in this transcendental Theism or Pantheism, and its success can only be attributed to its offering a diversion to the serious portion of the Moslem community, who fail to find rest in the dry and heartless system of the Koran. Sufiism however contributes its share to weaken the fanatical dependence upon the Koran, and this is especially the case among the higher classes of the Persian Moslemin; yet the leaven is not confined to them, and recent computations have estimated their number to be not less than 300,000 souls.[73]

21. There was indeed no small amount of religious dissension, and at times, cruel persecution between the various conflicting parties in the Christian Church; but whilst Christianity expelled or recalled many of its most dangerous sects by its *inherent* vitality and power, Islamism, destitute of power to subdue heresies in any other way than by fire and sword, sought only to maintain its warlike character in its

[72] Mrs. Meer Hassan Ali's Observations on the Mussulmans of India. II. p. 249.

[73] Dr. Pfander found a considerable number of *Sufis* among the lower classes. Sufi Mir Massum Ali Shah gathered 30,000 disciples in Shiraz, Malcolm II. pag. 417. and his follower, Nur Ali Shah after the execution of his master, could muster in 1800, double that number.

efforts to suppress them. The sects too generally caught up the spirit of the parent creed from which they sprang, and thus it was natural that religious wars, mutual persecutions and attempts at extermination were the necessary result of Moslem sectarianism. As long as the Kaliphate existed in full force, heresy was of course treated as *high treason*. The most fatal wound was however inflicted by the schism between the *Sonnite* and *Shiite* parties, which to this day are opposed to each other with the deadliest animosity. The anniversary of the murder of Hossein is sufficient to make the smouldering fire of mutual hatred burst forth with virulence. The Kaliphs of Bagdad executed thousands of Shiites, and declared their property, their wives and children to be the legal prey of the orthodox faithful; and even the fall of the Kaliphate was accelerated by these dissensions.[74] When religious wars penetrated the Turkish Empire in the sixteenth century, Selim I. caused a list of the Shiites to be executed by secret agency, and some 40,000 of them were slain or imprisoned.[75]

All this was perfectly consistent with the legislature of the Sonnites against the Shiites; the severities which were severally prescribed against idolaters apostates, blasphemers and infidels, were conjointly enforced against them: it is deemed more meritorious to kill one Shiite in war, than seventy Christians or other infidels, and their corpses are denied the honour of burial.[76] Even in recent

---

[74] Price's Moh. History II. 222. M. d'Ohsson I. 117.
[75] Hammer's Othoman. Reich. II. 402. [76] M. d'Ohsson III. 236.

times the Sonnite tribe *Gocklan,* was excommunicated by their brethren for acknowledging a Shiite power![77] Extermination was always the rule concerning *dissent,* whenever it was practicable, and in this, the sects themselves were in nowise behind the orthodox community. The sect of the Bargawata, which arose in the ninth century among the Berbers, lasted only about a century, but one of its leaders alone destroyed 387 towns, the inhabitants of which, were cut to pieces.[78] The African, Abdallah Ben Tamurt, founded a sect, in 1116, which was less distinguished by new doctrines than by a zeal for reforming abuses;[79] and it is related of this strict moralist, who severely punished the most trivial transgression of the precepts of the Koran, that he destroyed some 70,000 people, by causing them to be precipitated over a rock.[80] Even as late as the year 1625, it happened that a Shiite, who declined to abjure his religious views, was impaled alive in Mecca.[81] It would not be difficult to add other facts, but these may suffice to show the general tendency of Moslem sectarianism.

22. We have already seen how far the religion of the Koran has contributed to impress the character of despotism upon the Mohammedan Governments; and it may not be without interest to add a few remarks respecting the influence of that

---

[77] Fraser's Journey into Khorassan I. 143.

[78] Description de l'Afrique, Notices et extraits XII. 578—591.

[79] This founder of the sect of Mowaheddins, completed the conquest of Mauritia and Spain.

[80] Abulfeda III. 405. [81] Burkhardt's Travels in Arabia II. 12.

creed upon the history of Moslem states, and the frequent change of dynasties, to which they were exposed. According to a tradition mentioned by Siuti,[82] there have been only *five righteous Kaliphs* among the entire number: Abubeker, Omar, Othman, Ali and Abdelassis. Movia is accused of having introduced Pagan usages,[83] his son, Jezid, was an infidel who neglected the religious duties belonging to his office and spent his time in riotous living.[84] Abdelmalek increased the hatred which already rested upon his house, by avarice and cruelty; Omar Abdelassis was poisoned by his own family, on suspicion of having favoured the Shiites;[85] and the extravagant Walid II. was deprived of his throne and life by his relation Jezid III. The rule of the Abasside Kaliphs, commenced at a period when the Kaliphate was already sunk in the estimation of the people, by the godless and tyrannical rule of their predecessors; and their own immorality, tyranny and occasional heterodoxy mainly contributed to destroy whatever remained of that nimbus of sanctity, which once surrounded the Kaliph, as vice-regent and "shadow of God upon earth." It was therefore only natural, that the provinces, one by one, should become severed from the overgrown body of the colossal empire. There is, however, nothing which will better show the effects of Islamism upon

---

[82] History of the Temple of Jerusalem pag. 309.

[83] Ebn Hamsa, Notices et extraits IV. pag. 703.

[84] The Medinites declared him unworthy of the Kaliphate, Price's Moham. History I. pag. 414.

[85] Price's Mohammedan History I. pag. 526.

the history of the states and rulers, placed under its immediate protection and supervision, than the fact, that out of fifty-nine Kaliphs who ruled in the name of God and religion, thirty-eight died by violent means, and those who escaped the edge of the sword died of hunger or poison.[86] In the year 934 the dignity of the Kaliphate had sunk to such a depth, that Kaliph Kahir, who had been degraded and blinded, was seen every Friday for the space of fifteen years begging his bread at the entrance of the chief mosque of his capital![87]

Can it be wondered that dynasties founded by blood and rapine should succeed each other with unnatural rapidity? Copper-smiths and highway robbers, camel-drivers and adventurers were seen to raise themselves to be founders of royal houses.[88] That these violent changes of dynasties are attributable to the insufficient provision of the author of the religion, relative to the succession of power, no one will deny: Mohammed established a politico-religious system, but neglected to make the most necessary arrangements as to its future government. The instability of Moslem rule has been pre-eminently shown in the history of the Persian Empire. In the space of 900 years we have no less than fourteen different dynasties, which rapidly succeeded each other; and each was accompanied with the most startling convulsions of the

---

[86] In many cases, they were immured alive or thrown into ice-pits.
[87] Elmakin hist. Saracen. pag. 199. Price's Mohammed. Hist. II. pag. 177.
[88] Price's Mohammedan History II. pag. 231.

U*

state. The fact that in the Turkish Empire we have the same dynasty for the space of 500 years, has been already accounted for, by the religious awe with which the Sultan was regarded as the last heir of the heaven-ordained Kaliphate.[89]

23. Ask we for the durable effects of Islamism as regards the civilisation of the manners and customs of nations, and the cultivation of literature, science and art, it is only what we might naturally expect from such a religious system. It may be fairly asserted that the chief work of this creed was pulling down, rooting up and destroying, rather than planting and building up; and no one can say that we overstep the limits of moderation when we add, that it has destroyed more in eighty short years, than its united efforts could rear up in the space of twelve centuries. It is painful to read some elaborate rehearsals of the great things which moslem genius is said to have achieved; but it ought not to be forgotten that virgin soil is always productive for a season, till the inherent vitality be exhausted.[90] When in the day of visitation, God ploughed up the nations by the Moslem conquests, some fruit might naturally be expected to follow; but natural results must not be confounded with grace or blessing from heaven. As Islamism had no inherent vitality of its own to sus-

[89] The Kaliphate properly speaking was dissolved 1285 when Mostassem surrendered himself to Hulagus; the Sultan of Turkey therefore could only be *nominally* a successor to the ancient Kaliphs.

[90] It has been declared by agriculturists that even chaff will grow for a time being sown in the field, but that it soon withers.

tain the growth, the incidental beneficial effects soon died away. We would ask those authors who write, as if they were *almost* Mohammedans, whether it was probable that the Arabs, being an energetic and vigorous people, could be expected to conquer nations more civilised than their own, without acquiring accomplishments unknown in their native deserts? That it was only a concussion of various nationalities and a *temporary* impulse from without, which prompted the cultivation of sciences for a period, may be seen from the fact, that the Arabs live at this day in the most perfect simplicity, scorning everything which is not in accordance with patriarchal custom.

In proportion as barriers are broken down, commerce is likely to be extended among nations; but we do not observe the effects of any specially civilising influence, when we see their wretched boats creeping along the coasts inhabited by Moslemin;[91] and every one acquainted with Mohammedan trade will readily admit, that with the exception of a few articles of traffic, the *slave* trade is the most flourishing. Yet, the conquests of foreign lands, the slave trade, and the rite of pilgrimage could not fail to extend the science of geography;[92] nor is it just to disparage the services which they have rendered in this re-

[91] The writer has but too lively a recollection of the days when he was driven up and down in the Red Sea, in miserable boats, manned by people who never venture to lose sight of the shore.

[92] The author frequently gleaned most interesting facts from slaves and pilgrims from the interior of Africa.

spect.[93] The fine arts however, are utterly neglected by the Arabs, and their *music* is just that which is met with among every savage tribe; to assume, as some have done, that it exerted a favourable influence upon Italian music, is too preposterous to deserve a refutation. As regards the *mathematical* sciences which were not neglected in better days, we must remember that they were not the productions of the native mind, but the translations of Archimedes and Ptolemaeus on the one hand, and Marinus of Tyre on the other.[94] We must not forget that we are indebted to the Arabs for the transmission of our *cyphers,* which superseded the less convenient mode of arithmetical notation by the letters of the alphabet, in use among the Greeks and Hebrews; but as some ancient inscriptions found on stone and copper in Guzerat, contain those cyphers or hieroglyphics, now used as our figures with but little variation, we cannot well ascribe their invention to the Arabs. Among the *algebraic* discoveries, the solution of equations of the second degree, is ascribed to Mohammed Ebn Musa. The *astronomy* of the Arabs was derived from foreign sources;[95] they have however the merit, characteristic of their ingenious superstition, of perverting the science into astrology. The only science of which the Arabs

[93] Abulfeda, who visited England in the 14th century, in his work on Geography, quotes several authors in order to illustrate his explorations of the region beyond the Oxus.

[94] Al Hazan wrote a work on optical science and ably succeeded Ptolemy who lived 1000 years before him.

[95] The worship and study of the heavenly bodies were common in the south of Arabia; both were imported from the Babylonians.

can claim the discovery is that of *Chemistry*, which originated in their alchemical pursuits to discover the philosopher's stone.[96]

The translations into Arabic, of works on history, medicine, botany, geometry, algebra, astronomy, philosophy, jurisprudence, grammar, logic and rhetoric were so imperfect, that they only obscured the sense of their originals;[97] slavish dependence upon foreign sources, especially on the only half-understood Greek classics, precluded the possibility of a national literature. The partial benefit derived from the classics, was confined to the court and the higher classes of society; the people generally, contenting themselves with the beauties of poetry and the extravagant productions of romance, to enliven the dulness of a sterile and heartless creed.[98] The pursuit of knowledge among the Saracens was stimulated rather by pedantic eagerness to acquire information from foreign literature, than by a spirit of free, practical and independent inquiry; hence the utter decay of those institutions, anciently established for scientific and theological education. The schools and colleges in the metropolis of Islamism are mostly extinct, and

---

[96] More important still was their thirst for the *elixir* of immortality, in searching for which, they did service to Chemistry, and good was brought out of evil and superstition. Medical science was only a species of magic.

[97] Harun el Reschid appointed a body of learned men to procure them.

[98] The public schools at Bussora, Kufa, Damascus and other large cities, together with libraries, observatories and laboratories, established by some of the Kaliphs, form but a striking contrast to the usual neglect of national instruction.

ignorant fanaticism alone survives.[99] In *Cairo*, the classical seat of moslem learning, each mosque had its hospitium and library, but of all this scarcely any trace is left. The great school attached to the "Flower-mosque", which formerly provided Africa and Syria with Ulemas, numbered formerly 1200 students; but now for many years, it has only counted 500. Of 500 mosques only 150 are still opened, the remainder are decayed;[1] and of the hundred mosques of Alexandria, scarcely fifty continue to be frequented: and then it is customary almost throughout the East *for boys only* to study.

24. The depopulation and devastation of the country are also the direful effects of the sway of Islamism. The neighbourhood of *Aleppo*, as late as the beginning of the eighteenth century, could number 300 villages, but towards the end of it, only twelve remained![2] In the district of *Mardin* in Mesopotamia, were once 1600 villages, and now scarcely 500 are remaining.[3] Before the conquest by the Moslem armies, *Cyprus* had 1400 towns and villages, but in 1670 it could boast of only 700.[4] No better was the fate of the island of *Candia*, where at this moment a fierce excitement of the Mohammedans against the

---

[99] Travels of Ali Bey 1816. II. 136.

[1] Michaud VI. 4. 7. What a contrast this with the estimation, in which arts and sciences were held by the Romans! "Adolescentiam alunt, senectutem oblectant, secundas res ornant, adversis perfugium ac solatium praebent, delectant domi, non impediunt foris, pernoctant nobiscum, peregrinantur, rusticantur." Cic. Orat. pro Arch.

[2] Russel's History of Aleppo I. 339. [3] Niebuhr II. 320.

[4] Rycaut's State of the Greek Church pag. 91.

Christians is raging. Few only of the towns and cities, which were populous and flourishing at the time of the Kaliphate, are now existing; and how fearfully *Egypt* has suffered under the leaden sceptre of Islamism since its first conquest by the Saracens, is too well known to require any comment.[5] Persia is covered with ruins, and the remaining towns are in the saddest condition; even Shiraz and Ispahan present only the skeleton of their former grandeur and magnificence; and the once beautiful and fruitful province of Khorassan is reduced to utter poverty, wearing the aspect of a desert.[6] The once flourishing province of the Roman Empire of North-Africa, which even in the days of the Vandals gloried in more than 400 Episcopal sees, is reduced to misery and decay. Lastly, the *Turkish* Empire is brought to the very verge of political insolvency; its subjects are reduced to the most despicable condition, and the provinces, some of the finest in the world, are depopulated and left in an uncultivated state.[7]

---

[5] Before the Moslem invasion, the Coptic population amounted to 6 millions, but according to modern statistics, the Coptic Christians of Egypt, including probably those of Abyssinia are put down at the low number of 3,200,000! Dr. Newman says: "I might call your attention to particular instances of such atrocities, such as that outrage perpetrated within the memory of many of us, how on the insurrection of the Greeks at Scio, their barbarian masters carried fire and sword throughout the flourishing island, till it was left a desert, hurrying away women and boys to an infamous captivity, and murdering youths and grown men, *till, out of* 120,000 *souls in the spring time, not* 900 *were left them* when the crops were ripe for the sickle." Lect. on the Hist. of the Turks pag. 135. 136.

[6] Kinneir's Memoir of the Persian Empire 1813. pag. 117.

[7] The Turkish Empire would however be in a still more deplor-

Dissolution and decay then are the foot-prints of the religion of the crescent; but lest the philo-Mohammedan latitudinarians of Europe should be tempted to accuse us of narrow-mindedness, bigotry, or ignorance of the real state of things, we insert the testimony of a Moslem, the excellent Historian Ebn Chaldun, who enlarges upon the piteous spectacle of countries, conquered by the Saracens: "The cause of it, he adds, is in the fierce character of the people, whose wild habits are as much a part of their nature and inborn, as those of a wild beast; and such innate propensities are adverse to, and destructive of civilisation. The principal feature of their character is a love of change and revolution, one, utterly opposed to that quiet which civilisation requires. Their instinct leads to plunder; trade only prospers beneath the shadow of lances, their thirst for robbery knows no limits, they plunder whatever comes within their reach. Meditating only how they may possess themselves of the substance of others, they desist not from severities till they have obtained it; fiscal punishments are invented for gain and as a means of procuring money; vice and obscenities therefore are not suppressed but rather encouraged. The fact of the subjects being thus left to themselves, must be injurious to mankind and destructive to civilisation. Again, they have an aversion to all control, few submitting themselves to the command of a father or to the

able condition if it had not been for the wholesome influence of European diplomacy, and more especially for the large admixture of a *Christian* population among its subjects.

brother or elder of their tribe. .... Look only at the countries, which they conquer in the name of the Kaliphs, how they are stripped of cultivation, how the inhabitants are plundered, and the very soil has been entirely changed. Yemen the seat of their power is lying waste with the exception of certain tracts, cultivated by the Ansars; the same may be said of the Arabian Irak. The cultivation of Persia has ceased and likewise that of Syria. The African desert and Mauritia have been laid waste, since the Beni Hilal and the Beni Selim settled there; and how the country between Nigritia and the Mediterranean was formerly inhabited, may be seen from the ruins of buildings, and the deserted sites of villages and towns."[8]

Were we to collect what eyewitnesses and historians have recorded of the immorality, injustice, deceit, oppression and cruelty of the Moslem community, combining it with a religion either *too weak* to heal the evil which consumes the marrow of the nations, or *too accommodating* to the vilest passions of man, we should form a picture, the contemplation of which, would be truly appalling. The consideration of the *character* and *influence of Islamism* reminds us of the vision of the dry bones, and when here, as there, the question is asked: "*Son of man can these bones live*"? we also can only reply, in the words of the Prophet Ezekiel: "*O Lord thou knowest!*"

[8] Quoted in, and translated from von Hammer's Länderverwaltung unter dem Chalifate. 1835. Berlin pag. 62.

PART II.

CHRISTIANITY AND ISLAMISM CONTRASTED.

INTRODUCTION.

All false creeds, of comparatively modern date, endeavour to show that they are connected with the beginning of time, and that they have been preparatively introduced in by-gone ages. Nor could *Islamism* hope to prosper in the world without resorting to a similar expedient; it was therefore convenient and indeed necessary for Mohammed to rest his new creed upon the Jewish and Christian dispensations, and to do this consistently, he was compelled to admit their divine origin.[1] As the Jewish dispensation was of a temporary character being *superseded* by Christianity, so the Christian religion, according to Mohammed, was only to be in force till Islamism should appear to supplant it! There is however a strange inconsistency in Mohammed's claim to *succession*,

[1] Möhler's gesammelte Schriften Vol. I. pag. 350.

since it involves an entire change and *abrogation* of the previous dispensations. The immutability of Judaism and Christianity are asserted in the Koran,[2] yet we have seen, in the first part of this work, that they are both virtually ignored and abolished. The change which we recognise in the succession of the Christian to the Jewish dispensation, is analogous to that which takes place between the laying of the foundation of a building and its completion. The Jewish Church was the ground-work of that temple, of which Christ is the *"head-stone"*.[3] If change there be, it is this; in the Old Testament we have prophecy, in the New, fulfilment.[4] The bud gives place to the blossom, and the blossom to the fruit. We have a change, but only such as God had promised and foreshadowed. Nothing was abrogated by the Gospel, but the ritual ordinances and the ceremonial precepts, which being of a typical character, were necessarily transient.[5] Looking upon the whole Mo-

---

[2] "Wherefore be thou orthodox, and set thy face towards the true religion, the institution of God, to which he hath made mankind disposed; لا تبديل لخلق اللّٰه there is no change in what Allah created." Sur. XXX. 30.

[3] וְהוֹצִיא אֶת־הָאֶבֶן הָרֹאשָׁה Zech. IV. 7. That this refers to Christ who shall build and complete the temple, see chap. III. 8. and VI. 12. : הִנֵּה־אִישׁ צֶמַח שְׁמוֹ וּבָנָה אֶת־הֵיכַל יְהֹוָה

[4] Οὐκ ἦλθον καταλῦσαι τὸν νόμον ἢ τοὺς προφήτας· ἀλλὰ πληρῶσαι. Matt. V. 17. Zwar ist das alte Testament in der Einheit des Heilsbeschlusses und der Thatsache der Offenbarung mit dem neuen eines, aber nicht einerlei, sondern dieses verhält sich zu jenem wie die Vollendung zur Vorbereitung, wie die Entschränkung zur Beschränkung, wie das Unmittelbare zum Mittelbaren. Nitzsch.

[5] "Abrogatae sunt leges *ceremoniales*, exhibitio Messia, et *forenses*, sublata politia judaica; *moralis* non item. Lex moralis Mosaica

saic constitution with its personal and impersonal types, and with its figurative ceremonial, we find everywhere "a *shadow of things to come;*" the *body* of which was Christ. Every single hieroglyphic figure had its meaning; every historic character, event, and circumstance, down to the very items of the drapery and the ornaments of the temple, so minutely recorded, were divinely chosen symbols for conveying truths of lasting interest to the whole human race.[6] Whilst we recognise unity of purpose and harmony of design in both dispensations of the Bible,[7] in Islamism, we find a creed, which is radically different from the Old and directly opposed to the New Testament. If the Koran had merely abrogated a few ceremonial observances of the Christian religion, and if this abrogation had been predicted in the Gospel, as an event which would take place in a succeeding dispensation, then, there might have been less cause to dispute the claims of Islamism. But unhappily for the creed of Mohammed, we have nothing typical in the Gospel. . There is no shadow in Christianity for the substance and body of which, we might have to look in a subsequent dispensation. On the contrary, our expectation is

seu Decalogi eadem est cum lege Christi; illam enim a Pharisaicis corruptelis purgavit et rectius declaravit, non precepta moralia plane nova dedit fidelibus." Baier. Compare also Article VII, "Of the Old Testament."

[6] "Theologia typica, quae futurorum praedictionem, ex intentione Dei sub rebus, personis factisque latentum in V. T. scrutatur et explicat. Typus, σκια, ὑποδειγμα, est adumbratio, praefiguratio, praesignatio." Carpovius.

[7] Novum Testamentum in vetere latet (velatum est) vetus in novo patet (revelatum est). Augustine.

from heaven, "from *whence* also we *look for the Saviour;*" being taught "*to wait*" for Him from heaven. Instead therefore of having the fulfilment of type or promise in Islamism, the most essential truths of the Old and New Testament are denied and rejected. To assume that God is the author of Islamism, is to assume that He decreed yesterday, what to-day He abolishes; that He established the old and new dispensation, but, that after more mature consideration, He determined to give the world a better religion; that His legislation for mankind was imperfect, since He found it necessary to revoke what He before had solemnly ordained. That after the Gospel was preached and attested by signs and wonders, in various parts of the world, according to God's will and command,[8] this very Gospel was recalled and God promulgates through a certain Mohammed of Mecca, doctrines and laws directly opposed to it; and this changeableness of mind and purpose is to be proclaimed, if we may believe the Koran, not only to mankind but even to demons![9] If this principle of succession or rather abrogation be defended, as it is, on the ground of Christianity becoming unsound; we reply, that a distemper in the body or a disorder in any of its members does not of necessity prove fatal to existence.

---

[8] Πορευθέντες εἰς τὸν κόσμον ἅπαντα, no exception being made: κηρύξατε τὸ εὐαγγέλιον πάσῃ τῇ κτίσει. Mark. XVI. 15. That the κήρυγμα penetrated Arabia, is proved by the existence of an Arabian Church prior to Mohammed.

[9] قل اوحى الىّ انّه استمع نفر من الجنّ فقالو انّا سمعنا قرانا عجبا Sur. XXXII. 1. See also XLVI. 30. 31.

Neither the moral corruption of the Christians at the period of the rise of Islamism, nor the heresies which then infected the Church, could make the abrogation of the Christian religion requisite. It was foretold by Christ Himself, that there would be a mixture of good and evil within the Church, to the end of time; and that heresies would spring up, was predicted by the Apostles.[10]

The chief charge, brought by Mohammed against Jews and Christians, as the representatives of their respective dispensations, and for the sake of which, both were to be superseded, was that of *corrupting the Old and the New Testament*.[11] That Christians had altered the New Testament, Mohammedans profess to prove from their holding the doctrine of the Holy Trinity, and the Divinity of the Lord Jesus Christ, but most of all from their rejection of Mohammed, though required by the supposed *original* Gospels, to receive him. In order to justify their alleged errors and their rejection of Mohammed, the Christians are accused of having expunged from their Scriptures all that related to the prophet, and of having made such additions, as they deemed necessary. This objection, is constantly urged in religious disputations, and naturally falls first in our way when about to

---

[10] Matt. XIII. 24—30. 47—50. XXIV. 5. 11. 24. Act. XX. 29. 30. 2 Pet. I. 1.

[11] The *suppression* of Scripture passages, which were favourable to the cause of Mohammed, and the crime of *corrupting* them, are frequently censured in the Koran. Sur. II. 73. also 176—178. III. 188. V. 17. where it is fully stated that they "knowingly hide or conceal certain passages;" "pervert or dislocate the words out of their places," and corrupt the "signs of God for vile gain."

compare Islamism with Christianity. It must therefore be our first care to examine, whether there be *any ground* for so grave a charge as that made by Mohammed, and whether we can satisfactorily prove the *integrity* of the Holy Scriptures; for so long as the Bible lies under any such suspicion, we are deprived of our best and most valuable weapon. The Jews being first accused of having corrupted the Old Testament Scriptures, we shall in the next chapter endeavour to substantiate the integrity of that portion of the Bible, which for so long a period was entrusted to their guardianship.

CHAPTER I.

INTEGRITY OF THE OLD TESTAMENT.

"Verily I say unto you, Till heaven and earth pass, one jot or one tittle shall in no wise pass from the law till all be fulfilled. And it is easier for heaven and earth to pass, than one tittle of the law to fail." Matt. V. 18. Lu. XVI. 17.

1. That we may prove to better advantage the integrity of the *Old Testament*, it will be necessary to introduce some items respecting the *history* of that part of the Bible.[12] It is generally known as "the Scripture," "the Old Testament," "the book of the covenant," or simply "the Law,"[13]—the latter

---

[12] The entire Bible, so termed since Chrysostom: τὰ βιβλία sc. θεῖα; libri κατ' ἐξοχήν. Chrysost. in Suic. thes, eccles. pag. 696. Also ἱερὰ γραφή; ἁγία γραφή; θεία γραφή, and *Bibliotheca sancta*. Isidor. Orig. cap. IV. pag. 3.

[13] בְּתָב, Chald. בְּתִיבָה, בְּתָבָא, ἡ γραφή 2 Pet. I. 20; αἱ γραφαί

being the standing name in the Koran. After the Church had been without Scriptures for more than two thousand years, and when the word of God could no longer be orally transmitted with safety, Moses wrote the Pentateuch, and thus laid the foundation of that series of holy books which Malachi concluded in the year B. C. 397.—This collection of holy Scriptures is divided into the Law, the Prophets and the Psalms.[14]

The Law comprised the five books of Moses, and admitted of no other division. The Prophets were divided into "the former" and "the latter Prophets;" among the "former Prophets" were reckoned the book of Joshua and of Judges, the books of Samuel, and of the Kings. "The latter Prophets" are the Prophets properly so called, Isaiah, Jeremiah, Ezekiel and the twelve minor Prophets.[15] Amongst the *Psalms* or "other holy writings" are understood all the rest of the holy Scriptures, including also Daniel, whom the Christians, according to the Septuagint, count with the Prophets, there being a considerable difference as to the *order* in which these books are made to follow each other, with the Jews, the Sep-

---

Matt. XXII. 29; הַכְּתָבִים, γραφαὶ ἁγίαι Rom. I. 2; ἱερὰ γράμματα 2 Tim. III. 15, תורה, Sanhed. fol. 91. col. 2. ὁ νόμος, John XII. 34; סֵפֶר הַדָּבָר, βιβλίον διαθήκης, Exod. XXIV. 7; "vetus Testamentum" since the third century; ἡ παλαιὰ διαθήκη 2 Cor. III. 14.

[14] Our Lord's division: ὁ νόμος Μωσέως, οἱ προφῆται καὶ οἱ ψαλμοὶ Luke XXIV. 44. Or 1. תורה, 2. נְבִיאִים, 3. כְּתוּבִים, γραφεῖα, ἁγιόγραφα, ψαλμοὶ, also: καὶ τὰ ἄλλα βιβλία.

[15] נְבִיאִים אַחֲרוֹנִים so called in contradistinction to נְבִיאִים רִאשׁוֹנִים *priores* and *posteriores*.

tuagint, and the Fathers of the Church.[16] Again, from the fact of our Lord speaking of the "Psalms," as the "third division of the Old Testament, it would appear that the book of Psalms stood first on the list of *that division*, and thus gave its name to all the remaining books" or Hagiographa, as this section of the "sacred writings" has been called; just as we speak of the whole of the New Testament, as "the Gospel," because the portion so called stands first.[17] Others think that our Lord made use of the title of "the Psalms" to signify the entire division of the Hagiographa, not so much on account of its standing first on the list, as because of the poetical character, which distinguishes the greater part of this class of writings.[18] Both Josephus and Philo speak of the Hagiographa as containing chiefly hymns and praises to God.[19]

[16] The Talmud thus: "Ordo Prophetarum: Josua et Judices, Samuel et Reges, Jeremia et Ezechiel, Jesaia et duodecim Prophetae." Baba Bathra f. 14. cap. 2. The cause is thus stated: "Cum libri Regum finiantur in desolatione, et Jeremias totus versetur in desolatione, Ezechiel vero incipiat in desolatione et finiat in consolatione, et Jesaias totus versetur in consolatione, copulaverunt desolationem cum desolatione, et consolationem cum consolatione." J. G. Carpzov. Introductio ad libros can. III. 88.

[17] The Talmud, with the exception of Ruth, places them thus: "Ordo Hagiographorum: Ruth, Psalmi et Hiob et Proverbia, et Coheleth, Canticum et Threni, Daniel et Esther et Chronica." Baba Bathra f. 14. cap. 2.

[18] Josephus speaks of them as containing ὕμνους εἰς τὸν θεόν. Joseph. cont. Ap. §. 23.

[19] Μηδὲν εἰσκομίζοντες, μὴ ποτὸν, μὴ σιτίον, μηδέτι τῶν ἄλλων ὅσα πρὸς τὰς τοῦ σώματος χρείας ἀναγκαῖα, ἀλλὰ νόμους καὶ λόγια δεσπισθέντα διὰ προφητῶν καὶ ὕμνους καὶ τὰ ἄλλα οἷς ἐπιστήμη καὶ εὐσέβεια συναύξονται καὶ τελειοῦνται. Philo de vita contemplat. §. 13. p. 893 ed. Fref.

As the Psalms stood *first* on the list of the third division of the Old Testament, so the book of Chronicles appears to have stood *last* among the Hagiographa; that this book closed this division, and hence the entire Old Testament, is evident from our Saviour's words, in which He sums up the bloodshedding of martyr-prophets from the foundation of the world, to the last martyrdom recorded in the canonical books of the Jews, viz. "from the blood of Abel unto the blood of Zacharias, which perished between the altar and the temple."[20]

2. The *enumeration* of the books of the Old Testament has been variously made out; we mention this, lest the Mohammedans should rush to the conclusion, that there is either confusion or uncertainty respecting the real number of the canonical books. *Josephus*, to whom we are indebted for the first catalogue of these writings, with a view evidently, of making their number correspond with that of the letters in the Hebrew alphabet[21] reduces them to twenty-two combining the books of Ruth and the Judges into one, as also Jeremiah and the Lamentations, after the manner of the Septuagint.[22] If however the five books of Moses be counted separately, as they are by Jo-

---

[20] Luke XI. 50. 51. Matt. XXIII. 35. 2 Chron. XXIV. 20.

[21] Ὀυκ ἀγιοητέον δ' εἶναι τὰς ἐνδιαθήκους βίβλους, ὡς Ἑβραῖοι παραδιδόασιν, δύο καὶ εἴκοσι, ὅσος ὁ ἀριθμὸς τῶν παρ' αὐτοῖς στοιχείων ἐστίν. Origen. Euseb. II. E. VI. 25.

[22] Ὀυ γὰρ μυριάδες βιβλίων εἰσὶ παρ' ἡμῖν, ἀσυμφώνων καὶ μαχομένων· δύο δὲ μόνα πρὸς τοῖς εἴκοσι βιβλία, τοῦ παντὸς ἔχοντα χρόνον τὴν ἀναγραφὴν, τὰ δικαίως θεῖα πεπιστευμένα. Joseph. contra Apion. lib. I. cap. 8.

sephus, the rest may justly be counted singly; this being done in the Bibles of the present day, the number amounts to thirty-nine books.

The question now arises, when do we hear of their being *collected* together in the form in which we now possess them? We find the entire Old Testament deposited in the temple immediately after the Jewish captivity.[23] Again, at the time when the prologue was written to the apocryphal book of Sirach or Ecclesiasticus, which was about 130 years B. C. the collection of the canonical books had been accomplished.[24]

Josephus, born 37. B. C. quotes not only nearly all the books, but gives a detailed account of their names and number. He informs us that the above-mentioned twenty-two books of the Old Testament were completed in the days of Artaxerxes Longimanus, king of Persia, who in his twentieth year had commissioned Nehemiah to rebuild the walls of Jerusalem. Five of the books were written by Moses; thirteen viz. Joshua, Judges and Ruth, Samuel, Kings, Chronicles, Ezra and Nehemiah, Esther, Isaiah, Jeremiah and Lamentations, Ezekiel, Daniel, the twelve minor Prophets and Job, were added to the Pentateuch during the interval between Moses and Artaxerxes.

---

[23] Joseph. Antiquit. V. I. 17. de bello Jud. VII. 5. 5; traces of the holy Scriptures being preserved in the sanctuary before the Captivity 1 Sam. X. 23. Deut. XXXI. 26.

[24] The books were collected by Ezra and the other members of the *synagoga magna*, הַכְּנֶסֶת הַגְּדוֹלָה, συναγωγὴ γραμματέων in 1 Macc. VII. 12; but the conclusion of the canon is said to have been effected under Simon the Just. B. C. 292.

Josephus particularly mentions that the other four books were Hymns, being the Psalms proper, Proverbs, Ecclesiastes and Canticles. From Artaxerxes to his own day, he adds, that some others had been written, but that they were not worthy of the same faith as the preceding, not containing the same teaching as the prophetical books.[25]

3. The above twenty-two canonical books of the Jewish Church, of which Josephus wrote, were the same in the days of Christ, as they were at the time of Josephus. Our Lord and his Apostles fully acknowledged the integrity and completeness of the canonical books in the beginning of our era; and from that period, the Christians had an equal interest in watching over the Old Testament, having received it as the foundation of their faith. They read these books in their Churches from the very earliest times and their guardianship thus became divided between two rival parties.[26] The Law, the Prophets and

---

[25] After saying the Jews had only 22 divine books, he proceeds "Καὶ τούτων πέντε μέν ἐστι τὰ Μωϋσέως ἃ τούς τε νόμους περιέχει, καὶ τὴν τῆς ἀνθρωπογονίας παράδοσιν, μέχρι τῆς αὐτοῦ τελευτῆς· οὗτος ὁ χρόνος ἀπολείπει τρισχιλίων ὀλίγον ἐτῶν. Ἀπὸ δὲ τῆς Μωϋσέως τελευτῆς μέχρι τῆς Ἀρταξέρξου τοῦ μετὰ Ξέρξην Περσῶν βασιλέως ἀρχῆς (reign not beginning) οἱ μετὰ Μωϋσῆν προφῆται τὰ κατ' αὐτοὺς πραχθέντα συνέγραψαν ἐν τρισὶ καὶ δέκα βιβλίοις· αἱ δὲ λοιπαὶ τέσσαρες ὕμνους εἰς τὸν θεὸν, καὶ τοῖς ἀνθρώποις ὑποθήκας τοῦ βίου περιέχουσιν. Ἀπὸ δὲ Ἀρταξέρξου μέχρι τοῦ καθ' ἡμᾶς χρόνον γέγραπται μὲν ἕκαστα· πίστεως δὲ οὐχ ὁμοίας ἠξίωται τοῖς πρὸ αὐτῶν, διὰ τὸ μὴ γενέσθαι τὴν τῶν προφητῶν ἀκριβῆ διαδοχήν. Δῆλον δ' ἐστὶν ἔργῳ, πῶς ἡμεῖς τοῖς ἰδίοις γράμμασι πεπιστεύκαμεν." Joseph. contra Apion. Lib. I. cap. 8.

[26] Τῶν φερομένων γραφῶν καὶ ἐν πάσαις ἐκκλησίαις θεοῦ πεπιστευμένων εἶναι θείων οὐκ ἂν ἁμάρτοι τις λέγων πρωτογέννημα μὲν τὸν Μωϋσέως τόμον, ἀπαρχὴν δὲ τὸ Εὐαγγέλιον. Μετὰ γὰρ τοὺς πάντας τῶν προφητῶν καρπούς, τῶν μέχρι τοῦ

the Psalms or Hagiographa, were considered one and
the same Holy Scripture, having the same authority
and demanding the same faith.[27] As however the
Septuagint was used in the Churches, and as that
translation of the Old Testament contained the apocryphal books, these were read together with the canonical Scriptures, "for example of life and instruction
of manners, without applying them to establish any
doctrine."[28] We here have the key to the reading
of the apocryphal books in Churches; but to prevent
them gaining authority, as this seemed to be the case
in the Latin Church, and amongst the ignorant in
the East, fresh catalogues of the canonical books were
from time to time issued. The first of these Christian
catalogues of Jewish books was compiled by *Melito*
of Sardes, who died A. D. 171. In his epistle to
a certain Onesimus, who had made inquiries of him
respecting the books of the Old Testament, Melito
offers to give the names, the exact number, and the
order in which the books follow each other. We have
in his enumeration[29] all the books of the Jewish Ca-

κυρίου Ἰησοῦ, ὁ τέλειος ἐβλάστησε λόγος. Origen. Comm. in Joh.
tom. I. §. 4. Opp. IV. 4. Cont. Cels. III. 45. Opp. 476. ὅτι βούλε-
ται ἡμᾶς εἶναι σοφοὺς ὁ λόγος, δεικτέον καὶ ἀπὸ τῶν παλαιῶν
καὶ Ἰουδαϊκῶν γραμμάτων, ᾗ οἷς καὶ ἡμεῖς χρώμεθα, οὐχ
ἧττον δὲ καὶ ἀπὸ τῶν μετὰ τὸν Ἰησοῦν γραφέντων καὶ ἐν ταῖς
ἐκκλησίαις θείων εἶναι πεπιστευμένων.

[27] Clemens Strom. III. p. 455: Νόμος τε ὅμου καὶ προφῆται
σὺν καὶ τῷ εὐαγγελίῳ ἐν ὀνόματι Χριστοῦ εἰς μίαν συνάγονται γνῶ-
σιν. Irenaeus adds: "Cum itaque universae Scripturae, et Prophetiae
et Evangelia, in aperto sint, etc." Iren. II. 27. 2.

[28] "Libros legit quidam Ecclesia, sed inter canonicas Scripturas
non recepit." Hierony. praef. in libros Salomonis.

[29] Ἀνελθὼν οὖν εἰς τὴν ἀνατολήν, καὶ ἕως τοῦ τόπου γενόμενος

non with the exception of Nehemiah and Esther, which were sometimes considered to form an integral part of the book of Chronicles.[30] As Melito undertook a journey to Palestine in order to ascertain the correct number of books, his catalogue is endowed with special authority. A similar catalogue from *Origen*, who died A. D. 254, is still extant, it gives a double list of the Greek and Hebrew names of the two and twenty canonical books of the Old Testament.[31] At the *Council of Laodicea* held between 360—364 an other list was set forth, which entirely agrees with those which preceded or followed with this exception only, that it admits, *Baruch*, like the catalogue of Origen, among the canonical books.[32] Some time later, *Cyril*, the Patriarch of Alexandria, issued another index of the canonical writings of the Old Testament, which, omitting Baruch, numbered twenty-two books.[33] The catalogue of *Athanasius* agrees

ἔνθα ἐκηρύχθη καὶ ἐπράχθη, καὶ ἀκριβῶς μαθὼν τὰ τῆς παλαιᾶς διαθήκης βιβλία, ὑποτάξας ἐπεμψά σοι· ὧν ἐστι τὰ ὀνόματα· Μωϋσέως πέντε· Γένεσις, Ἔξοδος, Λευιτικόν, Ἀριθμοί, Δευτερονόμιον· Ἰησοῦς Ναυῆ, Κριταί, Ῥούθ, Βασιλειῶν τέσσαρα, Παραλειπομένων δύο· Ψαλμῶν Δαβίδ, Σολομῶνος Παροιμίαι, ἡ καὶ Σοφία, Ἐκκλησιαστής, ἄσμα ἀσμάτων, Ἰώβ· Προφητῶν, Ἡσαΐου, Ἱερεμίου, τῶν δώδεκα ἐν μονοβίβλῳ, Δανιήλ, Ἰεζεκιήλ, Ἔσδρας· ἐξ ὧν καὶ τὰς ἐκλογὰς ἐποιήσαμεν, εἰς ἓξ βιβλία διελών. Euseb. H. E. IV. 26.

[30] Eichhorn Einleit. in das Alt. Test. I. §. 52. Ewald I. 242.

[31] Euseb. H. E. VI. 25. See Lehrbuch der historisch-kritischen Einleitung in das Alte Test. von de Wette pag. 37. 38.

[32] The catalogue is introduced with these words: Ὅτι οὐ δεῖ ἰδιωτικοὺς ψαλμοὺς λέγεσθαι ἐν τῇ ἐκκλησίᾳ, οὐδὲ ἀκανόνιστα βιβλία, ἀλλὰ μόνα τὰ κανονικὰ τῆς καινῆς καὶ παλαιᾶς διαθήκης. Concil. Laodic. Cant. 59.

[33] Cyril. Hierosol. Catechs. IV. 33—36. pag. 67—69.

with that of Cyril, with this difference only, that it counts the book of Ruth separately and places the book of Esther amongst the apocryphal books.[34] To *Epiphanius* we are likewise indebted for an enumeration of the canonical books; who, after mentioning the twenty-two books of the Old Testament and the principle of their computation, adds a very brief and simple catalogue, in which we recognise the identical names, number, and order of arrangement, which we find in all the preceding lists.[35] Thus the catalogues of the fourth century show not only that the Scriptures of the Old Testament were read, and believed as the "fountains of salvation," but that they were ecclesiastically established under the term of canonical books.[36]

4. We enter upon these details with a view to prove, that no books were lost, and none were added since the Canon of the Old Testament was closed. We have the same number of Scriptures, with the same names, arranged in the same order. When

[34] Athan. epist. festalis Op. I. pag. 961. Edit. Bened.

[35] "Γένεσις —Ἔξοδος — Λευιτικὸν, Ἀριθμοὶ Δευτερονόμιον — ἡ τοῦ Ἰησοῦ τοῦ Ναυῆ, ἡ τοῦ Ἰώβ — ἡ τῶν Κριτῶν — ἡ τῆς Ῥοὺθ — τὸ ψαλτήριον — ἡ πρώτη τῶν Παραλειπομένων — Παραλ. δευτέρα — Βασιλειῶν πρώτη, Β δευτέρα, Β. τρίτη, Β. τετάρτη· ἡ Παροιμιῶν — ὁ ἐκκλησιαστὴς — τὸ Ἄσμα τῶν ἀσμάτων — τὸ Δωδεκαπρόφητον — Ἡσαΐου — Ἱερεμίου — Ἰεζεκιὴλ — ἡ τοῦ Ἔσδρα πρώτη — δευτέρα, ἡ τῆς Ἐσθὴρ. Epiphanius de mens. et pond. c. 22. 23. Op. II. 180.

[36] This is shown by the terms, βιβλία κανονιζόμενα, κεκανονιζομένα, ὡρισμένα and κανονικά. These Scriptures are not only πηγαὶ τοῦ σωτηρίου, according to Athanasius; but the Christian and Jew recognised in them τὸν κανόνα τῆς ἀληθείας. Isidor. Pelus. epist. 114.

Mohammed charged the Jews with withholding certain books, why did he not name the correct list, and pointing out the absent ones, request that such and such a missing Scripture might be brought forth? As we have the same books now, which the Jews and Christians had in the fourth century, they must have possessed the same Scriptures at and after the rise of Islamism. Possessing therefore, as we do, in the above catalogues the perfect skeleton, the complete framework of the Old Testament, can we prove that the *contents* of each book have escaped the corruption, which the Koran assumes to have taken place? In reply to this question we proceed to show, that with the exception of a few verbal and accidental differences, by which no single article of faith, nor any one historical fact is called in question, we possess the books of the Old Testament in their *original integrity*. These books, it will be remembered, were copied a thousand times; but the infallibility of the authors was not transferred to the men who copied them in after ages. Different readings would naturally arise from want of attention or judgment; but such mistakes may be remedied by an ordinary application of skill and the necessary amount of learning and intelligence. Errors committed through ignorance and carelessness, can always be repaired by learning and research.[37] — The

---

[37] "Observandum, in hac thesi de integritate Scripturae, questionem esse de tali corruptione, qua finis Scripturae, hoc est, salutaris illius usus, impediretur. Adeoque *variantes lectiones* integritati illi, quam nos tuemur, non satis perite objiciuntur: 1. quia quantacunque sit earum multitudo, nulla tamen historia scitu nobis necessaria, multo minus aliqua salutis doctrina intercidit; 2. quia ipsa

transcribers of the Hebrew original have occasionally "*seen amiss*," as a German writer quaintly but justly expresses it,[38] and exchanged letters of a similar form,[39] or transposed them, putting one letter in the place of another.[40] Another kind of oversight is observed, where letters were omitted, and whole words overlooked; especially in cases where two sentences end alike.[41]

Other examples of unintentional mistakes, in multiplying the Manuscripts of the Hebrew text, might be added, where the transcribers "*heard amiss*,"

lectionis varietas argumento est, mutationem non factam esse in omnibus qui supersunt codicibus; 3. quia eruditorum inter Christianos diligentia dubiis de genuina lectione sufficientem medelam, adhibita Crisi sobria, attulit. Supersunt quidem *affecti*, quos Critici vocant, *loci*, hoc est tales, quibus per media critica, collationem codicum, versionum, patrum, subveniri nondum ita potuit, quin etiamnum suspendi judicium debeat. Sed illi quidem perpauci sunt." Sartorius Comp. Theolog. Dogmat. II. p. 57.

[38] "Sie sahen falsch, und verwechselten ähnliche Buchstaben, versetzten sie, versetzten ganze Wörter oder Sätze, ließen Buchstaben, Wörter und Sätze aus, besonders wenn sich zwei Sätze gleich endigten." Dr. de Wette, Hist. krit. Einl. pag. 124.

[39] Frequently ר for ד, Ps. CX. 3. XIX. 4. cfr. LXX. ר for ב, Josh. XV. 47. ב for כ, Ps. 78, 69. ו for י, Gen. 36, 23. See also the numerical letter 2 Sam. 24, 13. נ for ז; hence seven years famine in Sam.; whilst LXX. in loco has τρία ἔτη λιμὸς, the same as 1 Chron. XXI. 12. Again ס for כ 1 King XII. 21. has 180,000 men whilst the LXX has 120,000 ἑκατὸν καὶ εἴκοσι χιλιάδας.

[40] שְׁבָטָי for שְׁבָטָיו Ezra II. 4. and Neh. VII. 48. *Algum* tree instead of *Almug* 1 Kings X. 11. 2 Chron. IX. 10. Ps. XVIII. 46. יַחְדָלוֹ and 2 Sam. XXII. 46. יַחְגְּרוּ.

[41] Asaiah in 1 Chron. IX. 5. Maaseiah Neh. XI. 5. See also Ps. XVIII. 42. 2 Sam. XXII. 42. יְשַׁוֵּעוּ; 2 Sam. 23, 25. with 1 Chron. XI. 27; Gen. 36, 11. 12. with 1 Chron. 1, 36; Josh. XXI. 23. with 1 Chron. V. 53. 54; 1 Chron. XI. 13. with 2 Sam. XXIII. 9—11.

and exchanged alike-sounding letters of the alphabet.[42] Again, mistakes were made where the copyist trusted too much to his memory, and exchanged synonymous expressions;[43] or altered the word after more frequent forms in parallel passages.[44] Again we recognise errors arising from want of sufficient knowledge of what they copied; these more likely occurred at a period, when the words were not yet divided, and the practice of writing the original text without the vowels was in vogue. Abbreviations for instance, were misunderstood and treated as ordinary letters.[45] It is obvious to all, that in copying a manuscript, mistakes may be easily and most unintentionally made; those above specified will sufficiently explain the existence of various readings; which being purely accidental, they are such, as Mohammed could neither have detected nor referred to, when he accused the Jews of wilfully suppressing prophecies, relating to himself, and of designedly corrupting the Old Testament.

5. The idea that the Jews falsified any portion of their sacred books, is in the first place, altogether at variance with, and opposed to their notorious and almost superstitious regard for the dead letter of the

---

[42] 1 Sam. XXII. 18. הֹרִיג Keri הָאֵג; Ps. LIX. 9. אֶשְׁמְרָה and אֲזַמֵּרָה: LXX. 1 Sam. XVII. 34. הַזֶּה in several Cod. instead of שֶׂה.

[43] Lev. XXV. 36, אַל instead of בַּל. 2 King. I. 10. וַיְדַבֵּר for וַיֹּאמֶר; and often יהוה for אדני.

[44] Isa. LXIII. 16. some have בַּיָּמִים instead of מֵעוֹלָם; just because the former is the more common.

[45] Jer. VI. 11. וְיהוה, חֲמַת־יְ was read חֲמָתִי, my wrath, like LXX. καὶ τὸ θυμόν μου. cap. XXX. 37. אַף־יְ, אַף, θυμοῦ μου; instead of אַף־יְהוָה.

law. The Talmud, which was concluded in the fifth century of our era, abounds with injunctions which tend to preserve the integrity of their holy Scriptures.[46] It speaks of most careful comparisons of divers Manuscripts,[47] and the most tedious and painful enumeration of verses, words and letters;[48] as the Mohammedans borrowed this practice from the Jews,

[46] "Ita autem scribendum vobis est; ut sit scriptura perfecta (בְּתִיבָה תַמָּה), ne scribatur Aleph pro Ain, et vice versa, Beth pro Caph, et v. v.; Gimel pro Zadeh, et v. v.; Daleth pro Resh, et v. v.; He pro Cheth, et v. v.; Vav pro Jod, et v. v.; Zain pro Nun, et v. v.; Teth pro Peh, et v. v.; incurvae litterae pro directis, et v. v.; Mem pro Samech, et v. v.; clausae litterae (ם finale) pro apertis (מ), et v. v.; sectio aperta ne fiat sectio clausa, et v. v." Tr. Shab. f. 103. c. 2. A Manuscript having only 3 mistakes on one leaf might be corrected, but if they amounted to 4, it was *hid* or put aside as inadmissible. Gemar. Babylon. Tract. Monachot. cap. III. sect. VII. Again: "Viginti de hoc praecepta enumerat R. Moyses in tractatu de lib. Leg. cap. 10. Inter quae X^{mum} est, ut ab homine Haeretico, vel profano exscribi non possint, XI^{mum}, *ut scriptor ita attentus sit, dum aliquod ex Dei nominibus exarat, vt si eo tempore a Rege Israelis salutetur*, salutem illi reddere non debeat. XII^{mum} et XIII^{mum}, et XIV^{mum} ac XVI^{mum}, ut si scribendo literula ulla per incuriam vel addatur vel detrahatur: si unus character ab alio nimis distet, vel eidem plus justo adhaereat, totus liber profanus habeatur." Maraccio, Prodrom. Part. I. pag. 9.

[47] "Tres libros invenerunt in atrio.... in uno invenerunt scriptum (Deut. XXXIII. 27.) מְעֹין, in duobus מְעֹנָה, et approbantes duos. rejecerunt unum. In uno invenerunt (Exod. XXIV. 5) scriptum זַעֲטוּטֵי, in duobus נַעֲרֵי, et approbantes duos, rejecerunt unum. In uno invenerunt scriptum, (Gen. XXXII. 23) תֵּשַׁע הִיא, (ed. Fr. אחד עשר הוא), in duobus אֶחָד עֶשְׂרֵה הִיא (ed. Fr. היא אחד) et approbantes duos, rejecerunt unum." Hieros. Tr. Taanith f. 68. c. 1.

[48] "Idcirco vocati sunt prisci, סֹפְרִים, Numeratores, quia numerarunt omnes litteras legis, dicentes: littera Vav vocis גחון Lev. XI. 42. est media littera libri legis: דרש דרש Lev. X. 16. media vox legis: Lev. XIII. 33.... medius versus in lege: Ps. LXXX. 14. י vocis יער est media littera in Psalmis: Ps. LXXVIII. 38. est medius versus in Psalmis." Kiddushin f. 30. c. 1.

and applied it to the Koran, they ought fully to appreciate this scrupulous anxiety of the Jews to preserve the integrity of the very letter of their law. In the Talmud, it is declared to be a sin altogether unpardonable to alter any thing in the Scriptures, and it is added, that to alter a single Hebrew word would endanger the existence of the world, as God had created this world on account of the Scriptures! If the sacred books accidentally fell to the ground, so great was their horror at this apparent desecration, that they appointed a fast to avert the judgment of heaven. The Talmudists added a notice at the end of Leviticus and some other books, that it was not permitted, even to the prophets, to make the very least alteration or innovation in the Law.

The assumption that the Jews intentionally corrupted Scripture, is further opposed to the *solemnity* with which some few mistakes which had crept into the text, were removed and corrected.[49] Nor can we omit to draw attention to the fact, that there are fifteen words in the Old Testament which are encumbered with a number of extraordinary dots,[50] concerning the meaning of which, both Jewish and Christian philologists and divines are to this hour at a loss.

---

[49] We refer to the "*ablatio scribarum*" עֲשֶׂרֶת סוֹפְרִים which removed the ו in Gen. XVIII. 5. XXIV. 55. Numb. XII. 14. Ps. LXVIII. 26. XXXVI. 7. And the "*correctio scribarum*" or תִּקּוּן סוֹפְרִים, which amended 18 passages; e. g. Gen. XVIII. 22. 1 Sam. III. 13. Numb. I. 1.

[50] These *puncta extraordinaria* are more ancient than the vowels. We find them Ps. XXVII. 13. לוּלֵא. Numb. XXI. 30. Gen. XIX. 33. בְּקוּמָהּ etc. etc.

Conjectures as to their origin and signification have not been wanting, yet no one has been able to unravel the mystery, and we are now, no wiser upon the subject than they were in the days of St. Jerome.[51] Yet as these points or dots stood for more than 2000 years, so they stand unmeaning but unaltered to this day."[52] Wherever the Hebrew text has been copied or printed, those extraordinary and practically useless points have been conscientiously transferred; but if they serve no other purpose, they at least act the part of most faithful and impartial witnesses to the integrity of the Old Testament, and to the reverence of the Jews for every "jot or tittle" of their law.

The Jews were indeed accused of having corrupted their Scriptures before Mohammed's time.[53] St. Jerome noticed that the Samaritan Pentateuch and the Septuagint read the passage Deut. XXVII. 26. "Cursed be *every man* that confirmeth not *all* the words of this law to do them;" whilst the Hebrew text merely says, "Cursed be he who confirmeth not the words

---

[51] "Appungunt desuper, quasi incredibile et quod rerum natura non capiat, coire quempiam nescientem." Hieron. quaest. in Gen. XVIII.

[52] Although the Jews crucified the Lord of Glory, yet they spare these useless dots: this is indeed straining a gnat and swallowing a camel! Matt. XXIII. 24.

[53] "Quando itaque, Patres nonnulli, ut *Justinus Martyr* in Dialogo cum Tryphone, Eusebius lib. IV. Hist. eccles. cap. 18. *Origenes* Homil. XII. in Jerem. *Chrysostomus* Homil. V. in Matth. et *Hieronymus* in Epist. 89 ad Augustinum in cap. V. Micheae.... asserunt; *a Judaeis textum biblicum esse corruptum*, non de textu Hebraeo, sed de versionibus praedictis loquantur. Vel de aliquibus saltem, non de omnibus Codicibus Hebraicis id intelligi debet." Quenstedt Theologia didactico-polemica Vol. I. pars I. pag. 195.

of this law to do them."⁵⁴ Upon this discrepancy he founds a grave charge against the Jews, maintaining that they probably expunged those two words which constitute the difference; a charge which it will be very difficult to establish. Some have suspected foul play on the part of the Jews, in the passage Ps. XXII. 16. where certain Manuscripts read, "The assembly of the wicked have inclosed me, like a lion, my hands and my feet;" instead of "they have pierced my hands and my feet;"⁵⁵ but whether this proceeds from a mistake of the transcriber, or from a wilful alteration must be left undecided. We cannot however reconcile *wilful* corruption with the fact, that owing to the scarcely perceptible difference of the respective words in the Hebrew characters, one reading may have passed into the other without in reality altering a single letter.⁵⁶

The Jews, during their contests with the Samari-

---

⁵⁴ "Incertum habemus, utrum LXX interpretes addiderint 5 Mos. XXVII. 26. *omnis homo* et *in omnibus*, an in veteri Hebraeo ita fuerit et postea a Judaeis deletum sit.... Quam ob causam Samaritanorum Hebraea volumina relegens inveni בכ scriptum esse, et cum LXX interpretibus concordare. Frustra igitur illud *tulerunt* Judaei, ne viderentur esse sub maledicto, si non possint omnia complere, quae scripta sunt: cum antiquiores alterius quoque gentis litterae id positum fuisse testentur." Hieron. Comm. in Gal. III. 10. The LXX has, Cursed be πᾶς ἄνθρωπος ὃς οὐκ ἐμμένει ἐν πᾶσι τοῖς λόγοις τοῦ νόμου.

⁵⁵ כָּאֲרִי sicut leo, as in Isa. XXXVIII. 13. Our version reads כָּאֲרוּ *perfoderunt*. So also the LXX. ὤρυξαν χεῖράς μου, καὶ πόδας. The Chaldee version unites both and translates "perfoderunt sic velut leo manus meas et pedes meas."

⁵⁶ Before the vowels were placed, the difference was simply in the ו; כארו and כארי. Besides ו and י are litterae ἐμεταβολοί sive invicem permutabilis.

tans, might have been tempted to corrupt certain passages, touching the points of difference between them, but they nobly resisted the temptation; whilst the Samaritans on the contrary, failed to preserve their Pentateuch in its original integrity. The Samaritans desiring to "worship on mount Gerizim" in opposition to the Jews who said that "Jerusalem was the place where men ought to worship"— in order to have some divine sanction for their choice, substituted "Gerizim" for "Ebal."[57] Here, indeed we discover *wilful corruption* of the sacred text; but the most profound examinations of the various editions of the Old Testament have proved, that those handed down by the Jews are the purest to be found; fewer inaccuracies having crept into their Manuscripts than in any others. Origen in his Hexapla and St. Jerome in his versions made use of Jewish editions, and they are still preferred by the most intelligent Divines.

Again, if the Jews had been desirous to corrupt the Scriptures, they would have found it impossible, from this circumstance; that after the first, and more especially after the second destruction of Jerusalem, they were dispersed all over the East. How, it may be asked, could they have met in conclave to agree upon what parts were to be altered, and in what the alterations should consist? After the advent of Christ, the Hebrew Scriptures were in the hands of the

---

[57] "Ye shall set up these stones which I command you this day in mount Ebal (Samaritan reading: in mount בְּהַרְגְּרִיזִים)..... and there shalt thou build an altar unto the Lord thy God;... and thou shalt offer burnt-offerings thereon unto the Lord thy God." Deut. XXVII. 4.

Christians as well as the Jews, and independently of the Jewish converts to Christianity, there have always been some in the Church, well versed in the Hebrew tongue, who would easily have detected any corruptions that might have been perpetrated. Again, Manuscripts became very early multiplied, a statute existing among the Jews to the effect, that no father of a family should be without a copy of the Law;[58] if therefore, corruptions could have been effected in some, or even in most of the Manuscripts, a considerable number must still have remained inaccessible to those who conspired to corrupt them.[59]

6. We have moreover *internal* proof, that the Jews abstained from making any alteration in their Scriptures, and that Mohammed's accusation falls to the ground. The books in question record their history with the utmost impartiality, neither favouring their prejudices, nor concealing their faults. Their holy Scriptures expose their pride, their rebellion, and their obstinate unbelief, and announce at the same time all the evils which should come upon them. Had the Jews been disposed to alter the sacred Scriptures, they would naturally have expunged those parts

---

[58] "Apud Judaeos legibus statutum, ne quis paterfamilias codice biblico destituatur." Gerhard. Loci Theolog. Vol. II. p. 260.

[59] "Si quaeram, quid sit credibilius Judaeorum gentem tam longe lateque diffusam, in hoc mendacium conscribendum uno consilio conspirare potuisse?..... Sed absit, ut prudens aliquis Judaeos cujuslibet perversitatis ac malitiae tantum potuisse credat in codicibus tam multis et tam longe lateque dispersis..... hoc de invidenda gentibus veritate unum communicasse consilium." August. lib. XV. de civit. Dei cap. 13. That there was a copy in Ethiopia, vide Act. VIII. 30.

which reflected dishonour on their character as a nation; and after the coming of Christ, they would most likely have made alterations concerning those prophecies which prove, that *Jesus of Nazareth was the Messiah* whose advent they had been led to expect. But all the prophecies concerning Christ, which were found in "Moses, the Prophets and the Psalms" before His coming, still exist in the Jewish Scriptures in all their integrity.[60] If the Jews corrupted the Scriptures, says Origen, it must have been done, either before or after Christ. If it was done before Christ, how is it, that our Lord and his Apostles fail to accuse them of this crime, whilst they charge them with all their other sins; if they altered them after Christ, how is it that we have the wonderful agreement between the original and the quotations in the New Testament?[61] The quotations in this case, must have been made prophetically, exactly as the Jews intended to falsify them, and not as they actually stood, when Christ and His Apostles made them!

[60] "Si voluisset Judaei divinas scripturas in odium christianorum corrumpere, praecipua vaticinia de Christo vel sustulissent, vel immutassent, quod tantum abest ipsos fecisse, ut ex textu hebraeo fortiora contra ipsos argumenta proferri possint." Gerhard. Loci Theol. Vol. II. pag. 259.

[61] "Quod si aliquis dixerit hebraeos libros postea a Judaeis esse falsatos, audiat Origenem quid in octavo volumine, explanationem Esaiae huic respondeat quaestiunculae: quod nunquam Dominus et Apostoli, qui caetera crimina arguunt, in Scribis et Pharisaeis, de hoc crimine, quod erat maximum, reticuissent. Sin autem dixerint post adventum Domini Salvatoris, et praedicationem Apostolorum libros Hebraeos fuisse falsatos, cachinnum tenere non potero, ut Salvator et Evangelistae, et Apostoli ita testimonia protulerint ut Judaei postea falsaturi erant." Hieron. Comm. in Esaiam cap. VI.

We shall now attempt to prove *historically*, that the accusation in the Koran of the corruption of the Law, is utterly without foundation. It cannot be said that the Jews failed to preserve the integrity of their Scriptures before Christ, for whilst our Lord rebukes their false interpretation; their "laying aside the commandment of God that they might keep their own traditions;" their "making the word of God of none effect" through their tradition; their "erring not knowing the Scriptures;"[62] neither He nor His Apostles ever accused them of either interpolating or subtracting any passage of their holy books. Christ urges His audience to "search the Scriptures," and argues that what the Scribes and Pharisees teach sitting in Moses' seat is to be heard, observed and obeyed;[63] the five brethren also of the rich man are required to "hear Moses and the Prophets." And is it to be supposed possible, that Christ, whom the Mohammedans themselves consider a great prophet should direct men to fountains that had been corrupted?— As if anticipating the rise of a false prophet, who would endeavour to destroy the antecedent dispensations, under the pretext of the Scriptures having been corrupted, our blessed Lord makes the emphatic declaration, "Think not that I am come to *destroy* the law and the prophets, I am *not come to destroy but to fulfil.*" For verily I say unto you till heaven and earth

---

[62] Καλῶς ἀθετεῖτε τὴν ἐντολὴν τοῦ θεοῦ .... ἀκυροῦντες τὸν λόγον τοῦ θεοῦ etc. etc. Mark VII. 9. 13. See also Matt. XXII. 29. πλανᾶσθε, μὴ εἰδότες τὰς γραφὰς..

[63] The Mosaical teaching to be observed and done πάντα οὖν ὅσα ἂν εἴπωσιν. Matt. XXIII. 2. 3.

shall pass, one jot or one tittle shall in nowise pass from the law, till all be fulfilled; whosoever therefore shall break one of these least commandments, and shall teach men so, he shall be called the least in the kingdom of heaven."[64] These remarkable words of Jesus put the seal to the integrity of the Old Testament in His day; and imply that it would be preserved in the same purity to the end of days; for how could the smallest *jot* which is here placed in juxtaposition with the universe, be fulfilled, were it not to retain its integrity?

The *Apostles* likewise acknowledged the Scriptures of the Old Testament to have come down to them unadulterated. Had the passage for instance, which the Ethiopian Eunuch was reading, been corrupted, Philip the Evangelist would have corrected, rather than expounded it. Again, how could the Bereans be praised Act. XVIII. 1. for testing the soundness of the doctrine which Paul preached, by searching the Scriptures daily, if those writings were themselves unsound? St. Paul supported his own testimony by declaring, that he preached "none other things, than those, which the prophets and Moses

---

[64] Matt. V. 18. *ίῶτα* in Alphabeto hebraico littera minima, maxime elementaris, et in qua Keri et Cethib persaepe differunt, ut promiscue videatur abesse vel redundare. In Codice Hebraeo 66420 jota numerantur. Graeci jota subscribunt aut praetermittunt. *κεραια*, apex, literae appendix, aut portio, linea, qua litera a litera, ut ב a כ vel ר a ד distinguitur, vel sonus a sono, ut punctum vocale aut accentus: denique quicquid ullo modo in lege pertinet ad divinam voluntatem significandam vel ejus significationem adjuvandam." Bengeli Gnomon ad locum. Rom. X. 4. τέλος γὰρ νόμου ΧΡΙΣΤΟΣ.

did say should come" Act. XXII. 22. The same Apostle testifies Rom. III. 2. that to the safe keeping of the Jews "were committed the oracles of God," and the fact of his numbering this, among the high privileges and honours of that nation, implies, that we are indebted to them for their having been preserved inviolate. Josephus, who although belonging to the Jewish communion, was in no way inclined to favour it,[65] makes the following remark, "During so many ages as have already passed, no one has been so bold as either to add anything to them, (viz. the 22 books) to take anything from them, or to make any change in them; but it is become natural to all Jews, immediately from their very birth, to esteem these books to contain divine doctrines, and to persist in them, and if occasion be, willingly to die for them."[66] Testimony from such an impartial authority, carries no small weight.

The early Fathers of the Church not only watched over the Old Testament in their day, but also gave credit to the unbelieving Jews for preserving their holy Scriptures in their original purity. *Eusebius*

---

[65] Josephus did not hesitate to confess of the mass of the people: "I cannot refuse to declare what the nature of the case demands; I believe if the Romans had hesitated to fall upon this frivolous nation, an earthquake would have swallowed, or a flood would have drowned them, or the lightening of Sodom would have burned them up. For this generation was more wicked, than all those could have been who suffered these things."

[66] "Τοσούτον γὰρ αἰῶνος ἤδη παρῳχηκότος, οὔτε προσθεῖναί τις οὐδὲν, οὔτε ἀφελεῖν αὐτῶν, οὔτε μεταθεῖναι τετόλμηκεν· Πᾶσι δὲ συμφυτόν ἐστιν εὐθὺς ἐκ τῆς πρώτης γενέσεως Ἰουδαίοις τὸ νομίζειν αὐτὰ Θεοῦ δόγματα, καὶ τούτοις ἐμμένειν, καὶ ὑπὲρ αὐτῶν, εἰ δέοι, θνήσκειν ἡδέως. Joseph. contra Apion. lib. I. cap. 8.

agrees with *Josephus* and *Philo*, that up to their time "for the space of more than two thousand years, not one single word in the law of the Hebrews had been altered, and that any Jew would rather die a hundred times, as was shown, than alter the law in the least degree."[67]

7. We have seen from a comparison of ancient catalogues of the Old Testament Scriptures, that the same books, bearing the same names which existed in the days of Josephus, were received by the Christians, and by them handed down to the present day; no books being lost, and none added to them. We have also shown, that although verbal differences arose from the neglect or ignorance of copyists, which gave rise to different readings in many passages, yet that none of these could be referred to by Mohammed who spoke of wilful corruptions; nor was any one dogma of the Jewish faith thereby affected.[68] Lastly, the foregoing testimonies of competent and impartial authorities are sufficient to convince us, that with no degree of justice can we accuse the Jews, at any period, of having altered their sacred books.

There is however another way of satisfying the

[67] Usque ad mea tempora per spatium amplius quam duorum millium annorum, ne verbum quidem fuisse unquam in lege hebraeorum mutatum et quemlibet Judaeum centies potius moriturum, quam ut pateretur, legem in aliquo mutari." Euseb. lib. III. Eccles. hist. c. 10. and lib. VIII. de praep. Ev. c. 2.

[68] God permitted these "variae lectiones" to adhere to His blessed book, to constitute a kind of likeness to the eternal Word, λόγος, when He had taken the form of a servant, μορφὴν δούλου λαβὼν, ἐν ὁμοιώματι ἀνθρώπων γενόμενος. It made the Bible "in fashion", σχήματι εὑρεθείς, as an ordinary production. Phil. II. 6—10.

most sceptical mind, that at no period could there have been the opportunity, even if there had been the desire on the part of the Jews, to corrupt their Scriptures. We possess *versions* of the Old Testament which agree with the original and with one another; *versions* too, which exist in Manuscripts, of dates prior to the rise of Islamism. We commence with those oriental translations, made by the Jews during their exile in Babylon, to supply a national want. Moses and the Prophets wrote in the Hebrew tongue, that the mass of the people might hear and understand the words of the law.[69] During the Captivity, the pure Hebrew dialect being lost for ever,— for it was never restored after their return to Palestine, —the Scriptures read in the synagogue had to be orally translated and explained in the *Chaldee* language, and ere long, we find written versions of the original in that tongue. These translations, owing to the analogy of the Hebrew and Chaldee languages, generally required no change of words, but merely an alteration in the grammatical construction.[70] All objections to the high antiquity of these Chaldee versions have been ably refuted.[71]

The first *Targum* or version of Jonathan,[72] was

[69] Deut. XXXI. 11. 2 Chron. XXXIV. 30.

[70] Targumim תַּרְגּוּמִים; a trace of Targumic version is recognised in Ἠλὶ Ἠλὶ, λαμὰ σαβαχθανί; Matt. XXVII. 46. אֵלִי אֵלִי לָמָה עֲזַבְתָּנִי׃ cfr. Psalm XXII. 1.

[71] Aug. Pfeifferi Critica sacra cap. VIII. sect. II. pag. 756. 896.

[72] Jonathan, the son of Uziel, was a disciple of Hillel, and lived about 42 years B. C. "Dicunt de Jonathane fil. Uzelis cum sederet et operaretur legi, quamlibet avem super ipsum voliantem sta-

made before Christ and comprised the entire Old Testament; but only the historical books, or the "former prophets," and the prophets properly so called, are now extant. The Jews considered this translation of great weight and authority, as appears from the many fables which they concocted about it; the work however, seems more a paraphrase than a literal version. The second Targum was made by *Onkelos*.[73] This version is four times mentioned in the Talmud, and is considered very faithful and literal. Among the other Chaldee versions, we only mention that, generally known as the *Targum of Jerusalem*; though not written in so pure Chaldee as the rest, yet it was no doubt made before the rise of Mohammedanism.

The *Greek translation* of the Old Testament, commonly called the *Septuagint*,[74] was executed under

tim combustam. Baba Bathra f. 134. c. 1. And in Megilla f. 3. c. 1. we read that he wrote his version from the mouths of Haggai, Zechariah and Malachi; adding: "tum commota est terra Israelis ad CCCC parasangas, egressa est filia vocis et dixit: Quis ille, qui revelavit secreta mea filiis hominum? Constitit Jonathan f. U. super pedes suos, et dixit: ego sum ille, qui revelavi secreta tua filiis hominum, verum non ad gloriam meam, neque ad gloriam patris mei, sed ad gloriam tuam."

[73] אֳנְקְלוֹס surnamed הַגֵּר the proselyte; said to be σύγχρονος with *Gamaliel senex.* That he was a Babylonian is inferred from his pure Chaldee. The Masora מָסֹרֶת, מְסֹרָה, מְסֹרֶת, from מָסַר *tradidit,* or the traditions respecting certain letters, words and verses — first handed down by oral communication and then collected by the Jewish Rabbis, chiefly of Tiberias, between the 3rd and the 6th century — was also of service in preserving the sacred text. The בַּעֲלֵי מָסֹרָה or Masorethae embodied their theological, critical, orthographical or grammatical notices in the so called קְרִי וּכְתִיב, always signifying that which they consider the more correct reading with ק, h. e. קְרִי *legito.*

[74] So called, not so much from "*septuaginta interpretes,*" who

Ptolemaeus Philadelphus, the generous protector of the Jews, 284 years B. C., and has done more to confirm the integrity of the Law than any other event. As the Chaldee versions were made for the benefit of the Jews in Babylon and Palestine, when Hebrew ceased to be a living tongue; so the Septuagint was made in Alexandria, on behalf of the Jews living in countries where *Greek* was spoken. If Kaliph Omar had been anxious to ascertain whether the Jews had corrupted their Scriptures, he might have convinced himself of the contrary, by the examination of the original Manuscripts of this version, which were probably deposited in that celebrated Library which his fanaticism caused to be burned. Happily for our argument and the interests of truth, the Septuagint version, at that period, was spread far and wide.[75] Josephus referred to this translation more than to the Hebrew, and Philo used it exclusively. It has been quoted on many occasions in the New Testament,

are said to have made this version, as from the fact of its having been approved of, and sanctioned by the Jewish Synedrium existing at Alexandria. There were at Alexandria LXXI seats for the great Synedrium. היו בה שבעים ואחת קתדראות של זהב כנגד שבעים ואחד של סנהדרין גדולה Gem. Succa fol. LI. c. 2. Quae Raschi in suis scholiis eodem modo exponit: כנגד ע' וא' זקנים שישרו להם סנהדרין: namely the Synedrium Alexandrinum. That this version was approved by the Jewish heads at Alexandria, appears from the following, "παρεκάλεσαν (Judaei) τε δοῦναι καὶ τοῖς ἡγουμένοις αὐτῶν ἀναγνῶναι τὸν νόμον: ἠξίωσάν τε πάντες, ὅτε ἱερεύς καὶ τῶν ἑρμηνέων οἱ πρεσβύτεροι καὶ τοῦ πολιτεύματος οἱ προεστηκότες ἐπεὶ καλῶς τὰ τῆς ἑρμηνείας ἀπήρισται, καὶ διαμεῖναι ταυθ' ὡς ἔχει καὶ μὴ μετακινεῖν αὐτά. Joseph. Lib. XII. c. II. p. 397.

[75] At the time of Christ it was quoted: "quia eo tempore illa erat in gentibus divulgata." Hieron. in cap. XLVII.

but without the defects having been adopted which crept into the translation.[76]

The *Syriac version* of the Old Testament comprises all the canonical Scriptures, and was in all probability a work of the Jews, from whom it received its name.[77] It was executed in the first, or certainly not later than the second century. Unlike the Chaldee versions, the *Peshito* had not only to adjust the grammatical construction, but to convey the sense of the original in a new form; hence perhaps the name of "*literal*" translation. If Mohammed had a suspicion of the Jews having corrupted their Scriptures, and if he could not satisfy his mind from an inspection of the Hebrew Manuscripts, he had opportunity during his commercial pursuits in Syria to institute a comparison between the Peshito and the original. The false prophet however, appears not at any time, to have "inquired diligently" for the truth.

The translation of *Aquila*, which was made for the use of the Jews, in the second century of the Christian era, is an exact and faithful rendering of

---

[76] They quoted according to this rule: "Ubicunque de veteri instrumento prophetae et apostoli testimonia protulerunt, diligentius observandum est, *non eos verba secutos* esse, sed *sensum*, et ubicunque septuaginta ab hebraeo discrepant, hebraeum sensum suis expressisse sermonibus." Hieron. Epist. 151.

[77] Peshito means "*the literal.*" תִּרְגּוּם, Targum, with the Jews, signifies every version into another language. Holy Scriptures are said by them to have a double meaning, viz. פְּשׁוּט the literal sense, and מִדְרָשׁ the learned or allegorical sense. The Hebrew פָּשׁוּט is turned פְּשִׁיט in Chaldee; and in the Syrian פְּשִׁיטָא. Hottinger, Thesaurus philologic. seu clavis sac. scripturae Lib. I. cap. II. sect. 7. pag. 233—237.

the original.[78] The translator was a native of Synope in Pontus, and his version was preferred by the Asiatic Jews to the Septuagint.[79] That Aquila himself was a Jew, is clear from the inimicial bearing which he frequently evinces towards Christianity. Mohammedans willingly admit that we have the genuine production of a Jew in this version; but though he strains a word here and there to favour the Jewish view of the text, Aquila cannot be charged by Christians with having corrupted the word of God.[80] Theodotion a proselyte of Ephesus, revised the Septuagint, and he was followed by Symmachus, who strove to give his version of the Old Testament a clearer and more classical finish, than it had previously received.[81]

At the beginning of the third century, we find a mighty work in the celebrated *Hexapla* of Origen.[82]

[78] עקילום in the Hieros. and אקילוס in the Babylon. Talmud Ἀκύλας ὁ Ποντικός; he also is called προσήλυτος. Iren. III. 24.

[79] Φιλοτιμότερον πεπιστευμένος παρὰ Ἰουδαίοις, ἡρμηνευκέναι τὴν γραφὴν, ᾧ μάλιστα εἰώθασιν οἱ ἀγροῦντες τὴν Ἑβραίων διάλεκτον χρῆσθαι. Origen. Epist. ad African. pag. 13.

[80] "Jam pridem cum voluminibus Hebraeorum editionem Aquilae confero, ne quid forsitan propter odium Christi synagoga mutaverit: et ut amicae menti fatear, quae ad nostram fidem pertineant roborandam plura reperio." Hieron. Epist. 74. ad Marcel. Op. IV. 2. 61.

[81] "Symmachus more suo manifestius." Hieron. Comm. in Jes. I.

[82] "Unde nobis curae fuit omnes veteris Legis libros, quos nos Adamantius in Hexapla digesserat, de Caesariensi Bibliotheca descriptos, ex ipsis authenticis emendare, in quibus ipsa Hebraea propriis sunt characteribus verba descripta, et Graecis litteris tramite expressa vicino. Aquila etiam et Symmachus, Septuaginta et Theodotio suum ordinem tenent. Nonnulli vero libri, et maxime hi, qui apud Hebraeos versu compositi sunt, tres alias editiones additas habent, quam Quintam et Sextam et Septimam translationem vocant,

In drawing attention to this undertaking, we furnish fresh evidence for establishing the integrity of the Old Testament Scriptures, upon a still broader foundation. All the translations we have hitherto mentioned, originated with the Jews; but the Hexapla was the work of a Christian, converted from Heathenism, and the weight of this testimony can scarcely be overrated. In placing the Hebrew, both in its own, and in Greek characters, parallel with the versions of Aquila, Symmachus, his own, that of Theodotion and the Septuagint, (and in some books of the Scriptures, with three other anonymous translations), Origen constructed an unparalleled bulwark against any attempts to undermine the integrity of the sacred text. There are only fragments of this valuable work remaining; the Hexapla itself no doubt perished with the Library at Alexandria.

At the time of Augustine, several *Latin versions* were in existence, among which, he gave the preference to the *Itala*, a work of the second century.[83] St. Jerome first revised this translation in the year A. D. 382, and whilst engaged in this work, he was requested by his friends to make a new Latin translation from the original, which was finished A. D. 405, and is known as the *Vulgata*.[84] Another trans-

auctoritatem, sine nominibus interpretum consequentas." Hieron. Comm. in Tit. III.

[83] "In ipsis autem interpretationibus *Itala* caeteris praeferatur: nam est verborum tenacior cum perspicuitate sententiae." August. de Christ. doctr. II. c. 15.

[84] "Desiderii mei desideratas accepi epistolas ... obsecrantis, ut translatum in Latinam linguam de Hebraeo sermone ... nostrorum auribus traderem." Hieron. praef. ad Pentateuch.

lation into *Ethiopic*—the language of the people who subdued the Jewish kingdom in the south of Arabia — was made in the fourth century. It is said to have been the work of Abba Salama. An entire copy of this version is now being printed in Germany.[85] *Egyptian translations* of the Old Testament are found as early as the third and the beginning of the fourth century; both the *Coptic* version and the translation into the language of Upper Egypt could therefore have been consulted by every one suspecting a corruption of the text of the Old Testament.[86] The *Armenian* Church received a version from *Miesrob* in the fifth century; the Septuagint from which this translation was made, was brought from the Council at Ephesus. Miesrob was assisted by two of his disciples whom he had sent to Alexandria to acquire a knowledge of the Greek.[87] There is only one more version of the Jewish Scriptures, made before the days of Mohammed, of which we have a detailed account, and that is the *Georgian;* it was finished in the sixth century.[88]

8. All these translations agree with each other, though made in different ages, by people of different views, and with different objects; they exist in Manu-

---

[85] The learned Orientalist, Dr. Dillmann, Prof. at Kiel, is engaged in carrying this version through the press, after a careful collation of the MSS. extant in Europe.

[86] Vide, Quinque II. Mosis Prophet. in lingua Aegypt. descripti et Lat. versi a David Wilkins, London 1731, as containing printed samples of the Coptic version.

[87] Mosis Chorenensis hist. Armeniae cap. 54. pag. 299.

[88] Allg. Biblioth. der biblischen Litterat. I. 153. von Eichhorn.

scripts considerably older than the Koran, and are accessible to any sceptic who may doubt the integrity of the Old Testament. As no dissentient voice then is heard, among all the witnesses that can be summoned by either party, the charge which Mohammed brought against the Jews, of corrupting their Scriptures, inevitably falls to the ground. But where, we may ask, is the *Arabic version* of the Old Testament?— Chaldee Targumim, Syriac, Ethiopic, Egyptian, Greek, Latin, Armenian and Georgian translations were made at an early period, and circulated before even the name of Mohammed was heard of; and yet we seek in vain for an *Arabic* copy of the Hebrew Scriptures, in the East, before the tenth century of our era, when the Hebrew prophets were translated into Arabic by a Christian priest at Alexandria.[89] The books of Solomon, the book of Ezra, and the Psalms — which as well as the Prophets just now mentioned, are found in the Paris and London Polyglotts — were rendered into Arabic by Abdallah ben Alfadi, in the eleventh century.[90] *Rabbi Saadias-Gaon*[91] who died A. D. 942

---

[89] Gabr. Sion. praef. ad Psalter. Syr. Par. 1625. In Spain indeed, we meet with an Arabic version in the middle of the eighth century, which had been made by John Bishop of Sevilia. "Joannes Hispalensis praesul divinos libros lingua arabica donabat utriusque nationis saluti consulens: quoniam Arabicae linguae multus usus erat Christianis aeque atque Mauris; latina passim ignorabatur. Ejus interpretationis exempla ad nostram aetatem conservata sunt; extantque non uno in loco in Hispanis." Mariana de rebus Hispan. lib. VII. cap. 3.

[90] The psalms were printed at Haleb 1706.

[91] Paulus Spec. vers. Pent. Arab. pag. 33.

[92] He was a native of Fayum in Egypt, and president of a school at Sora in Babylon. Some ascribe to him a translation of Job and Hosea.

left an Arabic Pentateuch, and the book of Isaiah with Targumic and Rabbinical explanations. Another Pentateuch was translated by an African Jew, in the thirteenth century.[93] In the year A. D. 1468 *Hareth ben Senan* translated the Psalms, Job, Proverbs, Canticles, Sirach, the minor Prophets, with Jeremiah, Daniel, Ezekiel and Isaiah.[94] Lastly, Arabic versions were made in behalf of the Roman Catholic Christians in the East, from the Vulgata; but the first of these bears no earlier date than A. D. 1671.[95] This version was reprinted by the British and Foreign Bible Society in 1822. The fact of there being no Arabic version of the Old Testament prior to the tenth century, seems incredible. We know that the Jews were sufficiently powerful to found a Jewish kingdom in the south of Arabia; how is it that they here, neglected to do, what they invariably did during their sojourn in other lands? For in Babylon, they made a Chaldee, in Egypt, a Greek, in Syria, a Syriac version of their holy books. We also know that there existed several *Bishoprics* in Arabia, prior to the rise of Islamism;[96] and it is certain that some Churches were there planted by the Apostles themselves. The question therefore arises

[93] Edited as "Pentateuchus Mosis Arabice "by Erpenius 1622.

[94] Copies are preserved in Manuscripts; 2 in Oxford, and 2 in Paris.

[95] Biblia Sacra Arab. s. Congregationis de propaganda fide jussu edita ad usum Eccles. orientalium, additis e reg. Bibliis Lat. Rom. typis sanct. Congreg. 1671. Vol. III.

[96] There was a Bishop of Dhafar, another of Hajran; the Jacobites had two Bishops, one at Akula, the other in Hira; and the Nestorians had one in the Peninsula. Sale's Prelim. Disc. pag. 17.

whether the Christians would not have translated the Old Testament into Arabic, within the space of 600 years, as they rendered them into the Syriac, Ethiopic, Egyptian, Armenian, Greek and Latin tongues. We can scarcely deem it possible, that a Church built upon the joint foundation of the Prophets and Apostles, could possibly exist for 600 years without a version of the Old Testament in the vernacular tongue!

We have moreover the testimony of the learned *Theodoretus*, who lived A.D. 450. that the Old Testament in his day, was translated into every language then spoken. We may then take it for granted, that the Jews and Christians, both of whom so strongly mustered in Arabia, would have made versions of the Old Testament, and that the Arabic though not specified by Theodoretus, A.D. 450 was included. That he did not mention all the translations by name is clear, from his omitting the Chaldee, Ethiopic and Syriac.[97]

Inference may in some cases amount to a moral certainty, and in this particular, it seems to justify our assumption of the existence of an Arabic version of Scripture. We have however direct and historical evidence, that the Old Testament had been translated into Arabic at the time when the Ethiopic version was being made. A poem and also a martyrology

---

[97] "Hebraici libri non modo in Graecum idioma conversi sunt, sed in Romanam quoque linguam, Aegypticam, Persicam, Indicam, Armenicam, et Scythicam, atque adeo Sauromaticam, semelque ut dicam in linguas omnes, quibus ad hanc diem nationes utuntur," εἰς πάσας τὰς γλώττας αἷς ἅπαντα τὰ ἔθνη κεχρημένα διατελεῖ. Theodoretus lib. V. de Curan. Graecor. tom. II. pag. 521.

in Ethiopic, both bear testimony that Aba Salama[98] translated the Scriptures into Geez, and that he made his version from an Arabic text.[99] The conclusion then to which we are driven by our argument is this, that there was an Arabic version of the Scriptures in existence before the rise of Islamism; and but little doubt can exist that Mohammed or his followers destroyed it, to remove the possibility of his charge against the "Scripturalists" being refuted.

9. If the Old Testament Scriptures be corrupted, as the Mohammedans will have it, then it must follow: that God either would not or could not preserve His own word in its original purity, which is opposed to either His goodness or power; again, the only source of our faith is for ever contaminated, since neither the original nor versions can be depended on; Christ and His Apostles stand convicted of blaming the Jews for minor offences; whilst they allowed so great a crime to pass unnoticed; the toil and study of Hebrew scholars in investigating and scrutinising the editions of the original have proved utterly unavailing; all that Philo, Josephus, Eusebius, Origen, Augustine, and others have stated of the scrupulous care of the Jews touching their Scriptures, is false, or the testimonies of these men have likewise been corrupted; the ho-

[98] Jobi Ludolphi historia Aethiop. Lib. III. cap. 2.

[99] "Die Habessinier nennen unter ihren ersten Glaubenspredigern mit vorzüglichem Ruhme einen gewissen Aba Salama, und diesem schreibt es auch ein inländischer Dichter und ein äthiopisches Martyrologium zu, daß er die Bücher des Gesetzes und Evangeliums aus der Arabischen in ihre Sprache übersetzt habe." Dr. Hug's Einleitung in die Schriften des neuen Testamentes. Vol. I. pag. 375. See also Ludolphi commentar. in histor. Aethiop. lib. III. cap. 4. pag. 295.

nour of keeping the oracles of God, as ascribed by St. Paul to the Jews, is nothing less than a cruel and unseemly satire; and Mohammed himself, in seeking to build upon Moses and the prophets has chosen but a rotten foundation. As these necessary sequences are utterly opposed to all sense and reason, still more absurd must be the assumption from which they are deduced.[1]

CHAPTER II.

THE INTEGRITY OF THE NEW TESTAMENT.

"Heaven and earth shall pass away but MY words shall not pass away." Mark XIII. 31.

1. Having repelled the charge of Mohammed against the Jews, we shall now proceed to remove the aspersions which he endeavoured to cast upon the Christians, who are likewise accused of having suppressed some of their Scriptures and corrupted others. In the time of Nero, the Christian Religion had spread not only over Palestine, but throughout the vast Empire of the Romans, aspiring to become, in the full acceptation of the word, the dominant creed of the world.[2]

That the New Testament Scriptures were written in the respective countries and ages ascribed to them by the Church, has been satisfactorily tested and in-

---

[1] Gerhardi Loci Theologici tom. II. pag. 261.

[2] Vide Tacitum lib. XV. Annal. cap. 44. Also: Suetonium in Nerone cap. 16. Plinii lib. X. Ep. 97.

controvertibly proved by internal and incidental evidence,[3] and also by external historical testimony.[4] It is not our intention to go over this ground again, but in order to obtain a solid foundation for our present argument, it will be requisite to premise some particulars relating to the early history of the sacred books, included in the New Testament.

2. We have many relics of ancient literature, concerning the genuineness and integrity of which, we are convinced without having any other, than internal evidence. Not so with the New Testament; there is no one book, among all the ancient works of the Greeks and Romans, which has an equal amount of historical evidence as regards its date and origin. Supposing the Scriptures of the Christians to have been written, the first under Nero, the last under Domitian, the witnesses, stretching as far down as Diocletian, would only be two centuries removed from the conclusion of the period in which they were composed. These early writers of the Church have been consulted, with a view to ascertain how soon the books in question had been circulated, and that with eminent success.[5] It may be added, that their

[3] This was happily done in many instances by *Paley*, in his "Horae Paulinae," and by *Hug*, "Einleitung in das neue Testament." Band I. pag. 9—32.

[4] Lardner's "Credibility of the Gospel History, or the facts occasionally mentioned in the New Testament, confirmed by passages of ancient authors." 1727.

[5] Lardner was followed by Ch. Fr. Schmid in the "Historia et vindicatio canonis." 1775. G. Less in his work: "Ueber Religion, ihre Geschichte und Bestätigung;" 1786. and Paley, "A view of the evidences of Christianity." 1797.

quotations are more exact in citing from the *didactic*, than from the *historical* portions of the New Testament; again, the Old Testament is more carefully quoted, than the New, simply because their readers were better acquainted with the latter than with the former.

Clemens Romanus, whose "name was in the book of life," Phil. IV. 3. speaks of the Epistle of "the blessed Apostle Paul;"[6] and faithfully quotes passages from the Epistles to the Romans and to the Hebrews.[7] *Ignatius*, Bishop of Antioch A. D. 69. who suffered martyrdom under Trajan at Rome, alludes to the didactic parts of the New Testament,[8] and also quotes St. Pauls words, "that ye all speak the same thing and be perfectly joined together in the same mind and in the same judgment."[9] In his Epistle to the Church of Philadelphia, he mentions the Gospel and the Apostolic writings conjointly, which implies, that he was acquainted with both.[10]

Polycarp, the disciple of St. John and Bishop of

---

[6] Ἀναλάβετε τὴν ἐπιστολὴν τοῦ μακαρίου Παύλου τοῦ Ἀποστόλου· τί πρῶτον ὑμῖν ἐν ἀρχῇ τοῦ Εὐαγγελίου ἔγραψεν; ἐπ᾽ ἀληθείας πνευματικῶς ἐπέστειλεν ὑμῖν περὶ αὑτοῦ τε καὶ Κηφᾶ καὶ Ἀπόλλω, διὰ τὸ καὶ τό ε ποσκλίσεις ὑμᾶς πεποιῆσθαι. Clem. Rom. I Epist. ad Corinth. cap. 47.

[7] Compare Clem. Rom. Epist. ad Cor. c. 35. with Rom. I. 29— 32. and cap. 36. with Hebr. I, 3—7.

[8] Παύλου συμμύσται τοῦ ἁγιασμένου..... ὃ ἐν πάσῃ ἐπιστολῇ μνημονεύει ὑμῶν ἐν Χριστῷ Ἰησοῦ. Ignat. Epist. ad Ephes. c. 12.

[9] Ignat. Ep. ad Ephes. cap. 2. with 1 Cor. I, 10.

[10] προσφυγὼν τῷ Εὐαγγελίῳ ὡς σαρκὶ Ἰησοῦ, καὶ τοῖς ἀποστόλοις ὡς πρεσβυτερίῳ ἐκκλησίας· Ignat. Epist. ad Philadelph. cap. 5. cfr. also *Ignat. ad Trall.* cap. XI. and *ad Philadelph.* cap. III. also *ad Smyrn.* cap. I. with Matt. XV. 13. III. 15. where two other quotations occur.

Smyrna, who became a martyr A. D. 169, likewise refers to the Epistles generally,[11] and to that of the Corinthians in particular.[12] In his Epistle to the Philippians, he writes, "Remember what our Lord said, when He taught,—Judge not that ye be not judged, forgive and it shall be forgiven you; be merciful and ye shall obtain mercy; with what measure ye mete, it shall be measured to you again."[13] Barnabas, the companion of St. Paul, and according to some, Bishop of Milan, refers to the following words of our Lord, "many are called but few are chosen;"[14] and "whosoever will come after me, let him deny himself and take up his cross and follow me."[15] Clemens Romanus bids the Corinthians remember the words of the Lord Jesus, and then rehearses several detached sentences from the sermon on the mount, especially as recorded by St. Luke.[16] In his second Epistle he adds, "And another Scripture saith.—I came not to call the righteous to repentance but the sinners."[17]

[11] Παύλου, ὃς γενόμενος ἐν ὑμῖν κατὰ πρόσωπον τῶν τότε ἀνθρώπων, ἐδίδαξεν ἀκριβῶς· καὶ βεβαίως τὸν περὶ ἀληθείας λόγον· ὃς καὶ ἀπὼν ὑμῖν ἔγραψεν ἐπιστολὰς. Polycarp. ep. ad Philip. c. 3.

[12] Compare Polycarp. ad Philip. c. 5. with 1 Cor. VI. 9.

[13] Μνημονεύσαντες δὲ ὧν εἶπεν ὁ κύριος διδάσκων· Μὴ κρίνετε, ἵνα μὴ κριθῆτε· κτλ. Polycarp. Epist. ad Philip. c. 2. Also Clem. Rom. ad Corinth. c. 13.

[14] "Attendamus ergo, ne forte, sicut scriptum est, multi vocati, pauci electi inveniamur." Epist. Barnab. cap. 4.

[15] Οὕτω, φησὶν (Ἰησοῦς) οἱ θέλοντές με ἰδεῖν καὶ ἅψασθαί μου τῆς βασιλείας, ὀφείλουσι θλιβέντες καὶ παθόντες λαβεῖν με. Epist. Barn. cap. 7. Vide Matt. XVI. 24. Mark. VIII. 34. Lu. IX. 23.

[16] Clem. Rom. Epist. ad Corinth. cap. 13. with Lu. VI. 36—38.

[17] Καὶ ἑτέρα γραφὴ λέγει, ὅτι οὐκ ἦλθον καλέσαι δικαίους, ἀλλὰ ἁμαρτωλούς. Clem. Rom. Epist. II. ad Corinth.

He also refers to the words of our Lord, touching faithfulness in little things, with the special addition that they were found in the Gospel.[18] More detailed evidence of the existence of the New Testament, than the above, may be deduced from the works of the early Fathers of the Church. Justin Martyr, born in Palestine A. D. 89. was well acquainted with the Gospels;[19] and whilst merely alluding to the existence of the Epistles, he ascribes the Apocalypse to St. John.[20] Athenagoras, who died A. D. 180. quotes the first Epistle to the Corinthians,[21] and shows a general acquaintance with the Epistles of St. Paul. Theophilus, who flourished A. D. 180. speaks of the Gospels, mentions that of St. John by name, refers to the Epistles of St. Paul to the Romans and to Timothy,[22] and is said to have made use of the Apocalypse. In the year A. D. 170. Dionysius, Bishop of Corinth, speaks of the New Testament Scriptures as the books of the Lord Jesus Christ.[23]

3. The above quotations prove two things, first,

---

[18] Clem. Rom. Epist. II. cap. 10. cfr. Lu. XVI. 11. 12.

[19] Οἱ γὰρ ἀπόστολοι ἐν τοῖς γενομένοις ὑπ' αὐτῶν ἀπομνημονεύμασι, ἃ καλεῖται Εὐαγγέλια, οὕτως παρέδωκαν. Just. Martyr. Apolog. I. cap. 66. pag. 83.

[20] Just. Mar. Dialog. cum Tryph. cap. 81. pag. 179.

[21] Εὔδηλον παντὶ τὸ λειπόμενον, ὅτι δεῖ κατὰ τὸν ἀπόστολον τὸ φθαρτὸν τοῦτο καὶ διασκεδαστὸν ἐνδύσασθαι ἀφθαρσίαν. Athenag. de resurrect. cap. 18. p. 531. and 1 Cor. XV. 54.

[22] ... τὰ τῶν προφητῶν καὶ τῶν εὐαγγελίων ἔχειν. Theoph. ad Autolyc. III. pag. 338. and pag. 389. he quotes as ὁ θεῖος λόγος what is written 1 Tim. II. 2. Rom. XIII. 7. 8.

[23] γραφαὶ κυριακαί. Euseb. H. E. IV. 23. where Dionysius is quoted.

that the books of the New Testament existed in the *first two centuries* and were known among the Christians, and secondly, that they had the same books then, as we have now. That these writings should have been corrupted during the above period, is clearly impossible. They could not have been corrupted during the lifetime of the Apostles, because these Scriptures were speedily multiplied and circulated among the Churches, and the greater the number of manuscript copies, the greater the difficulty to alter any portion of them. Nor did the Apostles, or their immediate disciples, the Apostolic Fathers, complain of any such corruptions, although they had occasion to censure many a disorder which had crept into the Churches. After the decease of the Apostles, the original Manuscripts of the various detached books of the New Testament, were reverentially preserved in the archives of the principal Churches, and served as a check against any alteration, which might be attempted.

Still more weighty, and in the eyes of the Mohammedans, more impartial, must be the evidence which is to be obtained from the *enemies* who assaulted, and the *heretics* who separated from the Church, during the first two centuries. Celsus, an Epicurean philosopher, wrote a work[24] against Christianity, which has been partially preserved in a refutation by Origen. He refers to the various miracles, wrought by our Lord, and gives many details of His passion; and all these things, he states, had been written by His dis-

---

[24] He gave it the arrogant title of "Ἀληθὴς λόγος."

ciples.[25] Although he speaks of these writings as *the Gospel*,[26] yet he plainly indicates two of the Evangelists, (St. Matthew and St. Luke), when he states, that those writers assume too much, who trace the lineal descent of Jesus, the one genealogically to the first man, the other, to the Jewish kings.[27] As Celsus refers, in one part of his work, to Christ being asked in the temple,[28] by the Jews for a sign to prove His divine Sonship; and in another part, to the fact of His showing His wounds in His side and hands after His Resurrection;[29] and also alludes to the *word*, being declared in the Gospel to be the Son of God;[30] we have a threefold proof that he was acquainted with the Gospel of St. John.

That Celsus was also in possession of the remaining Gospel of St. Mark, is placed beyond all doubt, by his urging it as a point of disagreement between the writers of the Gospel, that, "some say there were

---

[25] Τοὺς δὲ μαθητὰς, τοὺς κατὰ τὸν Ἰησοῦν ἀναγεγραφέναι περὶ αὐτοῦ τοιαῦτα. Celsus lib. II. 13. and lib. II. cap. 16. Shortly after he adds, "All these have we taken out of your own Scriptures; we need no other witnesses, as your own weapons are sufficient for your destruction." Lib. II. cap. 74.

[26] Ἐυαγγελιον; just as the most ancient Manuscripts are inscribed.

[27] Ἀπηυθαδήσθαι τοὺς γενεαλογήσαντες ἀπὸ τοῦ πρώτου φύντος καὶ τῶν ἐν Ἰουδαίοις βασιλέων τὸν Ἰησοῦν. καὶ.... ὅτι οὐκ ἄν ἡ τοῦ τεκτόνος γυνὴ τηλικούτου γενοῦς τυγχανοῦσα ἠγνόει. Celsus lib. II. c. 32.

[28] Ἐν τῷ ἱερῷ. cfr. John II. 18.

[29] Καὶ τὰ σημεῖα τῆς κολασέως ἔδειξεν ὁ Ἰησοῦς, καὶ τὰς χεῖρας ὡς ἦσαν πεπερονημέναι Celsus lib. II. cap. 59. with John XX. 27.

[30] After stating that λόγον εἶναι υἱὸν τοῦ θεοῦ, Celsus makes the Jew whom he introduces, blasphemously object, that "it was an impure and unholy λόγος, who was abused and executed."

two angels, and some, there was only one angel at the sepulchre of Christ."[31] To justify this expression, there must have been at least two writers on each side, and this accords with the four Evangelists.[32]

Without further examining the allusions of Celsus to Apostolic writings,[33] we hasten to notice, what this bitter and subtle enemy of Christianity neglected to do. Celsus assaulted Christ and Christianity, Christians and their Holy Scriptures with an extraordinary skill and virulence, but in all his attacks we seek in vain for any charge against the integrity of the Holy Scriptures. He ridicules the Christians, and nothing apparently would have given him greater satisfaction than to prove to the world, that from some motive or other they had corrupted their sacred books. His silence therefore must be considered the most convincing proof that up to that period, no alteration had been affected in the sacred text.

Scarcely less important is the testimony of the Christian heretics[34] of the first two centuries, both as to the early existence of the sacred books of the New Testament, and to their being preserved in their integrity during that period. In the fragments pre-

[31] Καὶ μὲν καὶ πρὸς τὸν αὐτοῦ τοῦδε τάφον ἐλθεῖν ἄγγελον, οἱ δὲ δύο τοὺς ἀποκρινομένους ταῖς γυναιξὶν, ὅτι ἀνέστη. Celsus lib. V. cap. 52.

[32] Matthew and Mark speak of one angel; Luke and John of two.

[33] Quotations of the Epistles of Paul are seen Celsus lib. V. cap. 64. lib. VI. cap. 12. lib. VIII. cap. 24.

[34] Tatian, Julius Cassian, Theodotus; anonymous heretics mentioned by Tertullian and Origen; Marcion, Ptolemaeus, Heraclion, Valentinus and his school, Basilides and Isidorus. Hug Vol. I. p. 38.

served of these heterodox teachers, we have numerous quotations from every book of the New Testament with the exception of the Epistle of St. Paul to Titus. Although some of these heretics altered or omitted both books and passages in their own Manuscripts, yet we recognise portions from the New Testament Scriptures, in most of the quotations which they made to support their own particular views.

4. It is not necessary here to show, how soon the early Churches interchanged and collected the various books of the New Testament, but it would appear, that it was fairly commenced in the lifetime of the Apostles.[35] Some of the Apostolic writings, specially those addressed to *private* individuals, were naturally slower than others in becoming known and circulated;[36] yet they too ere long were read in the Churches, and thus escaped being placed among the unknown or apocryphal books.[37] As however Epistles of the

---

[35] It was requested by St. Paul Col. III. 16. that Epistles should be exchanged. That the Epistle to the Laodiceans here mentioned was that to the Ephesians is clear from the fact that ἐν Εφεσω was not originally in the text Ephes. I. 1. Marcion altered it to "*ad Laodicenos*". The idea of Archbishop Usher seems to be the most natural, and agrees best with the whole tenor of the Epistle, viz. that it was an encyclical writing addressed to various Churches. That St. Paul's Epistles were at least partly collected when St. Peter wrote his second Epistle would appear from the expression ἐν πάσαις ταῖς ἐπιστολαῖς. 2 Pet. III. 16.

[36] Addressed to Timothy, Philemon, Titus, and the 2d and 3d Epistle of St. John.

[37] The word ἀπόκρυφον, *liber absconditus*, as Augustine has it, was taken from the Jews, who called those writings גנוזים; not being put with the sacred books in the holy chests, but separately in secret places; a manuscript having 4 mistakes in one leaf, was *hid*. Justin, Dialog. c. Tryph. translates with ἀφανὲς ποιεῖν; in op-

Apostolic Fathers were sometimes read in the Churches, it became necessary to set forth *catalogues* of those Scriptures which were to be considered canonical. The first of these is found in the Homilies of *Origen* upon the book of Joshua, where he gives an allegorical exposition of the seven trumpets of rams' horns." The first, he saith, who blew the trumpet, was Matthew, then Mark, Luke and John among the Evangelists; Peter in two Epistles, then James and Jude. John resumed the trumpet-call in his Epistles and the Apocalypse, and Luke in the Acts of the Apostles. But Paul, the last, threw every thing down before him with the twice seven-fold sound of his Epistles."

Eusebius in his Church History, classifies the entire body of the sacred literature of the Christians into *three divisions;*[38] the *first* of which, consisted of books which were universally acknowledged as divine, comprising the four Gospels, the Acts, the Epistles of St. Paul, the first Epistle of St. John, the first Epistle of St. Peter, and the book of Revelation. The *second* division,[39] embracing the Epistle of St. James, that of St. Jude, the second of St. Peter, and the

position to this, Origen uses the expression φανεϱὰ βιβλία; Epist. ad Afric. cap. 9. The first who uses ἀπόκρυφος is Clemens Alex. lib. III. cap. 4.

[38] Euseb. Eccles. Hist. lib. III. cap. 25. also explanatory lib. III. cap. 3. and cap. 24. The 3 divisions were ὁμολογούμενοι, ἀντιλεγούμενοι and νόθα.

[39] Not to be confounded with the παντελῶς νόθα; and held παρὰ πλείστοις τῶν ἐκκλεσιαστικῶν; γνώριμα πολλοῖς. Lib. III. cap. 25. μετὰ τῶν λοιπῶν ἐν πλείσταις ἐκκλεσίαις παρὰ πολλοῖς δεδημοσιευμένα. III. 31.

second and third of St. John, was received by many, but had been doubted by some. This uncertainty was removed by the Council of Nice, when they were received into the Canon. The *third* and last division of the Christian books by Eusebius, comprised writings of an apocryphal character, such as "the Acts of Paul," the "Shepherd of Hermes," the "Epistle of Barnabas," the "Apocalypse of Peter" and the "teachings of the Apostles."[40] With this third class of books we must not confound the many spurious Gospels, of Peter, Thomas and Matthias, or the Acts of Andrew, John and other Apostles; together with many other fabulous and heretical productions, which Eusebius pronounced to be godless and presumptuous, and unworthy to be classed among his third and last division.[41]

5. Thus we see, that no small care was bestowed upon the *collection* and *preservation* of the books of the New Testament. They were religiously set apart, and no other book could gain admission among their number, under whatever name it might claim to be admitted.[42] In proportion to the fear of the Catholic

---

[40] Ἐν τοῖς νόθοις κατατετάχθω καὶ τῶν Παύλου πράξεων ἡ γραφὴ, ὅ, τε λεγόμενος ποιμὴν, καὶ ἡ ἀποκάλυψις Πέτρου. Καὶ πρὸς τούτοις ἡ φερομένη Βαρνάβα ἐπιστολὴ, καὶ τῶν Ἀποστόλων, αἱ λεγόμεναι διδαχαί. Euseb. Hist. Eccl. lib. III. cap. 25.

[41] Ὅθεν ὂν δ' ἐν νόθοις αὐτὰ κατατακτέον, ἀλλ' ὡς ἄτοπα πάντη καὶ δυσσεβῆ παραιτητέον. Euseb. Hist. Ecc. lib. III. 25.

[42] "Sicut olim in populo Judaeorum multi prophetiam pollicebantur, et quidem erant pseudoprophetae...: ita et in N. Testamento multi conati sunt scribere Evangelia, sed non omnes recepti. Et ut sciatis non solum quatuor Evangelia, sed plurima esse conscripta, ex quibus haec, quae habemus, electa sunt et *tradita ecclesiis*, ex ipso

Church, lest a book should be received upon insufficient authority, was the zeal to *preserve* those which were admitted in their original integrity. Yet in spite of the greatest watchfulness, some discrepancies crept into the sacred text; partly through the inattention of the copyists, partly from other causes, which cannot be left unnoticed.

Unintentional "Variae lectiones" not unfrequently arose here, as in the Old Testament, from the copyists sometimes "seeing amiss," and so exchanging letters, transposing words and sentences, and making repetitions;[43] from *hearing amiss* they were also liable to commit numerous mistakes.[44] To these may be added, faults arising from want of memory, such as, misplacing words; and exchanging synonymous expressions;[45] faults arising from want of knowledge,

prooemio Lucae... cognoscamus... Hoc, quod ait, *conati* sunt, latentem habet accusationem eorum, qui absque gratia Spiritus S. adscribenda Evangelia prosilierunt. Matthaeus quippe et Marcus et Johannes et Lucas non sunt *conati* scribere, sed Spiritu S. pleni scripserunt Evangelia... Ecclesia (κατὰ τὸν ἐκκλεσιαστικὸν κανόνα Euseb. VI. 25) quatuor habet Evangelia, haereses plurima; e quibus quoddam scribitur secundum Aegyptios, aliud juxta duodecim Apostolos... Sed in his omnibus *nihil aliud probamus, nisi quod Ecclesia*, i. e. quatuor tantum Evangelia recipienda." Origen. Homil. I. in Luc. III. 933.

[43] *Exchanging letters:* Mark. V. 14. ἀνήγγειλαν for ἀπήγγειλαν. Act. XXVII. 6. ἀνεβίβασεν for ἐνεβίβασεν. Rom. XII. 13. μνείαις for χρείαις. *Transposing:* Rom. I. 13. καρπόν τινα for τινὰ καρπόν. *Repetition:* 1 Thess. II. 7. ἐγενήθημεν νήπιοι for ἐγένη. ἤπιοι.

[44] Thus Rom. II. 17: ἴδε for εἰ δέ. 1 John IV. 2: γινώσκεται for γινώσκετε. Matt. XXVII. 60: κενῷ for καινῷ.

[45] John XVI. 22. νῦν μὲν λύπην for λύπην μὲν νῦν. Rev. XVII. 17. τὰ ῥήματα for οἱ λόγοι.

where abbreviations were mistaken for single letters, or words were wrongly divided.[46]

More or less intentional, though certainly not malicious, were other mistakes committed in the act of transcribing the books of the New Testament. It was the natural wish of the early Christian transcriber and reader to render the text of the sacred books as plain as possible, and with a view to accomplish this object, they sometimes wrote a more intelligible word over, or on the margin of an unusual expression. A *Greek* reader for instance, considering that the term used for tribute-money was not generally intelligible, placed a more purely Greek word by its side, and a subsequent copyist introduced the word from the margin into the text, and thus caused a different reading.[47] Another took the events recorded Luke XII. 38. as happening during the daytime;[48] to prevent misunderstanding, he followed the computation of the Romans, who divided the day as well as the night into four watches, and instead of "the third watch" added by way of explanation, "the evening watch;" a mistake, afterwards copied into the text of several Manuscripts. Again, another reader conceiving that the thirty pieces of silver, Matt. XXVI.

[46] We refer only to 1 Tim. III. 16. where ΘΣ was taken ΟΣ or the reverse. Mistakes such as συνεπισκόποις for σὺν ἐπισκόποις Phil. I. 1. will easily be accounted for, when we remember that the original MSS. were not divided into words or sentences.

[47] Κῆνσος was superseded by ἐπικεφαλαίον. Mark. XII. 14. In Pet. II. 20. instead of κολαφιζόμενοι, some Codd. read κολαζόμενοι.

[48] The third Hebrew watch τρίτη φυλακή answers to the Greek μεσονύκτιον; the day being divided in *quatuor excubias;* the third of these day-watches was therefore the ἑσπερίνη φυλακή.

15. seemed to require explanation — being intelligible only to the Jews — ventured to subjoin the equivalent Greek sum of "thirty staters," in the margin, which was eventually substituted in the text of some Manuscripts for "thirty pieces of silver." Another critical reader of Mark X. 12. not finding it consonant to the taste and manners of the Greeks, that a woman should *"put away her husband,"* their laws endowing the *man* only with power, to put away his wife, the Cambridge Manuscript turns the sentence thus, "if a woman go forth from her husband, and be married to another etc."[49] The following expression, "to catch something out of His mouth," was considered too Hebraically idiomatic for the Greeks, and was therefore rendered in this form, "seeking occasion to find something to accuse him."[50] The many other Hebraisms, which constitute so striking a peculiarity of the New Testament, did not meet with greater indulgence from the fastidious Greek grammarians. The harsh inflexions and foreign combinations of the various parts of speech could not fail to create a desire for correction, in a people who thought so much of purity of style and diction; hence, the purely Hebraic expression, "and he added to send another servant"[51]

[49] Γυνὴ ἐὰν ἐξέλθῃ ἀπὸ τοῦ ἀνδρὸς καὶ γαμήσῃ, thus accommodating it to Grecian law, which only gives man the power of ἀπολύειν and ἀποπέμπειν.

[50] Ζητοῦντες θηρεῦσαί τι ἐκ τοῦ στόματος αὐτοῦ ἵνα, κτλ. becomes: ζητοῦντες ἀφορμὴν τινὰ λαβεῖν αὐτοῦ ἵνα εὑρῶσι κατηγορῆσαι. Lu. XI. 54.

[51] Καὶ προσέθετο πέμψαι ויסף שלח is rendered Lu. XX. 11. at once ἐπέμψεν. Mark. II. 15. ἐν τῷ κατακεῖσθαι αὐτὸν is made, κατακειμένων αὐτῶν. See also John XI. 33. where we read in

was more concisely rendered by, "and he sent another servant."

The rough *Hebrew* construction Lu. VII. 1. "now when He had ended all his sayings in the audience of the people," was rendered by the more smooth and classical Greek, "when He had finished speaking all these words, He came to Capernaum."[52] Other discrepancies arose, from the desire of making the text more clear and perspicuous; by adjoining parallel passages from the other Evangelists, merely for the purpose of illustration, and these notes gradually intruded into the text itself. To give only one striking instance,—Mark. XIII. 2. Our Lord speaking of the destruction of Jerusalem says, "there shall not be left one stone upon another," to which the Cambridge addition adds, "I will build it again in three days without hands;" absurdly interpolating these words from St. John II. 19. The *Diatessarons* of the Gospels also contributed their share to the variety of readings; one of these was made by the disciple of Justin Martyr, the heretical Tatian. The Cambridge Manuscript e. g. must have borrowed from one of them, the words in Matt. XXVII. 28: "And they put on Him a purple garment and clothed Him with a scarlet robe;" clearly a combination from the other Evangelists.[53]

Cod. D, ἐταράχθη τῷ πνεύματι ὡς ἐμβριμώμενος, instead of the *textus receptus*.

[52] Ἐπεὶ δὲ ἐπλήρωσε πάντα τὰ ῥήματα αὐτοῦ εἰς τὰς ἀκοὰς τοῦ λαοῦ εἰσῆλθεν εἰς Καπερ. is turned into the easy Greek sentence: ὅτε ἐτέλεσεν πάντα τὰ ῥήματα λαλῶν, ἦλθεν εἰς Καφερ, κ. τ. λ. Mark. XIV. 25. they put: οὐκέτι οὐ μὴ πίω instead of οὐ μὴ προσθῶ πιεῖν.

[53] Ἐκδύσαντες αὐτὸν, ἱμάτιον πορφυροῦν καὶ χλαμίδα κοκκίνην

Lastly, we find *omissions* where synonymous expressions occur; these being defects of composition which no polished Greek could permit, he would naturally eject, what in his opinion would be *tautological:* thus the synonymes in Mark. VIII. 15 — "*Take heed, beware* of the leaven of the Pharisees etc. etc." being looked upon in this light, the former one was omitted. In the passage Mark. XI. 28. "by what authority doest thou these things, and who gave thee this authority to do these things?" the second clause of the interrogation was considered redundant, and therefore struck out. For the same reason in Lu. XXI. 15.— "your adversaries shall not be able to gainsay or resist," the last verb was omitted.[54]

6. Among these "variae lectiones" justly complained of by *Clemens Alexandrinus, Origen* and others,[55] there is not *one* instance of wilful corruption, properly so called. Nor is it possible for Mohammed or any other enemy of Christianity to point out the malicious suppression, addition or perversion of any

περιεθήκαν αὐτῷ. Now Mark XV. 17. had a πορφύραν; Luke XXIII. 11. has the ἐσθῆτα; John XIX. 2. has the ἱμάτιον πορφυροῦν; the ἐνδύουσιν Mark had to give; and Mathew furnished the χλαμύδα κοκκίνην.

[54] Mark XII. 23. instead of ἐν τῇ ἀναστάσει, ὅταν ἀναστῶσιν several Codd. simply: ἐν τῇ ἀναστάσει.

[55] Μακάριοι, φησιν, οἱ δεδιωγμένοι ἕνεκεν δικαιοσύνης, ὅτι αὐτοὶ υἱοὶ θεοῦ κληθήσονται· ἤ, ὥς τινες τῶν μετατιθέντων τὰ εὐαγγέλια, Μακάριοι, φησιν, οἱ δεδιωγμένοι ὑπὸ τῆς δικαιοσύνης, ὅτι αὐτοὶ ἔσονται τέλειοι· Clem. Alex. Strom. I. IV. cap. 6. p. 490. Again: Νυνὶ δὲ δηλονότι πολλὴ γέγονεν ἡ τῶν ἀντιγράφων διαφορά, εἴτε ἀπὸ ῥᾳθυμίας τινῶν γραφέων, εἴτε ἀπὸ τόλμης τινῶν μοχθηρᾶς τῆς διορθώσεως τῶν γραφομένων, εἴτε καὶ ἀπὸ τῶν τὰ ἑαυτοῖς δοκοῦντα ἐν τῇ διορθώσει προστιθέντων ἢ ἀφαιρούντων. Origen. Comm. in Matt. XV. Vol. III. pag. 671. ed. Ruaei.

book or passage in the New Testament. It may not however be altogether inappropriate, to bring forward an example of such corruption, as might well justify the accusation of Mohammed, had it been perpetrated by *the Church*, instead of by a *heretic*, cast off from her communion.—*Marcion*, a heretic of the second century, made it his object to destroy what he considered the Judaism of Christianity; portions of his work, which he called *the Antitheses*, from its giving his view of the antithetical character of the New Testament, are handed down to us by Theodoretus.[56] He even went so far as to severally reject the Apostles, whom he considered imbued with Jewish prejudices, St. Paul, only excepted, whose Epistles he partially admitted. Of the Gospels, he considered St. Luke's the least to be suspected of Jewish tendencies, he being the friend and companion of St. Paul; nevertheless he altered passages and even expunged entire portions from St. Paul's Epistles, and still more from the Gospel of St. Luke, which to his mind were objectionable.[57] The Epistles to the Hebrews, Titus and Timothy he utterly rejected; and

---

[56] Theodoret. haeret. fab. lib. I. cap. 24.

[57] Marcion's followers maintained that the words of Christ Matt. V. 17. must be reversed: οὐχ οὕτως δὲ εἶπεν ὁ Χριστὸς, λέγει γὰρ, οὐκ ἦλθον πληρῶσαι τὸν νόμον, ἀλλὰ καταλύσαι. Dialog. (Pseudo-Origenis) contra Marcionitas Sec. II. pag. 63. How Marcion dealt with St. Luke's Gospel may be gathered from *Epiphan. adv. haeres.* XLII. §. 11. 12. A collation of the above, vide, Lehrbuch der historisch-kritischen Einleitung in die kanonischen Bücher des Neuen Testamentes von Dr. M. L. de Wette. 4. Aufl. pag. 106—112. His alterations of the Epistles were exposed e. g. *Iren. adv. haer.* I. 27. 1. *Tertull. adv. Marc.* I. V. *Epiph. adv. haer.* XLII. §. 9. *Hieron. comm. in Epist. ad Galat.*

this wholesale alteration or rejection was justified by the Marcionites, who considered this sacrilegious abuse in the light of extending to the New Testament "the benefit of medical treatment."[58]

The grounds upon which Marcion endeavoured to introduce his *new Gospel*, were in some respects similiar to those, upon which Mohammed ushered his Koran into the world: both pretended that the originals had been corrupted, but with this difference; that Marcion fixes his accusation upon the Apostles in particular, instead of the Christians in general.[59] In thus throwing the act of corruption upon the *authors* of the books,[60] he cuts off all possibility of showing to the world, by what means he himself obtained the original in its integrity. Hence Tertullian in his argument with him, asks, whether he does not see, that by his charge he reproached Christ Himself, for choosing such untrustworthy and faithless Apostles,[61] and requests to be informed, from what source he obtained the *true* Gospel; adding, that from the time of Tiberius to that of Antoninus, Marcion was the first who dared to take upon himself the office

---

[58] Tertull. lib. I. adv. Marcion cap. XX.

[59] In his "Antitheses" he starts from the charge of St. Paul against St. Peter Galat. II. 9—13. and suspects the Apostles in general of Judaising principles, which impelled them to corrupt the Gospels. "Praevaricationis et simulationis suspectos *queritur* usque ad depravationem Evangelii." Tertull. lib. IV. cap. 3.

[60] "Semetipsum esse veraciorem, quam sunt hi qui Evangelium tradiderunt Apostoli, suasit (Marcion) discipulis suis, non Evangelium, sed particulam Evangelium tradens eis." Iren. adv. haeres. lib. I. cap. 27.

[61] Tertull. lib. IV. cap. 3.

of *emending* the Gospels, nor indeed did they require emendation.[62]

Here then, we have an instance of the New Testament Scriptures having suffered corruption; not however from the parties, accused by Mohammed, but from an adversary of the Church, who at that perilous hour, when the truth was so fiercely attacked, wanted not champions, earnestly to "contend for the faith." In writings which are preserved to this hour, they pointed out what Scriptures had been altered, which portions omitted, and what passages were corrupted. This is what we might justly have looked for, from Mohammed: with his charge, we had a right to expect that kind of proof, which the Fathers brought forth conjointly with their charge against Marcion. But Mohammed failed to prove even the *existence* of those passages concerning himself, which he accuses the Christians of having suppressed; neither has he pointed out in what the alterations consist, nor where they are to be found.

7. We have now noticed the *early existence* of the books in question; and have repelled the charge of Mohammed from evidence, gathered out of the writings of *enemies* as well as of *friends,* during the

---

[62] "Emendator sane Evangelii a Tiberianis usque Antonina tempora eversi Marcion solus et primus obvenit, expectatus tamdiu a Christo poenitente, jam, quod Apostolos praemisisse properasset sine praesidio Marcionis; nisi quod humanae temeritatis, non divinae auctoritatis negotium est haeresis, quae sic semper emendat Evangelia dum vitiat..... itaque dum emendat, utrumque confirmat, et nostrum alterius, id emendans quod invenit: et id posterius, quod de nostri emendatione constituens suum fecit." Tertull. lib. IV. adv. Marcion cap. 3—4.

first two centuries. We have examined the most ancient *catalogues* of the New Testament Scriptures, and have found in them the *very same books*, which existed in the days of Mohammed, and which are in our possession at this day. Again, we have seen that the *different readings*, which had here and there crept into Manuscripts, could not possibly be, what Mohammed referred to in his charge against the Christians: for the *wilful* corruptions which were perpetrated by certain *heretics*, were detected and exposed by the Fathers of the Church, in a manner worthy of Mohammed's imitation, and long before he uttered his charge.[63]

For the further establishment of the *integrity* of the New Testament Scriptures, we now appeal to those venerable *Manuscripts*, written prior to the rise of Islamism. Their respective ages are indicated, by the changes which were effected from time to time in the shape of the letters, the style of the handwriting, the materials on which they were executed, as well as other particulars connected with their internal arrangement.[64] Auxiliary helps for the discovery of the

[63] "Etsi multa depravere conati sint haeretici," scribit Bellarminus lib. II. de Verbo Dei cap. 7, "tamen nunquam defuerunt catholici, qui eorum corruptelas detexerint, et non permiserint libros sacros corrumpi." Plurima ex toto nov. Test. abstulit, mutavitque Marcion, sed illa omnia fere notavit Epiphanius haeres. 42. et in nostris codicibus recte habentur." Gerhard. Loci Theolog. Vol. II. pag. 278.

[64] "Die ältesten Handschriften sind mit Uncialschrift geschrieben, welche jedoch nicht immer ein sicheres Zeichen des Alters ist, die jüngeren (vom 10. Jahrh. an) mit Cursivschrift. Leicht kann man den älteren aufrechten, viereckigen, runden Schriftcharakter vom spätern gedruckten unterscheiden: der geübte diplomatische Blick weiß noch feinere Unterschiede zu finden. Der

ages of Manuscripts are afforded by Church Almanacks, ecclesiastical registers, notices of the festivals, marginal explanatory notes, psotscripts, and other additions, which were frequently appended to these ancient documents by the calligraphers. Some *historical* hints may also be gathered, by which to judge of the age of the *Alexandrian Manuscripts*. Strabo for instance, mentions two cities, *Alexandria* and *Rome*, in which the making and selling of Manuscripts was a regular branch of trade.[65] Some celebrated names are met with among the Alexandrian calligraphers; one *Philodemus,* who became blind in the pursuit of his art,[66] and another, *Hierokas,* who prosecuted the tedious work of copying till his ninetieth year with unfailing sight.[67] But as we approach that period of decay which commenced with the conquest of Egypt by the Saracens, we find the Greeks withdrawing themselves from this laborious means of earning their bread; and leaving calligraphy to the native *Copts,*[68] they became soldiers and taxgatherers, by which they

Mangel der Wortabtheilung ist ein sichereres Zeichen des Alters als der der Accente und der Interpunktion, indem jene auch in jüngeren Handschriften fehlen, diese in älteren vorkommt. Unsicher ist das Merkmal der Stichometrie und der Kapiteleintheilung oder das Fehlen derselben. Die Rechtschreiberei läßt auf das Vaterland schließen. de Wette's Lehrbuch pag. 63.

[65] Strabo lib. XIII. p. 419. Whilst *Greek* MSS. were chiefly made and sold in Alexandria, *Latin* ones were made εἰς πρᾶσιν in Rome.

[66] Athol. Graec. H. Grotii lib. VI. epigr. Juliani Aegyptii 6. et 7. Brunck, analecta Tom. II. pag. 495. 496.

[67] Epiphanius Haeres. LXVII. §. 3. pag. 712. edit. Colon.

[68] Renaudot. Histor. Patriarchar. Alexandrinor. Benjamin Patr. XXXVIII. pag. 164. The author procured an Arabic MS. of this work from Egypt.

made themselves so hated that A. D. 641. they were all ultimately driven out of the country. The sale of Manuscripts was at length impeded through the Saracens having interrupted the connection with the Empire of Constantinople; in addition to which the Copyists were deprived of the beautiful originals, which were destroyed with the Alexandrian Library.

But few Manuscripts embrace the entire New Testament; most of them contain only parts, more frequently the Gospels and St. Paul's Epistles, many only the lessons and Gospels required to be read in Churches. Some give the text with a parallel version and explanatory notes. The *Codices* themselves, as regards their *form*, consist not of *rolls* as the Hebrew Manuscripts, but of, from four to eight sheets of *parchment*, silk, cotton or linen paper stitched together. The oldest Manuscript in our posession is that preserved in the Vatican Library at Rome,[69] consisting of the Old and the New Testament; though of the latter, the Epistles to Timothy, Titus, Philemon, the end of the Epistles to the Hebrews and the Apocalypse have perished. This Manuscript is written on the finest parchment, in the most simple, uniform and beautiful characters. All the letters are placed at equal distances, there being no division of words. To denote the beginning of a new section, the space of the breadth of a letter, or half a one, is left vacant. It has three columns on each leaf, and is broader

---

[69] Known as *Codex B.* or *Vatic.* 1209. The naming of MSS. with letters, probably commenced in some incidental way without any scientific definition.

than long. The ink, having grown pale by age, has been revived by a later hand, and in some places words and sentences have been re-written at the side of the original.[70] Whenever punctuation occurs, which is seldom the case, it has been added at a subsequent period. These are all marks of great antiquity; but there are *two points*, which will enable us to fix its age more definitely. St. Basil born at Cesarea A. D. 329. states, that according to the learned doctors of the Church who lived before him, the words "*in Ephesus*" Ephes. I. 1. had been wanting in the ancient *Manuscripts*, and he himself had seen them omitted *in Old Manuscripts*. The Vatican Codex therefore must have been *old in his day*, for it is without the words in question, which are only placed in the margin.[71]

The second point by which the date of the *Va-*

---

[70] The Manuscript has internal marks of its having been written by an Egyptian Calligrapher. Instead of συλλήψῃ, λήψεσθε, ληφθήσεται, ατελήφθη we have ουλλημψη, λημψεσθε, λημφθησεται and ατελημφθη. This *peculiar orthography* is only found in Graeco-Coptic monuments. In Coptic manuscripts we have ἀποκαλυμψις instead of ἀποκαλυψις. In Graeco-Thebaic fragments of St. John's Gospel VII. 52. we have ἀπεκρίθησαν καὶ εἶπαν. So Codex B. always writes εἰδαν, ἔπεσαν, ἦλθαν Lu. IX. 36. ἑώρακαν and Rom. XVI. 7. γέγοναν.

[71] Ἐν Ἐφέσῳ. He says: the Apostle called his readers ὄντας, and that he did so: ἰδιαζοίτως, exclusively or peculiarly, adding: οὕτω γὰρ καὶ οἱ πρὸ ἡμῶν παραδεδώκασι, καὶ ἡμεῖς ἐν τοῖς παλαίοις τῶν ἀντιγράφων εὑρήκαμεν. Basilius Editio princeps Vened. 1535. pag. 127. St. Jerome also assumes that the words were not in the text in the original MSS. He says, some think St. Paul would denominate the readers "*essentiae vocabulo, ut ab eo, qui est, qui sunt appellentur;*" but others hold, that the Epistle was not addressed "*ad eos qui sunt,*" but "*ad eos qui sunt Ephesi.*" Hieron. ad locum. Hug de antiquitate cod. Vatic. pag. 26.

tican Manuscript can be determined, is the order in which the Epistles are placed.⁷² The Epistles of St. Paul being taken as a whole, are divided into so many sections or chapters. Those to the *Romans, Corinthians, Galatians,* stand in the order in which we now have them. The last Epistle concludes at the fifty-ninth division; the next, that to the *Ephesians,* begins with the seventieth instead of the sixtieth section, the figures afterwards continuing regularly through the Epistles to the *Philippians, Colossians* and *Thessalonians,* the last ending with the ninety-third division. We naturally inquire, where are the missing sections, between the numbers fifty-nine and seventy, i. e. between Galatians and Ephesians? We find them in the Epistle to the *Hebrews,* which stands in this Manuscript, after those to the Thessalonians, but commences with the sixtieth instead of the ninety-fourth section, as we should expect. From this irregular enumeration we infer, that the Epistle to the *Hebrews,* in the original collection, stood immediately after that to the Galatians, but was subsequently placed, where we now find it in this Manuscript.⁷³ Now at the time when the Manuscript in question was written, it is evident, that this *transfer* must have been of so recent a date, that the former mode of reckoning the sections was retained, although the

---

[72] Dr. Hug, Einleitung in das Neue Test. Vol. I. 237.

[73] Epiphanius at a later period records, that there were two kinds of manuscripts, some of them placing Hebrews after the Epistles to Timothy, Titus and Philemon; others placing it after the second Epistle to the Thessalonians. Epiphan. Haeres. XLII. p. 373. juxta Petav. coloniens.

position of the Epistle itself had been altered. In the catalogue of *Athanasius*, we find the Epistle to the *Hebrews* placed after those addressed to the *Thessalonians*. Had this alteration taken place before the time of Athanasius born A. D. 296, the *Vatican Codex* must necessarily be of an earlier date than this; on the other hand, if Athanasius was the *first* who placed the Epistle to the *Hebrews* after *Thessalonians*, then the Manuscript may have been written during his lifetime, when the *new* arrangement had not yet become universal.[74] At all events, the arrangement of Athanasius was universally adopted in the fourth century;[75] and as it is clear that this Manuscript must have been written at a period prior to the universal adoption of the new arrangement, or at a time when it was first introduced, we must assign to it a date not later than the beginning of the fourth century.[76]

The so-called *Alexandrian Codex*, in the British Museum,[77] likewise comprises the Old and New Tes-

---

[74] Vide, Hug, de antiquitate Codicis Vaticani commentatio.

[75] Τὰ δὲ τῆς καινῆς διαθήκης ταῦτα Εὐαγγέλια τέσσαρα, κατὰ Ματθ., κ. Μαρκ., κ. Λουκ., κατὰ Ἰωάν. Πράξεις Ἀφοστόλων· Ἐπιστολαὶ καθολικαὶ ἑπτὰ, ὄντως· Ἰακώβου μία, Πέτρου δύο, Ἰωάννου τρεῖς, Ἰούδα μία· Ἐπιστολαὶ δεκατέσσαρες, ὄντως· πρὸς Ῥωμ. μία, πρὸς Κορ. δύο, πρὸς Γαλ. μία, πρὸς Ἐφεσ. μία, πρὸς Φιλ. μια, πρὸς Κολ. μία, πρὸς Θεσσ. δύο, πρὸς Ἑβρ. μία, πρὸς Τιμοθ. δύο, πρὸς Τιτ. μία, πρὸς Φιλημ. μία. Concil. Laodic. between 360—364 apud *Mansi*. Concil. nov. et ampliss. collect. II. pag. 574.

[76] Montfaucon places Cod. B in the 5th or 6th century; Blanchini in the 5th; Hug in the 4th century.

[77] *Codex Alexandrin. Mus. Britannic.* is known under the figure A. The N. T. begins Matt. XXV. 6. up to which it has been destroyed; otherwise it is complete with the exception of John VI.

tament. The order of the books is the same as in the Vatican Manuscript; *Hebrews* taking its place *after Thessalonians.* The letters are similar, only a little larger; the whole is written in two columns. We find no accents, aspirates or division of words; and the inscriptions are most simple. It was printed A. D. 1786.[78] The absence of the divisions of *Euthalius*, and of other marks of a later date, are sufficient evidences that it was written *before the second half of the fifth century.* The orthography indicates its Alexandrian origin.[79] The *Parisian Codex*[80] embraces parts of the Old, and the whole of the New Testament; and resembles, in all important points, the Vatican and Alexandrian Manuscripts. Considering that it has less of punctuation and fewer additions of a later time than the Alexandrian Codex, it is rightly considered the older of the two. That it was also of Egyptian origin is proved by its orthography.[81]

The *Dublin Manuscript* of the Gospel according

50 — VIII. 52. and 2 Cor. IV. 13 — XII. 2. It was given to Charles I. by Cyrillus Lucaris, first Patriarch of Alexandria, afterwards of Constantinople.

[78] Nov. Test. Graec. e cod. Alexandrino, qui Londoni in Bibliotheca Musei Britannici asservatur, descriptum a Godofr. Carolo Woide.

[79] Here also we have in Mark. XII. 40. λημψονται; XVI. 24. λημψεσθε. Lu. XIII. 11. ἀνακυμψαι. Act. X. 39. ἀνειλαν.

[80] Codex C. n. 9. Regio-Parisinus, also called rescriptus or palimpsestus, Cod. or Ephraem Syri, because the original having been partially effaced with a spunge, ascetical essays of Ephrem were written upon the parchment; but the original still shows through. It was written according to Wetstein before 542. Hug makes it older than Cod. A.

[81] Lu. I. 31. ἀναλημψεως. Act. I. 2. εἰπαν. Matt. X. 13. ἐλθατω.

to *St. Matthew* is of importance, inasmuch as it supplies the lost portion of the *Codex Alexandrinus*.[82] Judging from the absence of accents, the paucity of punctuation, and from other marks of antiquity which have been noticed in connection with the above-mentioned Manuscripts, we cannot ascribe a more recent date to this noble fragment of the New Testament than we assigned to the Parisian Codex.[83] The *Cambridge Codex*[84] contains the four Gospels and the Acts of the Apostles, and was written after *Stichometry* had come into practice. It presents the Greek text on one side, and on the other, one of those Latin versions which were in existence before St. Jerome executed the *Vulgata*. The calligrapher here, did his work mechanically; the internal and external arrangement clearly shows that the Manuscript was made after *Euthalius*, and before the rise of Islamism, about the end of the *fifth*, or at the latest during the *sixth* century, when the Greeks had given up the writing of Manuscripts to the Copts who understood but little of Greek and Latin. Of the same age is the Manuscript of the *Acts* of the Apostles, preserved in the *Bodleian Library* at Oxford;[85] both the Greek text

[82] It is called *Codex S. Matthaei Dublinensis rescriptus*. It was discovered and edited by Mr. Barret 1801. Like Codex C. it was partly obliterated and other essays written upon it; yet the original writing could easily be read; it is described: "*nec habet spiritus aut accentus omnino.*"

[83] Alexandrian forms are chap. X. 41. λημψεται; VII. 25. προσεπεσαν; XI. 7. 8. 9. εξηλθατε.

[84] *Codex Cantabrigiensis* or Cod. D., also called the Bezan MS., or *Codex Theodori Bezae Cantabrigiensis*, was edited 1793. in two beautiful folio-Volumes.

[85] Cod. E. or *Codex Laudianus*, because given by Archbishop

and the old Latin version were stichometrically written and executed in Alexandria.[86] As we can scarcely date it later than the *sixth*, or the beginning of the *seventh* century, it was in existence when Mohammed brought forward his charge against the Christians of corrupting their sacred books. As the Dublin Manuscript supplied the deficiency of the Alexandrian, so the *Codex Claromontanus*, preserved in the Library of Paris, supplies those *Epistles of St. Paul*, which are wanting in the Cambridge Manuscript.[87] Although not written in the same hand, they were executed in the *same period*, and upon the same principle, giving stichometrically both the Greek text and a Latin version. Fragments of another copy of the Epistles of St. Paul, in the Greek text only, written with accents on the stichometrical principle, were at one time preserved in the celebrated library of Bishop Coislin at *Metz*.[88] As it was written in Alexandria[89]

Laud; also Cod. Bodlei. It was printed at Oxford 1765. by Thomas Hearne. Written according to Hug and Woide in Alexandria; Marsh and Eichhorn suppose it to be the work of Western Europe, perhaps Sardinia or Gallia.

[86] See, specimens of MSS. *Montfaucon* palaeogr. gr., *Blanchini* Evang. quadrup. *Matthaei* ed. N. T.

[87] The *Codex Claromontanus* n. 107. is complete with the exception of the first and last leaf, which have been lost. It is marked with the figure D. Montfaucon places it within the 7th cent.

[88] This MS. is known as *Codex H*. Griesbach Symbol. crit. part II. pag. 85. It came originally from Mount Athos, A. D. 1218. where it was used as old parchment, with which to bind other books, as is proved by a note on a book, which it served as a cover. It was printed and published by Montfaucon, Biblioth. Coislin. Part II. pag. 253—256.

[89] The formation ἐκκαταλημτον, in the subscription, is purely Alexandrian.

in a genuinely antique style, it must have been copied during the sixth century, before the invasion of the Saracen army.

We have now noticed those Manuscripts of the New Testament, written *prior* to the rise of Islamism; and reckoning the last mentioned Codex from Mount Athos as supplementary to that of the Vatican, we obtain — the Apocalypse only excepted, — an entire copy of the New Testament. The Alexandrian and the Dublin Manuscripts form a second *complete edition*, whilst the *Parisian Codex* is entire in itself. Lastly, the *Cambridge* and *Clarmontane* documents of the sacred Scriptures constitute a *fourth edition*, which is however deficient in the general Epistles and the Apocalypse.[90] We can therefore produce *four* distinct copies of those New Testament Scriptures, the integrity of which, Mohammed so wantonly impeaches: amongst them are several bi-lingual Manuscripts, containing Latin versions, which were made at least in the beginning of the fourth century. These Manuscripts are found in regions the most remote from one another, cherished by Churches, which hold different shades of opinions upon some of the doctrines they contain; yet wonderful to say, there exists between them the most perfect harmony. On comparing these documents together, we find, — notwithstanding the different styles of calligraphy, the different methods of placing the books, and the different readings, which have accidentally found their

---

[90] The Codex Cantabrigiensis and the Codex Claromontanus, are both marked D, and have been considered by some, to belong together.

way into the text,—no trace of alteration or interpolation. Any attempt to corrupt these venerable Manuscripts, could easily be detected. Although the Parisian and Dublin Codices have been literally washed through, and other matter written upon the parchment, yet, the original writing is still almost as legible, as if no attempt had been made to efface it.

If these efforts to obliterate the sacred writings— springing as they did, from mere ignorance of their value—have failed, surely malevolent attempts to corrupt the text, would be attended with no better success. Should doubts of the integrity of these documents, still linger in the mind of any intelligent Moslem, we invite him to examine them for himself, as they are still accessible to every sincere inquirer for the truth.[94] Older witnesses however, than the most ancient Manuscripts which testify to the integrity of the New Testament, are to be found, among the *versions* of its sacred books; and to these, we shall next turn our attention.

[94] The following learned works relative to the collation of MSS. will show that this branch of Divinity has not been neglected: Hist. du *Card. Ximenes* par *Flechier*. 1502. *Rob. Stephan.* Novum Test. ad vetustissima exemplaria M. S. C. excusum. 1551. Novum Test. Parisiis, impensis viduae *Arnoldi Birkmanni*. 1549. Bp. *Fell* published his work "$T\eta_{\varsigma}$ $\varkappa\alpha\iota\nu\eta_{\varsigma}$ $\delta\iota\alpha\vartheta\eta\varkappa\eta_{\varsigma}$ $\alpha\pi\alpha\nu\tau\alpha$." 1675. *Mill*, encouraged by him, worked in the same line. *Bengel* took the lead among the Germans. 1734. *Wetstein* and *Griesbach* followed it up in a masterly manner. *F. Matthaei* of Moskau pursued the same path. 1782—1788. in the same age appears *Alter* of Vienna. Nor are *Treschow*, *Adler*, *Engelbreth*, *Scholz* and *Lochmann* to be forgotten. *Birch* compared the Vatican Cod. for the Royal Danish edition of the N. T. with the exception of Luke and John; of these he received a comparison which had been made for Mr. Bentley, and Woide published the whole of Bentley's comparison in appendice Cod. Alexand.

8. We are now to demonstrate the integrity of the New Testament from those *versions* made prior to the rise of Islamism. If the Christians corrupted their sacred Scriptures, as Mohammed alleges, those translations must support the accusation; for any alterations made in the original must appear in the versions made from it. The *Peshito*, comprising the New as well as the Old Testament, has been noticed in the previous Chapter.[92] This version was first cited in the works of Ephrem; a proof that it was used in the *first half* of the *fourth* century. Yet there is reason to assume its existence in the second century of our era, as Eusebius declares, that Hegesippus had quoted from a Gospel in Syriac.[93] From these and other data, too tedious to enter upon, we may reasonably infer, that this version was executed towards the end of the second century; a Syriac tradition mentions *Achaeus*, a disciple of St. Thaddaeus, as the author.[94]

---

[92] The Peshito omits the 2ᵈ Epistle of St. Peter, the 2ᵈ and 3ᵈ Epistles of St. John, and the Epistle of St. Jude. There are strong reasons for supposing that the Apocalypse formed part in the original version; Hug Vol. 1. 306. „Ich kann mich nicht bereden, daß die Peschito ursprünglich die Apokalypse nicht mit begriffen habe, da im Oriente so große Zeugen für sie sprachen wie Justin, der Märtyrer in Palestina, und Theophilus in Antiochien, das Oberhaupt der angesehensten Kirche in Syrien; es müßte nur sein, daß die Peschito erst nach den antiallegorischen Streitigfeiten des Nepos entstanden, was ich mich noch viel weniger bereden kann."

[93] Ἐκ τε τοῦ καθ' ἑβραίους ἐυαγγελιου και του συριακου· και ιδιως ἐκ τῆς ἑβραΐδος διαλεκτου τινα τιθησιν. Euseb. Hist. Eccl. lib. IV. cap. 22.

[94] „Alt ist sie theils darum, weil die genannten Antilegomenen keine Aufnahme in sie gefunden, theils weil sie von allen syrischen Kirchenparteien anerkannt, theils weil der ihr zu Grund liegende Text sehr alt ist; auch läßt

z

Another *Syriac version* was made on behalf of the Monophysite section of the Syrian Church, by *Polycarp*, at the request of the Patriarch *Philoxenus* A. D. 508.[95] This translation which was made from the Manuscripts of Origen, was improved by Bishop *Thomas* A. D. 616;[96] who compared it with two or three old Manuscripts in the Antonine cloister at Alexandria. It is not without interest for our argument to observe, that this rival translation of the Peshito, which was made by a sectarian branch of the Syrian Church, not only alters nothing in the sacred text to support its particular views, but in its scrupulous adherence to the original, does violence to the rules of the Syriac grammar.[97] The more studiously a version retains the grammatical and philological peculiarities of the original text, the more faithful must consequently be the translation.

A third, or the *Palestino-Syriac* version, was made either before the fall of the Roman Empire, or whilst

die frühe, nach der Mitte des 2. Jahrhunderts beginnende Literatur erwarten, daß diese früh auch das Bedürfniß einer syrischen Uebersetzung werden gefühlt haben." Lehrbuch von de Wette pag. 13.

[95] Vide, Versio Syriaca Philoxeniana ed. Jos. White. pag. 641.

[96] He was then only "the poor Thomas," also Thomas of Charkel. His version contains the ἀντιλεγόμενοι, which were omitted in the Peshito, excepting only the Apocalypse. The most perfect edition of this version is that of Glocester Ridley's, now preserved in the New College at Oxford.

[97] ὁ, ἡ, τὸ also ἐστι and εἰσι are scrupulously translated, although contrary to the pure Syriac idiom. The affixes ἀυτος and ἀυτη are likewise given, contrary to Syriac usage. Compositions with προ, συν, ἐπι, κατα, foreign to all Semitic tongues are rendered in a manner, too artificial to be consonant with good taste. Vide Mark II. 26. XII. 16.

that part of Syria, in which it was made, was still a Roman province. This is shown by several terms which are retained in the translation.[98] What the Peshito was to the region of Edessa, and what the Philoxenian version was to Antioch, the Palestino-Syrian translation was to Damascus, to the north of Palestine, and to the mountains of Assyria. The *Armenian* version was made by Mesrob, and the statement of some, that *Chrysostom* gave a translation to the same people, is probably explained by his having lent his assistance and encouragement to this version, during his exile in Armenia, which coincides with the period, in which the version was made.[99]

In Upper and Lower *Egypt* we meet with versions of the New Testament, at a very early period of the Christian era. We have seen, that the Old Testament was translated into the *Coptic* dialects in the *third* or the *beginning* of the *fourth* century; and the version of the New Testament was certainly not of a later date. That of Lower Egypt, following the text of Hesychius, could not have been made prior to the middle of the *third* century, but as we find a version in the fourth century,[1] it must have been made during

---

[98] Specimens from Matt. XXVI. 3—32. which were printed by Dr. Adler. The soldiers v. 27. are simply called *Romans;* σπεῖρα rendered *castrum;* as the garrison is called *castrum*, we may easily guess under what rule the country was at the time.

[99] That Chrysostom took a part in this work, whilst an exile in *Kukus*, appears from the passage — διακελεύεσθαι ποτὲ ψαλτήριον καὶ τὴν ἅπασαν διαθήκην τὴν ἐκείνων γλῶτταν μεταποιήσασθαι. Anonym. Vita Chrysostom. cap. 113.

[1] Palladius visits John of Lycopolis, who is unacquainted with Greek, and yet he was well versed in the New Testament. Palladii historia Lausiaca cap. XLIII. de Abbate Joanne urbis Lyco pag. 963.

that interval. Again, *Antonius,* the founder of a monastic order in Egypt, who died A. D. 356. though ignorant of the Greek language, yet hearing the Gospel read in a Church, the words Matt. XIX. 21. produced in him the resolution to part with his fortune and retire from the world; which resolution was further confirmed, by his entering the Church a second time, and hearing the Gospel, especially Matt. v. 34. A clear proof that it must have been read in the vernacular tongue.[2] In the desert of Central Egypt, to which he retired, he addressed his disciples in a long speech in the *Egyptian* tongue, quoting largely from the Old and the New Testament. Antonius was so well acquainted with the Bible, that he is said to have known the entire Volume by heart.[3] We have therefore a version of the New Testament, in Lower, and Central Egypt. That there was a translation in the *Thebaic* dialect of Upper Egypt, is clear from the rules, which, according to Palladius, Father *Pachomius* framed for his 7000 monastic brethren; one of which required, that all should learn to read the Psalter and the New Testament:[4] this requisition

[2] Εισῆλθεν εἰς τὴν ἐκκλησίαν, καὶ συνέβη τότε τὸ εὐαγγέλιον ἀναγινώσκεσθαι, καὶ ἤκουσε τοῦ κυρίου λέγοντος τῷ πλουσίῳ κ. τ. λ. Athanas. Vita S. Anton. cap. 3. cfr. Matt. XIX. 21. ὡς δὲ πάλιν εἰσελθὼν εἰς τὸ κυριακὸν ἤκουσε ἐν τῷ εὐαγγελίῳ κ. τ. λ. ditto cap. 3. Matt. V. 34.

[3] August. de doctr. Christ. lib. I. §. 4. That other Anachorites accomplished the same task, is known from their biographies. πα- λαίαν δὲ καὶ καινὴν γραφὴν ἀπεστήθισεν Palladius cap. 12. in Ammonio. And, Vita abb. Aphthonii cap. 33: ἀποστηθίζουσι πάσας τὰς γραφάς. Lastly: Epiphan. lib. III. haeres. LVIII. pag. 1071. ἐν στόματι δὲ σχεδὸν πᾶσαν θείαν γραφὴν ἀπαγγελοῦσι.

[4] See the 139th and the 140th sections of these rules. Hieronym. Praef. in reg. S. Pachomii.

would have been a mockery, if the latter had not been translated into the vernacular dialect of the Upper provinces.[5] In the collection of Cardinal *Borgia*, were found fragments of a third Egyptian translation, in the *Bashmurian* dialect, which was spoken in the eastern portion of the Delta.[6] To judge from the condition of the text which it followed, and the style of the language in which it is given, we cannot assign to it a later date than the first half of the third century.

On ascending the Nile, we discover the *Ethiopian version*, which like that of the Old Testament was executed by *Abba Salama*. The text follows sometimes one reading and sometimes another, and the opinion, previously alluded to, that it was translated from an *Arabic* version, gains some ground. These Arabic translations, either of the Old or of the New Testament, are however nowhere to be found. Having been pronounced corrupted, they were doomed to destruction, on the same principle, that prompted the infatuated Omar to destroy the Alexandrian library.

Latin versions were found in Africa, Italy, and Gallia, before the days of St. Jerome; but *when* they were made, it is difficult to guess. Augustine declares, that they were "*innumerable*" in his days, but gives

---

[5] Vide: Novum Test. Aegyptium, vulgo copticum ex MSS. Bodleianis descripsit cum Vaticano et Parisiensibus contulit, et in latinum sermonem convertit David Wilkins. 1716.

[6] Containing portions of St. John's Gospel, Isaiah, Corinthians, Ephesians, Philippians, Thessalonians, and Hebrews. Vide W. F. Engelbreth: fragmenta Basmurico vet. et nov. Test. quae in Museo Borgiano Velitris adservantur. 1811.

the preference to the *Itala*. That some of them were in use in the time of Tertullian, or at the end of the second century, is proved, by his speaking of a version, which to his mind misrepresented a certain passage of the New Testament.[7] The most enduring work of this kind was the well-known *Vulgata* of *St. Jerome*, which was sanctioned by Pope Gregory in the sixth century, and has ever since remained the authorised version of the Church of Rome. The *Gothic version* was given to the world, in the last half of the fourth century, by *Ulfila, Bishop of Moesia*.[8] We have some very old Manuscripts of this translation; the Silver Codex of Upsala, — so called from its being written in silver characters, upon fine purple parchment, — was executed at the latest, in the beginning of the sixth century, before the Goths were expelled from Italy, and therefore prior to the rise of Islamism.[9] As the Dublin and Parisian Manuscripts were discovered beneath writings of a later age; so, fragments of the Epistle to the *Romans* were happily detected beneath some of the writings of Isidorus.[10] In the year 1817, the several Epistles of St. Paul, belonging to *Ulfila's* version, were found in

---

[7] Tertullian. de monogam. cap. 11.

[8] Ancient writers extend his version to the entire Bible, as embracing severally τας γραφας θειας, ιερας βιβλους, divinas scripturas. Socrates hist. eccles. lib. IV. cap. 27. Sozomen lib. VI. cap. 37. The Cod. Argent. contains the 4 Gospels.

[9] The Codex Argent. was published by Mr. Ed. Lye in 1750: "Sacrorum Ev. versio Gothica ex codice Argento." Oxford.

[10] They were published in the year 1762 by Knittel, who had discovered them.

the Ambrosian library, beneath the "Homilies of Gregory upon Ezekiel," which had been written over the *washen* Manuscript.[11] A second copy of these Epistles, with the exception of those to the *Romans* and to the *Hebrews*, was found hidden under "St. Jerome's Commentary on Isaiah;" which was written over the original Manuscript.[12]

At the risk of being tedious, we have now gone through some of the particulars connected with the ancient versions of the New Testament. Had we to deal with an enemy unprejudiced and open to conviction, we might have been satisfied with a bare enumeration of their titles; but we must remember, that in dealing with Mohammedans, we may take *nothing* for granted. In countries, where Islamism supplanted Christianity, doubtless other versions existed: *Chrysostom* e. g. speaks of *Indian* and *Persian* versions which are no longer to be found; having probably shared the same fate as the Arabic versions.[13] According to *Theodoretus*, the words of the Gospel were already in his day "in the whole world under the sun;"[14] and the *Venerable Bede*, born 673, ac-

[11] This MS. was published at Milan 1819. "Ulphilae partium ineditarum in Ambrosianis palimpsestis ab Angelo Maio editum."

[12] The entire remains of Ulfila's version was collected and published by Gabelenz and Loebe: Ulfila's veteris et novi test. vers. Gothicae fragmenta, quae supersunt. 1843.

[13] "Syros, Aegyptios, Indos, Persas, Aethiopes et alias innumeras gentes, divina dogmata in suam linguam transtulisse atque ita homines barbaros philosophari didicisse." Chrysostom. homil. I. in Johan. tom. III. col. 15.

[14] "Universam faciem terrae, quantacunque soli subjicitur, ejusmodi verborum plenam jam esse." Theod. de Curan. Graeco. affect. lib. V.

quaints us, that the Scriptures were read in his time in *five* British dialects.[15] St. Jerome is said to have rendered the New Testament into the *Dalmatian* tongue; nor should we forget the *Georgian* version, which was made in the sixth century of our era.

9. These versions existed in the most remote countries of Christendom, during the lifetime of Mohammed. Most of them are preserved to this day, and they severally agree with each other, and with the venerable Manuscripts just examined; although they were made for the benefit of different Churches, among whom rivalries were not unfrequent. What a task then, to corrupt the New Testament in the seventh century! The zealous and enterprizing individual who accomplished this tremendous undertaking, must have collected every Manuscript, every copy of the many translations from every part of Christendom; he must have penetrated into every church, monastery, college, library and dwelling-place, for the purpose of altering or destroying them, as the case might be! It would be preposterous, to assume that nations of various tongues, characters, laws, and religious views should have agreed in so sacrilegious a cause; and this, on account of *Mohammed*, of whose existence they had not so much as heard, when the alleged corruption is stated to have taken place. Except in the case of Marcion, history affords no analogy to such a proceeding. Though the Arian heresy highly prospered for a time, being countenanced by mighty potentates, yet no-

---

[15] Beda lib. I. histor. cap. 1.

where do we hear of any attempt to alter those passages of the New Testament which assert the divinity of our Lord.[16] If therefore no permanent alteration of the Scriptures could be effected, at a period when the gates of hell sought, under the most favourable circumstances, to prevail against the truth; is it possible that under less temptation, prophecies of any kind should have been abstracted? Or, can we believe that the Jews and Christians in Arabia could have so done, in the expectation that all their brethren would acquiesce in the deed? Assuming it to have been the work of the Christians and Jews in Arabia, Syria, and Egypt, and supposing all the Manuscripts of the Bible to have been corrupted among the *Eastern,* would not the *Western* Churches have ultimately discovered these alterations, and charged their Eastern brethren with the crime? Had even corruption been *attempted,* and partially effected, by the Christians in the East and in the West, it must have met with instant resistance; for those Jews and Christians, who embraced Islamism, would undoubtedly have confronted them with the true copies of the sacred books; and thus at once have frustrated their

---

[16] The words 1 John V. 7. were said, to have been erased from old MSS. by the *Arians,* but says Gerhard: "piorum ecclesiae doctorum vigilans industria illud restituit." Vol. II. 278. Yet the passage was also omitted by Cyril lib. XIV. thesauri, by St. Augustine and Bede. St. Jerome says: In prologo sup. epist. can. "*ab haereticis eum erasit esse.*" As another proof that no alteration could be made in the hope of escaping detection, see also Ambros. de fide V. 8. "Scriptum est, inquiunt (Ariani): *De die autem illo et hora nemo scit, neque angeli coelorum, nec filius, nisi solus Pater.* Primum veteres non habent codices Graeci, *quod nec filius scit.* Sed non mirum, si et hoc falsarunt, qui Scripturas interpolavere."

intention. Again, though the early Christians were *hunted* and *burned* by some of the Roman Emperors, yet they would rather give up the ghost, than surrender their holy books; and is it probable that they should *alter* those Scriptures, at a period when as yet they were not exposed to the like persecutions? Nor have our adversaries shown us any *rival copies* of the New Testament, which would naturally have been the case, if *some,* or *most* of the copies had been corrupted; for it is unnatural to suppose that all the true, were suppressed, and all the spurious ones, were propagated. If the books which we possess are not the true and genuine copies, let Mohammed and his followers produce them in their original integrity, and point out in what, the alleged corruptions consist.

10. Lastly, the New Testament being suspected of corruption, is therefore deemed of no further service; yet Mohammed considers its Founder a great Prophet, calls Him the *"Word"* and *"Spirit of God"* and admits that He has wrought many miracles. Is it reasonable in the eyes of a Moslemin, that the Gospel, which he ascribes to "Jesus the son of Mary," should be permitted to be corrupted so as to become useless! If what Mohammed maintains of Jesus Christ be true, then the Gospel must have been preserved in its original integrity; if not, then is Mohammed a false witness, and if he be a false witness, he cannot be a true prophet. Again it is asserted, that Christ was sent into the world to bear *witness* of Mohammed, and that this was his peculiar mission; Sur. LXI. 6. but how could He fulfil this mission, if His testi-

mony in favour of Mohammed was lost? We recognise therefore a flagrant contradiction, in the Mohammedans alleging that Christ came to bear record of their prophet, and at the same time in their declaring the documents containing that record, to have been corrupted. The impossibility, moreover, of God's word being corrupted, is stoutly asserted in the Koran.[17] We might justly inquire, whether the followers of Mohammed are acting the part of rational beings, whilst persisting in the accusation that our Scriptures are corrupted; unless they have proof, that their prophet had examined, and by his examination, had placed himself in a position to point out what portions had been altered, and what prophecies respecting him had been expunged. If we may believe Mohammed and his followers, he could *neither read nor write*; hence he was directed in the Koran to *ask* those who had the Scriptures,[18] and not to *read*

[17] "Et jam quidem mendaces habiti sunt legati ante: sed patienter sustinuerunt, quod mendaces haberentur et vexarentur, donec veniret ad eos auxilium nostrum. ولا مبدل لكلمات اللّه *Et non est, qui immutet verba Dei.*" Sur. VI. 33. Again: وتمت كلمات ربك صدقا وعدلا لا مبدل لكلماته وهو السميع العليم *Et* completa sunt verba Domini tui quoad veritatem et aequitatem: *non est qui permutat verba ejus*, et ipse est audiens. sciens. Vers. 115. Sur. XXIX. 46. and XLII. 14. M. avows his belief in the Christian and Jewish Scriptures.

[18] "*Ask* those (God says to Mohammed) who are acquainted with the Scriptures, if thou doest not know it." Sur. XXI. 7. Again: فان كنت فى شك مما انزلنا اليك فسل الذين يقرءون الكتاب من قبلك Sur. X. 93. The charge of corrupting the Scriptures was fabricated when flattery failed to gain the "Scripturalists" and *after* M. had acknowledged the divine authority of the law and the Gospel.

them himself: how could a man charge a book with being corrupted, which he never saw, or if seen, he could not read; and even if he could read an Arabic version, could not examine, either the ancient Manuscripts of the original, or the numerous versions which existed in the world?[19]

Having thus *established* the integrity of the *Bible*, we finish the argument by impeaching that of the *Koran*. No one is able to prove that Mohammed is the real author of the Koran, as we now find it. After his death, detached fragments of it were discovered, and it must be left undecided what was from Mohammed, and what has been added by other hands. There being no system in the book, we may have *double* the amount of the original matter, or have lost *half*, and remain for ever ignorant of the fact; how could it be otherwise expected than that his followers should be thrown into confusion by this uncertainty? Nor can any one acquainted with the early history of the Saracens, have failed to notice the bloody *feuds* which succeeded each other, concerning the many editions and alterations of the Koran. The first Kaliphs successively took the matter in hand, and supplying from memory what seemed to be wanting, seven most con-

---

[19] What would the Mohammedans think of a Christian, who should charge them with having corrupted the Koran, but disclaiming at the same time, all knowledge of Arabic, and boasting that he could neither read nor write? The author of Islamism is called the "illiterate" by Allah himself: الذين يتبعون الرسول النبي الامي who shall follow the apostle, the illiterate prophet." Sur. VII. 158. and 159. "*Credite ergo in Deum et Legatum ejus prophetam idiotam.*" النبي الامي.

flicting editions of the Koran came into circulation, during the first century after Mohammed's death.[20] The edition of the Shiites differed so greatly from that of the Sonnites, as to affect the essential doctrines of Mohammedanism. It was not therefore without good reason, that the Mohammedans gave up the point, as to which was the *original* copy of the Koran, affirming that it was placed beneath the throne of Allah!

CHAPTER III.

THE BIBLE AND THE KORAN.

"Tekel; thou art weighed in *the Balance* and found wanting."
Dan. V. 27.

1. The concluding remarks of the previous chapter lead us to a closer comparison of the religious *documents* of Christians and Mohammedans. It is not within our present scope to enter upon a detailed examination of their respective doctrines, but even a cursory inspection will convince us, that we have

---

[20] Nay, according to the following tradition, there were seven editions before he died. "Jedes Jahr im Monat Ramadhan wiederholte Mohammed vor dem Engel Gabriel, was bis dahin von dem Koran geoffenbart worden; man sagt sogar, im letzten Lebensjahre habe er ihn zweimal wiederholt. So oft er eine neue Lesart hinzusetzte, oder etwas wegließ, woraus die ersten 7 Ausgaben entstanden, prägten seine Gefährten diese Varianten sogleich ins Gedächtniß ein und handelten diesen Zusätzen oder Veränderungen gemäß." Historisch-kritische Einleitung in den Koran von Dr. Weil pag. 49. These various readings, sanctioned by M. himself, were however destroyed by Othman, and one of his own; substituted instead. See pag. 106. 107. of this work. Where then, we ask, is Mohammed's original Koran?

to do with writings of a directly opposite character. — The first thing which strikes us, is the constant anxiety of the author of the Koran, to guard against objections, to justify his claims, to defend his conduct and to account for the absence of those seals, which always accompany the dignity of a true prophet.[21] How often he reiterates, that his declamations are true; how repeatedly he swears, that his words are those of a faithful messenger.[22] The author of the Koran betrays precisely that disquietude and suspicion, which invariably indicate *fraud*, and never exist in guileless, honest and truthful minds. Mohammed always anticipates contradictions and expects opposition.[23] Truth on the contrary, has no need of such apprehensions or precautions, therefore never uses them. The writers of our sacred Scriptures are "not careful" to obviate cavils, to anticipate objections, to remove doubts, or to explain what may seem strange

---

[21] "They have sworn by God, by the most solemn oath, that if a sign came unto them, they would certainly believe therein. Say verily signs are in the power of God alone." Sur. VI. 109. also XIII. 8. II. 112.

[22] Allah is made to say, "If he (Mohammed), had forged any part in his discourses concerning us, we should surely have taken him by the right hand, and cut in two the vein of his heart." Sur. LXIX. 42—50.

[23] "There is *no doubt* in this book, it is a direction to the pious." Sur. II. 1. This is the real beginning of the Koran; the first Sura being a doxology. "This is the mission of the book (Koran), from the Lord of all creatures, there is *no doubt* thereof. Will they say he (Mohammed) has forged it?" Sur. XXXII. 1. 2. "A book hath been sent down unto thee, and therefore let there be *no fear or doubt* in the breast concerning it." Sur. VII. 1. "Praise be unto God who hath sent down the Koran... which *deceives not*." Sur. XVIII. 1. also Sur. XIII. 1.

and incredible; and this, simply because they entertain no doubts themselves, knowing they record facts, which they allow to speak for themselves by their own intrinsic force and power.

There is in the Bible an artless relation of events; all bears the stamp of genuine simplicity; all is real and unaffected, free from every meretricious ornament; it is destitute in short, of all that highflown grandiloquence and declamation, so much studied in the Koran.[24] The sacred writers make no reflections on what they record; if we may be permitted the expression, they manifest a sublime indifference, which takes the heart by storm and inspires a feeling of confidence. We feel at once that we are reading facts not fictions, revelations from heaven, not the outpourings of a wild imagination, or a heated brain. How different for instance, must an impartial Mohammedan feel in reading *Livy,* and in perusing the *Gospel* according to *St. John*; it is as if the former was giving his ideas of the events he describes, and the latter was recording the events themselves, as they actually happened. Livy must ever retain his fame as an historian, but apart from all other considerations, one must instinctively give his preference to St. John's style of narration. If only compared with this or any other Pagan author, how tedious and unmeaning, how ambiguous and confused, is the style of this so

---

[24] St. Matthew thus records his own call to the Apostleship "As Jesus passed forth from thence, He saw a man named Matthew, sitting at the receipt of custom and He said unto him: follow me, and he arose and followed Him." Matt. IX. 9.

called *"perspicuous book* come down from heaven,"[25] betraying throughout that guarded and mistrustful tone which unmistakeably betokens it to be a fraudulent production.

2. Proceeding to investigate the *contents* of both documents, we shall first endeavour to trace out the vein of history, which from beginning to end runs through the Bible, and embraces the divine plan of salvation.[26] Soon after the fall, mankind came to be divided into two distinct branches, *"the sons of God"* and *"the children of men."* When at a future period they became united, it was only for evil, the rapid growth of which, ended with the destruction of the human race, by the flood; Noah and his family alone finding *"grace in the eyes of the Lord."* His descendants vainly sought to frustrate God's purpose that they should be scattered and replenish the earth; but after this dispersion, it being impossible that God should reveal Himself to each particular nation in the peculiar manner which His plan demanded, He chose one people to be the steward of His past, and the depository of His future revelations. As this chosen people were in all points to be educated for a peculiar purpose, the education commenced with a

[25] تلك ايات الكتاب وقران مبين Sur. XV. 1. a standing term. Sur. XXVI. 1. XLIV. 1. XII. 1.

[26] To select a few passages here and there, would lead to no definite and just appreciation of the books to be contrasted. This mode of dealing has been justly condemned with regard to Natural Science. *"Naturae rerum vis atque majestas in omnibus momentis fide caret, si quis modo partes ejus, ac non totum complectatur animo."* Pliny.

single individual; and Abraham that he might become "the father of them that believe," was trained by God to "walk by faith" in the land of promise; thus 'consecrating Canaan as the future home of his posterity.²⁷ To prevent a premature settling down in the promised land, and a possible intermixture with the idolatrous nations of Canaan, the people were sheltered for a period in the land of *Goshen*. Although the promise of a numerous posterity was speedily fulfilled, yet it might seem as if God had forsaken His people during their oppression in Egypt *Moses* therefore, on receiving the commission to lead them forth from the house of bondage, announced the God of their fathers to be the unchangeable *Jehovah*.²⁸

The Jews, by the *Exodus*, had become an independent nation, and having thus far grown up under God's fostering care, were now placed under the schoolmaster of the law to bring them unto Christ; but as no finite being could comprehend the tenor of their future constitution,— which should embrace all ages and meet all exigencies,— nor conceive the ultimate destiny of this people, God alone could be the lawgiver; thus their *private, civil* and *religious* character was formed upon a model, which He gave to Moses in the wil-

---

[27] Notice the contrast of the promise of God to Abraham וַאֲגַדְּלָה שְׁמֶךָ "I will make thy name great," and the resolve of those proud patriarchs, "let us make us a Shem, i. e. a name; וְנַעֲשֶׂה־לָּנוּ שֵׁם. How great a difference in the end! Gen. XII. 1—2. XI. 4.

[28] אֶהְיֶה אֲשֶׁר אֶהְיֶה ero qui ero; ὁ ὢν καὶ ὁ ἦν καὶ ὁ ἐρχόμενος; cfr. Exod. IV. 14. with Rev. I. 4.

derness. As these laws neither emanated from the nation itself, nor yet from any human legislator, it was natural that the *executive power* should remain in the hands of the Divine Sovereign, who framed them; hence it was an offence against God, when Israel demanded a king. The Divine plan of *educating* them required a *symbolical* instruction adapted to their childish perception; *types* and *symbols* are therefore employed, as the most natural mode of conveying divine truths. Israel being *like unto other nations*, the fact of their having been chosen, implied no miraculous translation from their days, to an epoch some thousand years in advance. To prescribe to them a religion in which the spiritual elements preponderated over external forms, types, rites and ceremonies would have been to apply moral force to produce a premature result, a plan which would have defeated its own object. Amongst all the emblems and types of good things to come, the appointed *priesthood*, with the prescribed *sacrifices*, was the most important. That the cause of their efficiency *was not in man*, but in the blood, of which God declared, "*I have given the blood to atone your souls*,"[29] is a point not to be overlooked. The means of atonement was something independent of man, he not having the principle of sanctification in himself; hence the person for whom the sacrifice was intended, was not permitted to assist in the services. *Another soul* was required for *his soul*, but this substitute being that of an *animal*,

[20] Lev. XVII. 11. כִּי נֶפֶשׁ הַבָּשָׂר בַּדָּם הִוא וַאֲנִי נְתַתִּיו לָכֶם עַל־הַמִּזְבֵּחַ לְכַפֵּר עַל־נַפְשֹׁתֵיכֶם כִּי־הַדָּם הוּא בַּנֶּפֶשׁ יְכַפֵּר׃

standing in no connection with man, it was inadequate to take away sin, Hebr. x. 4. and did no more than point to the blood of Christ, Who, pouring out His blood and giving His soul as a ransom for many, took away the sins of the world. Hebr. IX. 12.— Again, as it was God's purpose to keep the Jewish nation *separate* from all others, it is not surprising that its future *abode* was physically *guarded* from foreign influence. On the other hand, it possessed singular advantages for *spreading* that light amongst the surrounding nations of antiquity, of which the Jews were the chosen guardians. "Thus saith the Lord God, This is Jerusalem: I have set it in the midst of the nations and countries that are round about her." Ezek. v. 5.

The first period of Israel's possession of the country being the time of the *Judges,* was one of perpetual change and confusion; yet no epoch afforded so many striking evidences, that no vicissitudes could alter the purposes of the unchangeable Jehovah. To infuse new life into the Jewish church, neither the transitory enthusiasm of Jewish conquerors, nor yet the oracle of the Urim and Thummim was henceforth sufficient: it demanded something more spiritual and quickening; and this necessary, and extraordinary aid was imparted in the days of *Samuel,* when the *Spirit of Prophecy* supplied a living commentary to the law of Moses, and the symbolical forms of the constitution. Not less opportune was the introduction of this new element, in checking the influence of the political power which was added to the government of the

Jews, when—no longer satisfied with the priestly representative of Jehovah—they demanded a king, "to judge them like all the nations" 1 Sam. VIII. 5—7.[30] Scarcely had the nation reached its highest degree of worldly prosperity, under the peaceful reign of *Solomon*, than a fearful declension of spiritual life took place, and the Jewish kingdom speedily became ripe for judgment. Yet, as it would militate against the promise given to David, to allow an idolatrous power to destroy Solomon's temple, and to overthrow David's throne,[31] the kingdom was only weakened, being divided into a "house of Israel" and "a house of Judah," the latter retaining the temple and capital of the nation, whilst the former fell into idolatry.

But the wisdom of Jehovah, could not be baffled by the depravity of man; it was manifest that full scope was given to the passions of men, and yet that no human error could make void the purposes of God. The ten tribes of Israel, having lost their savour, are cast out, and driven back to that very land, from which Abraham was called forth. John XV. 2. 6. The house of Judah soon followed into captivity, but after being "purged," John XV. 2. it was to return for purposes set forth by Isaiah, who spoke of a *"branch out of a dry ground;"* of a *king*, whose throne no

---

[30] According to the original plan, the office of high priest comprised the threefold dignity of king, priest and prophet. Numb. XXVII. 21. Psalm LXXXII. 6. Exod. XVIII. 5. The regal dignity, as a separate office, not being originally included in the theocratical constitution, was after a short period, dissolved.

[31] וְחַסְדִּי לֹא־יָסוּר מִמֶּנּוּ כַּאֲשֶׁר הֲסִרֹתִי מֵעִם שָׁאוּל אֲשֶׁר הֲסִרֹתִי מִלְּפָנֶיךָ׃ 2 Sam. VII. 14. 15.

idolatry could undermine: of a *prophet* who would possess the Spirit without measure; and of a *priest* who would pass from death to life, and from humiliation to glory. When the civil power was dissolved as a cumbersome appendage, *Jeremiah* mourned upon the ruins of Jerusalem; *Daniel* watched on behalf of God's people near the Babylonian throne; and *Ezekiel* guarded the scattered and captive flock of the Almighty on the shores of the Chaboras. Nor could this apparent breaking up of God's long cherished plan of education endanger the safety of the remnant, upon whose preservation the issue depended; for there exists no record of their falling into idolatry during their captivity.

When the *house of Judah* returned, their condition was by no means encouraging; a shadow only being left of the house of David, and the second temple could not be compared to the glory of the first; yet a living hope and prospects of a brighter nature were still preserved.[32] When the house of David had fallen into oblivion, the guardianship of the prophets over the political power was no longer required; besides, all that was needful had been uttered respecting the advent and work of the Messiah. The Spirit of Prophecy fled, and in its flight, nothing more is said of a "*house of David,*" but it prophesied of "*the ruler desired,*" Mal. III. 1—4. IV. 5. 6. Who would come to His temple as a purifier of the nation, Who would

[32] Jehovah who chooses "*things which are not,*"—the words Isa. XLV. 1. being uttered 176 years before the birth of Cyrus — put it into Cyrus' heart to grant permission for the return of Judah. Ezra I. 1. 2.

separate the gold from the dross, and be introduced by a man of the spirit of Elias.

3. The time between *Malachi* and the forerunner of Christ was a time of *deep silence*, in which, "the kingdom of heaven was like unto a man travelling into a far country, who called his servants and delivered unto them his goods."[33] They were to keep fast what they had already received: the last prophet departing with the injunction, *"Remember ye the law of Moses,* my servant, which I commanded you in Horeb, with the statutes and judgments." The period immediately preceding the advent of Christ, was the time when the *blossoms* of the theocratical constitution had fallen off, and the *fruit* had not yet appeared. That it must have added to the trial of the nation to see their ancient privileges, *one by one,* die away, can easily be conceived. Nor was this all; the feeling of disappointment and misery which prevailed on the eve of the long expected advent of the Messiah, was such, that nothing short of the appearance of *"the Lord from heaven"* could satisfy the wants, and allay the intense *desire* of the Jewish

---

[33] This period of silence which lasted 400 years has its parallels. The Jews were in Egypt about 400 years without a voice of comfort or advice from the God of Abraham. Such a period also, was the time of the Judges, which lasted above 300 years. How inexplicable these periods of captivity, silence and apparent neglect seem to the natural man, may be seen e. g. from the celebrated conversation of Caecilius with Octavius: "Unde autem, *vel quis ille, aut ubi Deus* unicus, solitarius, destitutus, quem non gens libera, non regna, non saltem Romana superstitio noverunt? Judaeorum sola et misera gentilitas unum et ipsi Deum, sed palam, sed templis, aris, victimis, caerimoniisque coluerunt: *cujus adeo nulla vis nec potestas est, ut sit Romanis hominibus cum sua sibi natione captivus.*" Minuc. Fel. cap. X.

nation.[34] But here again we begin with small things, *a babe in swaddling-clothes lying in a manger.*[35] We have to do, not with rhythmical effusions, nor with metaphysical disquisitions upon divine things, nor yet with an unheard-of aggregate of moral precepts, from which the salvation of the world was expected. On the contrary, we have a sober, calm and simple narration of historical facts, "which were not done in a corner;" not a solitary, but a fourfold record of the leading events, words, deeds, and sufferings of the Son of God. Christianity was

[34] That Christ had become *"the desire of all nations,"* was proved by the general expectation of the world. The *Chinese* at that period looked for "the Holy one who was to appear from the West." The *Persian* Sosiosh was then expected as the Oshanderbega, or "man of the world." The *Buddhist* waited for a new Buddha, and the *Hindoos* for a fresh Avatar or incarnation of the Deity. The *wise men* in the East watched for the star of the king of the Jews. The *Romans* were not behind: "Percrebuerat Oriente toto vetus et constans opinio, esse in fatis, ut eo tempore, Judaea profecti rerum potirentur." Suetonius in Vita Vesp. Vide also Com. Tacit. Hist. I. 5. Virgil nat. 70. A. D. wrote at the time of Herod the Great:

"Ultima Cumaei venit jam carminis aetas:
Magnus ab integro saeclorum nascitur ordo.
Jam nova progenies coelo demittitur alto.
Tu modo nascenti puero, quo ferrea primum
Desinet, ac toto surget gens aurea mundo —
— Nec magnos metuent armenta leones.
Occidet et serpens, et fallax herba veneni occidet.
Aggredere O magnos (aderit jam tempus) honores,
Chara Deum soboles, magnum Jovis incrementum!
Aspice convexo nutantem pondere mundum,
Terrasque, tractusque maris, coelumque profundum:
Aspice venturo laetentur ut omnia saeclo.
Pauca tamen suberunt priscae vestigia fraudis,
— Erunt etiam altera bella.   Virgil. Eclog. IV.

[35] "Ut homines nascerentur ex Deo, primo ex ipsis natus est Deus. Descendit Deus, ut assurgamus."

based upon the foundation of the historical facts recorded in the four Gospels; and these books, with their contents, indicate "the fulness of time," and constitute the very centre of all ancient and modern history. The Koran itself, in speaking of the Law and the Gospel, as two distinct dispensations which chronologically succeeded each other, virtually acknowledges the beginning of a new epoch with the coming of Christ. Nor is it possible that any general history of the world, though written in a spirit directly opposed to Christianity, could fail to recognise the natural division of time, at the commencement of our era.

The supernatural conception of the Lord Jesus, and His manifestation of miraculous power are admitted by the Koran, though His death and resurrection are denied. In the Gospel, all these dogmas rest upon one and the same foundation; but the Koran rejects the death and resurrection of Christ, as being the groundwork of Redemption; since He gave His life *"by the eternal Spirit,"* [36] His blood is the blood of *the Son of God* which cleanseth from all sin. 1 John I. 7. All types and prophecies being *in Him* fulfilled, the distinctive rites of the Old Testament were no longer required: for the Gentiles being admitted to the blessings of the Gospel, the partition wall between them and the Jews was broken down, and Christ thus made in Himself, of twain one new body to be henceforth called by a new name. [37] The

---

[36] "Mors Christi vita mundi." Also John XII. 24.

[37] Compare Isa. LXV. 15. where the name of the Jews was to

order in which the Apostles were to bear witness, after having received the power of the Holy Ghost, was,—first at *Jerusalem*, then in *Judea*, then in *Samaria*, and after that, in the *uttermost parts* of the earth;³⁸ thus making fully known the mystery, "that the Gentiles should be fellow-heirs and of the same body, and partakers of His promise in Christ by the Gospel."³⁹

It must be considered one of the greatest marvels in history, that a nation should exercise the greatest influence upon the rest of mankind, only *after* it was destroyed; having during its existence remained comparatively unknown. Possessing for ages the secret of the world's salvation, the Jewish nation lost its importance on that secret being divulged. It then became manifest, that it was not partiality which prompted the choosing of this remarkable people. As the Jewish Scriptures have the peculiarity of being read *backwards, from right to left*, so, God's dealings with that people can only be understood, when they are retrospectively considered; thus St. Paul regarded the Ephesians, when saying they were "built upon

---

be left for a curse, לִשְׁבֻעָה, and His servants called by another name, שֵׁם אַחֵר, with the fact of the disciples being called χριστιανους first in Antioch. Act. XI. 26.

³⁸ The Semi-pagan Samaritans and the Semi-Jewish Ethiopians served as the medium for the transmission of the Gospel from the Jews to the Gentiles. After the baptism of the proselyte Eunuch, follows the conversion of the Apostle of the Gentiles, Act. IX. and cap. X. St. Peter preaches the Gospel to the Gentiles "without respect of persons."

³⁹ ουκ εγνωρίσθη: non notificatum est. Non dicit: ουκ απεκαλύφθη: non revelatum est. Beng. Gnom. ad Ephes. III.

the foundation of the *Apostles* and *Prophets*."[40] It was only through the Gospel that they became possessed of the key to the Old Testament.

The Koran contains no evidence, that prior to Islamism, a similar training of the Arabs took place, to fit *them* to convey a new dispensation to the world; and until this point be established, the Moslem has no right to place Islamism in the same category with the Law and the Gospel. The Arabs doubtless have a mission to fulfil in God's *providential* government of the world, like any other nation;[41] but as regards their instrumentality in the *salvation* of mankind, had they not hitherto existed, no nation under heaven would have sustained any loss whatever. Not so with the Jews; if we suppose that they had never existed, all would necessarily have taken a different course. Idolatry must have prevailed, and no element would have remained to serve as a foundation for the recovery of mankind. The history of the Jews, considered in this light, eclipses in importance the combined history of all other nations of antiquity. But the Jews in rejecting the Messiah, forfeited their right to national independance and the possession of the land of their inheritance, and thus lowered themselves beneath those nations from whom they had been so honorably distinguished.

[40] To use another simile: the Old Testament was written without vowels; these being added in the beginning of the Christian era. The Gospel supplied the vowels to the Old Testament, "so that he may run, that readeth."

[41] كذلك زينّا لكلّ امةٍ عملهم "We have given a work to every nation." Sur. VI. 108.

Lastly, we find not only an *organic* connection of the several parts of the Bible, which we vainly seek in the Koran or in any other religious document, but that each historical feature has a *prophetical* or *typical* character which embodies a miniature of the whole, and so anticipates the final consummation of the entire counsel of God. Thus, in reading the *last three Chapters* of the book of *Revelation*, we observe every single incident brought into close connection with something which has been recorded in the *first three Chapters* of *Genesis;* so that the beginning and the end of the Bible are linked together by an indissoluble bond of divine perfection and harmony.[42]

4. This *organic* connection and harmony between the Old and the New Testament are fully acknowledged in the Koran, "we also caused Jesus the son of Mary to follow the footsteps of the prophets, confirming the law which was already in their hands, and we gave him the Gospel, containing direction and light, confirming also the law which was given before it."[43] It would undoubtedly serve as a confirmation of the

[42] Gen. I. 1. and Rev. XXI. 1. Rev. XXI. 2. and Gen. I. 3. Gen. I. 14. and Rev. XXI. 23. Gen. I. 9. 10. and Rev. XXI. 1. Gen. II. 9. and Rev. XXII. 2. Gen. II. 10. and Rev. XXII. 1. Gen. II. 7. and Rev. XX. 13. Gen. II. 22. and Rev. XXI. 1. Gen. III. 8. and Rev. XXI. 3. Gen. II. 2. 3. and Rev. XXII. 14. Gen. I. 28. and Rev. XX. 4. Gen. III. 3. and Rev. XXI. Gen. III. 15. and Rev. XX. 2. 10. Gen. III. 16—19. and Rev. XX. 12. Gen. III. 17. 16. and Rev. XXI. 4. Gen. III. 17. and Rev. XXII. 3. Gen. III. 19. and Rev. XXI. 4. Gen. III. 21. and Rev. XIX. 7. XXI. 2. Gen. III. 24. and Rev. XXII. 14.

[43] وقفينا على اثارهم بعيسى ابن مريم مصدقا لما بين يديه من التوراة Sur. V. 54. See also XII. 111.

claims of Mohammed and his alleged revelations, could it be proved, that the Koran stands in the same relation to the Gospel, as the Gospel stands to the Old Testament: although this is the pretension of the Koran from beginning to end,[44] yet the completeness of the historical and doctrinal character of the Bible at once precludes the assumption. The Old and New Testament appear as a perfect whole, which requires no fresh revelation, nor the introduction of any new dispensation, excepting that only, which will unfold with the end of the world. Not only have we no single truth revealed in the Koran which we have not already in the Bible, but there is an absolute abrogation of some of the essentials of the preceding dispensations; there is no *historical vein* in the Koran, which would either lead back to the Gospel era or to the beginning of the world; but a direct denial of some of the most important historical facts recorded in the Gospel, and confirmed, as we shall see, by the testimony of profane writers.

It is not our design to compensate for weakness of argument by applying aspersive epithets to Islamism; it would be not only unseemly in any

---

[44] The same terms, which are used to signify the relation of the Gospel to the law, are applied to the Koran *confirming* the law and the Gospel. وانزلنا اليك الكتاب بالحق مصدقاً لما بين يديه من الكتاب Sur. V. 56. Again, "This book, which is blessed, we have sent down, *confirming* that which was before it." Sur. VI. 92. Again, "The Koran could not have been invented by any other, but it is from God; a *confirmation* of that which was revealed before it, and an *explanation* of the Scripture. There is no doubt, that it come from the Lord of all creatures." Sur. X. 38.

work of a religious or theological character, but would only defeat our object, by closing the mind to the power of truth and strengthening the prejudices of those, whose conversion we have in view. Yet the interests of truth must not be sacrificed to the desire of maintaining peace. After studiously perusing the Koran, with a view to ascertain whether the book had any pretext to consider itself as supplementary to the law and the Gospel, we are compelled to confess, that the judgment of the sober-minded enemies of Mohammed, as preserved in the Koran, is the most correct estimate which can be formed of its contents.[45] The Koran ostensibly professes to be of an historical character, but when the author borrowed a few fragments from sacred history, it was with the pompous claim to revelation, — "This is out of the secret *histories*, and we reveal the same," —forgetting that it had been already preached throughout the world as a matter of history, not revelation for the period of 600 and 2000 years![46] If any person ventured to question the pretensions of the "perspicuous book sent down from heaven," Mohammed, instead of meeting rational objections with rational arguments, enveloped himself in his alleged prophetical dignity, and in the name of Allah he

---

[45] "But they say, the Koran is a confused heap of dreams, nay he hath forged it; nay he is a poet." Sur. XXI. 5. Again: "They also say, These are fables of the ancients, which he hath caused to be written down; they are dictated to him morning and evening." Sur. XXV. 5.

[46] ذلك من انباء الغيب hoc est ex historiis arcani. Sur. III. 44.

poured forth a volley of maledictions upon his opponents and condemned them to be roasted in hell.[47]

To trace any fixed plan or system of doctrines in the Koran or to discern an *historical* thread of any kind is simply impossible. Some of the events connected with Noah, Abraham, Ishmael, Moses, and other distinguished characters of the Bible are repeatedly related in different parts of the Koran, and always with a painful admixture of fabulous additions. Sur. XII. introduces the history of Joseph as a fresh *revelation*, although it had happened 2870 years before Mohammed's time, and was written 200 years after it occurred. The conclusion therefore, to which we must of necessity arrive, is this, that there is no historical feature whatever in the Koran; on the contrary the matter is thrown together in the utmost confusion: historical events of the day are amalgamated with traditions of the most remote antiquity; biblical characters are brought forward in utter defiance of the order of their chronological succession.[48] In the midst of declamations against his enemies, Mohammed suddenly alludes to a period, when some

---

[47] I will afflict him with grievous calamities... may he be cursed! And again may he be cursed..... He looked and frowned and put on an austere countenance; then he turned back and was elated with pride, and he said, This is no other than a piece of magic, borrowed from others, these are only the words of a man. But such a one will I roast in hell. And who will say, in what this hell consists? It leaves nothing unconsumed, and nothing escapes. It scorcheth all the flesh of the human body; 19 angels have we appointed over them." Sur. LXXIV. 16—30.

[48] Contrast the apology of St. Stephen. Act. VII. and the lucid record of Peter in Acts II. and III. Or the historical sketch of the Psalmist Psalm CV. and CVI.

of the disobedient Jews were turned into monkeys and pigs, leaving his readers at a loss where to find an authenticated record of so extraordinary a metamorphosis! Sur. v. 65, vii. 166, ii. 61. Though divided into chapters and verses, no arrangement of subject is perceptible in the Koran. Invectives and curses against enemies are interwoven with instructions for fighting with infantry or cavalry. The history of the *Red Cow* of the Israelites is thrown together with charges against Jews and Christians and the usual denunciations of hell-fire; conversations of the damned are mingled with challenges to produce a Koran like his own; incidents from the Gospels and the apocryphal books of the New Testament are linked together with precepts for fasting, and promises of the material pleasures of Paradise. Asseverations of the truth of Mohammed's pseudo-revelations and lamentations at being considered an impostor, are coupled with the enaction of civil laws and the terrors of the day of Judgement.[49]

5. The next point of contract, to be observed is, —*the Bible, a standing miracle of God's power and wisdom*,[50] and the so called *miracle of the Koran*. Beginning with the former, we notice the *miraculous* character of the Old and New Testament.—Unlike the alleged nightly visions of Mohammed, the manifestations of Jehovah in the Bible were for the most

---

[49] The learned Hinkelmann declared A.D. 1694, when the Koran was less known: "*negotium nobis est cum libro, quem legere et detegere est refutare.*"

[50] Vide, Koppen, Die Bibel ein Werk der göttlichen Allmacht und Weisheit. 2 Bänd.,

part of a tangible and public nature. The cloudy pillar, the smoke, the thunder and lightening on mount Sinai, accompanied with the voice of the living God and the song of the angels at the birth, with the visible and audible manifestations at the baptism of the Lord Jesus, well befitted the respective introductions of the two dispensations. Whenever visions to *single* individuals are recorded in the Bible, such as vouchsafed to Moses in the bush, to Isaiah in the temple, to Ezekiel in Chaldea, to Zacharias during his ministrations and to Mary in her house, although not attested by others, yet they are invariably proved by their mighty *results;* a proof, for which we fruitlessly search to corroborate any one of Mohammed's visions.

Another class of miraculous demonstrations recorded in the Bible were those witnessed in the *sun, moon and stars*; it being the prerogative of the Lord of hosts "to bring out their hosts by the greatness of His might," and to cause them to hide themselves at His bidding, as was the case during the darkness which covered Egypt before the Exodus and which enveloped Palestine during the Crucifixion. As instances of Jehovah's sovereign power over the elements, we may remember that *Sodom* and *Gomorrah* were miraculously overthrown by *fire;* and *Nadab* and *Abihu* were killed by the same element. Elijah's prayer was answered by *fire;* the two companies of fifties, sent to the same prophet by the superstitious king Ahaziah, were consumed by *fire:* and Daniel's three friends were presented "in the midst of fire."

Marvels were also wrought in the *air*. Moses prophesied a destructive hail, which fell in some localities, whilst others were spared. A similar miracle was performed in the days of Samuel to ensure the victory to Israel. *Rain* from heaven ceases and falls upon the "fervent and effectual prayer" of the prophet Elijah. At another time, *dew* fell upon a fleece of wool, when the whole earth round about was dry, and again, upon all the earth, leaving the fleece dry. Lastly, our Lord rebuked the wind and it was calm. *Water* at one time is changed into blood, at another, into wine. A dry path is opened by Jehovah in the sea, and on three occasions through the river Jordan; again, Christ and Peter are seen walking on the lake of Galilee. In the days of the *Flood*, a miraculous interposition of Jehovah embraced both the dry *earth* and the water. The earth swallowed up Korah, Dathan, and Abiram with their rebellious followers, and all their substance. The *rocks* at one time were rent assunder, at other times, fire and water issued from them. *Iron* is made to swim; chains fall from the hands of holy prisoners, and an iron gate opens of its own accord. The *Rod* of Moses becomes a serpent, and that of Aaron "budded, and brought forth buds, and bloomed blossoms and yielded almonds" in a single night; and at another time a green fig-tree withered within the same period, at the Saviour's command. The *Manna* which for forty years was the miraculous food of the Israelites, falls on some days and not on others, remains good over the Sabbath, yet becomes foul, if kept on other days.

Poisonous herbs become wholesome: the *barrel of meal* and the *cruise of oil* never fail. A hundred men are fed upon scanty provisions, and Jesus feeds at one time 5000, at another, 4000 men, with a few loaves and a few fishes. Moses, Elijah, and Christ, live without food, during forty days in the wilderness. Again, a disobedient prophet is *killed* by a *lion*, whilst his ass stands by unharmed; but the prophet Daniel is *safe* in a *den* of lions. *Bears* are commanded to kill forty-two wicked children; two milch *kine*, upon which there had come no yoke, conduct the ark of the covenant in safety; *quails* are sent, at the prayer of Moses; Elijah is fed by *ravens;* an *ass* speaks with man's voice; Jonah is cast alive on the sea-shore by a *fish;* another fish supplies the tribute money; and others are found in a disciple's net in miraculous abundance. *Locusts, frogs, fiery serpents* and other creatures suddenly appear as judgments upon guilty nations. The greater number of the miracles of the Bible were wrought upon *man*. *Languages* are suddenly confused; people with open eyes, fail to find their way; a proud monarch is degraded to the condition and instincts of a beast of the field, and after seven years, is restored to his reason and kingdom; *Bezaleel* and *Solomon* are endued with supernatural wisdom. Sennacherib's host is miraculously destroyed in one night; Ananias and his wife fall down dead at an Apostle's feet; Miriam and Gehazi are punished with leprosy. Zacharias is suddenly struck dumb, and Elymas is struck blind. As bodily powers are miraculously taken away, so are they given; as in the case of David, and Samson. Still more numerous are the miracles of *Mercy*. Devils are cast out, lepers are cleansed, fever and palsy are removed, the bloody flux and the issue of blood are staunched, the deaf hear, the blind see, the lame walk, the ear cut off is replaced, withered limbs are cured, the dying are restored to health at a word, and the dead, even in a state of corruption, are instantly recalled to life.[51]

These miracles are distributed over the visible and invisible world, among animate, inanimate, rational and irrational creatures; thus setting forth the illimitable supremacy of Jehovah over the *whole universe*. The Koran, having no miracles of its own, relates some of the above-mentioned, with the most grotesque and fabulous exaggerations; while others recorded for the first time, have never been authenticated, and are invariably of an undignified, puerile and incongruous character, such as would worthily form a part of "the Arabian Nights" or any like fiction.[52] The Biblical miracles, on the other hand, although wrought in different parts of the world, amidst an endless diversity of circumstances, in different ages, by different persons, and for different purposes, yet are each, severally impressed with a

[51] Josh. VII. 14—21. Exod. XVII. 2. Judg. VII. 1—6. 16—20. 2 Chron. XX. 1—30. XII. 1—16. *wonderful* battles are recorded.

[52] See Abraham's deliverance from fire Sur. XXI. 69; the metamorphosis of the Jews into apes and swine Sur. V. 65; Solomon's power over demons, spirits and birds Sur. XXVII. 7—20; the story of Ezra, his ass, his basket of figs and cruise of wine Sur. II. 261; Job's cure on washing in the fountain which sprang up after stamping on the ground, Sur. XXXVIII. 43—46; the miraculous virtue of the shirt of Joseph. Sur. XII. 93—96—99.

BB*

peculiar stamp and significance.—Here then, the question arises, how comes it that these miracles form such a well ordered, highly diversified, duly proportioned and completely organised system of wonderful deeds? As it was impossible that they could have been fortuitously thrown together in the Bible, they doubtless were recorded under the immediate direction of God Himself, in the manner in which we find them, and in the order in which they were wrought. Since no human prescience could foresee what kind, and what number of miracles would be wrought, and no human wisdom could suggest how many of them should be selected, and in what manner they should be recorded so as to produce a collection not wanting in any of the essential links of the entire system, and yet, not needlessly replete with wonders of the same type and character; and since *God* alone could both work such miracles, and cause them to be so recorded, it unquestionably follows, that the *Bible,* in which we find them, must in *itself be a stupendous miracle of God's absolute power and wisdom.*

6. The Bible more especially appears a miracle of God's *wisdom*, when we examine its fulfilled prophecies. The prediction of the Flood; the numerous posterity of Abraham; the prophetic definition of the period, during which the Israelites were to be in bondage in a strange land; the announcement of the seven years' famine in Egypt; the threatening of the dispersion of Israel among all nations, in case of disobedience; and the still greater marvel,—one indeed without parallel in the annals of nations,—their re-

maining amidst the widest possible dispersion, a *distinct* people; all these predictions were clearly beyond the scope of human penetration to anticipate. The same may be said of Deborah's prediction that Jehovah would sell Sisera into the hand of a woman; of Samuel's telling Saul what should befall him on the way; of the message of Ahijah to the wife of Jeroboam; of the prophecy which *Elijah* conveyed to Ahab and Jezebel; of that of Elisha concerning the king of Samaria; of the promise of sons to Sarah, to the Shunamite, and to Elizabeth. Again, 300 years beforehand, it was predicted that *Josiah* would sacrifice the priests of Baal upon a certain altar; and the victory of Judah over the Moabites was prophesied by Jehaziel, under most improbable circumstances. The prophet *Isaiah* described the glory of Babylon, 250 years beforehand, and that, when it was yet an insignificant place; and he also predicted its ultimate downfall and conquest by the Medes. The same prophet mentioned Cyrus by name, as the person who should destroy Babylon, grant permission to the Jews to return from their captivity, and rebuild Jerusalem and the temple of Jehovah. *Jeremiah* foretells the captivity of Judah for the space of seventy years, and the lasting destruction of Babylon by the *Medes* and *Persians;* he also prophesies the early death of the false prophet, who had announced the destruction of Babylon within two years. The destinies of the four empires which succeeded the Babylonian, were unmistakeably pourtrayed by the prophet *Daniel;* he also foretold the destruction of the holy City by one of these four powers, and fixed the time of the *advent* of the Messiah.

Our *Lord* prophesied the details of His passion; His death, His resurrection, and ascension with a fearful precision; the locality where these events would take place, the persons who would take part in them; the denial of Peter, the betrayal of Judas and the flight of all His disciples. The pouring out of the Holy Ghost, the endowment of the Apostles with miraculous power; the manner of the death of Peter; his prominent part in the founding of the Church; the growth of God's kingdom; the prolonged existence of good and evil; the offence which the Gospel would cause, and the universality of its proclamation, as a witness among all nations; the duration of the Church in spite of opposition; the rising of false Christs and false prophets; the fate of the Jewish polity; the dispersion of the Jewish people; the call of the Gentiles, and the establishment of a new dispensation, in which men would no longer worship God in Jerusalem only; all these, and other events were foretold and fulfilled with wonderful exactitude.

As it could not be the work of man, in the first instance, to distribute the foregoing predictions over a space of thousands of years, giving to each its proper position in the economy of grace; and then to insert their respective fulfilments in after ages, so as to constitute that comprehensive organism which we find in the Bible; it *must* of necessity be the immediate work of *God*. Containing *such* marvellous *revelations* of future events as no finite intelligence could conceive, or human foresight prognosticate, revelations moreover, constituting a well-ordered *system* amidst an endless diversity of circumstances, the Bible bears in itself incontestible proof of being of *divine origin*; and we are thus led to the same conclusion, we arrived at with regard to the *miracles*, viz. that the Bible can be nothing *less, than a miracle of God's infinite wisdom and power.*

7. To start a comparison on these points with the Koran, is impossible, from the simple fact of Mohammed denying that he ever possessed the gift of prophecy, or the power to work miracles.[53] In the absence of these two kinds of evidence in favour of the Koran, Mohammed and his followers insist upon the *book itself being a miracle,* such as no previous prophet had wrought. Mohammed thus harangues the men of Mecca; "If ye be in doubt, concerning that which we sent down unto our servant (Mohammed) produce a chapter like unto it, and call upon your witnesses . . . . but if ye do not, nor shall be able to do it, justly fear the fire, whose fuel is men and stones, prepared for the unbelievers." Sur. II. 21. 22. In another place, he is made to say, "Ve-

---

[53] ويقول الّذين كفروا الّا انزل عليه اية من ربه اتّما انت منذر Sur. XIII. 9. In XLVI. 23. A prophet is made to declare "Surely the knowledge of the future standeth only with God. But I only show you for what I am sent." Mohammed is told to say verse 9: "Say I am not singular among the Apostles, neither do I know, what will be done with me or with you hereafter." The alleged predictions Sur. XXX. 1—3; XLVIII. 27. 28. and III. 108. alluded to by Ebn Abdolhalim in his *Apologia*, pag. 355. thus falling to the ground, need no refutation.

rily if men and genii were purposely assembled, that they might produce a book like this Koran, they could not produce one like it, although the one of them assisted the other."[54] It seems that Mohammed was confirmed in the belief of his being inspired, when, on the appearance of Sur. II. Labid Ebn Rabia tore down his own prize-poem, which had been affixed to the walls of the temple of Mecca, declaring that only a *divine* pen could produce such a composition as that of Mohammed.[55] Every chapter and verse of the Koran is hence considered a no less striking miracle, than the leprous hand of Moses was to the beholders; and this, chiefly on account of the *beauty* and sublimity of its style and language. Mohammed, it is argued, was an *illiterate* person, and as the Koran could not be the production of an illiterate man, it must necessarily be from God; the miracles recorded in the Bible, they assert, will become less and less striking in the lapse of ages; but that of the Koran will become more and more convincing, in proportion as learned men multiply to appreciate its merits, and to admit their inability to produce one equal to it!

[54] Sur. XVII. 90. See also Sur. X. 38. ام يقولون افتريه قل فاتوا بسورة مثله An dicent: confinxit eum (Mahumetus)? Responde, atqui afferte Suram unam, sicut (Suras) illius.

[55] "So selbst genugsam sich Mohammed, durch Labids Schmeichelei verführt, für einen wirklichen, ja sogar für den größten Dichter hielt, und die Schreibart in seinen Suren so entzückend schön fand, so können wir ihm doch beides durchaus nicht eingestehen, und dürfen es nicht verschweigen, daß seine Schreibart von einigen Stellen selbst für Prosa zu niedrig ist." Wahl's Einleitung pag. 87.

Although the beauties of the Koran were acknowledged by some of Mohammed's contemporaries, yet we have proof from the Koran itself, that this was rather the exception than the rule. Sur. VIII. 31. Several Arab writers have maintained, that the Koran could be surpassed in beauty and elegance; e. g. *Ishmael Ebn Ali* held, that being human, it might be equalled. The author of the work "Sharah al Mukaf," asserted that it was possible to surpass it. *Alnodham*, and others expressed similar sentiments. European authors of the highest reputation, who must be considered competent judges of the language and style of the Koran, have not failed to destroy the evidence, upon which, the divinity of the Koran has been mainly established. To quote one amongst many, the celebrated Dr. Lee says, "no one who can read the "*Mukamal of Hamadavi*" and "*Hariri*," will doubt, that the Koran has been surpassed."[56] The admission that the Koran contains many elegant and sublime portions, does not prove its superiority to any other work; nor does the allegation that Mohammed was an *illiterate* man, prove it to be miraculous. Many unlearned men have distinguished themselves, so as to command the admiration of posterity. Again, the alleged ignorance of Mohammed is incompatible with the fact of his being considered by his followers

---

[56] *Maraccio*: "Ego sane a capite ad calcem totum legi ac multoties relegi; atque ut melius intelligerem adhibui praecipuorum doctorum Moslemorum glossas et commentaria et neque in unica Sura, neque in decem, neque in omnibus, *miraculum ullum*, vel *umbram miraculi* potui reperiri, imo plures ineptias, nugas, fabulas, errores, mendacia inveni."

the *wisest* and most *enlightened* of men; if then, the Koran be the production of so wise and enlightened a man, it ceases to be a miracle; but it is admitted, that Mohammed was assisted by various individuals.[57]

The fact that Mohammed was a member of the tribe of Koreish, amongst whom, poetry and rhetoric were favourite studies, and the circumstance of his having retired to the celebrated cave near Mecca, greatly diminish the so-called miracle of the Koran. Supposing that the Koran has hitherto been unsurpassed, this does not imply the impossibility of its being eclipsed at a *future* period: but assuming that this will never be the case, the assumption affords no proof that the Koran was *inspired;* if so, we should be compelled to acknowledge the divinity of the Hindoo *Vedas* and the classical writings of the *Greeks* and *Romans*, since they are never likely to be surpassed or equalled; there being in every production of genius an individuality which cannot be reproduced. Again, elegance of style being the result of good taste and mental cultivation, cannot reasonably constitute a *proof* of *divine* inspiration; and to determine the divinity of the Koran by the rules of rhetoric, is to argue strongly against the supposition of its being a miracle. As all the rules of Arabian rhetoric

---

[57] Sur. XVI. 105. Cl Zamakshari, Bedawi and Yahia say it was a Greek, Zabar, who could read and write well. Another tradition says, that Jabar and Yesar often read the Old and New Test. to M. Yaish, a man of some learning, is also mentioned. Jellalodin says that M. frequented Kais's house, who was a Christian. Yahia also mentions Addas and Salman a Persian. Christian writers mention as coadjutors, Abdallah, the Jew, and the Nestorian monk Sergius, called Boheira. Sale's Koran pag. 223. note.

are taken from the Koran, and established by quotations from that book, and as it is understood among Mohammedans, to contain the best laws of grammar, it must follow, that every composition which is not in perfect accordance with it, is inelegant and objectionable. The absurdity of proving a book to be divine from its language is still more apparent, when we remember that all language is composed of changeable elements, and subject to changeable laws, so that a book may be considered elegant in one age, and rejected as inelegant and unpolished in another. In addition to this, it will be admitted, that the most pernicious sentiments and doctrines may be clothed in language surpassingly beautiful. — Again, the Koran having been written in Arabic, how could the world at large be satisfied of its divine origin? The *style* of the book, as one of the chief evidences of its inspiration, has been most inappropriately chosen, since its peculiar beauty could only be appreciated by the *Arabs*, or the few learned, acquainted with their tongue. If the evidence be intended for none but the Arabs, then the Koran is destined for their nation only; and if so, the book cannot be true, because it professes to be a revelation for all nations. Lastly, if the excellence and merit of the Koran consist in so high a degree in the beauty of its language, this certainly would be perceptible in its translations; but it is in the *versions* that the real poverty of the book is especially apparent. Hence probably, the prohibition among Mohammedans to render the Koran into any vernacular tongue.

The reasons assigned by Moslemin for deeming the Koran a miracle, are thus diametrically opposed to the grounds upon which the Bible may be so considered. Mohammed's chief object was to charm the ear and to beguile the mind. The Bible, on the contrary, uses a speech, which all may understand, and disdains enticing words of man's wisdom.[58] Yet it will be admitted by every competent and impartial judge, that it has a loftier style, and more beautiful passages in the fortieth chapter of Isaiah, than can be found in the celebrated second Sura of the Koran.[59] The Bible, indeed, can well afford to yield the palm in point of elegant composition, to books which, in the absence of real worth, require such means to recommend them; yet, in point of vigorous expression and innate power, as well as in simplicity of style, it stands unparalleled.

8. The historical feature of the Old and New Testament has now been examined, and the absence of this element in the Koran, has been demonstrated. The Bible, regarded as a miracle of God's power and wisdom, has been contrasted with the alleged miracle of the Koran. We will now consider the *in-*

---

[58] "*Verbis appertissimis et humilimo genere loquendi se cunctis praebens et exercens intentionem eorum, qui non sunt leves corde ut exciperet omnes populari sinu.*" Aug. Conf. lib. VI. cap. 5. The preaching is not καθ' ὑπεροχὴν λόγου ἢ σοφίας, οὐκ ἐν πειθοῖς ἀνθρωπίνης σοφίας λόγοις, ἀλλ' ἐν ἀποδείξει Πνεύματος καὶ δυνάμεως. 1 Cor. 11. 1—5.

[59] In spite however of all the inspired rhetoric of the Koran it declares that none besides God can understand it. وما يعلم تاويله الا الله Sur. III. 7.

ternal connection subsisting between the several books of the *New Testament*, as opposed to the *contradictory character of the contents of the Koran.* — The Gospel according to *St. Matthew* sets forth the Lord Jesus as the *promised* Redeemer, and recognises throughout His life, death, and resurrection the fulfilment of the law and the prophets.[60] The genealogical descent of the Saviour from David and Abraham; the history of the wise men from the East; the sermon on the mount as the re-edition of the law on mount Sinai; the numerous quotations from the Old Testament; Christ's prophecy regarding Jerusalem, as the centre of the Jewish economy; — all represent Christ as the promised seed of Abraham. The meekness and humility of His human nature; His character as the Messiah of Israel; His spotless purity and holiness as the Lamb of God; these, and similar features in our blessed Lord's life, shine forth with peculiar lustre in this Gospel. — Though the Gospel according to *St. Mark* has some features in common with that of St. Matthew and St. Luke, yet being written with a special reference to the apostolical work among the Gentiles, it condenses select portions of the life of Christ. Omitting frequent allusions to the Old Testament and the longer addresses of our Lord, it vividly sketches the most important scenes and graphically records many of the smaller incidents, in such a manner, as to form distinct and perfect

---

[60] Hence the constant repetition of the formula: I. 22. ἵνα πληρωθῇ τὸ ῥηθέν; II. 17. τότε ἐπληρώθη τὸ ῥηθέν; II. 23. ὅπως πληρωθῇ τὸ ῥηθέν.

pictures. — *St. Luke*, commencing with the forerunner of Christ, goes through the life of Jesus with chronological precision, and terminates with the Ascension; his object is to "*set forth in order*" the gradual development of the life of the God-man Jesus, to the Gentile converts. It supplies St. Matthew and St. Mark, yet, so that each of the three maintains a position of its own. — The Gospel according to *St. John* was not written to any particular class of people, but to the Church at large, united as it was into one body, after the destruction of Jerusalem. This Gospel was supplementary to the preceding ones; omitting what has in them been fully stated, it presents Christ in a new aspect, and starts with what has been made the scope and end of the other Evangelists. Hence St. John gives all those discourses of our Lord, relative to His person, and connection with the Father. Hence the detailed evidence of the *reality* of Christ's Death and Resurrection; the omission of the parables; the relation of a few only of the miracles,[61] and lastly, the record of the Saviour's intercessory prayer and valedictory addresses to His disciples.

These four records were called *the Gospel*[62] *of*

[61] *Nazianzenus* thus: Παῦρα δ' Ἰωάννου δήεις ἱερῇ ἐνὶ βίβλῳ, θαύματα δὴ πολλοὺς δὲ λόγους Χριστοῦ ἄνακτος.

[62] Ἐυαγγέλιον Ἰησοῦ Χριστοῦ κατὰ Ματθαῖον, Μάρκον, Λουκᾶν, καὶ Ἰωάννην. As the fourfold figure of the cherubim constitute the throne of the Divine Majesty of Jehovah, so, the 4 Gospels support the throne of the revealed Majesty of the incarnate Son of God, agreeably to the ancient view of the Church, which led to the symbolic representation of St. Matthew under the figure of a man, St. Mark under that of a lion, St. Luke under that of an ox, and St. John under that of an eagle. Ἐπειδὴ τέσσαρα κλίματα τοῦ κόσμου, ἐν ᾧ ἐσμέν, εἰσί, καὶ τέσσαρα καθολικὰ πνεύματα, κατέσπαρται δὲ

Jesus Christ to intimate their close connection and unity. Four men were moved by the Holy Ghost to write the life of Jesus, doubtless because, one individual would have been incapable of representing all its fulness; since it is not within the grasp of a single mind to receive and reflect *all* the rays of the "*Sun of righteousness*". Each *Evangelist*, as a distinct mirror, reflected the image of the glory of Christ in a different light; each writing for a different class of readers, and with a special object in view. Not as if there were any essential difference in the Redeemer's character, as severally pourtrayed by the four Evangelists, for they were equally inspired; yet each brings out one or other of the leading features of the history of Christ, in a more prominent degree. The *Acts of the Apostles* together with the Gospels, form the historical foundation of the New Testament. The Apostolic writings represent Christ in His Church and people, as the Son is in the Father. The Acts show to the world, in what manner Christ became the Shepherd of the flock, which was gathered into one fold from Jews and Gentiles; thus, connecting the Acts of the Apostles with the *Gospels* and the *Epistles*. Some of these exhibit the true nature of a living *faith* in Christ Jesus;[63] others exemplify the working

ἡ ἐκκλησία ἐπὶ πάσης τῆς γῆς, στύλος δὲ καὶ στήριγμα ἐκκλησίας τὸ εὐαγγέλιον καὶ πνεῦμα ζωῆς· εἰκότως τέσσαρας ἔχειν αὐτὴν στύλους, πανταχόθεν πνέοντας τὴν ἀφθαρσίαν καὶ ἀναζωπυροῦντας τοὺς ἀνθρώπους. Ἐξ ὧν φανερόν, ὅτι ὁ τῶν ἁπάντων τεχνίτης Λόγος, ὁ καθήμενος ἐπὶ τῶν Χερουβὶμ — — ἔδωκεν ἡμῖν τετράμορφον τὸ εὐαγγέλιον. Iren. adv. haer. III. 11. 8.

[63] This is the case in the Epistles to the Romans, Corinthians, Galatians, Ephesians and Philippians.

of faith by *love;*[64] others again, hold forth to the believer the *hope* of glory, amidst the distress, vanity, and opposition of the world.[65]

We admit that a single book might not probably be missed, if absent from the Canon, especially as the others belonging to the same class, would in a measure supply the deficiency; if however entire sets, as for instance the *Gospels,* or the *Acts* of the Apostles, or the *Epistles,* exhibiting the *faith,* the *love* or the *hope* of the Church were wanting, the rest of the Scriptures could *not* supply the deficiency. Though we willingly admit, that none might be able to discover, which *link* or *member* of the organism of Gospel truth were wanting, yet this does not affect our argument; since the question is not what books we may deem necessary *a priori,* but whether the existing Scripture form an organic whole. It might, for instance, be difficult for the naturalist to point out a gap, and to specify a missing member in the systems of natural science, yet, he would nevertheless be justified in insisting upon the systematic union of the respective families and species of botany and zoology.[66]

[64] This particularly in the Epistle of St. John. In those to Titus, Timothy, Philemon and the Thessalonians the work of Christ in single individuals and whole communities is made manifest; whilst the writings of St. Jude and St. James describe the new life in Christ as opposed to the carnal life, the snares and seductions of the world.

[65] This the scope of the Epistles of St. Peter, the Epistle to the Hebrews and the book of Revelation. The latter sketches the future history of the Church up to the final consummation of Christian hope.

[66] The same argument holds good as regards the Old Test. A book was considered a revelation from God, as far as it partook of

9. Moslem divines have never yet attempted to trace any connection between the 114 Suras of the Koran; such a task would be impracticable, since they form a confused mass of heterogeneous matter. That a book with *no connection* and with direct *contradictions* cannot be from God, is acknowledged by the Koran itself;[67] and that the followers of Mohammed made no attempt to disguise its contradictory character, may be inferred from the fact of their having recognised 225 instances, in which the author abrogated passages previously revealed, in consequence of a change in his policy.[68] In the Koran, all the patriarchs and prophets are considered Moslemin, Sur. III. 60. and yet Mohammed was ordained to be the first to confess Islamism. Sur. VI. 14. At one time, "Christians, Jews, and Sabeans" are promised deliverance at the day of Judgment, as well as Mohammedans, Sur. V. 73. III. 109. at another, the Koran urges a fierce and exterminating war against them as "unbelievers, whose dwelling shall be hell." Sur.

---

the theocratical character and expressed the *hope of Israel.* Christ is the head, under which both Testaments are united; each single book forming an essential part of the organic whole. "Das ist der rechte Prüfstein alle Bücher zu tadeln, wenn man siehet, ob sie Christum treiben oder nicht, sintemal all Schrift Christum zeigt. Röm. III. 21. Was Christum nicht lehrt, das ist nicht apostolisch, wenn es gleich St. Peter und Paulus lehrte." Luther.

[67] افلا يتدبرون القران ولو كان من عند غير الله لوجدوا فيه اختلافا كثيرا "Will they attentively consider the Koran? Were it from any other but God, they would certainly have found therein many contradictions." Sur. IV. 81.

[68] Möhler, Ueber das Verhältniß des Islams zum Evangelium. pag. 361—385.

C C

IX. 74. *Force*, in religious matters, is prohibited in one Sura; Sur. II. 257. in another, believers are commanded to fight against the unbelievers "with whatever *force* they may be able." Sur. VIII. 40. 62. God is said to have implanted into man power to choose, and liberty to act for good or evil; Sur. XCI. 7. 8. but in Sur. VI. 39. and elsewhere, we read, that Allah will lead into error or into the right way, whom he will. Sur. II. 6. 7. VII. 176. Lastly, the duration of the last Judgment is estimated Sur. XXXII. 4. to last 1000, but Sur. LXX. 3. it is prolonged to 50,000 years!

To these examples of *contradictions,* we add some specimens of gross *mistakes.* These, according to the to the Koran, are common to all prophets, and therefore claim our indulgence. "We have sent no apostle or prophet before thee, but when he read, Satan suggested some error in his reading." Sur. XXII. 51. The case of John the Baptist, amongst others, has already been referred to. *Alexander the Great* is represented as a worshipper of the true God, who enjoyed prophetical communion; whereas he was an idolater: pretending to be the son of Jupiter, he caused coins to be struck of himself with two horns, hence his name of *Dhulkarnain* in the Koran, or the *master of two horns.*[69] In his marches, which are likewise misrepresented in the Koran, Alexander came to a place "where the sun setteth, and he found it to set in *a spring of black mud.*" Another error seems to have

---

[69] ذوالقرنين, δικεραιος, bicornis. Sur. XVIII. 85—98. has been invariably applied to الاسكندر, Alexander.

been "suggested by Satan," when the prophet fabled of the conqueror's raising a wall of iron and brass to check the inroads of Gog and Magog. Not to refer to ancient mythologies, which severally embody traditions respecting the *Deluge,* the Pentateuch was read in the days of Mohammed by Jews and Christians throughout the world; yet the Koran in describing the flood, professes to *reveal* an unheard-of secret! Sur. XI. 51. Again, the Israelites are stated to have *returned* to Egypt after the passage of the Red Sea, to take possession of gardens, houses, and fountains. Sur. XXVI. 57—59. As samples of *anachronism,* which abound, we only mention that *Pharaoh* and *Haman* are made contemporaries, Sur. XXVIII. 5. and the *Virgin Mary* is called the sister of Aaron! Sur. XIX. 17.

If the Koran being the work of *one* individual, contain so many contradictions, anachronisms, blunders and incongruities,[80] what would have been the result, had it been written by many authors, in different countries, languages and ages, like the Bible!

[70] We avoid entering into further details, referring the reader to the Koran itself, or to Maracc. Prod. Pars IV. cap. XVII. *Fabula, falsa, impia ac superstitiosa, quae in Alcorano continentur, ex parte referentur.*

CHAPTER IV.

TRINITY OF THE BIBLE AND UNITY OF THE KORAN.

"The *natural man* receiveth not the things of the Spirit of God: for they are *foolishness* unto him: neither can he know them, because they are spiritually discerned." 1 Cor. II. 14.

1. It behoves us to approach this subject with befitting reverence, lest we reduce the transcendent Majesty of the triune God to an idol, the work of our own imagination. The nature of God is so far beyond, and above all similitude and comparison, that in attempting to consider it, we stand in imminent danger of putting forth a set of arbitrary notions concerning the Deity, of making His divine character the subject of ordinary reflection and reasoning, and of creating an image of God which would fall infinitely short of Him, who "dwelleth in the light which no man can approach unto."[71] Specially important is a just appreciation of those *symbolical* anthropomorphisms, in which the *Bible* transfers upon God human passions, such as anger and jealousy; or human relations, such as His being the *Father* of the human family, and in a special sense, the *Father* of our Lord Jesus Christ. The attributes of God,[72] have been divided into *mo-*

---

[71] "*Anthropomorphismus dogmaticus* i. e. ea cogitandi ratio perversa, quae humani et imperfecti aliquid ad Deum transfertur." Hutterus Redivivus pag. 148.

[72] Attributa divina, νοήματα ἀξιώματα, i. e. conceptus essentiales, quibus notio Dei absolvitur; as they are styled by the old divines.

ral and *metaphysical;*[73] the moral attributes comprise His holiness, justice, mercy, and truth; whilst His metaphysical perfections refer to the *physical* world and are known as His omnipotence, omnipresence, omniscience, and eternity. All these perfections are revealed in the Bible in due proportion, and what is more important, in perfect harmony with each other.[74] But the Koran passes over the moral attributes, and treats almost exclusively of the metaphysical perfections of the Godhead; thus producing a fearfully distorted image of the Divine nature. When the Bible declares, "God is light," it gives a symbolical definition of His glorious majesty,[75] a beautiful illustration, not only of the harmony between the divine attributes, but also of the manner, in which, if we may be allowed the expression, we may analyse the glory of God, and separately consider its component rays. As by the aid of the prism, a ray of light may be reduced to its primitive colours, and as we can make one of these colours the object of distinct contemplation, so may we bring each of the divine attributes under our se-

[73] *Attributa metaphysica* (physica, naturalia); and *attributa moralia;* to them are added: *attributa mixta*, spirituality, wisdom and happiness.

[74] "*Harmonia* attributorum in eo consistit, quod omnia rite inter se comparanda sint, ne uni tantum tribuatur, ut alterum tollatur, vel evertatur. Sic de misericordia div. ita censendum, ne quidquam detrahatur justitiae, et vice versa, de justitia, ne quidquam detrahatur misericordiae." Buddeus Dogmat. pag. 214.

[75] The question, so much agitated by the schoolmen, whether the difference of the attributes was *real*, or *nominal*, was decided by the old divines, to be neither *realiter* nor yet merely *nominaliter* but *formaliter*, i. e. no real difference in God Himself, but only necessary to our apprehension. This their *unity* in God implies the necessity of the mutual *harmony* of the divine attributes.

parate and special consideration: yet it is the union and harmony of these colours, which produce the clear, pure and colourless ray of light. Were one of the primary colours disproportionably strong and prominent, the appearance of light would be necessarily changed. In like manner, if one of the attributes of God be unduly set forth to the prejudice of the rest, we shall consequently have a distorted and imperfect representation of the Divine character.

The undue predominance which the Koran gives to God's omnipotent power, presents a painfully one-sided view of the Divine character. In its efforts to represent God as an incomprehensibly powerful Deity, the Koran withholds the gracious and loving attributes of God; hence the frigid nature of Islamism. In thus destroying the glorious harmony of the divine perfections, the Koran deprives the sinner of all true comfort, as well as of every incentive to a holy life. Instead of announcing the divine attributes as *abstract* ideas, after the manner of the Koran, the Bible presents them as historically exemplified in creation, providence and redemption; and although infinite and incomprehensible in themselves, they thus, at once assume an intelligible and practical form. In the Koran, an unknown God speaks of what "he is to himself," entirely omitting what he is pleased to be unto man.[76] How fearfully true are here proved the

---

[76] "Qualiter cognovi te? Cognovi te in te! Cognovi te non sicut tibi es, sed certe sicut mihi es; et non sine te, sed in te, quia tu lux, quae illuminasti me. Sicut enim tibi es, soli tibi cognotus es; sicut mihi es secundum gratiam tuam et mihi cognotus es; — cognovi, quoniam Deus meus tu!" Augustine.

words, "Whosoever denieth the Son, the same hath not the *Father*." The Moslem indeed has not *the Father*, that consoling name never crosses his lips; and there is so far consistency, since in Christ Jesus only, God is a Father. We ask, what comfort can the brokenhearted sinner derive from approaching a Deity, such as described in a Persian treatise on Divinity: "God is not a body that can be measured; He possesses neither length nor breadth, depth nor height; it is impossible, that there should exist in His nature any necessity to possess the properties of any thing; and He is no line, that is, a thing which can be divided in but one direction; nor is He a flat surface; that is, a thing which can be divided in both directions. He, the great God, is neither heavy nor light; He is neither in motion nor at rest; He is neither in space nor in time. Before Him the past and future are but the eternal present, and He is free from all properties of the creatures."![77]

Widely different from Allah, *Jehovah* in the administration of His providence "declares His Almighty power most chiefly in showing mercy and pity." The omnipotence of God is manifested by redeeming His people, by upholding them that are ready to fall, by raising up them, that are bowed down, by giving meat to all in due season, by satisfying the desire of every living soul, by showing Himself nigh to all that call upon Him, by preserving the righteous, and by finally destroying the evil doers.[78] The providential care of

[77] Pfander's Remarks pag. 11.
[78] Psalm LXXVII. 12—15, CXLV. 8. 13—20. Matt. V. 17. Act. XIV. 17.

Allah is partial, being confined to the Mohammedans; whilst Jehovah makes "His sun to shine upon the evil and the good, doing good, giving rain from heaven and fruitful seasons and filling all hearts with food and gladness.

2. If then, the Theology of the Koran be unsound in its *best* points, viz., the metaphysical perfections of God, still more unsound is it as regards those attributes which bear upon the *moral* nature and the spiritual wants of man. Islamism confines itself to those points of faith, which may be found with more or less clearness, in natural religion; but these cannot lead to a saving knowledge of God:[79] since it is not "God reconciling the world to Himself" who is revealed in natural religion, but only the omnipotent and eternal Creator, manifesting Himself by "*the things that are made.*" Rom. I. 19. 20. The world's Redemption being connected with the revelation of God, as *Father*, as *Son*, and as *Holy Ghost*, belief in the *triune God* is *alone* of saving efficacy. John V. 23. XVII. 3. 1 John II. 23. This blessed doctrine in which all the divine attributes are practically displayed in perfect harmony, could not be gathered from *nature* or *reason*; because neither of them could anticipate

---

[79] "Die natürliche Gotteserkenntniß ist ein angebornes, durch Betrachtung der Natur und Geschichte ausgebildetes Bewußtsein von Gott, das zwar den Begriff des vollkommensten Wesens enthält, aber im sündigen Menschen nicht hinreicht zum Heile, sondern nur den Abfall von Gott darthut, und dadurch die Sehnsucht weckt nach der übernatürlichen Offenbarung. Diese allein als Offenbarwerden der Trinität ist befeligend." Hutterus Redivivus pag. 121. "Notitia Dei *naturalis* ad salutem procurandam, aut saltem damnationem arcendam, sufficiens non est, nec ullus mortalium per eam solam vel ad salutem perductus fuit, vel perduci potuit." Quenstedt I. pag. 261.

the mystery of Redemption; and it could not be placed before the tribunal of man's finite intellect;[80] since it is revealed in the Gospel, not in the form of a *doctrinal system*, but as the merciful achievement of Divine love, wisdom, holiness, justice and power. The triune God is revealed in the Bible, as the Father who resolves upon our redemption; as the *Son* who accomplishes the blessed work, and as the *Holy Ghost* who communicates its gracious and sanctifying influences to the Church in all ages; hence the formula of baptism, expressive of our Christian faith. To defend the doctrine of the holy Trinity by arguments drawn from reason, cannot then be our object, being avowedly above its power and beyond its sphere.[81]

It would have been better for the interests of truth, if Christian apologists and Missionaries had never attempted to make this mystery acceptable to Mohammedans by illustrations and comparisons, which, moreover, have not always been the happiest or most elevated. The Scriptures simply reveal the fact, and

[80] "Mysterium Trinitatis quod est ὑπὲρ νοῦν, ὑπὲρ λόγον καὶ ὑπὲρ πᾶσαν κατάληψιν ex ratione naturali oppugnari non potest." Quenst.

[81] "Es widerspricht 1) dem Denkgesetze, daß ein Theil gleich dem Ganzen, das Ganze gleich dem Theile sei; 2) dem Gesetze der Causalität, [baß *generatio*, wie auch gedacht, eine ursächliche Handlung außer der Zeit erfolge; 3) der Idee des Absoluten, indem der *character hypostaticus* entweder etwas Zufälliges, sonach Unvollkommenes ist, das in Gott nicht gedacht werden kann, oder etwas Wesentliches und Vollkommenes, dann würde diese Vollkommenheit den andern Personen abgehen. Das Dogma ist daher Mysterium, als über allen Verstand erhabenes Postulat des Christenthums, wenn die Gottheit des Sohnes und Persönlichkeit des Heiligen Geistes im religiösen Leben und der Heiligen Schrift nachgewiesen ist, so ruhig in seiner unvereinbaren Dreiheit und Einheit aufzustellen, als die gleichfalls in der Demonstration unvereinbaren Freiheit und Vorsehung." Hase.

demand simple and childlike faith; any attempt therefore to expound a mystery therein revealed, must only "darken counsel by words without knowledge."[82] We *believe* it to be so; *how* it is, we are not ashamed to say we cannot tell; nor can we understand why we should be expected to explain it. A *revelation without miracles*, and a *faith without mysteries*, such as is found in Islamism, present a most unreasonable anomaly. How little this was felt by the *eclectic* prophet of the Arabs, is clear, from his anxiety to expunge from his creed, every article which he could not square with his sharp but unsanctified intellect. As the doctrine of man's Redemption is so intimately connected with that of the holy Trinity, both were struck out from his system of faith. The belief of the Trinity will *always* be rejected, where neither the burden of sin is felt, nor the authority of Scripture acknowledged.

As if to revenge himself upon the holy *mysteries* of our faith, both the dogma of the *Trinity,* and the doctrine of the *Incarnation* of the Son of God were grossly and blasphemously misrepresented by Mohammed. It would be unjust to lay the teaching of a Moslem heresy to the charge of orthodox Islamism: equally unfair is it, to borrow from the Colyridian heresy,— which flourished in Arabia and was convicted of Mariolatry,— and to set forth its teaching as a *Chris-*

---

[82] The philosophical theory concerning the Λόγος; the ancient comparison of fire, brightness and heat in light, and the mysterious harmony of three sounds and forms, which run through creation, have been vainly resorted to, with a view to ellucidate this mysterious dogma.

tian dogma. Mohammed, therefore, from whom we might have expected a better knowledge, is alone responsible for this misrepresentation. Our Lord and His Apostles might as well have rejected the old dispensation as unsound and heretical, because at certain periods the Israelites worshipped *Baal* and served the *host of heaven*. Mohammed however was determined to reject certain doctrines; and the heretical views, which were current in his corrupt age within the Church, afforded him a plausible reason for so doing.—All the Christian Missionary can do in this momentous dispute, is to remove those *erroneous* notions and prejudices, which the Koran has taken such pains to impress upon the minds of its followers; and to show that there is nothing *unworthy* of God in the teaching: that from God, the *Father* are all things, that by the *Son* are all things and that to the *Holy Ghost* are all things; and also that it is not *blasphemy* to preach "the grace of our Lord Jesus Christ, the love of God and the fellowship of the Holy Ghost;" avoiding "*profane questions*" upon so sacred a subject; and shunning illustrations and comparisons with a view to render the mystery comprehensible to the limited powers of human intellect.[83]

---

[83] "Mysterium hoc ex naturali ratione nec a priori, nec a posteriori demonstrari potest; non *a priori*, quia Deus in se et prout ipse est, in hac imbecilitate cognosci nequit, quicquid de Deo scitur, id omne a posteriori tantum scitur. *Non a posteriori* h. e. *ex operibus et creaturis Dei, nulla enim vera et plena similitudo vel imago Trinitatis in creaturis est expressa* ... *Illaeque congruentiae naturales et analogia rerum creatarum cum hoc fidei mysterio non divinam fidem, sed opinionem tantum humanam generant* ...... Imo ne quidem possibilitas hujus mysterii e naturae lumine haberi potest, cum rationi,

3. In perfect accordance with this view, the Church in her *symbols* endeavours to express the mystery, as set forth in Scripture; not to embrace it with the intellect, but to protect it both against *Unitarianism* and *Tritheism;* so that a Christian may possess saving faith in the triune God, Father, Son and Holy Spirit without the knowledge of these dogmatic forms; yet no one can reject these, without rejecting the Trinity. When modern theologians endeavour to shake these venerable safe-guards of our holy faith, we can only ascribe it to a secret leaning to *Unitarianism;* hence we have sufficient reason to hold fast the dogmatic representation of this doctrine in our creeds.[84] That neither the doctrine of the Incarnation nor that of the Trinity are in themselves *irrational*, may be inferred from the religious speculations of Pagan antiquity. As true religion commenced with manifestations of the Deity and ended with the Incarnation of the blessed Godhead, so Paganism commenced with oracles and pseudo-prophetical revelations, and

propria principia consulenti: ἀδύνατον καὶ ἀντιφατικὸν, absurdum et impossibile videatur." Quenst. Theolog. Didactico-polemica Vol. I. pag. 318.

[84] "Fides Catholica non in hac loquendi formula praecise sita est, quod tres sint *personae* in una div. *essentia*, sed in eo ut sincere credamus, Patrem, Filium et Spiritum S. unum esse Deum, — ut per omnia et unitatem in Trinitate et Trinitatem in unitate veneremur. Gemina illic loquutionis illius necessitas statuitur a S. Augustino: altera ab humani eloquii inopia, altera ab haereticorum versutia. Primo dictum ita fuit, quum non liceret aliter, ut aliquo saltem modo explicaretur ineffabilis illa Unitatis et Trinitatis ratio, non ut illud *diceretur*, sed ne *taceretur*.... Patet igitur, quo pacto necessaria sint illae formulae, non quidem *absolute*, sed ex *hypothesi* tum declarandae ὀρθοδοξίας, tum dignoscendae ἑτεροδοξίας, tametsi hujus videatur potior esse, quam illius ratio." Calovii Dog. III. pag. 4.

ended with incarnations of the Deity. Again, may we not go further, and admit that some *image*, ideal or material, exists in almost every false creed, by which the blessed Trinity is adumbrated. We find in almost every Mythology a divine *Triad*, and in some cases even a *Monad* in connection with a *Triad;* we refer to the *Trimurti* of the Hindoos, the *Triads* of the ancient Egyptians, and Scandinavians, also to the Neo-platonic philosophy. To this may be added the remarkable fact, that the Jewish philosophers B. C. assumed three lights, three names and one substance in God.[85] Errors, when universal, may be invariably traced to some perversion of truth; if so, we may recognise a corruption of the Trinity in all these Triads, if not in Polytheism itself.

As far then as the philosophico-religious speculations of the Pagan and Jewish world have any weight, we have their testimony, that it is precisely the *abstract metaphysical Monotheism* of the Koran which satisfies neither faith nor reason.[86] Waving however the question, whether the dogma of the Trinity or this rigid Unitarianism be the more opposed to rea-

---

[85] See Maraccio Prodrom. Pars III. cap. IX. *Ex veterum Hebraeorum doctrina, Sanctissimae Trinitatis Mysterium comprobatur.* pag. 26—28.

[86] „Es ist weniger Menschensache, den spekulativen Werth eines Lehrgebäudes zu verfolgen und zu ergründen; die Bemerkung dürfte demnach für Viele völlig unnütz sein, daß der Monotheismus des Islam die philosophirende Vernunft nicht befriedige und gerade dann verworfen werden müsse, wenn von der Denkbarkeit oder Unbenkbarkeit einer bestimmten Vorstellung von Gott die Rede ist. Daß die Gottheit Eine Person sei, ist eben das ganz und gar Undenkbare, durchaus Unvernünftige, und aller wahren Spekulation Entgegengesetzte. Daß Gott nicht Mensch geworden, ist eben das Widersinnige." Möhler's Gesammelte Werke pag. 397.

son, let it suffice us to know and to feel that the Holy Trinity is what the human *heart* practically *needs*. Indistinct and undefined as were the longings expressed in Pagan errors, and far beyond the power of human reason to anticipate, yet they gave loud utterance of the real wants of man.

Lastly, our opponents have in themselves a species of unity in trinity, which though unable to understand, they will have some difficulty to deny. We do not allude to the human constitution in its threefold aspect, as an illustration of the Divine Trinity, but we would ask those, who consider that doctrine unreasonable, to explain how the human *spirit* acts upon the *soul,* and how the soul acts upon the *body;* let them define how their *reasonable* thoughts upon the Trinity produce the words, with which they oppose the truth, and how these words call forth corresponding thoughts in the minds of others, and when they have satisfactorily explained this mystery, we will undertake to explain the mystery of the holy Trinity.[87] "If I have told you of earthly things, said our Lord, and ye believe not, how shall ye believe, if I tell you of heavenly things?"

[87] "1. Dieses Geheimniß bewahrt die Idee des göttlichen Lebens ohne die unstatthafte Annahme einer ewigen Schöpfung; 2. erleichtert den Gedanken der Offenbarung Gottes, ohne aufzuheben den Gedanken seiner Unerforschlichkeit; 3. stellt Gott in seiner Offenbarung, insbesondere im Sohne, als uns verwandt nahe, ohne aufzuheben die Idee der Unermeßlichkeit seines Wesens." Hahn.

CHAPTER V.

CHRIST THE SON OF GOD AND MOHAMMED THE SON OF ABDALLAH.

"What fellowship hath righteousness with unrighteousness? And what communion hath light with darkness? What concord hath Christ with Belial? What hath he that believeth with an infidel? 2 Cor. VI. 14. 15.

1. The comparison which devolves upon us in this chapter, is of a character from which we naturally recoil; but the interests of truth, and the arguments of our adversaries compel us to point out the infinite difference, existing between *the prophet of the Arabs* and the *Messiah of the world:* since it is against the *Divine Sonship* of the Redeemer, that the Koran chiefly levels its concentrated wrath. The Koran asserts that Christ is nothing but a messenger; Sur. V. 79. those are infidels, that confess Christ the son of Mary to be truly God. Sur. V. 19. Allah has no son, Sur. XXIII. 93. and the impossibility of this is proved from the fact of his having no partner. Sur. LXXII. 2.[88] It is foreign to our intention to exhaust

[88] "Offendi se ajunt Mahumetistae, quod Deo filium demum cum uxore non utatur; quasi filii vox in Deo non possit diviniorem habere significationem. At ipse Mahumetus multa Deo ascribit non minus indigna, quam si uxorem habere diceretur: puta manum ipsi frigidam esse, idque se tactu expertum: gestari in sella et his similia. Nos vero cum Jesum Dei filium dicimus, hoc significamus, quod ipse cum eum Verbum Dei dicit: verbum enim ex mente, suo quodam modo gignitur: adde jam, quod ex virgine, sola Dei opera vim paternam supplente, natus est, quod in coelum evertus Dei potestate, quae et ipsa Mahumeti confessa ostendunt Jesum singulari quodam jure Dei filium appellari posse et debere." Grot. de veritat. relig. Christ. pag. 288.

the subject in all its bearings; all that we contemplate, is to furnish hints and supply materials for the inexperienced Missionary, or any other Christian man who may have occasion to sustain an argument with Mohammedans on these momentous subjects. The Divine Sonship of Christ may be sometimes proved from the admissions, which the Koran has hazarded, respecting the dignity of "the son of Mary." That mode of reasoning, which carries the argument within the camp of our opponents and fights with their weapons, if ably conducted, is one of the most powerful, which can be adopted; and is moreover accompanied with this singular advantage, that the Koran is proved to be inconsistent and false, if its admissions do not imply that Jesus is the Son of God.

When Christ is styled "the *Word*," not only His prophetical character, but also His pre-existence with the Father is admitted. If Jesus be the Word, in the sense of St. John, from whom alone, Mohammed could have borrowed the expression, He must have been with God from the beginning, and by Him all things were made. Christ could not be the Word, if he was not God or the Son of God; Mohammed therefore, either declared a falsehood when he admitted Christ to be the Word, or he is wrong in denying Him to be the Son of God.[89]

---

[89] "Si interrogatus es a Saraceno, quis sit Christus? respondi ei: Verbum Dei, nec existimes peccare quia et verbum dicitur in Scriptura et brachium et potentia Dei et multa alia. Vicissem autem interroga ipsum et tu: a Scriptura quid dicitur Christus? Tum forte volet interrogare te et ipse aliud, cupiens sic effugare te: non vero

Again, Mohammed having asserted Sur. LXI. 6. that his coming had been predicted by Christ, clearly admits the dignity of Christ as a prophet, and the divine character of the New Testament. Jesus, whose prophetical character is thus granted, asserted more than once, that He is the Son of God, and that He and the Father are one; His testimony of Himself, must equally be true; if it be not, Christ could not have been a true prophet, and Mohammed

tu respondens ei, donec utique respondeat tibi, dicens: a Scriptura mea Spiritus et Verbum Dei dicitur. Dum rursus interroga ipsum: Verbum a Scriptura tua creatumne an increatum? Et sic dicat: increatum, dic ipsi: Ecce consentis mihi; omne enim non creatum sed increatum Deus est. Si autem dixerit: creata esse Verbum et Spiritum, tum quaere: et quis creavit Verbum et Spiritum? quod necessitate coactus responderit: Deus ipse creavit; tum tu rursus: ergo antequam creavit Deus Spiritum et Verbum, non habuit Spiritum neque Verbum? Quod quum audierit, fugiet a te, non habens, quod respondeat. Disceptantes enim sunt tales secundum Saracenos et omnino abominabiles et abjecti. Quod si vero tu interrogatus fueris a Saraceno: *Verba* Dei creatne sunt an increata? Haec enim proponunt adversus nos Saraceni problemata, potentius volentes ostendere creatum Verbum, quod non est. Et si dicas: creata, dicet tibi: ecce dicis creatum Dei verbum. Si autem dicas: increata, dicet tibi: 'quoniam ecce omnia verba Dei increata quidem sunt, Dii autem non sunt. Ecce tu confessus es, quoniam Christus Verbum est Dei, non Deus est.' Propter quod neque creata dicas, neque increata, sed sic responde ei: ego *unum solum Verbum* Dei confiteor increatum ens, omnem autem scripturam meam non dico λoγους i. e. verba, sed ῥήματα i. e. sermones Dei. Et Saracenus: qualiter dicit David: verba Domini casta? Dic ei, quod propheta tropolice locutus sit, et non cyrologice, i. e. non propria et firma verborum significatione." Disceptatio Christiani et Saraceni, Joan. Damascenus pag. 477. ed. Bas. With this may be compared: "Respondet Gelaleddinus: سمى كن بكلمة خلق لانّه اللّه كلمة, *nominatus est Verbum Dei, quia creatus est per verbum, Esto.* Sed hoc modo *omnia* dici poterunt Verbum Dei... Eadem ratione, qui per aquam mundatur, aqua dicendus erit; et qui ignem calefit, ignis: et qui per pharmacum sanatur, pharmacum appellandus erit." Maraccio Prod. Pars III. pag. 61.

DD

in declaring Him to be such, has proved himself a false witness.—Christ is also styled, in the Koran, the *Spirit* of God; Sur. IV. 169. whilst the first man Adam is said only to have received of the divine breath. If the Spirit proceed from God, and if Christ be that Spirit, the Koran establishes the Divinity of "the son of Mary." Supposing however, that the Holy Spirit only *dwelt* in Christ, it would at least imply what is otherwise stated in the Koran, viz. that Christ was a true prophet: for the Holy Spirit can neither dwell in a false prophet, nor speak false things through a true prophet. If therefore, Christ had the Spirit of God, and spoke through the same Holy Spirit, all that He said of His coming from God, and of His equality with the Father, must be true. Christ then, was either not the Spirit of God, and in that case the testimony of the Koran is false; or, He was the Spirit of God, and in this case, His record of Himself is true; and Mohammed thus in vain denies His Divine character and Sonship.

The son of Mary performed many miracles, as the Koran expresses it, "by the permission of God." If miracles, therefore, can only be performed by persons who receive the gift from God, they are witnesses to the truth of the doctrine which is preached. The miracles of Christ then, were seals to the truth of His teaching. In His teaching He openly declared Himself to be the Son of the Most High God; if this His teaching be true, that of Mohammed must be false. If on the contrary the teaching of Mohammed be true, that of Jesus must be false. As the testimony of Christ is proved by miracles, the testimony of Mohammed, which has no such seal, must be false; for if Christ be not the Son of God, God has put his seal to a false testimony. As God cannot attest what is false, Christ could have wrought no miracles; and if he wrought no miracles, the Koran is a false witness, and Mohammed, who wrote it, a false prophet.

Again, our Lord is generally called "*the son of Mary.*" From this extraordinary appelation, it appears that Mohammed did not consider Jesus the Son of Joseph, nor indeed, have we any suspicion thrown out on this subject, in any part of the Koran; on the contrary, Mary is always spoken of as the woman who preserved her virginity. In Sur. xxi. 91, it is fully admitted that Christ was miraculously conceived of the Holy Ghost, and Mary is held up as the most distinguished person of her sex, beloved of God, praised as a miracle and honoured in all ages. Sur. iii. 42. God appointed the Son of Mary and His mother for a sign. Sur. xxiii. 52. That Mohammed did not look upon Joseph, as the Father of Jesus, will appear from the fact, that he is not even so much as once mentioned in the Koran. Yet if we had no further evidence of Mohammed's admission of the supernatural origin of Christ, the standing appellation of "*the son of Mary*" would in itself, be sufficient to mark Him as the Son of God. The ancient oriental custom, which prevails to this day, of always associating a man's name with that of his father, proves that Mohammed held, that *Jesus* had no earthly father; since, against all usage, ancient and modern, he calls Christ "the son of Mary," thereby indicating, that he had no earthly father; we may therefore regard this singular departure from a customary practice, as tantamount to calling Him the *Son of God.*

2. Mohammed, elevating himself to the same position of Christ, challenges the world to examine his claims, and to ascertain, by what evidence, his pretensions to be considered the prophet of the last age, are supported. His followers urge two things on his behalf, viz. the *miracles* he is said to have performed, and the *prophecies* which are alleged to have been fulfilled in his person. As Mohammed was considered the greatest of the prophets, he was also represented as having performed more miracles than all of them.[90] The commencement of the old and new dispensation were acknowledged in the Koran to be miraculous; and although Mohammed constantly excused himself for not working miracles, yet his followers could not resist furnishing Islam with this dispensable prerequisite to every creed; and thus it came about,

---

[90] "Si recenseremus omnia miracula et signa ejus, de quibus mentionem fecerunt historici in libris suis, certe excresceret tomus. Nam propheta noster faustae memoriae reliquos prophetas in multitudine miraculorum superavit. Et quidam auctores asserunt, miracula ejus ad numerum millenarium pervenisse." De signis directionis. Marac. Prod. P. II. pag. 30. Some authors count 4440, others 60 millions of miracles.

that as early as the second century, when the first biographers of Mohammed appeared, the prophet's life was so overcharged with miraculous tales, that even the keenest European eye is often unable to distinguish between historical facts and legendary fictions. As an act of justice to our opponents, we give some of the currently received miracles of Mohammed.

A camel weeps and is calmed at the touch of Mohammed; the hair grows upon a boy's head when the prophet lays his hand upon it; a horse is cured from stumbling; the eye of a soldier is healed and made better than the other. He marked his sheep in the ear, and the species retains the mark to this day; he milked an emaciated goat with marvellous success. A stick turns into a sword; one palm-tree sings, another walks up with a great noise and bears testimony to Mohammed's Mission. On his entrance into Mecca, his majesty the prophet, was saluted by all mountains and trees, saying, "Peace be with thee, O prophet of God!"[91] He put his toes and fingers over empty vessels, and so copious were the fountains flowing from his extremities, that camels were in danger of being drowned; or he spits into a pool of water and it becomes sweet. He fed 130 men upon the liver of a sheep, and two dishes remained over and above what they had eaten. Once, a million of people were fed on a few loaves and a lamb, and many fragments were left. On a different occasion, eighty men fed upon a crust of bread which Mohammed had

---

[91] Mishcat Vol. II. pag. 717. Achmed Ebn Abdolhalimi's Apologia pag. 382. classifies the miracles of Mohammed.

blessed. A woman having offered him melted butter from a leathern bottle, the butter continued to flow till the woman pressed it, and it is added, the bottle would *still* flow, had the woman abstained from squeezing it.[92]

Another miracle, the returning of the sun, is related in the following manner; "One day his majesty the prophet had laid his blessed head on the skirts of Ali's cloak and slept, and receiving a revelation he wrapt up his head in the cloak, and was engaged in hearing the revelation till the sun had nearly gone down. When he had received his revelation, he got up, and said, 'Ali, have you performed the evening prayers?' He said, 'No, O prophet of God, for I could not remove thy blessed head from the skirts of my cloak.' His majesty then said, 'O Lord, bring back the sun.' Asman said, by God, I saw, that the sun returned and got high. And after his majesty had performed the prayer, the sun went down again.' Once, Mohammed went, accompanied by his followers, who were a large number, to the house of Abdallah. After he and Ali had eaten of the dish prepared for him, consisting of a roasted lamb, he gave it to his followers, and they all ate and were satisfied, leaving nothing but the bones. They said then; 'O prophet of God, we want some milk to drink.' His majesty having spread his handkerchief over the bones said, 'O Lord, in like manner as Thou didst send Thy blessing on this animal and satisfy us with its meat, so bless it again, and do such an act, that we may

[92] Maracc. Prodrom. Pars II. cap. VI.

drink of its milk.' Accordingly through the divine power, flesh grew on those bones, and the animal began to move, and got up, and its udder became full of milk. They then all drank, and filled besides all the basins in the house with its milk."[93]

It is superfluous to multiply specimens, or to enlarge upon the frivolous and puerile character of the miracles ascribed to Mohammed. There is not a shadow of proof for any one of them; but could it even be proved, that Mohammed had wrought miracles, he would still be what he was before, viz. a false prophet, who "speaks his own words and prophesies out of his own heart;" for miracles *alone*, furnish no proof of divine Mission, since they may be performed by false prophets, to establish false doctrine, through the agency of Sátan.[94] But the prophet himself repeatedly asserts, in the clearest possible language, that he never possessed the power of working miracles, declaring that he was not a worker of miracles, but was commissioned only to preach;[95]—we must therefore either believe Mohammed and reject the above miracles, as mere fabrications, or, believe the miracles, and reject him as a *lying* prophet.

3. It is admitted by the Koran that the divine

---

[93] Pfander's Remarks pag. 23—30, Hayat ul Kulub Vol. II. leaf 126. 127.

[94] Deut. XIII. 1—5. 2 Thess. II. 9. 2 John IV. 1. Rev. XIII. 13. 14. Exod. VII. 22. 2 Tim. III. 8. Act. VIII. 9.

[95] وقالوا لولا انزل عليه ايات من ربّه قل آنما الايات عند الله وانما انا نذير مبين Sur. XXIX. 50. See also XIII. 8. XVII. 92—95. VI. 57. 58. 109. XXI. 5—6.

Mission of our Lord was accredited by miracles; but the question arises, whether they are sufficient to prove His Divine character or not. Before this can be answered in the affirmative, it must be decided, whether the miracles of Jesus Christ can in any way be compared with those, wrought by prophets and apostles who claimed no such distinction; and here it will be granted, that our Saviour's miracles differ not so widely in character, from those wrought by the prophets of the Old, and the Apostles of the New Testament, as to bear no comparison with them; on the contrary there is a great similarity to them. The highest order of miracles, that of raising the dead, was wrought by messengers of God, who laid no claim to Divinity. A second point to be decided, before we admit our Lord's miracles to be a conclusive proof of His Divine character, is this; whether there be any external mark, through which, miracles wrought by God, can be distinguished from miracles wrought by satanic agency. As regards this question, it cannot be denied that in many cases, they are perfectly alike; Exod. VIII. 11; in some, a criterion is added, which is too vague to be generally applicable; Deut. XIII. 1—3. in others, the power by which miracles are wrought, will not be revealed before the day of Judgment. Matt. VII. 23. 24. Again, miracles are wrought by the powers of darkness, without any distinguishing mark being given, as to the source from whence they spring. Lu. XI. 19. Matt. XXIV. 2.

Again, if miracles were meant to prove the Divinity of Christ, He and His Apostles would undoubtedly have appealed to them, as unerring credentials of His Divine character. Our Lord indeed appealed to His *works*, but not exclusively to those of a miraculous character.[96] When asked whether He was the promised Messiah, Jesus refers to His mighty deeds; but rehearsing these in gradation, He signifies the last mentioned to be the highest and most convincing—"to the poor the Gospel is preached."[97] The Apostles also refrained from appealing to the miracles of Christ, as an irrefragable evidence of His Divine nature.[98]

Again, if miracles were *alone* sufficient to establish His Divinity, Christ would have desired their becoming as extensively known as possible: in many instances however, we know this was just what He sought to prevent. Matt. IX. 30. XII. 15. 16. Miracles, moreover, failed to accomplish their object, for Christ had to upbraid the cities, "wherein *most* of His mighty works were done, because they repented not." Hence, our Lord uniformly repels a craving after signs and wonders; complying in no one instance with the repeated request to show "a sign from heaven." When

---

[96] When Christ speaks: τὰ ἔργα ἃ ἐγὼ ποιῶ μαρτυρεῖ περὶ ἐμοῦ ὅτι ὁ πατήρ με ἀπέσταλκε: or when He exhorts: διὰ τὰ ἔργα αὐτὰ πιστεύετέ μοι, He refers to His miracles, but not to them alone. John V. 36. XIV. 11.

[97] Matt. XI. 3—5. with this *climax* He refers likewise to the prophecy, in which His divine glory and excellency is set forth: יְרָא׃ כְּבוֹד־יְהוָה הֲדַר אֱלֹהֵינוּ Isaiah XXXV. 2. LXI. 1. 2.

[98] Where this seems to be the case: the λόγος σωτηρίας, spoken by the Lord, and confirmed unto us by them that heard Him, is the chief thing; συνεπιμαρτυροῦντος τοῦ θεοῦ σημείοις τε καὶ τέρασι, καὶ ποικίλαις δυνάμεσι is superadded: *Christi* est, *testari*: Dei est, συνεπιμαρτυρεῖν, *testimonium superaddere.*" Hebr. II. 3. 4. Beng. Gnomon ad loc.

at one time He had wrought a double miracle, and at another, cured a man, who was possessed, blind, and dumb, the Jews ask, "what sign showest thou then that we may see and believe thee?" When they reiterate their demands, our Lord invariably directs their attention to the "*signs of the time*" in which they lived, to the singular dignity of His person, to His *death* and *resurrection*;[99] and when Herod, on the eve of these crowning signs of His wonderful life, hoped to have seen a miracle done by Him, He answered him nothing.[1] These numerous solicitations for fresh signs clearly demonstrate, that the many miracles which had been wrought, did *not in themselves suffice* to prove Christ to be the Messiah; but to give them their peculiar value, as infallible demonstrations of Divinity, they must needs be connected with a distinctive dignity in His person.

Christ never appears in the Bible, as the worker of single miracles; He is on the contrary represented as the *Sign of signs*, and is called "*Wonderful*."[2]

---

[99] John VI. 1—14. 18—21. 30. Matt. XII. 13. 22. 38. 39. 40. John II. 18. The same Matt. XVI. 1—4. John IV. 48.

[1] It seems Herod was most importunate in *asking* Him for a sign: ἐπηρώτα δὲ αὐτὸν ἐν λόγοις ἱκανοῖς. Lu. XXIII. 8. 9. "He questioned with Him in many words," does not convey the exact meaning.

[2] שְׁמוֹ פֶּלֶא, His name is called *Wonderful*, as much as Messiah or Ἰησοῦς, Isa. IX. 6. From Him emanate all that may be called פֶּלֶא, θαυμάσιον, miraculum; אֹת, whence آية, σημεῖον, signum, ostentum, portentum; מוֹפֵת, τέρας, monstrum, prodigium; גְּבוּרָה, δύναμις; He is the mediator of all the מִפְעֲלוֹת יְהֹוָה, ἔργα τοῦ Θεοῦ, or simply ἔργα κατ' ἐξοχήν; also called by the Fathers, sacramenta, mysteria visibilia.

Being Himself the fountain-head of all that is *wonderful*, in the truest sense of the term, signs and miracles, in Christ's life, were but the natural manifestation of His Divine character, and the necessary mode of operation: the absence of miracles and signs in His life and history, would have been most wonderful, and inexplicable. In working miracles, the Prophets and Apostles exhibited their *seal* of office to the Church; but Christ, in contradistinction to all duly accredited messengers of God, revealed His *glory*.

We can but admire the divine sobriety of Holy Scripture, in never appealing to a miracle as a sufficient proof of our Lord's Divine character. The single wonders performed by our Lord are so many distinct rays of His Divine Majesty, and though essentially belonging to His work of Redemption, they are unable to reflect the whole fulness and glory of the person of Christ.[3] They were indeed, proofs to the disciples, serving to confirm their already existing belief; but only those who already believed in Christ, recognised in His person, "a man approved of God among them by miracles and wonders and signs which God

[3] There is no order or system in our Lord's miracles, if we examine them simply as "*facta inexplicabilia, quae admirationem excitaverunt spectatoribus;*" or in which "*naturae leges suspenduntur.*" But we observe both harmony and *order*, when we regard them as expressive of our Lord's work of Redemption. It begins with changing water into wine in the hour of need; then follow healings of the sick; cleansing of lepers; casting out of devils; and it finishes with raising the dead. When Lazarus was raised, "*many believed in Him.*" The last miracle, on the fig-tree, expressed the judicial power of Jesus over those that believe not. Here we have a system of miracles, expressive of a *wondrous Redemption*. When preparatory signs were repeated, it was in places, where the first were as yet unknown.

did by Him in the midst of them."[4] Instead, therefore, of enlarging upon the miracles, in their discourses, the Apostles simply preached "Christ and the Resurrection."

Thus we consider the miracles of Christ, not only as a proof, that He was a teacher come from God, but as the manifestation of the glory of the incarnate Redeemer, which can only be appreciated in connection with His entire life. Amongst the things testified by St. John, that we might believe, are not only signs and wonders, but many other things, which Jesus did, and taught.

4. Having glanced at the miracles of Christ and the alleged prodigies of Mohammed, we next examine the *prophecies*, said to be fulfilled in the respective founders of Christianity and of Islamism. Our Lord prophesied, and as prophecy is only a miracle of another kind,[5] we might fairly introduce a summary of His predictions in this place; as however, Mohammed disclaims the gift of prophecy, we shall pass it over and confine ourselves to those predictions or prophecies

---

[4] Act. II. 22. Hence it is also stated, that Christ in certain places did not many miracles "because of their unbelief." Matt. XIII. 58. That it was *expected* in every prophet to have this seal, accounts for John the Baptist denying that he was a prophet. John I. 21.

[5] נְבוּאָה, προφητεία, are "*miracula vaticana aut praescientiae sunt perspicuae rerum futurarum earumque contingentium praedicationes, quibus eventus respondit, per div. omniscientiam.*" *Hume* asserts in his Essays on miracles: "All prophecies are *real* miracles, and as such only, can be admitted as proofs of any revelation. If it did not exceed the capacity of human nature to foretel future events, it would be absurd to employ any prophecy as an argument for a Divine mission or authority from heaven."

which are respectively said to have been fulfilled in Christ and Mohammed. We have already noticed that the Arab prophet claimed to have been predicted by our Lord, John XV. 26. and that by name.[7]

This blasphemous misappropriation of the prophetic promise of the Holy Ghost is too revolting to dwell on; but were it possible to apply it to any mortal, Mohammed, of all men in the world, has the least claim to be considered the *Comforter*, which Christ promised to send to His Church. Our Lord required His disciples to *wait* in Jerusalem; if Mohammed, therefore, had been the promised Pareclete, he would have appeared *in Jerusalem*, not in Mecca, and that, 600 years earlier than he did. Again, if the prophet of the Arabs were the Paraclete, it was his part, according to the tenor of the promise of Christ, that he should abide with the Church for ever. The promise, moreover, was made to the Church of Christ; Mohammed therefore ought to have come to the *Christians*, not to the Pagan Arabs. Then, the office of the promised Paraclete was to *glorify Christ;* to take of the things of Jesus and show them unto

---

[6] ومبشرا برسرل ياتى من بعدى اسمه أحمد Annunciaturus Legatum, *qui veniet post me: nomen ejus Ahmad.* Sur. LXI. 6. Now τὸ πνεῦμα τῆς ἀληθείας is in Hebrew רוּחַ אֱמֶת and in Arabic الروح عامة; from this, Moslem subtilty made *Achmed* or *Mohammed.* The παράκλητος was likewise shrewdly turned into περικλυτὸς, id est *inclytus, valde inclitum*, which agreed again with أحمد or محمّد with the sense *laudabilis, laudatum, multa dignus;* cfr. also חָמַד, desire after; חֶמֶד, the dearest, most beautiful. מַחְמָד, desire, darling.

His people; now where does Mohammed glorify Christ? The Gospel of Jesus is altered into "another Gospel," His divine character is denied, His truth perverted, His Church destroyed, His work of Redemption disowned, and the glorious dispensation of the New Testament is considered to be superseded! Had Mohammed represented the promised Comforter, he would not have been guilty of elevating himself above the Lord Jesus. The Holy Ghost glorified Christ, bore witness of Him, taught many things concerning Him; remained with the Church for ever, and called the things of Christ to the remembrance of the disciples; but Mohammed, under the impulse of another, than the *"Spirit of truth,"* maintained throughout a contrary part.[7]

Another fulfilment of prophecy is found by Mohammedans, in the blessing of Moses, where the three mountains, *Sinai, Seir,* and *Paran* are considered to be typical of three successive dispensations: *Judaism, Christianity,* and *Islamism.*[8] Independently however of the fanciful and arbitrary character of this exposition, it is unfortunate for those who urge it, that Seir is in Idumaea, instead of Galilee or Judea; and Paran between mount Seir and Sinai, about 500 miles from Mecca! Such is the perversion of the words of Moses, who refers to the mountains which

---

[7] Very significant is the expression: τὸ πνεῦμα τῆς ἀληθείας: "*Alias est quaedam falsa cognitio, falsa fides, falsus amor, falsa spes; sed non falsa veritas.*" Bengelius.

[8] "The Lord came from Sinai, (*Judaism*); and rose up from Seir, (*Christianity*); He shined forth from mount Paran, (*Islamism*)." Deut. XXXIII. 2.

witnessed God's works during the march of the Israelites. The next prophecy referred to Mohammed, is the celebrated prediction of Moses, that God would raise up a prophet from among Israel like unto him. Deut. XVIII. 15. But Mohammed was not like Moses; nor was he raised up among Israel; nor can the Arabs be said to be brethren of the Jews; nor does Mohammed come before the world with the like credentials as Moses; nor can any one reason be demonstrated in his person, his creed or his Koran, why we should "hearken unto him."

Another misapplication of prophecy, or rather of a plain description, was perpetrated by the Moslem doctors, when with the aid of the Syriac, they endeavour to wrest the words, *"perfection of beauty,"* Ps. L. 2, being a descriptive epithet of Zion,[9] and make them to signify, *"the crown of Mohammed."* This shows, their extreme anxiety to establish the point, that Mohammed had been prophesied in the Old and New Testament. We shall notice but one other attempt to support Mohammed's dignity, by evidence derived from prophecy, one, which has at least this in its favour, that it is the most ingenious. In the following passage from Isaiah, "he saw a chariot with a couple of horsemen, a chariot of asses, and a chariot of camels,"[10] the learned Mohammedans see a clear

---

[9] The Moslem doctors read thus, with the Syriac version: اكليلا محمودا اظهرو اللّه من صهيون *Coronam laudatam Deus manifestavit ex Sion.* Were the version correct, which it is not, the *coronam laudatam* comes not from Mecca but from Sion.

[10] It is said of the watchman: וַיַּרְא רֶכֶב צֶמֶד פָּרָשִׁים רֶכֶב חֲמוֹר

prediction of Christ, who rides into Jerusalem upon the ass; and Mohammed, who frequently rode upon a camel! But the chapter contains burdens of prophecy against Babylon, *Duma* and *Kedar*, the two latter being the descendants of *Ishmael;* and Babylon was taken by the Medes and Persians *precisely* as here prophesied.[11]

Mohammed, might however, have been prophesied by name, — as was the case with Cyrus, the "servant" of God, — centuries before he was born, and yet be in the same predicament, in which he now stands: for it does not necessarily follow, that the person predicted must be a true prophet of God. *Antichrist* is prophesied in the Old and New Testament, but this in nowise puts a divine seal upon his work, or makes him the less "that man of sin, and the son of perdition." Nor shall we contradict the Koran, when it repeatedly asserts, that we find Mohammed "written down in the law and the Gospel." Our Lord bids us to "beware of false prophets;" He prophesies, that "many false prophets shall rise and deceive many;" "false Christs and false prophets shall rise, and shall

רֶכֶב בְּנֵי. Isaiah XXI. 7. Vulgate: "*Et vidit currum duorum equitum, ascensorem asini, et ascensorem cameli.*" The LXX read: καὶ εἶδον ἀναβάτας ἱππεῖς δύο, καὶ ἀραβάτην ὄνου, καὶ ἀραβάτην καμήλου. German version: "Er siehet aber Reiter reiten und fahren auf Rossen, Eseln und Kamelen." Vitringa: "*vecturam asinorum, vecturam camelorum.*"

[11] Babylon being taken when feasting in security. cfr. Isa. XXI. 5—10. "Prepare the table; watch in the watch-tower; eat, drink: arise ye princes and anoint the shield. For thus hath the Lord said unto me. Go set a watchman, let him declare what he seeth." This watchman then sees, what is here alleged to be a prophecy of Christ and Mohammed.

show signs and wonders, to seduce, if it were possible, even the elect." His Apostles agree with their Master in warning the Church of *false* teachers and prophets, who shall bring in damnable heresies; adding that "many shall follow their pernicious ways."

In proving from the Scripture that "Jesus is the Christ," especially to unbelievers, we have to place prophecy and fulfilment, before our opponents, in its *totality*, without giving undue prominence to isolated predictions fulfilled in the person of the Messiah. We proceed therefore to take a succint view of the leading prophecies, concerning Christ, which are fulfilled in Him.—Beginning with those, which describe His human nature, as the promised "*seed of the woman*," no Moslem will fail to recognise "the son of Mary," who "preserved her virginity." That He was to be born of a virgin was however specially added. The *genealogy* of Christ is minutely predicted; He was to spring from the family of *Shem*, the seed of *Abraham*, the line of *Isaac*, the tribe of *Judah* and the house of *David*. It was predicted that the Messiah should appear, at the period when the tribe of Judah should have lost its political independence. The *place* of His birth, and the circumstances connected with it, were likewise given. Again, we have a prophetic description of the person and character of the forerunner of Christ; also of the commencement of our Lord's public ministry; the places He was to visit; the condition of His life; the miracles He would perform; the nature

EE

and mode of His teaching; the details of His passion; and of His death on the cross; together with the specific mention of the time when He should give up the ghost. We would call particular attention to those prophecies concerning the *violent* death of Christ, which the Koran thought fit to deny. Again the *entombment* of Christ was distinctly foretold by the Spirit of prophecy,—" His grave was *appointed* Him with the wicked, but with the rich man was His tomb in His death." His flesh however should only rest in hope, and not see corruption; He was to rise from the dead, prolong His days, and ascend into heaven.

5. It is not without instruction to observe how the *Person* and the *Work* of the Redeemer is the point in religious controversy, around which, all antagonistic powers seem to rally, for the doctrine of the *cross* will ever be rejected as irrational, where man's sinfulness and helpless condition is unfelt, and denied, as is the case in the Koran. The Moslem looks upon sin, as an external act, to be estimated merely by its results. Since sin is not regarded as sin, by Mohammed, he could not admit the crowning act of Christ's sacerdotal office, namely, His death upon the cross, by which an atonement was made for the sins of the world. Had Mohammed assumed our Lord's body to have been a mere phantom, as was the case with some of the early heretics, we could account for his denial of the death of Jesus; but the Koran insists upon the purely *human* nature of Christ, and in apparent contradiction with the **view**

that our Lord had a mortal body, yet with a fearful and well-calculated consistency, the Koran denies the *Crucifixion*. The death upon the cross was an historical fact, attested, not only by the Gospels, which he considered interpolated, but by profane testimony, of *Jews*, and *Pagans*.[33] Yet Mohammed preferred opposing a well authenticated historical fact, rather than admit the death upon the cross; because he clearly saw, that with it, he would be compelled to acknowledge its *meritorious character*, which rested entirely upon the innocent and violent death of "the Lamb of God which taketh away the sins of the world."

If Christ were no more than an ordinary prophet, and if His death be not the crowning part of His vicarious work, why should Mohammed deny it, any more than the violent death of other prophets? But having rejected the doctrine of the atonement, he was led to adopt the view of an ancient heresy, in preference to the truth. Had he admitted the Crucifixion, he could not have denied, that our Lord's

[33] Moses ben Maimones in lib. Jud. cap XI. says: "Jesus Nazarenus visus est Messias, et occisus est per domum Judaicii, at illa causa fuit ut Israel destruetur in gladio et disperguntur, relinquae ipsorum et deprimerentur." Again, "Jesus Nazarenus propinquus fuit regno (idest fuit familia Regia) et in vespere Paschae crucifixerunt eum." Sanhed. distinct. Nigmar Hadin. See also Joseph. Archaeolog. lib. XVIII. cap. III. 3. Again Tacitus writes: "Auctor nominis ejus Christus Tiberio imperitante per procuratorem Pontium Pilatum supplicio affectus erat; repressaque in praesens exitiabilis superstitio rursus erumpebat, non modo per Judaeam, originem ejus mali, sed per urbem etiam, quae cuncta undique atrocia aut pudenda confluunt celebranturque. Corn. Tac. lib. XV. cap. 44.

person and work were far superior to the person and work of any other apostle of God; and he would thus have involved himself in a contradiction and inconsistency which would undoubtedly have proved ruinous to his creed.

CHAPTER VI.

CHRISTIAN MISSIONS TO MOSLEMS.

"Why will ye not willingly contribute of your substance for the true way of God, or the carrying on of war against the unbelievers, since God alone is the possessor of heaven and earth? Whosoever will lend unto God an acceptable loan, to him he will double it again and he shall receive moreover an honourable reward."
Sur. LVII. 10. 11.

1. The zeal of Moslems in proselytizing was not extinguished, when they ceased to conquer. The duty of spreading the faith is still made paramount in the education of every Mohammedan; and it is equally incumbent on the governor, the soldier, the merchant, the captain of the ship, and the Sheich or Mollah, to watch every opportunity of disseminating the doctrines of the Koran. It cannot be without humiliation, that we contrast this zeal, with the culpable apathy of Christians concerning the souls of Mohammedans. Although the first tide of Moslem invasion had been successfully repelled, some of the Saracen settlements continued to exist for centuries in Europe; and the closing conquest

of European Turkey with Constantinople in the fifteenth century, perpetuated the approximation of Christianity and Islam. During those twelve centuries that the Church of Christ stood face to face with her gigantic foe, should we not have expected that many a David would have gone out to meet this blaspheming adversary, " in the name of the God of the armies of Israel ?" But how little was attempted in comparison with the magnitude of Christian responsibility![64] Yet to our shame must confess, that our forefathers did more in darker ages, than has be accomplished, or even attempted, in this our self-conceited generation. We have, for instance, noble relics of the eighth century,[65] and subsequent ages were not altogether inactive in the word of converting the Moslems.[66]

This may be proved by an example of burning zeal for the conversion of the Moslems in the thirteenth century. Raymond Lully, to whom the Arabic Professorship at Oxford owes its origin, was born of noble parents, in 1236, in the capital of Majorca, and when more than 30 years of age, conceived a strong

[64] Maraccio, in his preface, justly remarks, "Contra Mahumetum, Mahumeticamque superstitionem, quae per annos supra mille perseverat, qui scripserint, sive ex antiquioribus, sive ex recentioribus, pauci, ne dicam paucissimi."

[65] *Disceptatio Christ. et Saraceni exstat.* Tom. I. *oper. Joann. Damasceni.*

[66] A list of works is found in *J. Alb. Fabric. syllab. Script. de ver. relig. Christ. cap. L. pag.* 735. *Eusebii Renaudoti historia patriarcharum Alexandrin. pag.* 377, may also be consulted, as mentioning various works against Islam. But still, how true it is, *"Apparent rari nantes in gurgite vasto."*

desire to proclaim the message of the cross to the Saracens. He became a mendicant; studied Arabic, wrote a controversial work to convince the Moslem doctors, induced the king to found and endow a monastery in Majorca, where thirteen Franciscan monks should be trained as missionaries to the Moslems. He then went to Rome to obtain the aid and the sanction of Honorius IV., for founding Mission schools and colleges, on behalf of the Moslems, in various parts of Europe. When none cared for his project, he determined to set out himself and attempt, alone and single-handed, the propagation of the faith among the Moslems in Africa. In Tunis, whither he went, he invited the Moslem doctors to a conference, and preached Christ. He was imprisoned for his boldness, and at that time was only saved from death, by a Moslem counsellor reminding his sovereign, that a professor of their own faith would be held in high honour, if he imitated the self-devotion of the prisoner in propagating *their* doctrines among the Christians.

When shipwrecked near Pisa, after many years of missionary labours in other parts, though upwards of seventy, the ardour of Raymond Lully was unabated. "Once," he writes, "I was fairly rich; once I had a wife and children, once I tasted freely of the pleasures of this life. But all these things I gladly resigned that I might spread abroad a knowledge of the truth. I studied Arabic, and several times went forth to preach the gospel to the Saracens; I have been in prisons; I have been scourged; for years I have striven to persuade the princes of Christendom *to befriend the common cause of converting the Mohammedans.* Now, though old and poor, *I do not despair,* I am ready, if it be God's will, to persevere unto death." [67]

Again he appeals in vain to the Pope, then to the General Council at Vienna, to urge the opening of missionary colleges all over Europe *for the conversion of the Moslems;* and it was at this Council that he at last prevailed: a decree being then passed by which professorships of the Oriental languages, especially Arabic, should be founded and endowed in the Universities of *Paris, Salamanca,* and *Oxford,* and in all cities where the papal court resided.

Instead of now reposing upon this success, he was again more active for God. "As the needle," he says in his contemplations, "naturally turns to the north when it is touched by the magnet, so it is fitting, O Lord, that thy servant should turn to love and praise Thee, seeing that out of love to him, Thou wast willing to endure such grievous pangs and sufferings." And, "preferring to die in the glow of love" to his Lord he, in 1314, again sailed for Africa, gathered a little flock of converts at Bugia, where, in the following year, he was stoned to death.

The decree of the Council at Vienna, to form Arabic professorships, remained without effect until Francis I. called it into life; the result however of these feeble efforts was scarcely perceptible. There

[67] See Maclear's Missions of the Middle Ages.

was no *practical* tendency which could lead to any tangible issue; and a few learned works on the Arabic language, some translations of Arabic authors, and a couple of commentaries of small value, alone remain to testify to the deplorably inert condition of the Church.

It could not however fail that some would be stirred up by the noble example of Raymond Lully, to obtain the crown of martyrdom in the like cause. Thus we read of a monk who penetrated the great mosque at Cairo in 1345, to require the Sultan himself to become a follower of Christ crucified ; and so powerful was his appeal that a renegate, who had lapsed into Islam, returned into the bosom of the Church.

Ethier, the Father Confessor of the Infanta of Arragonia, preached Christ to the Moslems in the year 1370 ; and his example was followed 1439 by the Papal Legate, Albert, of Larzana, who was assisted by two monks. Again, in 1540, two Capuchin friars attempted to convert the governor of Cairo. Less to the purpose was the public burning of a Venetian Edition of the Koran in 1530.

The *chef-d' oeuvre* is however to this day the well known version and refutation of the Koran, by Maraccio, yet he had to struggle with unheard-of difficulties to procure permission to print his work from Pope Innocent XI. whose father-confessor he was. Amongst other writings against Islam,[67] that

---

[67] We might mention "*Triumphus catholicae fidei contra sectam Mahumetanam;*" also, *Manuductio ad conversionem Mahumetano-*

of *Philippo Guadagnoli* deserves to be mentioned; it was printed in Arabic and Latin, being intended as a reply to a Persian work by Achmed Ebn Zini, which was written in golden characters and sent to Pope Urban VIII. with a challenge to refute its contents.

We dare not omit some mention of that mistaken yet honest missionary zeal, which burning for three centuries, impelled some of the noblest monarchs of Europe to make the greatest sacrifices, in order to rescue the Holy Land from the hands of the Saracens.

Christendom was never so deeply roused by either Jews or Gentiles as it was in former ages by the Moslems. Primarily excited by the accounts of the persecutions inflicted on Christian pilgrims by the Saracens, the bare idea of the Holy Land remaining in the hands of these infidels could be no longer tolerated. When we reflect on those three centuries in which some of the noblest armies went to the *then* unknown East, and when we remember the personal sacrifices made by those champions of the Cross, and the unbounded enthusiasm which turned women into soldiers, and pressed children into the ranks of the Crusaders, it behoves us to inquire whether the mistaken missionary zeal of darker ages in so hotly contesting for the Holy *Land*, or the apathetic indifference of a self-indulging and self-appreciating age in so feebly contending for the *Faith*, be the more reprehensible in the sight of God.

rum;" by the Spanish Jesuit P. Turs. Gonzales.

If Christian Europe, in that period of the Church, was kindled with so fervent a zeal to reclaim Jerusalem and its sacred places from the power of the Saracens, we naturally look for a corresponding, but more spiritual zeal, for the Redeemer's Kingdom, to reclaim the souls of Moslems from the power of Satan. Surely the all-constraining love of our crucified Saviour, and the quickening presence of our risen Lord, cannot prove less powerful to stimulate holy exertion, and to prompt self-sacrificing devotion, than the interest which attaches to His empty sepulchre and to the place of His crucifixion.

In the defence of Rhodes, in 1524, several English Knights distinguished themselves at "the great siege, cruel oppugnation, and piteous taking of the noble and renowned city of Rhodes, the key of Christendome, the hope of many poor Christian men withholden in Turkie, to save and keep them in their faith—the refuge and refreshing of all Christian people having course of merchandize in the ports of Levant." Again, Queen Elizabeth petitioned for the release of some of her Christian subjects from the bondage of Sultan Murat III.; and Bishop Cosin bequeathed £500 towards the redemption of Christian captives at Algiers.

The first allusion to anything like a recognition of our duty towards the Moslems, occurs in 1649, when Edward Terry preached a sermon before the Governor and company of merchants trading in India, and when speaking of the Mohammedans of that country, he enforced a need of holiness of life, lest what he had sometimes heard from their lips, should be repeated, *i.e.*, " Christian religion, devil religion ; Christian much drunk, much rogue, much nought, very much nought."

2. In noticing some of the feeble attempts of Missionary labour in recent times, we cannot fail to mention *Henry Martyn*, died 1812, as one of the principal champions for Christianity against Islam. Situated as that devout man was in Persia, *alone*, with no other assistance in the unequal contest, than what he could derive from a small tract on Mohammedanism, and oppressed by the burden of a weak constitution, the course which he took, was perhaps, under such circumstances, the only one practicable. In perusing his arguments we are struck with the skill and wisdom which they display; and his reasoning appears generally conclusive; yet probably, few will doubt that many a Missionary, not excluding Henry Martyn himself, might have rendered more effectual service to the cause of Christianity among Moslems, had they possessed a more thorough acquaintance with the tenets of Islam. Henry Martyn will always be looked upon as a model of a devoted missionary, but he has not always taken the most advantageous grounds in arguing. The editor of his Controversies, Dr. Lee, adopts a different line of argument; having exposed the insufficiency of the evidence upon which the Mohammedan builds his faith, he substitutes in the place of erroneous principles, the true laws of evidence, as enforced by Locke's six considerations.

He then devotes some parts to the integrity of the Scriptures; after this, he foregoes the proof by miracles, and lays down from Scripture that a true prophet must prophesy, and that even then, if he opposes a previous revelation, he is not to be credited.

The first effort which was made by any Society towards the conversion of the Mohammedans subsequent to this single-handed but powerful effort of Henry Martyn was made on the continent. The *Evangelische Missions Gesellschaft*, founded at Basle 50 years ago, 1816, and which has sent out about 600 Missionaries—in 1822 commenced its operations, at the suggestion of British Christians, among the Moslem Circassians. The Mission prospered greatly, till in 1833 by an Imperial Ukase the devoted band of Missionaries was suddenly banished from the country. It is remarkable that about thirty years later these same tribes, who to their great grief had been thus deprived of their teachers, should themselves be driven from their mountainous homes by the same Russian Government! It deserves also to be recorded that Dr. Pfander, who has done so much in the way of writing controversial works for the use of the Moslems was one of those who was engaged in that enterprize.

3. Until quite recently it was deemed impossible to undertake direct Missionary work among the Moslems, because their respective Governments had always visited apostasy from Islam with capital punishment. Yet even amidst these difficulties in-

action was unjustifiable. Were we to believe the diffusion of Christianity impossible, without the sanction or co-operation of secular power, we should be imitating those followers of the Koran who relied upon the sword for success. Henry Martyn sacrificed his life to the Moslems for Christ's sake, when the laws of Moslem bigotry were yet in full force, and when there seemed no possible access to the Mohammedans in the East.

Neither the Apostles nor their successors in martyrdom waited till any one of the governing powers had withdrawn active opposition to Christianity. The Church for 300 years had all governments of the world, and all courts of justice against her, yet she conquered, and survived all the opposing powers. To hold that Christianity without secular aid can neither extend its boundaries nor protect its articles of faith, is to confess to a weakness of which it cannot be guilty. It was just between the third and the sixth centuries, when the Church was placed under the immediate protection of the civil government, that those "damnable heresies" were brought in which could alone render the rise of Islam a possibility.

If difficulty and discouragement were fitting arguments against the performance of a duty, any Society, or any number of Societies, might well shrink from the task of repairing the breach which the Church, through Islam, has for the last twelve centuries sustained. But our Lord bids us to "go into *all* the world, and to preach the Gospel to *every* creature;" and unless it can be satisfactorily proved that the 200 millions who profess Islam are not expressly excluded, we dare not refuse to deliver God's message of mercy to them, "whether they will hear or whether they will forbear."

4. It is recorded as a matter of gratitude to God that neither the two oldest Missionary Societies of the Church of England, nor the Missionary Societies of other denominations were altogether insensible to our duty in this respect. Yet what a fearful neglect of the Moslems would the statistics of the world present to our view?

The non-Christian population of the globe naturally divides itself into Jews, Pagans, and Mohammedans. But a single glance will convince us that these three distinct masses are of very unequal magnitude, or, in the language of the parable, the three measures of meal which are to be leavened are of very unequal size. It will also appear that Missionary zeal, even since its recent revival, has been distributed with still greater disproportion.

The Jewish population numbers about five millions; and for their conversion seven large Societies, or, counting the less important Associations, as many as thirty-three Societies, with a staff of 200 Missionaries are employed.

Among the Pagans—numbering, according to various estimates, from 300 to 500 millions—the different Protestant denominations of Europe and America support, without counting the less noted organizations, thirty-six Missionary Societies.

CHAP. VI.] AWAKENING OF MISSIONARY ZEAL. 479

The Moslems, as far as any approximate calculation can be made, cannot be reckoned at a lower figure than 200 millions of souls. Of these five millions are within the borders of Europe; fifteen millions are subject to the British Crown, and unnumbered millions are settled in Palestine, Syria, Asia Minor, Arabia, Egypt, and North Africa, the remainder being scattered like so many lost sheep over the rest of the world. Although these millions have a substantial claim upon Christian sympathy, they have received only a partial recognition in countries such as India and Turkey, where they happened to be living among Christians or Pagans amidst whom Missions had been planted.

The "Moslem Mission Society" recently established stands alone among the host of kindred associations, as addressing its attention altogether and exclusively to the Mohammedans. It has therefore no need to apologize for its existence. As regards the Church of England Societies and their Missions to Colonists, Pagans, and Jews, the "Moslem Mission Society" has entered on no other man's labours, but only supplies the fourth wheel, so to speak, which was lacking to complete "the differences of administration and the diversity of operation" in the Church.

A similar division of labour was made in the days of the Apostles. "When James, Cephas, and John, who seemed to be pillars, perceived the grace of God which was given unto Paul, they gave to him and Barnabas the right hand of fellowship, that they should go unto the heathen, and themselves unto the circumcision."

If no Missionary had as yet be sent; if there were as yet no school or station with some few genuine converts to cheer the undertaking, the obligation to go and do as we are bid, would still be binding. For many a century has the Church annually put up the prayer that God would "have mercy upon all Jews, Turks, infidels (*i.e.*, Pagans), and heretics, and take from them all ignorance, hardness of heart, and contempt of His Word." But the time, it is felt, had come when we ought to "*live more nearly as we pray.*" The members of the Moslem Mission Society, as members of the Church, remembered the solemn offices which the prayer necessarily involved; for it would be mockery, not prayer, to ask that God would take away "all ignorance" of the Gospel, "all hardness of heart," and "all contempt of His Word," and yet do nothing to reduce that "contempt," to remove that "ignorance," and to soften that "hardness."

5. That the Mohammedan world is, at last, accessible to evangelistic labour is not the mere assumption of an interested Society: the public press gives constant records of the wide-spreading changes in Turkey and in Egypt, where commerce, education, social and political reforms are sapping the foundations of Islam. In the Turkish empire, and in Egypt, electric Telegraphs and steam appliances are ploughing up the stiff soil of a petrified fanaticism and bigotry. Nor is this great change confined to the social, intellectual, and political life: there is a spirit of inquiry pervading the religious element. In

CHAP. VI.   AWAKENING OF MISSIONARY ZEAL.   481

Egypt, we find a Moslem writing a theological work to disprove the verasity of his own religion. At Constantinople, answers are being written to Dr. Pfander's controversial writings. In India a bilingual Commentary on the Holy Bible in English and Urda, is written by one of the most learned and zealous Moslem doctors of the present age, Syud Ahmud Khan, P. Sudder Ameen. In this work, the Bible and the Koran are placed upon the same footing, being regarded as equally inspired, and equally binding upon the Moslems.

The following letter received by the author from the above-named Moslem Theologian, written in English, shows, beyond doubt, that there is no one isolated mass of the human family which preserve its immobility for ever. He says :—" You are right in your supposition that no Moslem divine has ever written a Commentary on the Holy Bible. There may have been some reasons for which our Moslem ancestors could not undertake such work; but an obstacle, a great obstacle to that step, being, as regards the present Moslems of India, that they have always considered and believed the Scriptures to be a worthless, fabulous, and useless collection of books; and that this mischievous belief of theirs has sometimes been seen supported and strengthened by the imprudent and immature arguments proceeding from some missionaries,—arguments that would do nothing but create an undesirable dissension and prejudice, opposition and rancour, between the parties, and injure them seriously at heart. So it will

FF

be now easy for you to consider and to conclude that, if in such a position of the parties, a Mohammedan were to undertake a work like that of supporting and recognizing the Holy Bible, by commenting on it, what would be his situation and estimation among his co-religionists—indeed, nothing, but he will be generally abused and hated by them. For instance, I was an object of such treatment with them in the commencement of my undertaking. But I cheerfully bore and happily tolerated all their unjust insults, unfounded threatenings, and other similar excesses, merely to fear from nothing in announcing what I believe to be true and divine. The reward that was awarded to me, but only in the beginning of my career, by Christians, was indeed no less than what I received from my co-religionists.

"But, thank God, after part first of my Commentary was published, it was made known to the Mohammedans that all that I professed in favour of the Bible was grounded on the Holy Koran itself, and other as well respectable authorities. Then most of them came forward to applaud and join in my faith of, and respect for the Holy Scripture, and which diminished a great deal of the vague and absurd ideas they constantly cherished respecting them; as will appear from the following quotation from a letter of a great Moulvi to my address:—'I have read your Commentary, which is, no doubt, I must openly confess, a book without its rival, and that defends and maintains the Mohammedans' faith. Praise be to God, repeated praise to God that you only are the person in this age who leads to the right way. The work is perused every Tuesday (a day considered holy by some Moslem divines for preaching) when a recital of its praiseworthy passages fills the heart with thousands of thanks to God, and a warm prayer in your behalf.'—There are certain passages in the Holy Bible which have led the Moslems to a strange tendency against it. For example, Ibrahim's being said to tell a lie in Egypt. The Christian commentators have simply touched upon these subjects, but I being against them all, demonstrate that the Bible itself does not imply such meanings to such passages as are universally adopted. Hence, I hope, after the second part of my work is published, the prejudices of Moslems against the Scriptures will be further removed.

"Notwithstanding all this, I am sure that my life will fail before I could get rid of the abuse and hatred of the Mohammedans in general. Christians can by no means be satisfied with my Commentary; for, although I uphold the Bible to be true and upright in all it teaches, yet I do not believe in the Trinity of God; since I observe it nowhere supported, or even established in the Scriptures. I am certain the Mohammedan faith is true, and that its veracity and existence are founded in the Holy Bible itself. Wherefore, I do not care to be interested with either party—Moslems or Christians—but with the truth alone, and with that all true God before whom all are once to appear.

"Of course, I have always desired to see the

maintenance of a friendship between Mohammedans and Christians, since, if according to the Holy Koran, there can be any friends to us, they can be Christians only. This desire of mine will be well revealed to you by your perusing the few pamphlets published by me on the subject, now forwarded to you. I have also dispatched to your address a copy of the part I. of my commentary, the acceptance of which, by you, no doubt will add to my honour. The part second, when ready, shall also be sent you.

"I am, doubtless, as staunch an adherent and defender of the Bible as yourself. I have resolved to reply to Doctor Colenso's objections in the proper parts of my Commentary, as I come to pass by them."

If these views prevail, and it seems they are making way among the Moslems of India, they will not only make them loyal, but it will be simply a question of time when the great rupture caused by the rise of Islam shall be healed up. The Commentary, asserting as it does the authority of the Bible, and proving such from the Koran itself, in opposition to the hitherto assumed corruption of the Christian Scriptures, deserves to be translated into every tongue spoken by Moslems, especially into Arabic; for no greater service could be rendered them, than of raising the Bible in their estimation to the same level as the Koran. Let this be done by the Moslems themselves, and it will then demand little ingenuity or zeal on the part of Christians to prove, that if the Bible be true, the Koran must be false.

6. Although arguments are frequently provoked by the cavils and objections of the Mohammedans, yet Islam is not the creed to court enquiry or encourage a free discussion upon religious subjects. The Arab prophet repeatedly enjoins his followers to abstain from discussions, and he makes Allah require him to recede from those who dispute about the Koran. Sur. vi. 65. Arguments with the Scripturalists are especially discountenanced, Sur. xix. 46; disputes are to be settled by imprecations on those invited to meet for argumental inquiry, Sur. iii. 59; discussion is postponed, upon the grounds that God would decide differences on the day of Judgment, Sur. xxii. 65; a term, certainly too late for those in the wrong. Again we read, "As to those who dispute concerning God, after obedience hath been paid him, their disputing shall be vain in the sight of their Lord, and wrath shall fall upon them, and they shall suffer a grievous punishment." Sur. xlii. 14.

The Christian missionary is not to *seek* for arguments; but where they cannot be avoided, he is not to shun the contest, remembering the example of St. Paul who frequently "reasoned out of the Scriptures, disputing and persuading the things concerning the kingdom of God." Where discussion is entered upon in the like spirit of love, and zeal for the salvation of souls, we shall be guarded against a display of vanity, in gaining a victory which may simply prove a superiority in education, or philosophical acemem. The main point at issue will never be forgotten in the heat of the contest; and controversial disputations will always on that account, be as *short*, as *kind* and as *seldom* as possible. 1 Pet. iii. 15. We shall never be drawn aside to non-essential or frivolous discussion, neither shall we be tempted to excite or wound our opponents by using harsh, satirical and unbecoming expressions. Missionaries are frequently exposed to the most wanton insult, purely with a view of provoking resent; but to fall into the snare thus laid, is to inflict an irretrievable injury on their cause.

As a rule, it is well to commence our discourse upon subjects in which both parties agree, and to proceed from similarities to differences; or we may approach the heart of the Moslem in an indirect way by bringing forward a parable, which we lead him to admit. Thus, in arguing for the impossibility of the Bible being corrupted, the missionary may ask the Moslem, whether he has ever read Abulfeda, adding, that some individual had questioned its integrity, but that he had defended it by putting forth Abulfeda's general credibility as an author, that he showed him several manuscripts, which all agree to a word; that these manuscripts were written in several centuries, and among various nations; that he adduced several other testimonies from writers of acknowledged worth; that he obtained a collection of quotations, made in various writings, which all agree with the text; that he exhibited versions of the work in divers languages, all of a different date, but harmonizing with the original; yet in spite of all that was advanced, the sceptical man persisted in declaring that Abulfeda's work was corrupted. When the wrath of the Moslem has run as high as that of David, the missionary like Nathan, may turn round upon him and say, 'Thou art the man,' and this is precisely your obstinacy in refusing to admit the integrity of the Bible."

Again, supposing a Moslem assert the divine character of his creed, and the infallibility of the Koran, he may be asked, whether Islam was designed for the whole race of man, and whether all its precepts, not excluding the fast of the Ramadhan, are equally binding upon every true Moslem. When the universality of the creed is affirmed and the binding nature of the precept of fasting from sunrise to sunset, admitted, the missionary may remind his opponent of the geographical fact, that in the arctic and antarctic regions, the period from sunrise to sunset extending to several month's duration, the observation of this fast would there be a physical impossibility. The inference may then be urged, that the Koran cannot be intended for all climes and nations, and consequently cannot be divine. That further, the author of the Koran could not possibly have been inspired; but must have been a man ignorant of the first principles of geography, with which every Christian school-boy is acquainted.— This circuitous mode of reasoning is the most peaceable, perhaps also the most difficult, yet at the same time, forcible, and perfectly legitimate.

Above all, we must not withhold any one of the leading truths of Christianity with a view to conciliate Moslem animosity. In order to win souls, we cannot with a good conscience, yield one iota of the truth; for such an act of perfidity on our part, would involve our own souls in a snare of the devil, and after all defeat our object. There has been a considerable amount of this kind of Jesuitical accommodation in the missionary labours of the Church of Rome; yet even Xavier admitted, that Christianity resembled a good physician, who administers nothing but wholesome medicine to his patient, however distasteful it may be to his palate; whilst Islam played the part of a cook, who studied the likings of his master.

7. It is natural that the *hopes* and *fears* of the Church, with regard to ultimate success, should be differently expressed. Some writers entertain remarkably sanguine views upon the subject, assuming that Islam has been doing the work in God's providence, which the Jewish dispensation did in the Old Testament, viz., preparing the way of the Gospel, where the minds of the people were incapable of receiving the full light of the truth.

Professor White, in a sermon appended to his "Bampton Lectures," spoke hopefully of the chances of converting Moslems. Mr. Foster maintains that Islam must eventually prepare the way for the missions of the cross and claims the support of Mede and Warburton for his opinion. Dr. Mohler who regarded the subject from a point of view precisely opposite to that of Mr. Foster, yet agrees with him, that Islam in Africa is doing the work of Judaism.

Whilst first rejecting the plausible and purely gratuitous assumption, that any preparation in the Pagan world is required for the preaching of the Gospel, we are bound to add, that the practical experience of every missionary who has confronted this apostacy, has proved the fallacy of this view.[74] If ever there were "*enemies of the cross*," the Moslem deniers of the *Crucifixion* must be considered as such; and admitting that they have *frequently* fought against idolatry, we cannot forget, that they have *constantly* and upon principle fought against the Cross. Since Christianity has suffered a most fatal check by the spread and continuance of Islam, whilst the latter has suffered no check, and sustained no real loss by conversions from their ranks to Christianity, we are not justified in adopting Mr. Foster's assumption. It is confirmed by every Missionary who has had to deal simultaneously with Pagans and Moslems, that a perfectly barbarous and superstitious people will be more easily gathered into the folds of Christ's Church, than the proud and self-sufficient Mohammedans, who are indeed, in possession of some fragments of truth, but hold that truth is unrighteousness.

Our fears of success ought not however to overbalance our *hope* of winning converts from Islam; more especially as our confidence rests on no slender grounds. One encouraging fact is, that the Koran

---

[74] According to Archdeacon Grant, the system of the false prophet "offers the most formidable obstruction to the faith of Christ, from the fact of its being, as it is, a counterfeit of the truth itself." Bampton Lectures Lect. VII. pag. 227.

has laid the foundation of its own destruction, in ascribing considerable authority to the Law and the Gospel, without in any degree establishing its own assumed superiority.

The intelligent Moslem, on reading the Bible, cannot fail to discover the sophistry of the Koran, in professing to confirm the foregoing revelations, whilst it virtually abrogates them; and thus the charm which rivets him to that book will be inevitably destroyed. We remind the reader of the conversions of Kabis Effendi, d'Ohsson Tom. I. that of Abdrllah and Sabat, many others of more recent date, not excluding those made by the Moslem Mission Society.

Again, the intimate connection of religion and state must not only prove irksome to both, but eminently dangerous to the existence of Islam. It is impossible that no reforms should be required in the political affairs of a nation, especially when brought under foreign influences, as is the case with the Ottoman Empire; but to reform a Moslem state is to undermine the religion, since they are so inseparably bound together that the one cannot be altered in the remotest degree without detriment to the other. The very fact of the decay of the civil polity proves the untenableness of the creed, since both date their origin from the same source.[77]

It would have been utterly impossible for the late Sultan to have carried out the many innovating measures, which he had done, without endangering

---

[77] Möhler's gesammelte Schriften Vol. I. pag. 390.

his throne, had it not been for the foreign influence which supported his exertions : since the strength of a Moslem state consists only in being stationary, and Mohammedans consider that the sovereign who enacts reforms, betrays his trust and has himself become a Kaffer.

There can be no doubt that the present artificial existence of the Ottoman government can be only of very short duration; and the prevalent feeling among the Turks is, that the termination of their political power is at hand; an event which they anticipate with the calmest resignation, as one of the things which are written in the book of decrees. If a feeling of instructive fear take possession of brute beasts before the earthquake, or in birds and bees before the coming of a storm, may we not consider the presentiments and traditions so rife among Moslemin, as significant of the approaching decay of Islamism?

The oldest prediction was recorded as early as the year 1548.[78] Another Turkish prophecy more clearly states that the "fair sons of the North" would be the destroyers of the Osmanic Empire. In 1678, *Rycaut* speaks of a special liking for the Moscovites on the part of the Greek, because they were destined, according to ancient prophecies, to become their deliverers and avengers.[79]

Another prediction says, "The fair-haired race

---

[78] Ludovico Domenichi in his, *Profetie dei Maometani*, Firenze. 1548.

[79] Rycaut "State of the Greek Church," pag. 83.

with all their associates will overthrow the Empire of Ishmael, and conquer the seven-hilled city with its imperial privileges."[80] In Jerusalem, the gate on Mount Moriah towards the Mount of Olives, is walled up, because of the tradition, that whenever a Christian shall pass through the gate, the Moslem religion and empire will go down.

Within the mosque of Omar, there is said to be a board containing so many nails which mysteriously disappear one by one; and when all shall have vanished the Moslem rule will come to an end. As another presentiment of their ultimate expulsion from Europe, may be mentioned the fact, that the Turks always bury their dead on the Asiatic side of Hellespont.[81]

An Austrian *savant* Dr. Kotschy, who has just travelled over Asia Minor a second time, in his work upon *Natural History*, states, that *the entire Moslem community* expect a speedy dissolution of the Turkish Empire, and this upon the ground of ancient traditions.—On a *Sunday* it will happen that the Christians will receive back all that was taken from them by the Moslems.

Not only European Turkey, but the whole of Asia

---

[80] Walsh's Journey from Constantinople to England, pag. 436. Michaud II. 254, observes, "D'après d'anciennes prédictions les Turcs sont persuadés, que la ville de Constantinople tombere au pouvoir des Francs."

[81] The Moslems in India hold that, "When all four parts of the world contain Christian inhabitants, and the Christians approach the sacred territory of the Kaaba, then people might look out for the long expected Imam." Mrs. Hassan Ali's Observations I. 136.

Minor, and Syria, with the exception of Damascus, will be restored to the Christians, and Arabia alone will constitute their inheritance. During the appearance of the last Comet, addresses were delivered in the mosques at Constantinople till late at midnight, of which, approaching destruction of Islam and the Turkish empire formed the chief subject.

How great will be the change in the position of Islam, when the ruins of the Ottoman Empire shall fill considerable portions of Europe, Asia, and Africa, and how encouraging to the Christian to look forward to the breaking up of the old, and the commencement of a new order of things!

8. There are however additional reasons, why we should no longer neglect the posterity of Ishmael. It cannot be without deep meaning to us, that for the *first time* in the history of divine revelation Christ should appear to Hagar as "the Angel of Jehovah."[84] It is also in a high degree significant, that the very first occasion in which *Jesus-Jehovah* is revealed, should be to seek and bring back the haughty mother of the Ishmaelites, when she had gone astray! Calling her by name and styling her "Sarai's maid," Christ gently reminded her of her sin, and commanded her to return, and to submit herself to her mistress: a touching beautiful example for us, as to how we are to deal with her erring, but equally haughty and posterity!

[84] The Angel of Jehovah, who here as the good Shepherd goes after that which is lost until He find it, is invariably the Lord Jesus, and here, Gen. xvi. 7, the appellation occurs for the first time.

The Angel of Jehovah had never prior to this, personally manifested Himself; it being merely said, "Jehovah appeared unto Abraham," or "the word of the Lord came unto him;" but now, after God had made a *covenant* with Abraham, Gen. xv. He showed Himself to Hagar, Gen. xvi. as the *Angel of the covenant* or as the Angel of Jehovah. That the manifestations of the second Person of the Trinity, which now opens a long series of revelations, were ordinarily in *human* form, is clear from several accounts. Jacob speaks of Him as the "Angel who redeemed" him from all evil. He called Moses; He led the Israelites in the wilderness; He fought for them as "the Prince of the Lord of hosts" on their taking possession of Canaan; He guided the people in the days of the Judges, and took up his abode in the Most Holy of the Temple.

The Angel of Jehovah is one with Jehovah, and yet different from Him; He is called by Isaiah "the Angel of His presence;" at a later period He promises to "search His sheep and seek them out" as the good Shepherd; and in Malachi He declares, "Behold I will send my messenger, and he shall prepare the way before me, and the Lord whom ye seek, shall suddenly come to His temple, even the *Messenger or the Angel of the covenant*, whom ye delight in: behold He shall come, saith the Lord of hosts." Whilst the angels nowhere speak in the name of Jehovah without drawing a broad line of demarcation between themselves and Him, by whom they are sent, "the Angel of Jehovah" who appears to *Hagar;* speaks *as Jehovah.*

The reason why Christ the Angel of Jehovah, first appeared to Hagar, was doubtless, because He is "the same yesterday, to-day and for ever." It befitted the Friend of sinners to condescend to appear in *human form* to the erring mother of the Saracens, as He afterwards appeared in *human nature* to men and women who were sinners. She was, moreover, in affliction and probably already conscious of her guilt, Gen. xvi. 2, and was therefore permitted to see God's face, as it only can be seen, in Christ. By this manifestation to the proud and rebellious bondmaid of Sarah, it was shown to the world, that whilst *Jehovah* was pre-eminently the God of the Hebrews, *Jesus-Jehovah* was the Saviour of the *whole* world. They who cannot understand why Christ should first appear to the Egyptian Hagar, instead of to Abraham or Sarah, forget or disown the *love of Jesus to the most reprobate of sinful humanity.* Hagar was the mother of a posterity which more than any other have distinguished themselves by their animosity to Christ, their hatred to Christians, and their enmity to the Gospel: hence the appearance of Christ to her, as "the Angel of Jehovah," thus taught the same truth in the Old Testament, which is taught in the Gospel by the parables of the lost and the prodigal son.

The strong motives which are here supplied by our Lord's example, for Missionary enterprise among the sons of Hagar, are further supported by special *promises*, that they shall be re-admitted into the family of Abraham, from which, for a season they were expelled. Neither the Jews nor the Israelites are everlastingly excluded from the blessings of the Gospel; and as in the end "all Israel shall be saved," Rom. xi. 11—32, so will also be fulfilled what is written of the future conversion of the posterity of Ishmael. " The multitude of camels shall cover thee, the dromedaries of *Midian* and *Ephah*, all they from *Sheba* shall come, they shall bring gold incense ; and they shall show forth the praises of the Lord. All the flocks of *Kedah* shall be gathered unto thee, the rams of *Nebaoth* minister unto thee : they shall come up with acceptance on mine alter, and I will glorify the house of my glory." Isa. lx. 6, 7, crf. Gen. xxv. 2, 4.

As Israel "shall look upon Him, whom they have pierced and shall mourn for Him ;" so shall the house of *Ishmael* mourn, when their eyes shall be opened, and they think upon the gracious appearance of Christ to their mother Hagar, and His giving her a blessing, by which they multiplied, and upon which they shall continue to subsist to that very hour. For as Hagar returned and submitted herself, " not being disobedient to the heavenly vision," so may we hope that her sons will return ; and when they return and submit to Christ's yoke, then will be solved the great mystery, why God has blessed Ishmael with so numerous a posterity.

FINIS.

www.ingramcontent.com/pod-product-compliance
Lightning Source LLC
Chambersburg PA
CBHW020858020526
44116CB00029B/388